THE ANALYTIC HIERARCHY PROCESS

**McGRAW-HILL
INTERNATIONAL
BOOK COMPANY**

New York
St. Louis
San Francisco
Auckland
Bogotá
Guatemala
Hamburg
Johannesburg
Lisbon
London
Madrid
Mexico
Montreal
New Delhi
Panama
Paris
San Juan
São Paulo
Singapore
Sydney
Tokyo
Toronto

THOMAS L. SAATY
*The Wharton School
University of Pennsylvania*

The Analytic Hierarchy Process

Planning, Priority Setting, Resource Allocation

British Library Cataloguing in Publication Data

Saaty, Thomas Lorie
    The analytic hierarchy process
    1. Decision-making—Mathematics
    I. Title
    153.8′3′018   HD30.23   79-41060
    ISBN 0-07-054371-2

THE ANALYTIC HIERARCHY PROCESS

1 2 3 4 MPMP 8 2 1 0

Typeset in Great Britain by Eta Services (Typesetters) Ltd., Beccles, Suffolk
Printed and Bound in the United States of America

CONTENTS

PREFACE

The decision-maker, be he motivated by the need to predict or to control, usually faces a complex system of interrelated components, such as resources, desired outcomes or objectives, persons or groups of persons, etc.; and he is interested in analyzing this system. Presumably, the better he understands this complexity, the better his prediction or decision will be. In this book we present a theory, whose application reduces the study of even formidably intricate systems to a sequence of pairwise comparisons of properly identified components.

This theory had its beginnings in the fall of 1971 while I was working on problems of contingency planning for the Department of Defense. It had its adolescence in 1972 in a study for the NSF (and later also ERDA) on rationing electricity to industries according to their contribution to the welfare of the nation. The origins of the scale which relates judgments to numbers date back to the serious events of June and July, 1972, in Cairo while I was there analyzing the effects of "No Peace, No War" on Egypt's economic, political, and military status.

The application maturity of the theory came with the Sudan Transport Study in 1973, which I was directing. Its theoretical enrichment was happening all along the way, with greatest intensity between 1974 and 1978. The applications so far have been many and varied, ranging from an analysis of terrorism for the Arms Control and Disarmament Agency (published in a book edited by Dr. Robert Kupperman of the Agency) where I worked in Washington for seven years, and several other studies of conflict (e.g., the conflict in Northern Ireland) to allocating resources according to priority for large private, governmental, and international concerns.

The theory reflects what appears to be an innate method of operation of the human mind. When presented with a multitude of elements, controllable or not, which comprise a complex situation, it aggregates them into groups, according to whether they share certain properties. Our model of this brain function allows a repetition of this process, in that we consider these groups, or rather their identifying common properties, as the elements of a new level in the system. These elements may, in turn, be grouped according to another set of properties, generating the elements of yet another "higher," level, until we reach a single "top" element which can often be identified as the goal of our decision-making process.

What we have just described is commonly called a hierarchy, i.e., a system of stratified levels, each consisting of so many elements, or factors. The central question is, in terms of this hierarchy: how strongly do the individual factors of the lowest level of the hierarchy influence its top factor, the overall goal? Since this influence will not be uniform over the factors, we are led to the identification of their intensity or, as we prefer to call it, their priorities.

This determination of the priorities of the lowest factors relative to the goal, can be reduced to a sequence of priority problems, one for each level, and each such priority problem to a sequence of pairwise comparisons. These comparisons remain the central ingredient of our theory, even if the original problem should have been complicated by feedback relations between various levels or factors.

Let us return to our suggestion that our theory is a model of the way in which the human mind conceptualizes and structures a complicated problem. We were influenced by the following observations:

(1) When we watch people participating in the process of structuring and prioritizing a hierarchy, we find that they engage naturally in successive grouping of items within levels and in distinguishing among levels of complexity.
(2) Individuals informed about a particular problem may structure it hierarchically somewhat differently, but if their judgments are similar, their overall answers tend to be similar. Also, the process is robust. In other words, fine distinctions within the hierarchy tend in practice not to be decisive.
(3) In the course of developing the theory we find a mathematically reasonable way to handle judgments.

Participants tended to find that the process captures their intuitive understanding of a problem. Furthermore, the psychological limits seem to be consonant with conditions for mathematical stability of the results.

In his beautiful book *Number the Language of Science*, The Macmillan Company, New York (3rd ed. 1939), Dantzig observes that the human mind has a sense for numbers which is primitive and predates true counting; namely, the ability to recognize that a small collection of objects has increased or decreased when things are added to it or subtracted from it. This is an intuitive talent which is not the same as counting. He points out that individuals and even some animals have this talent. Finally, he speculates on whether the concept is born of experience or whether experience merely serves to render explicit what is already latent in the mind. On reflection it appears that it is the latter; that consciousness is a process of identifying events and distinguishing the intensity or degree of differences among them according to whatever properties they have in common. Thus, what we know as "qualitative" is a fuzzy way of acknowledging differences. Since our survival requires that we be more specific, we have developed the talent of number sense.

When a single experience involves a variety of different sensations or activities and some kind of integrated interpretation or action is needed, these activities must be combined somehow. How we combine them depends on the purpose they are supposed to serve; our objectives dictate where we place the emphasis. We need the idea of priority and its measurement.

The methodology should then be useful to model problems incorporating knowledge and judgments in such a way that the issues involved are clearly articulated, evaluated, debated, and prioritized. The judgments can be refined through a continuous application of a feedback process, each application leading to a refinement and sharpening of the judgments. We have even used the Analytic Hierarchy Process to obtain group judgments through consensus. There is no such thing as *the* answer but *an* answer, which with constant exposure, develops into *the* answer for the decision-maker. In whatever form the final judgment is cast, there will always be people whose judgments differ from any particular outcome but when a group was involved in formulating judgments a synthesis of interests would have been created.

We show that the age old adage that one cannot compare apples and oranges is not true. An apple and an orange have many characteristics in common: size, shape, taste, aroma, color, seediness, juiciness, and so on. We may prefer an orange for some characteristics and an apple for others. In addition, the strength of our preference for these characteristics may vary. We may be indifferent to size and color but may have a strong preference for taste which again may vary with the time of day. It is our thesis that this sort of complicated comparison occurs in real life over and over again, and some kind of a mathematical approach is required. We will also develop a dynamic method for such comparisons.

The practice of decision-making is concerned with weighting alternatives, all of which fulfill a set of desired objectives. The problem is to choose that alternative which most strongly fulfills the entire set of objectives. We are interested in deriving numerical weights for alternatives with respect to sub-objectives and for sub-objectives with respect to higher order objectives. We would like these weights to be meaningful for allocating resources. For example, if they are derived to represent the value of money or distance or whatever physical quantity is being considered, they should be the same, or close to, what an economist or a physicist may obtain using his methods of measurement. Thus our process of weighting should produce weights or priorities that are estimates of an underlying ratio scale. At the same time in situations with physical interdependence among activities, high priority activities which depend on low priority ones must not inadvertently be short-changed by reducing the resource allocation to the low priority ones. That is why resource allocation must be made subject to interdependence constraints.

Even with the same constraints there exist a variety of decision-making styles.

One Korean economic planner—the man who thought his country should do better than Japan—said:

In Japan, the decision process is talk, talk, talk until you reach consensus. In Korea and in China, it is talk, talk, but then somebody on top makes a decision. You see that in the humblest Korean peasant's home, where he is master. You see it, and criticize it, in our politics. We see it in our big business where there is excellent research, but the final decision is the president's. This can create problems as our pattern of industry becomes more complicated. But it is very good in the early states of industrial growth.

This fits well with the comments of a senior Japanese civil servant on the decision process in Japan:

Every decision in Japan is taken by consensus. In Japanese government most policies are originally suggested by officials. Their suggestions then go through many forums, of which the cabinet is only the last. Even in cabinet, talk can continue for hours without anybody being very precise. Then at the end, the prime minister says: this is our consensus. He is not very precise either. But action can then be taken in line with that unprecise consensus, and with everybody feeling he has had some say in what is being done. The consequence is that in Japan every decision is mediocre. But execution is then excellent. (*The Economist*, 7 May 1977, p. 46.)

Sometimes decisions taken by large organizations or governments appear to ignore human beings. Emilio Daddario in one of his papers says that:

Because of the uncertainties of political decision-making, society does not perform up to its technical capabilities. . . . Until the political process provides a clear ranking of priorities, the contributions of science and technology to specific problems of public welfare will probably remain random and unsystematic. . . . The political decision-makers must take care that, in adopting a systematic approach to the ranking of priorities, they do not abdicate their primary function of defending human values. In using this approach to solve large social problems, the decision-makers are learning how to resolve quantitatively many decisions previously left to intuitive or normative judgments. (Emilio Daddario, *Ventures*, Magazine of the Yale Graduate School, Spring, 1971.)

Perhaps, our quantitative approach is a process which avoids the dehumanizing dangers of which Daddario speaks.

This book is intended for readers of diverse backgrounds and intentionally involves some repetition of ideas. It is not solely aimed at people doing research or colleagues who have distinguished themselves in the area of measurement.

I am indebted to my colleagues, Dr. James P. Bennett and Dr. Carter C. Waid for stimulating discussion and challenging ideas, and to my friend Dr. Jeorg Mayer for reading the manuscript, rearranging it, and rewriting some sections to tighten the exposition. I am also grateful for a rearrangement and edition of an earlier draft by my ex-student and collaborator in making applications to conflict resolution, Dr. Joyce Alexander. To seven lively young minds, my students past and present, I want to express my lasting gratitude for interaction, rising to challenges, and helping with the computer. They are Dr. Peter Blair, Dr. Kun-Yuan Chen, Anand Desai, Dr. Eren Erdener, Dr. Fred Ma, Dr. Reynaldo Mariano, and Dr. Luis Vargas. Finally, to my secretary, assistant, and willing helper, Mrs. Mary Lou Brown, goes my deep appreciation for her high quality work on the manuscript.

For his appreciation of these ideas and the opportunity to apply them in significant ways in human affairs in the international field I dedicate the book to Abdlatif Y. Al-Hamad. It is for this kind of man that Proverbs 18:24 was meant: "There is a friend that sticketh closer than a brother."

Thomas L. Saaty
University of Pennsvlvania

PART

ONE

THE ANALYTIC HIERARCHY PROCESS

THEME Decomposition by hierarchies and synthesis by finding relations through informed judgment.

When economic factors have been reduced to numbers measured in dollars, when numbers of objects, their weight in tons, and the time needed to produce them have been calculated and when probabilities have been estimated, our modeling of complex human problems often would have reached the limits of its effectiveness. It depends strongly on what factors we can measure.

If then the models do not work well because we have left out significant factors by making simplifying assumptions, at least in the social sciences, we blame the result on politics and on capricious human behavior and other factors regarded as annoying aberrations of human nature which will disappear in time. But these are precisely the controlling factors that we must deal with and measure in order to get realistic answers. We must stop making simplifying assumptions to suit our quantitative models and deal with complex situations as they are. To be realistic our models must *include* and *measure* all important tangible and intangible, quantitatively measurable, and qualitative factors. This is precisely what we do with the analytic hierarchy process (AHP). We also allow for differences in opinion and for conflicts as the case is in the real world. We intend to develop this approach and show the reader how effective it is as a tool.

Chapter 1 gives a general introduction to the subject followed by examples in Chapter 2. Chapter 3 provides background on scales and consistency and Chapter 4 is concerned with hierarchic structures and their consistency.

1

ONE

HIERARCHIES AND PRIORITIES:
A FIRST LOOK

1-1 INTRODUCTION

When we think, we identify objects or ideas and also relations among them. When we identify anything, we decompose the complexity which we encounter. When we discover relations, we synthesize. This is the fundamental process underlying perception: decomposition and synthesis. The elaboration of this concept and its practical implications interest us here.

We all experience reality sufficiently close, so that even though our decompositions of it may differ, our evaluations at the operational level tend to be close, particularly when it is supported by successful experience in fulfilling our common purposes. Thus we may model reality somewhat differently, but we manage to communicate a sense of judgment which involves common understanding (but not without differences). We need to exploit this manifestation of judgment and of learning.

Our purpose is to develop a theory and provide a methodology for modeling unstructured problems in the economic, social, and management sciences. Sometimes we forget how long it took the human race to evolve measurement scales that are useful in daily living. The evolution of monetary units with wide acceptance has taken thousands of years of barter and legislation in a successive approximation process to design a medium for exchange which we call money. Money also serves as a basis of measurement of all kinds of goods and services. This evolution of a measurement scale, i.e., money, has helped to structure economic theory, making it amenable to empirical tests. The development of money has been an interactive process refining human judgment and experience on the one hand, and the medium of measurement on the other. This process has also established a framework which incorporates both philosophy and mathematics in the challenging science of economics. Economic theory is tied today very strongly to its unit of measurement, but has problems in dealing with political and social values that do not have economic implications.

Social values in our complex society call for a convenient method of scaling to enable us, on a daily basis, to evaluate tradeoffs between money, environmental quality, health, happiness, and similar entities. Such an approach should facilitate interaction between judgment and the social phenomena to which it is applied. We need such an approach precisely because there are no social measurement scales that have acquired popular use, although there have been several attempts in the social sciences to lay a foundation for a theory of measurement.

The acid test for a new tool is how "natural" and easy it is to understand and how well it *integrates* within existing theory, whether it is accepted by those who need to use it, and how well it *works* in solving their problems.

Our theory was developed to solve a specific problem in contingency planning (Saaty, 1972) and a later major application was to design alternative futures for a developing country, the Sudan (Saaty, 1977d). The result was a set of priorities and an investment plan for projects to be undertaken there in the late 1980's. The ideas have gradually evolved through use in a number of other applications ranging from energy allocation (Saaty and Mariano, 1979), investment in technologies under uncertainty, dealing with terrorism (Saaty and Bennett, 1977), buying a car, to choosing a job and selecting a school. Using pairwise comparison judgments for input, we can cope (in what we see as a natural way) with factors which, in the main stream of applications, have not been effectively quantified. Naturally, one has to be concerned with the ambiguity which occurs whenever numbers are associated with judgment; otherwise, one may fall in the trap of the modern epithet: "Garbage in, garbage out." Judgment is difficult to work with and widely variable. But we can study the consistency of judgment and its validity.

Various applications of the theory have involved the participation of lawyers, engineers, political, social and physical scientists and mathematicians, and even children. All felt comfortable with the easy and natural way they were to provide pairwise comparisons in their areas of expertise, and with the explanation of the method which was usually interpreted to them nontechnically.

But why this obsession with numbers and measurement? How do we hope it will help us and how will it work? We are constantly offered techniques to cope with every phenomenon we face today. But the techniques cannot cope with entities for which there are no measures. Here we have an effective way to create measures for such entities and then use them in decision making.

Our approach, which is sufficiently general to use both known measurements and judgments, may be better appreciated through the following quotation (Churchman and Eisenberg, 1969):

... It seems almost obvious that we cannot solve present-day major political and organizational problems simply by grinding through a mathematical model or computer a set of accepted inputs. What we require besides is the design of better deliberation and judgment. Once we begin to understand the process of deliberation and judgment we may converge on a better objective method, that is, a way to express optimal deliberation in a precise and warranted form.

In general, decision making involves the following kinds of concerns: (1) planning; (2) generating a set of alternatives; (3) setting priorities; (4) choosing a best policy after finding a set of alternatives; (5) allocating resources; (6) determining requirements; (7) predicting outcomes; (8) designing systems; (9) measuring performance; (10) insuring the stability of a system; (11) optimizing; and (12) resolving conflict.

Solving decision problems has suffered from an overabundance of "patent medicine" techniques without any holistic cure. The recommendations to solve one problem may leave the whole system more disturbed than it was to begin with.

In recent decades, the "systems approach" to problems in the social and behavioral sciences has found its place next to the older reductionist methods which seem more appropriate to the physical sciences. Basically, a system is an abstract model for a real-life structure such as the nervous system of a human, the government of a city, the transportation network of a state, or the ecosystem of the marshlands of New Jersey. In systems language we evaluate the impact of various components of a system on the entire system and find their priorities.

Some people have defined a system in terms of the interactions of its parts. But a much richer definition of a system can be given in terms of its *structure*, its *functions*, the *objectives* set for it in the *design* from the *perspective* of a particular individual or group (hence the possibility for conflict), and finally the *environment* (the larger surrounding system) of which it is a subsystem. For practical purposes a system is often regarded in terms of its

(1) *Structure* according to the physical, biological, social, or even psychological arrangement of its parts and according to the flow of material and people which define the relations and dynamics of the structure, and
(2) *Function* according to what functions the components of the system, whether animate or inanimate, are meant to serve; what these functions are and what objectives they are intended to fulfill; what higher objectives these objectives are part of (leading up to an overall purpose of the system); whose objectives are being satisfied; what conflict among individuals may have to be resolved.

Actually, the structure and function of a system cannot be separated. They are the reality we experience. What we would like to do is look at them simultaneously. In doing this the structure serves as a vehicle for analyzing the function. The functioning modifies the dynamics of the structure.

A hierarchy is an abstraction of the structure of a system to study the functional interactions of its components and their impacts on the entire system. This abstraction can take several related forms, all of which essentially descend from an apex (an overall objective), down to sub-objectives, down further to forces which affect these sub-objectives, down to the people who influence these forces, down to the objectives of the people and then to their policies, still further down to the strategies, and, finally, the outcomes which result from these strategies. It is worth noting that there is a degree of invariance to this structure whose highest levels represent environmental constraints and forces descending to levels of actors, their objectives, the functions of the system, and, finally, to its structure which may be modified or controlled.

Two questions arise in the hierarchical structuring of systems:

(1) How do we structure the functions of a system hierarchically?
(2) How do we measure the impacts of any element in the hierarchy?

There are also relevant questions of optimization with which we may wish to deal. They are meaningful after we have answered the above questions. We shall have a number of things to say later about the structure of hierarchies.

1-2 MEASUREMENT AND THE JUDGMENTAL PROCESS

Let us examine three related problems which have interesting applications. The *first* is concerned with measurement. Suppose we are given a set of objects which are all sufficiently light and can be lifted by hand. In the absence of a weighting instrument we wish to estimate their relative weights. One way would be to guess the weight of each object directly in pounds, for example, by lifting it (perhaps using the lightest one as the standard), comparing the whole class, and then dividing the weight of each by the total to get its relative weight. Another method which utilizes more of the available information in the experiment is to compare the objects in pairs, by lifting one and then lifting another and then back to the first and then again the second and so on until we have formulated a judgment as to the relative weight (ratio) of each pair of objects. The problem then is to adopt a meaningful scale for the pairwise comparisons. This second process has the advantage of focusing exclusively on two objects at a time and on how they relate to each other. It also generates more information than is really necessary since each object is methodically compared with every other.

For problems where there is no scale to validate the result, the pairwise comparison process can prove to be an asset, because although the steps are more numerous, they are simpler than in the first process.

We note that consistency in any kind of measurement cannot be taken for granted. All measurement, including that which makes use of instruments, is subject to experimental error and to error in the measuring instrument. A serious effect of error is that it can and often does lead to inconsistent conclusions. A simple example of the consequence of error in weighing objects is to find that A is heavier than B, and B is heavier than C but C is heavier than A. This can happen particularly when the weights of A, B, and C are close, and the instrument is not fine enough to distinguish between them. Lack of consistency may be serious for some problems but not for others. For example, if the objects are two chemicals to be mixed together in exact proportion to make a drug, inconsistency may mean that proportionately more of one chemical is used than the other, possibly leading to harmful results in using the drug.

But perfect consistency in measurement, even with the finest instruments, is difficult to attain in practice; what we need is a way of evaluating how bad it is for a particular problem.

By consistency we mean here not merely the traditional requirement of the transitivity of preferences (if apples are preferred to oranges and oranges are preferred to bananas, then apples must be preferred to bananas), but the actual intensity with which the preference is expressed transits through the sequence of objects in the comparison. For example, if apples are twice as preferable as oranges and oranges are three times as preferable as bananas, then apples must be six times as preferable as bananas. This is what we call cardinal consistency in the strength of preference. Inconsistency is a violation of proportionality which may or may not entail violation of transitivity. Our study of consistency demonstrates that it is not whether we are inconsistent on particular comparisons that matters, but how strongly consistency is violated in the numerical sense for the overall problem under study. An exact definition of a numerical index for consistency will be given later.

Note that there need be no relationship between consistency and tests of how closely a measurement duplicates reality. Thus, an individual may have excellent consistency but not know anything about the real situation. Usually, though, the more a person knows a situation, the more consistent one would expect him to be in representing it. Pairwise comparisons enable one to improve consistency by using as much information as possible. To represent reality with measurements, we assume the following:

(1) At least physical "reality" is consistent and can be counted on to yield similar results from trial to trial under controlled conditions.
(2) Judgment must strive towards consistency. Consistency is a desirable objective. It is necessary for capturing reality but not sufficient. An individual may have very consistent ideas which do not correspond to the "real" world situation. Consistency is a central question in concrete measurement, in judgments, and in the thinking process.
(3) To obtain better estimates of reality, we should channel our impressions, feelings, beliefs in a systematic way in providing judgments. The object is to enhance objectivity and downplay too much subjectivity.
(4) To get good results (which correspond to reality) from our feelings, we need: (a) to use mathematics to construct the right kind of theory to produce numerical scales of judgments and other comparative measurements, (b) to find a scale which discriminates between our feelings, whose values have some kind of regularity so that we can easily rely on making the correspondence between our qualitative judgments and these numbers, (c) to be able to reproduce the measurement of reality which we have already learned in physics and economics, and (d) to be able to determine how inconsistent we are.

In passing, we note that measuring instruments are not and cannot be means of absolute measurement, but themselves have been the object of scientific study and analysis and have been constructed with consistent behavior in mind, and have come to serve as vehicles in other scientific research. If these instruments are for any reason inadequate (and one can always devise an experiment for which there is no satisfactory instrument for measurement) then we must keep inventing new instruments. It is not difficult to imagine some important experiment for which no sufficiently fine instrument can ever be found from which consistent answers can always be obtained. In that case the entire problem is shifted to the study of consistency and evaluating the seriousness of inconsistency. The maximum eigenvalue approach to estimate ratio scales which we study here gives rise to a measure of departure from consistency enabling comparison between informed and random or unrelated judgments and serves as a vehicle for estimating departure from the underlying ratio scale.

In the measurement of physical quantities it is usually possible to set down a dimension or property such as length, which remains the same in time and space, and devise instruments to measure this property. Naturally it would be more difficult to make an instrument which adjusts its scale to changing circumstances before making a measurement. For example, length and mass vary at speeds near that of light and an instrument that directly measured these properties at near the speed of light may require some kind of variable scale.

This is precisely the problem in the social sciences. When we deal with properties that change not only in time and space but also (and far more seriously) in conjunction with other properties, their meaning also changes. We cannot improvise universal scales for social events. Social phenomena are more complicated than physical phenomena because they are harder to replicate in abundance. Too much control must be imposed and controls in themselves often destroy the very social behavior one is trying to measure. Our judgments must be sufficiently flexible to take into consideration the contextual setting of the property being measured.

Consider the problem of measuring achievement and happiness. Both may be called relative properties in that the unit of measurement may have to be adjusted to compare, for example, the degree of happiness in one setting with that in another. As we shall see, it is possible to do this with the pairwise comparison technique. A powerful instrument which varies its scale with the relativeness of the circumstance can be the human mind itself, particularly if it turns out that its measurement is sufficiently consistent to satisfy the requirements of the particular problem. The intensity of our feelings serves as a scale-adjustment device to put the measurement of some objects on a scale commensurate with that of other objects. In fact, as the mind improves its precision, it becomes the required tool for relative measurement as no instrument except our very personally designed one (our own mind) can be made to suit our particular experience and viewpoint. A group must coordinate their outlook to produce results acceptable (in some sense) to them.

We now turn to our *second* problem, which is concerned with providing greater stability and invariance to social measurement. Granted that the dimensions or properties are variable, how do we measure the impact of this variability on still other higher level properties and, in turn, these on still higher ones. It turns out that for a very wide class of problems we can usually identify overall properties (or one property) which remain the same sufficiently long, i.e., for the duration of an experiment. This approach leads us to the measurement and analysis of impacts in hierarchies as discussed earlier.

We can then study the invariance of the derived measures by reorganizing the hierarchy in different ways. The results of the measurement may be used to stabilize the system or to design new goal-oriented systems. They can also be used (as priorities) to allocate resources.

Here again, as in the monetary system described earlier, the measurements derive from judgments based on experience and understanding. These measurements are obtainable only from relative comparisons and not in an absolute way.

Our *third* problem is to set up the right conditions for people to structure their problems and to provide the necessary judgment to determine their priorities.

We assume that the pairwise comparisons are obtained by direct questioning of people (a single individual if the problem is his sole concern) who may or may not be experts, but who are familiar with the problem. A central point in our approach is that people are often inconsistent, but priorities must be assigned and things done despite inconsistency.

We also assume that all the alternatives are specified in advance, and that not all the variables need to be under the control of each of the parties involved in affecting the outcomes of the alternatives. It is desirable to know if the priority of an alternative is due to the influence of a more powerful outside party. The object may be to improvise policies and establish communication to influence that party to produce a more favorable outcome to the stakeholders. The stability of the results due to changes in judgment evaluation is of interest.

The expressed preferences are assumed to be deterministic rather than probabilistic. Thus, a preference remains fixed and is not contingent upon other factors not included in the problem.

If several people are involved, they can assist each other in sharpening their judgments and also divide the task to provide the judgments in their areas of expertise, thus complementing each other. They may attempt consensus. Failing that, a bargaining process, particularly for people in a dispute, enables one group to yield when the pair being compared is of no significance to them and in return ask for similar concessions from the opposition when that party's interest is involved. When each of several individuals does his own evaluation, the separate results may be compared from the standpoints of their individual utilities to obtain a synthesis performed by an outside party of what they would do jointly.

Still another way to use the method would be to have each member of a group with conflicting interests develop the outcome using his judgments and assuming judgments for the other parties, note the outcome, and compare it (perhaps with the aid of a computer) with what the others arrive at. The process reveals what outcome each party is exerting pressure to achieve. The crucial upshot of this is to induce cooperation.

10

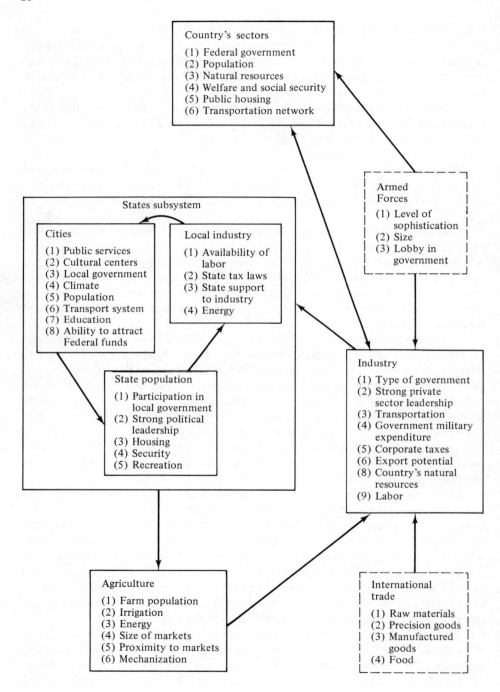

Country's sectors

(1) Federal government
(2) Population
(3) Natural resources
(4) Welfare and social security
(5) Public housing
(6) Transportation network

States subsystem

Cities

(1) Public services
(2) Cultural centers
(3) Local government
(4) Climate
(5) Population
(6) Transport system
(7) Education
(8) Ability to attract
Federal funds

Local industry

(1) Availability of
labor
(2) State tax laws
(3) State support
to industry
(4) Energy

State population

(1) Participation in
local government
(2) Strong political
leadership
(3) Housing
(4) Security
(5) Recreation

Armed Forces

(1) Level of
sophistication
(2) Size
(3) Lobby in
government

Industry

(1) Type of government
(2) Strong private
sector leadership
(3) Transportation
(4) Government military
expenditure
(5) Corporate taxes
(6) Export potential
(8) Country's natural
resources
(9) Labor

Agriculture

(1) Farm population
(2) Irrigation
(3) Energy
(4) Size of markets
(5) Proximity to markets
(6) Mechanization

International trade

(1) Raw materials
(2) Precision goods
(3) Manufactured
goods
(4) Food

Figure 1-1

1-3 HIERARCHIES

Very often, as one analyzes the structure of interest, the number of entities and their mutual relations increases beyond the ability of the researcher to comprehend distinct pieces of information. In such cases, the larger system is broken up into subsystems, almost as the schematic of a computer consists of blocks and their interconnections, with each block having a schematic of its own.

Figure 1-1 represents a very rough representation of the various subsystems which, in their collection and interrelations, make up the trade system of a country today. We will be treating systems like this (which have cycles) in a later chapter.

Now let us turn to the more straightforward hierarchical representation of problems.

A hierarchy is a particular type of system, which is based on the assumption that the entities, which we have identified, can be grouped into disjoint sets, with the entities of one group influencing the entities of only one other group (in a separate chapter we study the interaction between several groups), and being influenced by the entities of only one other group. The elements in each group (also called level, cluster, stratum) of the hierarchy are assumed to be independent. If there is dependence among them we study independence and dependence separately and combine the two as in Chap. 6. The following is an elementary example of a hierarchy.

The welfare of the city-states of medieval Europe depended mostly on the strength and ability of their rulers. The general structure of a city-state may be represented in the hierarchical form shown in Fig. 1-2.

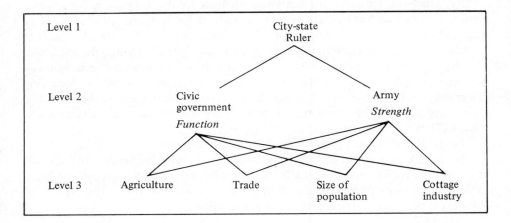

Figure 1-2

We have grouped agriculture, trade, size of population, and cottage industry into one set, or level, because in this model they share the property of being the most fundamental factors in the economic strength of the city-state. They determine the strength of the civic government function, and the army; these two, in turn, influence the welfare of the city-state.

Several observations are in order. Obviously, the model is too simplistic; many more entities could be identified, and more levels. This we can do depending on what question we are attempting to answer. The model can easily expand in complexity and become tedious to deal with. Thus we should construct the hierarchy carefully, choosing between faithfulness to reality and our understanding of the situation from which we can obtain answers. Experience has shown that even seemingly too rough an idealization can yield significant insights.

Second, we have not incorporated the evident fact that not only is the civic government influenced by trade, for instance, but civic government also has its impact on trade. This "reverse" impact, or feedback, while often important, is not as significant as it may seem at first. We have analyzed several problems first without taking feedback into account, and then with feedback. The first results were sufficiently close to allow the assumption that a well-constructed hierarchy will, in most cases, be a good model of reality even if possible feedback relations are ignored. However, as the initial example of this section indicates, some situations may be so complex that their representation by a hierarchy may be deceptively simplistic.

Perhaps another example will further clarify the notion of a hierarchy. The reality we are interested in is a college; we seek to determine the scenario which will most likely secure the continued existence of the college. Let us call the Focus the welfare of the college. It is influenced by the following forces: instruction, social life, spirit, physical plant, and extracurricular activities. These forces are determined by the following actors: academic administration, non-academic administration, faculty, students, trustees. We omit the obvious feedback between forces and actors. The various actors have certain objectives; for instance, the faculty may want to keep their jobs, grow professionally, offer good instruction, or, the students may be interested in obtaining a job, getting married, becoming educated, etc. Finally, there are various possible scenarios, such as: status quo, emphasizing vocational training, or continuing education, or becoming a bible school. The scenarios determine the likelihood of achieving the objectives, the objectives influence the actors, the actors guide the forces, which, finally, impact on the welfare of the college. Thus we have the hierarchy of Fig. 1-3.

Let us give this concept of hierarchy a closer look.

We have a tendency to think that hierarchies were invented in corporations and governments to take care of their affairs. This is not so. These hierarchies are basic to the human way of breaking reality into clusters and subclusters. Here is a brief eloquent expression in defense of this point of view.

"The immense scope of hierarchical classification is clear. It is the most powerful method of classification used by the human brain-mind in ordering experience, observations, entities and in-

Focus   Welfare of the college

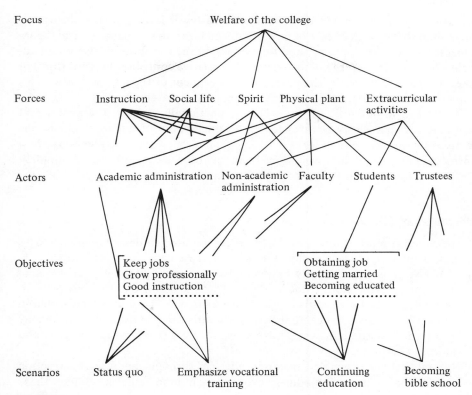

Figure 1-3

formation. Though not yet definitely established as such by neurophysiology and psychology, hierarchical classification probably represents the prime mode of coordination or organization (i) of cortical processes, (ii) of their mental correlates, and (iii) of the expression of these in symbolisms and languages. The use of heirarchical ordering must be as old as human thought, conscious and unconscious . . ." (Whyte, 1969)

The basic problem with a heirarchy is to seek understanding at the highest levels from interactions of the various levels of the hierarchy rather than directly from the elements of the levels. Rigorous methods for structuring systems into hierarchies are gradually emerging in the natural and social sciences and in particular, in general systems theory as it relates to the planning and design of social systems.

Direct confrontation of the large and the small is avoided in nature through the use of a hierarchical linkage (see Simon, 1962; Whyte et al., 1969). Conceptually, the simplest hierarchy is linear, rising from one level of elements to an adjacent level. For example, in a manufacturing operation there is a level of workers dominated by a level of supervisors, dominated by a level of managers, on to vice presidents and the president. A nonlinear hierarchy would be one with circular arrangements so that an upper level might be dominated by a lower level as well as being in a dominant position (e.g., in case of flow of information). In the mathematical theory of hierarchies we develop a method for evaluating the impact of a level on an adjacent upper level from the composition of the relative contributions (priorities) of the elements in that level with respect to each element of the adjacent level. This composition can be extended upwards through the hierarchy.

Each element of a hierarchy may belong functionally to several other different hierarchies. A spoon may be arranged with other spoons of different sizes in one hierarchy or with knives and forks in a second hierarchy. For example, it may be a controlling component in a level of one hierarchy or it may simply be an unfolding of higher or lower order functions in another hierarchy.

Advantages of Hierarchies

(1) Hierarchical representation of a system can be used to describe how changes in priority at upper levels affect the priority of elements in lower levels.
(2) They give great detail of information on the structure and function of a system in the lower levels and provide an overview of the actors and their purposes in the upper levels. Constraints on the elements in a level are best represented in the next higher level to ensure that they are satisfied. For example, nature may be regarded as an actor whose objectives are the use of certain material and subject to certain laws as constraints.
(3) Natural systems assembled hierarchically, i.e. through modular construction and final assembly of modules, evolve much more efficiently than those assembled as a whole.
(4) They are stable and flexible; stable in that small changes have small effect and flexible in that additions to a well-structured hierarchy do not disrupt the performance.

How to Structure a Hierarchy

In practice there is no set procedure for generating the objectives, criteria, and activities to be included in a hierarchy or even a more general system. It is a matter of what objectives we choose to decompose the complexity of that system.

One usually studies the literature for enrichment of ideas, and often, by working with others, goes through a free wheeling brainstorming session to list all concepts relevant to the problem without regard to relation or order. One attempts to keep in mind that the ultimate goals need to be identified at the top of the hierarchy; their sub-objectives immediately below; the forces constraining the actors still below that. This dominates a level of the actors themselves, which in turn dominates a level of their objectives, below which is a level of their policies, and at the bottom is a level of the various possible outcomes (scenarios). (Refer to the college hierarchy, Fig. 1-3). This is the natural form that planning and conflict hierarchies take. When designing a physical system, the policies can be replaced by methods of construction. This needs to be followed by several intermediate levels culminating in alternative systems. Considerable criticism and revision may be required before a well-defined plan is formulated.

There is sufficient similarity between problems that one is not always faced with a completely new task in structuring a hierarchy. In a sense the task for the experienced becomes one of identifying the different classes of problems which arise in life systems. There is such a variety of these that the challenge is to become versed with the ideas and concepts which people, living within such a system, encounter. This requires intelligence, patience, and the ability to interact with others to benefit from their understanding and experience.

The overall purpose and other criteria of a hierarchy in socio-political applications may not be unique. They depend on what to examine. This situation is not peculiar to hierarchies and is intrinsic to life situations. For example, in chess we have what is known as the *constant* (a priori) values of the pieces useful in the opening game. There are also the *current* (a posteriori) or empirical values of the pieces as they engage in the confrontations of the end game. Both types of values may be obtained under the following two assumptions: (1) in terms of how many squares they control when placed on each square and (2) in terms of their being able to check the king without being captured. We have the following relative values for the knight, bishop, rook, and queen (Ball, 1947, p. 162).

	Case 1 Controlling squares	Case 2 Threatening king
Constant value	3, 5, 8, 13	12, 13, 24, 37
Current value (empirically)	350, 360, 540, 1000	12, 13, 18, 33

Although the results in Case 2 are close, those in Case 1 are different. The analysis gives rise to the question: "What really is the relative worth of pieces in chess?" Obviously there is not a unique answer. However, in terms of relative orders of magnitude the answer may be acceptable.

Our sensory perception operates in specialized ways to serve our survival needs. Therefore, however we try to be objective in interpreting experience, our understanding is perceived and abstracted in a very subjective way, normally to serve our needs! Our survival seems to be a meaningful basis for devising purposes. Shared subjectivity in interpretation is actually what we mean by objectivity. Thus the hierarchies we form are objective by our own definition because they relate to our collective experience.

A valuable observation about the hierarchical approach to problem solving is that the functional representation of a system may differ from person to person, but people usually agree on the bottom level of alternative actions to be taken and the level above it, the characteristics of these actions. For example, the bottom level may consist of alternate traffic routes which can be taken between two points, and the level of characteristics may include travel time, bottlenecks, potholes, safety, and the like. Table 1-1 indicates levels for different types of hierarchies, but the person formulating the hierarchy must always be comfortable that the levels relate naturally to each other. If necessary a level may be expanded into two levels or more or completely taken out.

Table 1-1 The general format for hierarchies and decomposition

	Environmental constraints and forces	Perspective (actors)	Objectives of actors	Policies	Outcomes	Resultant outcome
Generic for a system						
Hierarchy for Conflict	Constraints	Actors	Objective	Policies	Outcomes	Compromise or stable outcome
Forward or projected planning	Present organizational policies	→ Other actors	→ Other actor objectives	→ Policies	→ Scenarios	→ Logical future
Backward or idealized planning	Organizational response policies ←	← Other actors	← Other actor objectives	← Other actor policies	← Scenarios	← Desired future
Portfolio Cost-benefit Analysis	Criteria	Sub-criteria	Objectives	Policies	Options	Best option or mix
Investment choice	Risk level	Major forces	Criteria	Problem areas	Specific projects	
Prediction	Risk level	Major forces	Criteria	Problem areas	Categories	

1-4 PRIORITY IN HIERARCHIES

A hierarchy, as presented in the last section, is a more or less faithful model of a real-life situation. It represents our analysis of the most important elements in the situation and of their relationships. It is not a very powerful aid in our decision-making or planning process. What we yet need is a method to determine the potency with which the various elements in one level influence the elements on the next higher level, so that we may compute the relative strengths of the impacts of the elements of the lowest level on the overall objectives.

By way of clarification, let us return to the college hierarchy of the last section. As stated here, we are interested in "the scenario which will most likely secure the continued existence" of the college. In order to determine this scenario, we begin by finding the strength of importance of the forces with respect to the focus. Then, for each force in turn, we determine the strength of influence of the actors on that force. Simple computation will give us the strength of influence of the actors on the focus. Then, we find the strength of the objectives for each actor; and finally, we determine, with respect to each objective, the efficacy of the various scenarios in assuring that objective. Repetition of the computation mentioned above several times will yield the "best" scenario.

How, then, do we determine the "strengths", or the priorities, of the elements in one level relative to their importance for an element in the next level. At this point, we will present only the most elementary aspects of our method. The psychological motivation for our approach and the mathematical foundation will have to wait.

A few terms must be introduced first. A matrix is an array of numbers, arranged in a rectangle, as in

$$\begin{bmatrix} 1 & 0 & 2.9 & 6 \\ 3 & 3.5 & 7 & 1 \\ 2.1 & 2 & 0 & 1.1 \end{bmatrix}$$

A horizontal sequence of numbers in a matrix is called a row, a vertical one is called a column. A matrix consisting of one row or one column only is called a vector. A matrix is called a square matrix if it has an equal number of rows and columns. It is useful to note that associated with a square matrix are its eigenvectors and corresponding eigenvalues. The reader need not be discouraged with these concepts as we will be developing and explaining them at length in other chapters.

Our method can now be described as follows. Given the elements of one level, say, the fourth, of a hierarchy and one element, e, of the next higher level, compare the elements of level 4 *pairwise* in their strength of influence on e. Insert the agreed upon numbers, reflecting the comparison, in a matrix and find the eigenvector with the largest eigenvalue. The eigenvector provides the priority ordering, and the eigenvalue is a measure of the consistency of the judgment.

Let us determine a priority scale in the following example. Let A, B, C, D stand for chairs, arranged in a straight line, leading away from a light. We develop a priority scale of relative brightness for the chairs. Judgments will be obtained from an individual who stands by the light source and is asked, for example, "How strongly brighter is chair B than chair C?" He will then give one of the numbers for comparison described in the table and this judgment will be entered in the matrix in position (B, C). By convention, the comparison of strength is always of an activity appearing in the column on the left against an activity appearing in the row on top. We then have the pairwise comparison matrix with four rows and four columns (a 4×4 matrix)

Brightness	A	B	C	D
A				
B				
C				
D				

The "agreed upon" numbers are the following. Given elements A and B; if

A and B are equally important, insert 1
A is weakly more important than B, insert 3
A is strongly more important than B, insert 5
A is demonstrably or very strongly more important than B, insert 7
A is absolutely more important than B, insert 9
in the position (A, B) where the row of A meets the column of B.

An element is equally important when compared with itself, so where the row of A and column of A meet in position (A, A) insert 1. Thus the main diagonal of a matrix must consist of 1's. Insert the appropriate reciprocal 1, 1/3, ..., or 1/9 where the column of A meets the row of B, i.e., position (B, A) for the reverse comparison of B with A. The numbers 2, 4, 6, 8 and their reciprocals are used to facilitate compromise between slightly differing judgments. We also use rational numbers to form ratios from the above scale values when it is desired to force consistency on the entire matrix from a few judgments, i.e., a minimum of $n-1$.

In general, what we mean by being consistent is that when we have a basic amount of raw data, all other data can be logically deduced from it. In doing pairwise comparison to relate n activities so that each one is represented in the data at least once, we need $n-1$ pairwise comparison judgments. From them all other judgments can be deduced simply by using the following kind of relation: if activity A_1 is 3 times more dominant than activity A_2 and activity A_1 is 6 times more dominant than activity A_3 then $A_1 = 3A_2$ and $A_1 = 6A_3$. It should follow that $3A_2 = 6A_3$ or $A_2 = 2A_3$ and $A_3 = \frac{1}{2}A_2$. If the numerical value of the judgment in the (2, 3) position is different from 2 then the matrix would be inconsistent. This happens frequently and is not a disaster. Even if one has the whole real numbers to use for judgments, unless he occupies his attention methodically to build up the judgments from $n-1$ basic ones, his numbers are not likely to be consistent. In addition, for most problems it is very difficult to identify $n-1$ judgments which relate all activities and of which one is absolutely certain.

It turns out that the consistency of a positive reciprocal matrix is equivalent to the requirement that its maximum eigenvalue $\lambda_{\max}$ should be equal to n. It is also possible to estimate the departure from consistency by the difference $\lambda_{\max} - n$ divided by $n-1$. We note that $\lambda_{\max} \geqslant n$ is always true. How bad our consistency may be in a given problem may be estimated by comparing our value of $(\lambda_{max} - n)/(n-1)$ with its value from randomly chosen judgments and corresponding reciprocals in the reverse positions in a matrix of the same size. We have a table for such entries on page 21 from which the figures may be taken. Consistency will be dealt with more precisely in later chapters.

Let us now return to our chair brightness example. There are sixteen spaces in the matrix for our numbers. Of these, four are predetermined, namely, those in the diagonal, $(A, A), (B, B), (C, C), (D, D)$, and have the value 1, since, for example, chair A has the same brightness as itself. Of the remaining twelve numbers, after the diagonal is filled in, we need to provide six, because the other six are reverse comparisons and must be reciprocals of the first six. Suppose the individual, using the recommended scale, enters the number 4 in the (B, C) position. He thinks chair B is between weakly and strongly brighter than chair C. Then the reciprocal value $1/4$ is automatically entered in the (C, B) position. It is not mandatory to enter a reciprocal, but it is generally rational to do so.

After the remaining five judgments have been provided and their reciprocals also entered, we obtain for the complete matrix

Brightness	A	B	C	D
A	1	5	6	7
B	1/5	1	4	6
C	1/6	1/4	1	4
D	1/7	1/6	1/4	1

The next step consists of the computation of a vector of priorities from the given matrix. In mathematical terms the principal eigenvector is computed, and when normalized becomes the vector of priorities. We shall see in the next chapter that the relative brightness of the chairs expressed by this vector satisfies the inverse square law of optics. In the absence of a large scale computer to solve the problem exactly, crude estimates of that vector can be obtained in the following four ways:

(1) *The crudest* Sum the elements in each row and normalize by dividing each sum by the total of all the sums, thus the results now add up to unity. The first entry of the resulting vector is the priority of the first activity; the second of the second activity and so on.
(2) *Better* Take the sum of the elements in each column and form the reciprocals of these sums. To normalize so that these numbers add to unity, divide each reciprocal by the sum of the reciprocals.
(3) *Good* Divide the elements of each column by the sum of that column (i.e., normalize the column) and then add the elements in each resulting row and divide this sum by the number of elements in the row. This is a process of averaging over the normalized columns.
(4) *Good* Multiply the n elements in each row and take the nth root. Normalize the resulting numbers.

A simple illustration which shows that methods (1), (2), and (3) produce the expected answer uses an urn with 3 white (W), 2 black (B), and 1 red (R) balls. The probabilities of drawing a W, B, or R are, respectively, 1/2, 1/3, 1/6. It is easy to see that any of the first three methods gives these probabilities when applied to the following consistent pairwise comparison matrix. Method (4) gives a good approximation.

	W	B	R
W	1	3/2	3
B	2/3	1	2
R	1/3	1/2	1

It is important to note that these methods give different results for the general case where a matrix is not consistent.

Let us now apply the different methods of estimating the solution to the chair example.

Applying method (1), the sum of the rows of this matrix is a column vector which, to save space, we write as the row (19.00, 11.20, 5.42, 1.56). The total sum of the matrix is given by summing these vector components. Its value is 37.18. If we divide each component of the vector by this number we obtain the column vector of priorities, again written as a row, (0.51, 0.30, 0.15, 0.04) for the relative brightness of chairs A, B, C, D, respectively.

Applying method (2), the sum of the columns of this matrix is a row vector (1.51, 6.43, 11.25, 18.00). The reciprocals of these sums are (0.66, 0.16, 0.09, 0.06), which when normalized become (0.68, 0.16, 0.09, 0.06).

Applying method (3) we normalize each column (add its components and divide each component by this sum) obtaining the matrix

$$\begin{bmatrix} 0.66 & 0.78 & 0.53 & 0.39 \\ 0.13 & 0.16 & 0.36 & 0.33 \\ 0.11 & 0.04 & 0.09 & 0.22 \\ 0.09 & 0.03 & 0.02 & 0.06 \end{bmatrix}$$

The sum of the rows is the column vector (2.36, 0.98, 0.46, 0.20) which when averaged by the sample size of 4 columns yields the column vector of priorities: (0.590, 0.245, 0.115, 0.050).

Method (4) gives (0.61, 0.24, 0.10, 0.04).

The exact solution to the problem, as will be described later in the book, is obtained by raising the matrix to arbitrarily large powers and dividing the sum of each row by the sum of the elements of the matrix. To two decimal places it is given by (0.61, 0.24, 0.10, 0.05).

By comparing these results we note that the accuracy is improved from (1) to (2) to (3), although they increase in complexity of computation. If the matrix is consistent all these four vectors would be the same. Method (4) only gives a very good approximation.

If we may assume that the reader knows how to multiply a matrix by a vector, we can introduce a method for getting a crude estimate of consistency.

We multiply the matrix of comparisons on the right by the estimated solution vector obtaining a new vector. If we divide the first component of this vector by the first component of the estimated solution vector, the second component of the new vector by the second component of the estimated solution vector and so on, we obtain another vector. If we take the sum of the components of this vector and divide by the number of components we have an approximation to a number λ_{max} (called the maximum or principal eigenvalue) to use in estimating the consistency as reflected in the proportionality of preferences. The closer λ_{max} is to n (the number of activities in the matrix) the more consistent is the result.

As will be clear from our theoretical discussion in a later chapter, deviation from consistency may be represented by $(\lambda_{max}-n)/(n-1)$ which we call the *consistency index* (C.I.).

We shall call the consistency index of a randomly generated reciprocal matrix from the scale 1 to 9, with reciprocals forced, the *random index* (R.I.). At Oak Ridge National Laboratory, colleagues (see Chap. 3) generated an average R.I. for matrices of order 1–15 using a sample size of 100. One would expect the R.I. to increase as the order of the matrix increases. Since the sample size was only 100, there remained statistical fluctuations in the index from one order to another. Because of these, we repeated the calculations at the Wharton School for a sample size 500 up to 11 by 11 matrices and then used the Oak Ridge results for $n = 12$, 13, 14, 15. The following table gives the order of the matrix (first row) and the average R.I. (second row) determined as described above.

1	2	3	4	5	6	7	8	9	10	11	12	13	14	15
0.00	0.00	0.58	0.90	1.12	1.24	1.32	1.41	1.45	1.49	1.51	1.48	1.56	1.57	1.59

The ratio of C.I. to the average R.I. for the same order matrix is called the *consistency ratio* (C.R.). A consistency ratio of 0.10 or less is considered acceptable.

To illustrate our approximate calculation of C.I. with an example we use the above matrix and the third column vector derived by method (3) to find λ_{max}. We had (0.59, 0.25, 0.11, 0.05) for the vector of priorities. If we multiply the matrix on the right by this vector we get the column vector (2.85, 1.11, 0.47, 0.20). If we divide corresponding components of the second vector by the first we get (4.83, 4.44, 4.28, 4.00). Summing over these components and taking the average gives 4.39.

This gives $(4.39-4)/3 = 0.13$ for the C.I. To determine how good this result is we divide it by the corresponding value R.I. = 0.90. The consistency ratio (C.R.) is $0.13/0.90 = 0.14$ which is perhaps not as close as we would like to 0.10.

These comparisons and computations establish the priorities of the elements of one level of a hierarchy with respect to one element of the next level. If there are more than two levels, the various priority vectors can be combined into priority matrices, which yield one final priority vector for the bottom level.

1-5 INTUITIVE JUSTIFICATION OF THE METHOD

Assume that n activities are being considered by a group of interested people. We assume that the group's goals are:

(1) to provide judgments on the relative importance of these activities;
(2) to insure that the judgments are quantified to an extent which also permits a quantitative interpretation of the judgments among all activities.

Clearly, goal (2) will require appropriate technical assistance.

Our goal is to describe a method of deriving, from the group's quantified judgments (i.e., from the relative values associated with *pairs* of activities), a set of weights to be associated with *individual* activities; in a sense defined below, these weights should reflect the group's quantified judgments. What this approach achieves is to put the information resulting from (1) and (2) into usable form without deleting information residing in the qualitative judgments.

Let $C_1, C_2, \ldots, C_n$ be the set of activities. The quantified judgments on pairs of activities C_i, C_j are represented by an n-by-n matrix

$$A = (a_{ij}), \qquad (i, j = 1, 2, \ldots, n)$$

The entries a_{ij} are defined by the following entry rules.

Rule 1. If $a_{ij} = \alpha$, then $a_{ji} = 1/\alpha$, $\alpha \neq 0$.
Rule 2. If C_i is judged to be of equal relative importance as C_j, then $a_{ij} = 1$, $a_{ji} = 1$; in particular, $a_{ii} = 1$ for all i.

Thus the matrix A has the form

$$A = \begin{bmatrix} 1 & a_{12} & \cdots & a_{1n} \\ 1/a_{12} & 1 & \cdots & a_{2n} \\ \vdots & \vdots & \ddots & \vdots \\ 1/a_{1n} & 1/a_{2n} & \cdots & 1 \end{bmatrix}$$

Having recorded the quantified judgments on pairs (C_i, C_j) as numerical entries a_{ij} in the matrix A, the problem now is to assign to the n contingencies $C_1, C_2, \ldots, C_n$ a set of numerical weights $w_1, w_2, \ldots, w_n$ that would "reflect the recorded judgments."

In order to do so, the vaguely formulated problem must first be transformed into a precise mathematical one. This essential, and apparently harmless, step is the most crucial one in any problem that requires the representation of a real-life situation in terms of an abstract mathematical structure. It is particularly crucial in the present problem where the representation involves a number of transitions that are not immediately discernible. It appears, therefore, desirable in the present problem to identify the major steps in the process of representation and to make each step as explicit as possible in order to enable the potential user to form his own judgment on the *meaning and value* of the method in relation to *his* problem and *his* goal.

The major question is the one concerned with the meaning of the vaguely formulated condition in the statement of our goal: "these weights should reflect the group's quantified judgments." This presents the need to describe in precise, arithmetic terms, how the weights w_i should relate to the judgments a_{ij}; or, in other words, the problem of specifying the conditions we wish to impose on the weights we seek in relation to the judgments obtained. The desired description is developed in three steps, proceeding from the simplest special case to the general one.

Step 1 Assume first that the "judgments" are merely the result of precise physical measurements. Say the judges are given a set of pebbles, $C_1, C_2, \ldots, C_n$ and a precision scale. To compare C_1 with C_2, they put C_1 on a scale and read off its weight—say, w_1—305 grams. They weigh C_2 and find $w_2 = 244$ grams. They divide w_1 by w_2, which is 1.25. They pronounce their judgment, "C_1 is 1.25 times as heavy as C_2" and record it as $a_{12} = 1.25$. Thus, in this ideal case of *exact measurement*, the relations between the weights w_i and the judgments a_{ij} are simply given by

$$\frac{w_i}{w_j} = a_{ij} \qquad \text{(for } i, j = 1, 2, \ldots, n) \tag{1-1}$$

and

$$A = \begin{bmatrix} w_1/w_1 & w_1/w_2 & \cdots & w_1/w_n \\ w_2/w_1 & w_2/w_2 & \cdots & w_2/w_n \\ \vdots & \vdots & & \vdots \\ w_n/w_1 & w_n/w_2 & \cdots & w_n/w_n \end{bmatrix}$$

However, it would be unrealistic to require these relations to hold in the general case. Imposing these stringent relations would, in most practical cases, make the problem of finding the w_i (when a_{ij} are given) unsolvable. First, even physical measurements are never exact in a mathematical sense; and, hence, allowance *must* be made for deviations; and second, because in human judgments, these deviations are considerably larger.

Step 2 In order to see how to make allowance for deviations, consider the ith row in the matrix A. The entries in that row are

$$a_{i1}, a_{i2}, \ldots, a_{ij}, \ldots, a_{in}$$

In the ideal (exact) case these values are the same as the ratios

$$\frac{w_i}{w_1}, \frac{w_i}{w_2}, \ldots, \frac{w_i}{w_j}, \ldots, \frac{w_i}{w_n}$$

Hence, in the ideal case, if we multiply the first entry in that row by w_1, the second entry by w_2, and so on, we would obtain

$$\frac{w_i}{w_1} w_1 = w_i, \qquad \frac{w_i}{w_2} w_2 = w_i, \ldots, \frac{w_j}{w_j} w_j = w_i, \ldots, \frac{w_i}{w_n} w_n = w_i$$

The result is a row of identical entries

$$w_i, w_i, \ldots, w_i$$

whereas, in the general case, we would obtain a row of entries that represent a statistical scattering of values around w_i. It appears, therefore, reasonable to require that w_i should equal the average of these values. Consequently, instead of the ideal case relations (1-1)

$$w_i = a_{ij}w_j \qquad (i, j = 1, 2, \ldots, n)$$

the more realistic relations for the general case take the form (for each fixed i)

$$w_i = \text{the average of } (a_{i1}w_1, a_{i2}w_2, \ldots, a_{in}w_n)$$

More explicitly we have

$$w_i = \frac{1}{n} \sum_{j=1}^{n} a_{ij}w_j \qquad (i = 1, 2, \ldots, n) \tag{1-2}$$

While the relations in (1-2) represent a substantial relaxation of the more stringent relations (1-1), there still remains the question: is the relaxation *sufficient* to insure the existence of solutions; that is, to insure that the problem of finding unique weights w_i when the a_{ij} are given is a solvable one?

Step 3 To seek the answer to the above essentially mathematical question, it is necessary to express the relations in (1-2) in still another, more familiar form. For this purpose we need to summarize the line of reasoning to this point. In seeking a set of conditions to describe how the weight vector w should relate to the quantified judgments, we first considered the ideal (exact) case in Step 1, which suggested the relations (1-1). Next, realizing that the real case will require allowances for deviations, we provided for such allowances in Step 2, leading to the formulation (1-2). Now, this is still not realistic enough; that is, that (1-2) which works for the ideal case is still too stringent to secure the existence of a weight vector w that should satisfy (1-2). We note that for good estimates a_{ij} tends to be close to w_i/w_j and hence is a small perturbation of this ratio. Now as a_{ij} changes it turns out that there would be a corresponding solution of (1-2), (i.e., w_i and w_j can change to accommodate this change in a_{ij} from the ideal case), if n were also to change. We denote this value of n by $\lambda_{\max}$. Thus the problem

$$w_i = \frac{1}{\lambda_{\max}} \sum_{j=1}^{n} a_{ij}w_j \qquad i = 1, \ldots, n \tag{1-3}$$

has a solution that also turns out to be unique. This is the well-known eigenvalue problem with which we will be dealing.

In general, deviations in the a_{ij} can lead to large deviations both in $\lambda_{\max}$ and in $w_i, i = 1, \ldots, n$. However, this is not the case for a reciprocal matrix which satisfies rules 1 and 2. In this case we have a stable solution.

Recall that we have given an intuitive justification of our approach. There is an elegant way of framing this in mathematical notation. It is given in detail in later chapters. Briefly stated in matrix notation, we start with what we call the paradigm case $Aw = nw$, where A is a consistent matrix and consider a reciprocal matrix A'

which is a perturbation of A, elicited from pairwise comparison judgments, and solve the problem $A'w' = \lambda_{\max}w'$ where $\lambda_{\max}$ is the largest eigenvalue of A'.

We have sometimes been interested in the opposite question to dominance with respect to a given property. We have called it recessiveness of one activity when compared with another with respect to that property. In that case we solve for the left eigenvector v in $vA = \lambda_{\max}v$. Only when A is consistent are the elements of v and w reciprocals. Without consistency they are reciprocals for $n = 2$ and $n = 3$. In general one need not expect them to have a definite relationship. The two vectors correspond to the two sides of the Janus face of reality—the bright and the dark.

1-6 HIERARCHICAL COMPOSITION OF PRIORITIES BY EXAMPLE

School Selection Example

Three highschools, A, B, C, were analyzed from the standpoint of the author's son according to their desirability. Six independent characteristics were selected for the comparison—learning, friends, school life, vocational training, college preparation, and music classes (see Fig. 1-4). The pairwise judgment matrices were as shown in Tables 1-2 and 1-3.

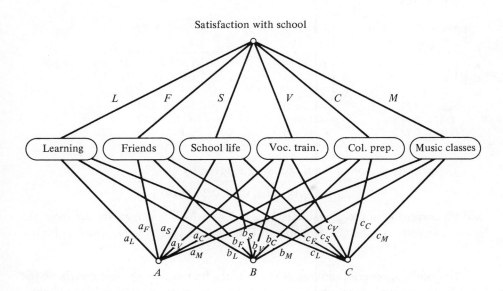

Figure 1-4 School satisfaction hierarchy

Table 1-2 Comparison of characteristics with respect to overall satisfaction with school

	Learning	Friends	School life	Vocational training	College preparation	Music classes
Learning	1	4	3	1	3	4
Friends	1/4	1	7	3	1/5	1
School life	1/3	1/7	1	1/5	1/5	1/6
Vocational training	1	1/3	5	1	1	1/3
College preparation	1/3	5	5	1	1	3
Music classes	1/4	1	6	3	1/3	1

$$\lambda_{max} = 7.49, \text{ C.I.} = 0.30, \text{ C.R.} = 0.24$$

Table 1-3 Comparison of schools with respect to the six characteristics

	Learning				Friends				School life		
	A	B	C		A	B	C		A	B	C
A	1	1/3	1/2	A	1	1	1	A	1	5	1
B	3	1	3	B	1	1	1	B	1/5	1	1/5
C	2	1/3	1	C	1	1	1	C	1	5	1

$$\lambda_{max} = 3.05 \qquad \lambda_{max} = 3.00 \qquad \lambda_{max} = 3.00$$
$$\text{C.I.} = 0.025 \qquad \text{C.I.} = 0 \qquad \text{C.I.} = 0$$
$$\text{C.R.} = 0.04 \qquad \text{C.R.} = 0 \qquad \text{C.R.} = 0$$

	Vocational training				College preparation				Music classes		
	A	B	C		A	B	C		A	B	C
A	1	9	7	A	1	1/2	1	A	1	6	4
B	1/9	1	1/5	B	2	1	2	B	1/6	1	1/3
C	1/7	5	1	C	1	1/2	1	C	1/4	3	1

$$\lambda_{max} = 3.21 \qquad \lambda_{max} = 3.0 \qquad \lambda_{max} = 3.05$$
$$\text{C.I.} = 0.105 \qquad \text{C.I.} = 0 \qquad \text{C.I.} = 0.025$$
$$\text{C.R.} = 0.18 \qquad \text{C.R.} = 0 \qquad \text{C.R.} = 0.04$$

The priority vector of the first matrix is given by

$$(0.32, 0.14, 0.03, 0.13, 0.24, 0.14)$$

and its corresponding eigenvalue is $\lambda_{max} = 7.49$ which is somewhat far from the consistent value 6. The C.I. is 0.30 and C.R. is $0.30/1.24 = 0.24$, which is high.

To obtain the overall ranking of the schools, we multiply the last matrix on the right by the transpose (column version) of the row vector of weights of the characteristics. This is the same as weighting each of the above six eigenvectors by the priority of the corresponding characteristic and then adding (made possible by the

Table 1-4

Learning	Friends	School life	Vocational training	College preparation	Music classes
0.16	0.33	0.45	0.77	0.25	0.69
0.59	0.33	0.09	0.05	0.50	0.09
0.25	0.33	0.46	0.17	0.25	0.22

independence of the characteristics (see below for further elaboration). This yields

$$A = 0.37$$
$$B = 0.38$$
$$C = 0.25$$

The son went to school A because it had almost the same rank as school B, yet school B was a private school charging close to \$1,600 a year and school A was free. This was a conflict problem between the author's son and wife; the first preferred school A, and the second school B, but neither took money into consideration as important. Although the C.R. for the second level was high they took the decision anyway despite protestations from the author about high inconsistency.

Explanation using Fig. 1-4 If the weights of the criteria and the schools with respect to each criterion are as indicated along each line segment in the figure, then

$$\text{Overall rank of school } A = a_L L + a_F F + a_S S + a_V V + a_C C + a_M M$$
$$\text{Overall rank of school } B = b_L L + b_F F + b_S S + b_V V + b_C C + b_M M$$
$$\text{Overall rank of school } C = c_L L + c_F F + c_S S + c_V V + c_C C + c_M M$$

The previous calculations are the same as the following matrix multiplication

$$\begin{bmatrix} 0.16(a_L) & 0.33(a_F) & 0.45(a_S) & 0.77(a_V) & 0.25(a_C) & 0.69(a_M) \\ 0.59(b_L) & 0.33(b_F) & 0.09(b_S) & 0.05(b_V) & 0.50(b_C) & 0.09(b_M) \\ 0.25(c_L) & 0.33(c_F) & 0.46(c_S) & 0.17(c_V) & 0.25(c_C) & 0.22(c_M) \end{bmatrix} \begin{bmatrix} 0.32(L) \\ 0.14(F) \\ 0.03(S) \\ 0.13(V) \\ 0.24(C) \\ 0.14(M) \end{bmatrix}$$

To find out the measure of satisfaction of a candidate with a school, first we need to list the important criteria which characterize schools and compute the relative desirabilities of these criteria to the candidate. Desirability would vary from one candidate to another. For example, one student may find friends more attractive than college preparation while another may feel the opposite way. The criteria are denoted by L, F, S, V, C, and M in the figure.

The second step is to compute the relative standing of each school with respect to each criterion. For example, one school may have better music classes while another is well known for its vocational training.

To get the overall ranking of each school, first we need to multiply the weight indicating the qualification of that school with respect to the criterion by the weight of that criterion. We then add these values for each school with respect to all the criteria. For example, for school A, a_L is the relative weight of learning in that school. Since the relative weight of learning is L, $a_L L$ is the overall weight of learning for school A. By the same argument we calculate $a_F F$, $a_S S$, $a_V V$, $a_C C$, and $a_M M$. Therefore, the overall rank of school A is the sum of the overall weights of the activities mentioned previously, i.e., overall rank of school $A = a_L L + a_F F + a_S S + a_V V + a_C C + a_M M$.

The reader who is interested in the perversity of youthful judgment may wish to see what the priorities look like three years after (Table 1-5). The young man (now aged 18) no longer considers friends or vocational training as important. His interest in college and music seem to dominate. They have become urgent needs rather than long range aspirations. Consistency has also improved tremendously.

The priorities of the schools with respect to the characteristics are the same as before and it is now much clearer that the right choice was made then. The priorities of the schools are $A = 0.40$, $B = 0.36$, $C = 0.25$.

1-7 PROTOCOL OF A PRIORITIZATION SESSION

The first requirement in the analysis of the functions of a system is to construct the hierarchy representing these functional relations. So far it has been found that for most simple systems, the hierarchy suggests itself in a natural correspondence with the functions of the system. However, the system may have a high degree of complexity and it may not be easy to find the hierarchical structure which corresponds to this system. In a more direct approach we have often resorted to the process of brainstorming, by putting down all elements relevant to that hierarchy. We then arranged these in groups according to dominance among the groups. These groupings served as the hierarchy levels. This process of grouping can be better accomplished by a technical procedure described later. It may be useful to mention that

Table 1-5 Overall satisfaction with school

	Learning	Friends	School life	Vocational training	College preparation	Music classes
Learning	1	5	7	5	3	1
Friends	1/5	1	3	1/5	1/6	1/6
School life	1/7	1/3	1	1/4	1/5	1/5
Vocational training	1/5	5	4	1	1/5	1/6
College preparation	1/3	6	5	5	1	1
Music classes	1	6	5	6	1	1

The eigenvalue of this matrix is $\lambda_{\max} = 6.68$, C.I. $= 0.14$, C.R. $= 0.14$.
The corresponding eigenvector is (0.33, 0.05, 0.03, 0.09, 0.23, 0.27)

two properties of a hierarchy level which have strong overlap should be grouped together as a single more general property for the comparison. For example, quality and size often go together and may be grouped together as suitability.

To assist with the quality of informed judgment inputs, it is essential that the hierarchy of activities, objectives, and still higher objectives be set up with care. A study may be required to identify and characterize those properties in the levels of the hierarchy which affect the performance of the higher level properties or the fulfillment of higher level objectives.

After dividing the ideas into categories, the process of defining the purposes for which the problem is being studied and structuring the hierarchy is carefully and methodically carried out. Tentativeness in the structuring process is essential. What is most important is that an individual's knowledge and judgments or those of a group have a fair chance of being adequately and correctly expressed. This is not a task for a weary and short tempered director. Diplomacy and concern for the feelings of the people involved are paramount. Yet the leader himself must make sure that differences do not cause the process to deteriorate. Occasionally it helps to remind the participants that someone has to do something about the problem, and that if they are not able to crystallize their ideas, the result may come out contrary to what they might desire to see happen in a fair process.

Before proceeding with prioritization, we urge that an attempt be made to write down a definition of the elements introduced to avoid controversial arguments later on.

The same approach may be used to assist a single decision maker in organizing the complexity he faces and derive priorities which reflect his beliefs and attitudes. In a complex situation there is little hope that problems can be resolved by an internalized mystical, but not articulated, understanding of the important factors. It may be counterproductive to be perpetually concerned that the process may leave out some important factors. If an individual really understands the process he would have to be aware of the important factors and keep examining his feelings for residual factors that are important but not yet included. That is one reason why one should take time to study a problem and not rush through it.

The quality of the output may be evaluated by how logically satisfactory the answers are. They must, in some sense, conform with the original input. For example, a member of a level that is favored over the other members through the original pairwise judgments should come out with the highest ranking and so on down the line. Of course, it is the very purpose of the model to develop a consistent order. Note that the total ordering is *not* known at the beginning, but only pairwise comparisons which may in fact be inconsistent. The results must conform with what one intuitively expects as a reasonable outcome. Otherwise, there would be discrepancy between the judgments provided and the operations of the theory.

It is important to remark that the numbers used in the scale are absolute magnitudes and not simple ordinal numbers. This says that our scale does not allow comparisons whose intensity exceeds 9. As we have indicated, elements must be put into clusters within each of which the elements are comparable with this scale, and then the clusters in turn must also be compared with this scale. Note that it may be necessary to invent or introduce intermediate clusters in order to be able to make relative comparisons which lead from the cluster with the smallest (or weakest) elements to the cluster with the largest (or strongest) elements. This is the natural way we do things and not an artifice adopted for the theory. We cannot directly compare the weight of a grain of sand with that of the sun. We need a gradual transition between them.

One must prioritize very carefully the highest levels of the hierarchy because it is there that concensus is most needed since these priorities drive the rest of the hierarchy. In each level one must ensure that the criteria represented are independent or at least are sufficiently different, and that these differences can be captured as independent properties in the level. Revision of the elements may be necessary to capture independence successfully. Since there are times when dependence is holistic and cannot be removed, our approach can also be adapted to handle interdependence, as we shall see in Chap. 6. As one goes farther down the hierarchy one expects greater variability of opinion among compatible people as we reach the operating level. In that case, each person wants a piece of the action. To the extent that people agree about the meaning as well as the importance of the elements more resources should be allocated to that area; to the extent that people disagree about either meaning or importance, their judgments tend to nullify each other and the area tends to get a smaller share of the action until greater support for it is obtained. If an area is important to our needs, but there is disagreement on implementation, we would have to withhold action until people develop a better appreciation for the need and can induce more cohesive action. This is a logical outcome of the hierarchical approach. Where there is disagreement, people will tend to be dissatisfied because they don't see realization of their judgments. Otherwise, with agreement there is greater satisfaction.

A large audience of diverse backgrounds would require a great deal of time to structure a hierarchy and provide judgments. Wear and tear may set in early and the meeting may not lead to fruitful results in the allotted time. The best way to engage a large group is either to choose a narrow focus for the discussion or, better, to have them generate the hierarchy (or provide them with one for debate) and then divide them into homogeneous groups and let each group provide the judgments in those parts of the hierarchy which relate to their special interest. People should be told that some may feel frustrated during the process; they could go out for a walk or participate in a discussion in a separate room while the others carry on, and then return when they feel reinvigorated. This avoids deterioration of the process.

Of course there are times when political favors, hidden agenda, disruption, and other political processes may be in operation and group interaction and cooperation would be difficult. We have encountered such problems in our experience using the Analytic Hierarchy Process (AHP). Our conclusion is that the AHP is a powerful tool for those who want to assess their own and their opponent's strategies. Those who do not wish to participate cannot be forced to, but they can sometimes be coaxed to do so.

In cooperative undertakings, the process moves faster when the participants have in common: (1) shared goals; (2) intimate long term contact; (3) work in a climate of social acceptance; and (4) have equal status when participating.

A final observation is that group interaction is not unlike a marriage, about which people tend to have romantic feelings at the start, but as they get into it they find that there is a good deal of friction, feuding, and dissent. However, overall, life moves on and there are fundamental points of agreement and mutual needs which keep people together. Thus one must not enter any group interaction process with too much idealism and a strong predisposition for propriety and order.

We now turn our attention to the next step in the process, which is to solicit informed judgments from people.

We are given the elements of a hierarchy level and wish to construct the matrix of pairwise comparisons among these elements in relation to each element of the next higher level which serves as a criterion or property with respect to which they are compared. The individuals, who give the judgments, are asked the following type of question: Given a pair of elements of the matrix, which one do you believe is more dominant in possessing or contributing to the property in question? How strong is this dominance: equal, weak, strong, demonstrated, or absolute, or is it a compromise between adjacent values in this strength comparison?

The question must be carefully phrased to evoke the judgment or feeling of the individuals involved. Uniformity should be maintained in the questions asked. It is essential to focus on the property involved as people's minds may wander fuzzily to more general properties.

REMARK In order to obtain a set of priorities that reflect the merit or positive impact of the activities, the set of properties with respect to which they are compared must be formulated in such a way that the desirable attributes of the activities are brought out. For example, the cost of going on vacation would yield a high priority number for the more expensive vacation spot but, in fact, this priority should be low. In that case, the question to ask is: Which vacation place *saves* more on cost rather than which one costs more?

If the individuals differ in their judgments, they are allowed to make a case for themselves by either reaching consensus (which sometimes happens even after a heated debate) or by following whatever ground rules there are for reaching a single judgment, such as a majority vote. Individuals have been known to change their position. In some cases a whole group changed their position after listening to reasons given by one member. Bargaining is possible whereby people accept the judgments given by others in return for using their judgment in another area more important to them.

When people are reluctant to volunteer their judgment, an auction-type procedure may be followed by proposing a judgment value and asking people how they feel about it. Lack of inclination to discriminate between two elements often means that they share the property equally among them. When there is no agreement, each individuals records his judgments and the solutions are examined for a clearer understanding of what (if anything) can be done. There are times when differences in the world of people cripple action.

When the entire set of judgments has been obtained, people are asked about how faithfully they feel their understanding and judgments have been represented. This avoids hard feelings arising out of being ignored. Debates might be shortened if time is limited, but people should be reminded that it is their problem and requires sufficient time to get good results. The participants should always be consulted about the adequacy of the hierarchical structuring of their problem and the representation of their judgments. If there are objections, they should be carefully and patiently considered. If revisions are desired, they may be assigned as subtasks to be performed soon and reported on to the group.

Frequently, one can note areas of greatest difference in judgment and bring them up again later in the session for review.

The procedure may begin by focusing on the rows of the matrix in the order of believed dominance of their corresponding elements essentially implying that people can probably tell the ordinal dominance of the elements in advance. The strongest and the weakest elements are compared first to provide a guidepost for the other values. Of course, this may not be always possible. Another way is to try and fill out those comparisons which people are sure of.

The numerical values and their reciprocals are entered in the matrix each time a judgment is obtained and soon people learn to give the numbers directly. The geometric means of the judgments may be used when people don't want to enter into debate. This is probably a less desirable alternative. Sometimes one can obtain the individual priority vectors and take their geometric mean for an answer.

It is worth noting that at times lower priority criteria finally determine the choice of alternatives. Consider an average family of four buying a car. The most important criterion is the budget (priority 0.52) they have available. Next is the price of the car (priority 0.23). A relatively low priority is the style and size (priority 0.16) and, finally, economy of operation (priority 0.09). Once they have selected several cars of the same price range allowed by their budget, the final selection of one of this group is dictated by the style and economy. The higher priority criteria help in choosing the suitable and affordable class of car; the lower priority criteria help in choosing the individual car from among the brands.

Four types of questions are sometimes raised with regard to the judgment process: (1) the primary effect, or whether providing judgments may not bias the outcome toward what is examined first; (2) the recency effect, or the influence of the latest information over what went before, (3) the out-of-role-behavior where people assume the role of others and provide judgments for them without full appreciation of the people they represent; and (4) personal bias while participating in group decision making. Most of these phenomena can occur in an ordinary group session. Their influence is diminished if more time is taken with repeated interaction and people are cautioned about personal bias. In other words to correct problems of handling information different repetitions of the problem should highlight these difficulties leading to a final exercise considered by the group to be most representative of the problem.

For the Decision-maker

If you are faced with a number of options to choose from and you have a maze of criteria to judge with, do the pairwise comparison of the criteria with respect to *short* and *long*-range efforts, *risks* and *benefits*, and also make a pairwise comparison matrix with respect to effectiveness and success. Finally, on the lowest level, compare the options with respect to each criterion, compose the weights hierarchically, and select the highest priority. If you have canvassed enough judgments so that you are sure you have considered all the relevant factors and good judgments, stop agonizing over your choice. You have done your human best to make the right choice. For quick decisions in day-to-day operations maintain a file of your working hierarchies, their judgment and resulting priorities. Change the necessary judgments for that decision to obtain the result or note which judgments have to be changed to obtain a desired result. Finally, add elements with their relevant judgments if necessary to obtain new priorities. This can also be done by interacting with a computer which has the information stored. For portfolio selection, a benefits hierarchy and a costs hierarchy are needed. The ratios of benefits to costs are then used for decision purposes.

1-8 SUMMARY

The eigenvalue approach to pairwise comparisons provides a way for calibrating a numerical scale, particularly in new areas where measurements and quantitative comparisons do not exist. The measure of consistency enables one to return to the judgments modifying them here and there to improve the overall consistency. The participation of several people makes it possible to make tradeoffs between different entries. It can also create a dialogue for what the real relation should be: a compromise among the various judgments representing diverse experience.

The steps of the process proceed as follows.

(1) State the problem.
(2) Put the problem in broad context—embed it if necessary in a larger system including other actors, their objectives, and outcomes.
(3) Identify the criteria that influence the behavior of the problem.
(4) Structure a hierarchy of the criteria, sub-criteria, properties of alternatives, and the alternatives themselves.
(5) In a many party problem the levels may relate to the environment, actors, actor objectives, actor policies, and outcomes, from which one derives the composite outcome (state of the world).
(6) To remove ambiguity carefully define every element in the hierarchy.
(7) Prioritize the primary criteria with respect to their impact on the overall objective called the focus.

(8) State the question for pairwise comparisons clearly above each matrix. Pay attention to the orientation of each question, e.g., costs go down, benefits go up.
(9) Prioritize the subcriteria with respect to their criteria.
(10) Enter pairwise comparison judgments and force their reciprocals.
(11) Calculate priorities by adding the elements of each column and dividing each entry by the total of the column. Average over the rows of the resulting matrix and you have the priority vector.

For (12)–(15) see later chapters.

(12) In the case of scenarios calibrate their state variables on a scale of -8 to 8 as to how they differ from the present as zero.
(13) Compose the weights in the hierarchy to obtain composite priorities and also the composite values of the state variables which collectively define the composite outcome.
(14) In the case of choosing among alternatives select the highest priority alternative.
(15) In the case of resource allocation, cost out alternatives, compute benefit to cost ratio and allocate accordingly, either fully or proportionately. In a cost prioritization problem allocate resources proportionately to the priorities.

1-9 HIERARCHIES AND JUDGMENTS BY QUESTIONNAIRE

It is possible to elicit the hierarchy concerning an issue by questionnaire, synthesize the result, and follow up by another questionnaire to elicit judgments.

We give a simple illustration of how judgments may be obtained for a single matrix by using a questionnaire. The same method can be applied to a hierarchy. Let us consider the optics example to obtain judgments on the relative brightness of chairs. We indicate scale values ranging from one extreme down towards equality and then again rising to the extreme. In a left column we list all the alternatives to be compared for dominance with other alternatives in the right column. In all, each column contains $[n(n-1)]/2$ alternatives. We then ask people to check the judgment which indicates the dominance of the element in the left column over the corresponding one in its row in the right column. If in fact there is such dominance some position in the set of values to the left of equality is checked. Otherwise equality or a position in the right set of values is checked. The same is done for all alternatives.

Relative brightness

Column I	Abso-lute	Very strong	Strong	Weak	Equal	Weak	Strong	Very strong	Abso-lute	Column II
C_1	—	—	—	—	—	—	—	—	—	C_2
C_1	—	—	—	—	—	—	—	—	—	C_3
C_1	—	—	—	—	—	—	—	—	—	C_4
C_2	—	—	—	—	—	—	—	—	—	C_3
C_2	—	—	—	—	—	—	—	—	—	C_4
C_3	—	—	—	—	—	—	—	—	—	C_4

TWO

INSTRUCTIVE EXAMPLES

2-1 INTRODUCTION

In this chapter, we shall develop our method further, primarily with the help of examples. First, we shall relate the "illuminated chairs" experiment and show that the relative brightness of the chairs, as determined by the subjective pairwise comparisons, are very close to those predicted by the inverse-square law of optics. As a further indication that our method produces, in cases where the actual figures are known, a close approximation to these values, we shall reproduce the results of the elementary study of the influence of nations through their wealth. Following that is an example estimating the relative distance of six cities from Philadelphia. We then distinguish between complete and incomplete hierarchies.

We close the chapter with two further examples. They were chosen in order to demonstrate how one determines an overall priority of the bottom level elements in a hierarchy with more than two levels. The first one gives us the opportunity to make some observations of more general interest.

2-2 TESTS FOR ACCURACY, RMS AND MAD

Of considerable interest to us must be the issue of how closely the priority vector developed by our method matches the "real" priority vector. One way to ascertain this is to apply the method to situations which allow determination of the actual numbers. In such cases, we wish to check how accurate the priority vector is.

To test for accuracy we must compare estimates in experiments with real answers that are known. Comparison of numbers involves the use of statistical measures. There are not many measures for validating theoretical results against reality. Two are the root mean square deviation and the median absolute deviation about the median. They are usually used for comparison purposes among several sample estimates to choose the one closest to reality and not as absolute measures.

Both are a means of measuring the spread of a set of measurements from a known set of underlying values.

Deviations between small numbers are apt to be small. To see how significantly small they are in absolute terms they must be divided by the average size number they are taken from. In our case it would be $1/n$ where n is the number of items being compared. Incidentally, one measure of error might be to take the differences (or absolute differences), weight them by the priorities, take their average, then divide by $1/n$, i.e., use $\sum_{i=1}^{n} w_i|w_i - x_i|$ where w_i are the priorities and x_i are their estimates.

The root mean square deviation (RMS) of two sets of numbers $a_1, \ldots, a_n$ and $b_1, \ldots, b_n$ is

$$\sqrt{\frac{1}{n} \sum_{i=1}^{n} (a_i - b_i)^2}$$

The median of a set of n numbers is obtained by arranging the numbers in increasing order and taking the middle term if n is odd and the average of the two middle terms if n is even. The median absolute deviation about the median (MAD) of a set of numbers $a_1, \ldots, a_n$ and $b_1, \ldots, b_n$ is given by median $\{|(a_i - b_i) - \text{median } (a_i - b_i)|\}$. As an illustration, see the illumination intensity example in the next section.

2-3 ILLUMINATION INTENSITY AND THE INVERSE SQUARE LAW

In Chap. 1 we presented the chair brightness example and proceeded as far as filling in the judgments and solving for the relative brightness. Four identical chairs were placed on a line from a light source at the distances of 9, 15, 21, and 28 yards. The purpose was to see if one could stand by the light and look at the chairs and compare their relative brightness in pairs, fill in the judgment matrix and obtain a relationship between the chairs and their distance from the light source. This experiment was repeated twice with different judges whose judgment matrices we now give. The first of these was given in Chap. 1.

Relative visual brightness (1st Trial)

	C_1	C_2	C_3	C_4
C_1	1	5	6	7
C_2	1/5	1	4	6
C_3	1/6	1/4	1	4
C_4	1/7	1/6	1/4	1

Relative visual brightness (2nd Trial)

	C_1	C_2	C_3	C_4
C_1	1	4	6	7
C_2	1/4	1	3	4
C_3	1/6	1/3	1	2
C_4	1/7	1/4	1/2	1

The judges of the first matrix were the author's young children, ages 5 and 7 at the time, who gave their judgments qualitatively. The judge of the second matrix was the author's wife, who was not present during the children's judgment process.

Relative brightness eigenvector
(1st Trial)

0.61
0.24
0.10
0.05

$\lambda_{max} = 4.39$
C.I. = 0.13
C.R. = 0.14

Relative brightness eigenvector
(2nd Trial)

0.62
0.22
0.10
0.06

$\lambda_{max} = 4.1$
C.I. = 0.03
C.R. = 0.03

Table 2-1 Inverse square law of optics

Distance	Normalized distance	Square of normalized distance	Reciprocal of previous column	Normalized reciprocal	Rounding off
9	0.123	0.015 129	66.098	0.607 9	0.61
15	0.205	0.042 025	23.79	0.218 8	0.22
21	0.288	0.082 944	12.05	0.110 8	0.11
28	0.384	0.147 456	6.78	0.062 3	0.06

First and second trial eigenvectors should be compared with the last column of the Inverse Square Law Table (2-1) calculated from the inverse square law in optics. It is interesting and important to observe that the judgments have captured a natural law here. It would seem that they could do the same in other areas of perception or thought, as we shall see later.

Note the sensitivity of the results as the object is very close to the source, for then it absorbs most of the value of the relative index and a small error in its distance from the source yields great error in the values. What is noteworthy from this sensory experiment is the observation or hypothesis that the observed intensity of illumination varies (approximately) inversely with the square of the distance. The more carefully designed the experiment, the better the results obtained from the visual observations.

The RMS of (0.62, 0.22, 0.10, 0.06) and (0.61, 0.22, 0.11, 0.06) is $\{\frac{1}{4}[(0.01)^2 + 0 + (0.01)^2 + 0]\}^{1/2} = 2.23 \times 10^{-3}$. The MAD is as follows. The differences between the two vectors are given by (0.01, 0, −0.01, 0). The median of these numbers is $0 + 0/2 = 0$. The deviations about this median are (0.01, 0, −0.01, 0). Their absolute value is taken and the median of the result is $(0.01 + 0)/2 = 0.005 = 5 \times 10^{-3}$. The significance of both RMS and MAD may be determined by dividing their values by the average value of the vector components which is simply $1/n$, where n is the number of components. Two vectors are nearly the same if either or both ratios are, for example, less than 0.1.

2-4 WEALTH OF NATIONS THROUGH THEIR WORLD INFLUENCE (Saaty and Khouja, 1976)

A number of people have studied the problem of measuring world influence of nations. We have briefly examined this concept within the framework of our model. We assumed that influence is a function of several factors. We considered five such factors: (1) human resources; (2) wealth; (3) trade; (4) technology; and (5) military power. Culture and ideology, and potential natural resources (such as oil) were not included.

Seven countries were selected for this analysis. They are the U.S., U.S.S.R., China, France, U.K., Japan, and West Germany. It was felt that these nations as a group comprised a dominant class of influential nations. It was desired to compare them among themselves as to their overall influence in international relations. We realize that what we have is a very rough estimate, mainly intended to serve as an interesting example of an application of our approach to priorities. We will only illustrate the method with respect to the single factor of wealth. The more general problem is studied in the paper referenced above.

In Table 2-2, we give a matrix indicating the pairwise comparisons of the seven countries with respect to wealth. For example, the value 4 in the first row indicates that wealth is between weak and strong importance in favor of the U.S. over the U.S.S.R. The reciprocal of 4 appears in the symmetric position, indicating the

Table 2-2 Wealth

	U.S.	U.S.S.R.	China	France	U.K.	Japan	W. Germany
U.S.	1	4	9	6	6	5	5
U.S.S.R.	0.25	1	7	5	5	3	4
China	0.11	0.14	1	0.2	0.2	0.14	0.2
France	0.17	0.2	5	1	1	0.33	0.33
U.K.	0.17	0.2	5	1	1	0.33	0.33
Japan	0.2	0.33	7	3	3	1	2
W. Germany	0.2	0.25	5	3	3	0.5	1

$$\lambda_{max} = 7.608, \text{ C.I.} = 0.10, \text{ C.R.} = 0.08$$

Explanation of Table
The first row compares the wealth influence (e.g., the Marshall Plan, A.I.D., etc.) of the U.S. with the other nations. For example, it is of equal importance to the U.S. (hence, the unit entry in the first position), between weak and strong importance when compared with the U.S.S.R. (hence, the value 4 in the second position), of absolute importance when compared with China (hence, the value 9 in the third position). We have values between strong and demonstrated importance when compared with France and the U.K. (hence a 6 in the next two positions), strong importance when compared with Japan and Germany (hence, a 5 in the following two positions). For the entries in the first colunn we have the reciprocals of the numbers in the first row indicating the inverse relation of relative strength of the wealth of the other countries when compared with the U.S. and so on for the remaining values in the second row and second column, etc.

Table 2-3 Normalized wealth eigenvector

	Normalized eigenvector	Actual GNP† (1972)	Fraction of GNP Total
U.S.	0.427	1,167	0.413
U.S.S.R.	0.230	635	0.225
China	0.021	120	0.043
France	0.052	196	0.069
U.K.	0.052	154	0.055
Japan	0.123	294	0.104
W. Germany	0.094	257	0.091
Total		2,823	

Note: Root Mean Square Deviation = 0.024.
Estimates of the GNP of China range from 74 billion
to 128 billion. Those of Russia are also uncertain.
† Billions of dollars.

inverse relation of relative strength of the wealth of the U.S.S.R. compared to the U.S.

Note that the comparisons are not consistent. For example, U.S.:U.S.S.R. = 4, U.S.S.R.:China = 7 but U.S.:China = 9 (not 28). Nevertheless, when the requisite computations are performed, we obtain relative weights of 0.427 and 0.230 for the U.S. and Russia, and these weights are in striking agreement with the corresponding Gross National Products (GNP) as percentages of the total GNP (see Table 2-3). Thus, despite the apparent arbitrariness of the scale, the irregularities disappear and the numbers occur in good accord with observed data. Thus wealth influence is proportional to actual wealth.

Compare the normalized eigenvector column derived by using the matrix of judgments in Table 2-1 with the actual GNP fraction given in the last column. The two are very close in their values. Estimates of the actual GNP of China range from 74 billion to 128 billion.

The value for China is more than it is for Japan in that our estimate is half the (admittedly uncertain) GNP value. Japan's value is a third over the true value. China probably does not belong in this group of nations.

2-5 ESTIMATING DISTANCES

Six cities were chosen: Montreal, Chicago, San Francisco, London, Cairo, and Tokyo. Their distances from Philadelphia were compared, pairwise by an experienced air traveler, who thought only of the airplane boredom and did not think of actual times or distances. The distance comparison matrix shown gives the judgments. The other matrix gives the actual distances, their normalized values, and the eigenvector derived from the judgment matrix.

Comparison of distances of cities from Philadelphia	Cairo	Tokyo	Chicago	San Francisco	London	Montreal
Cairo	1	1/3	8	3	3	7
Tokyo	3	1	9	3	3	9
Chicago	1/8	1/9	1	1/6	1/5	2
San Francisco	1/3	1/3	6	1	1/3	6
London	1/3	1/3	5	3	1	6
Montreal	1/7	1/9	1/2	1/6	1/6	1

$$\lambda_{max} = 6.45, \text{ C.I.} = 0.09, \text{ C.R.} = 0.07$$

City	Distance to Philadelphia (miles)	Normalized distance	Eigenvector
Cairo	5 729	0.278	0.263
Tokyo	7 449	0.361	0.397
Chicago	660	0.032	0.033
San Francisco	2 732	0.132	0.116
London	3 658	0.177	0.164
Montreal	400	0.019	0.027

2-6 TYPICAL HIERARCHIES

Figures 2-1 and 2-2 are illustrations of two different hierarchies.

In Fig. 2-1 the first hierarchy level has a single objective; the overall welfare of a nation. Its priority value is assumed to be equal to unity. The second hierarchy level has three objectives, strong economy, health, and national defense. Their priorities are derived from a matrix of pairwise comparisons with respect to the objective of the first level. The third hierarchy level objectives are the industries. The object is to determine the impact of the industries on the overall welfare of a nation through the intermediate second level. Thus their priorities with respect to each objective in the second level are obtained from a pairwise comparison matrix with respect to that objective, and the resulting three priority vectors are then weighted by the priority vector of the second level to obtain the desired composite vector of priorities of the industries.

In Fig. 2-2, the hierarchy consists of four levels, the first being the overall welfare of a nation, the second a set of possible future scenarios of that nation, the third level the provinces of that nation, and the fourth are transport projects which are to be implemented in the provinces. Note that not every province affects each scenario nor does each project affect every province. The hierarchy in Fig. 2-2 is not a complete one. The object is to determine the priorities of the projects as they impact on the overall objective. Here one must weigh the priorities of each comparison set by the ratio of the number of elements in that set to the total number of elements in the fourth level. This is done occasionally when the hierarchy is not

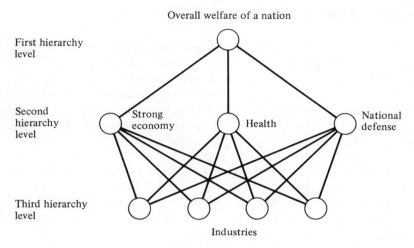

Figure 2-1 A complete hierarchy for priorities of industries

complete. Sometimes an incomplete hierarchy may be studied as a complete hierarchy but using zeros for the judgments and their reciprocals in the appropriate place.

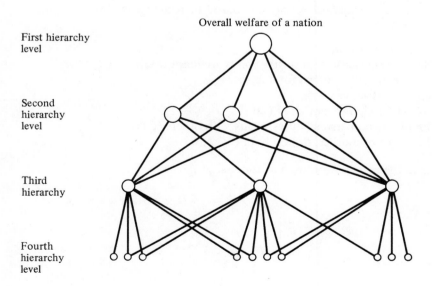

Figure 2-2 A hierarchy for priorities of transport projects in national planning

2-7 PSYCHOTHERAPY

The Analytic Hierarchy Process may be used to provide insight into psychological problem areas in the following manner. Consider an individual's overall well-being as the single top level entry in a hierarchy. Conceivably this level is primarily affected by childhood, adolescent, and adult experiences. Factors in growth and maturity which impinge upon well-being may be the influences of the father and the mother separately as well as their influences together as parents; the socio-economic background; sibling relationships, one's peer group, schooling, religious status, and so on.

The above factors which comprise the second level in our hierarchy, are further affected by criteria pertinent to each. For example, the influence of the father may be broken down to include his temperament, strictness, care, and affection. Sibling relationships can be further characterized by the number, age differential, and sexes of siblings; peer pressure and role modeling provide a still clearer picture of the effects of friends, schooling, and teachers.

As an alternative framework of description for the second level, we might include self-respect, security, adaptability to new people and new circumstances, and so on, influencing or as influenced by the elements above.

A more complete setting for a psychological history might include several hundreds of elements at each level, chosen by trained individuals and placed in such a way as to derive the maximum understanding of the subject in question.

Here we will consider a highly restricted form of the above, where the individual in question feels his self-confidence has been severely undermined and his social adjustments impaired by a restrictive situation during childhood. He is questioned about his childhood experiences only and asked to relate the following elements pairwise on each level.

Level 1. Overall well-being (*OW*)
Level 2. Self-respect, sense of security, ability to adapt to others (*R, S, A*)
Level 3. Visible affection shown for subject (*V*)
       Ideas of strictness, ethics (*E*)
       Actual disciplining of child (*D*)
       Emphasis on personal adjustments with others (*O*)
Level 4. Influence of mother, father, both (*M, F, B*)

The replies in the matrix form were as follows.

OW

	R	S	A
R	1	6	4
S	1/6	1	3
A	1/4	1/3	1

$\lambda_{max} = 3.26$
C.I. = 0.07
C.R. = 0.12

	R			
	V	*E*	*D*	*O*
V	1	6	6	3
E	1/6	1	4	3
D	1/6	1/4	1	1/2
O	1/3	1/3	2	1

$\lambda_{max} = 4.35$
C.I. = 0.12
C.R. = 0.13

	S			
	V	*E*	*D*	*O*
V	1	6	6	3
E	1/6	1	4	3
D	1/6	1/4	1	1/2
O	1/3	1/3	2	1

$\lambda_{max} = 4.35$
C.I. = 0.12
C.R. = 0.13

	A			
	V	*E*	*D*	*O*
V	1	1/5	1/3	1
E	5	1	4	1/5
D	3	1/4	1	1/4
O	1	5	4	1

$\lambda_{max} = 5.42$
C.I. = 0.47
C.R. = 0.52

	V		
	M	*F*	*B*
M	1	9	4
F	1/9	1	8
B	1/4	1/8	1

$\lambda_{max} = 4.00$
C.I. = 0.33
C.R. = 0.57

	E		
	M	*F*	*B*
M	1	1	1
F	1	1	1
B	1	1	1

$\lambda_{max} = 3.00$
C.I. = 0.0
C.R. = 0.0

	D		
	M	*F*	*B*
M	1	9	6
F	1/9	1	1/4
B	1/6	4	1

$\lambda_{max} = 3.11$
C.I. = 0.06
C.R. = 0.10

	O		
	M	*F*	*B*
M	1	5	5
F	1/5	1	1/3
B	1/5	3	1

$\lambda_{max} = 3.14$
C.I. = 0.07
C.R. = 0.12

The eigenvector of the first matrix, *a*, is given by

$$
OW \\
\begin{array}{c} R \\ S \\ A \end{array}
\begin{bmatrix} 0.701 \\ 0.193 \\ 0.106 \end{bmatrix}
$$

The matrix, *b*, of eigenvectors of the second row of matrices is given by

$$
\begin{array}{c} \quad R \quad\quad S \quad\quad A \end{array} \\
\begin{array}{c} V \\ E \\ D \\ O \end{array}
\begin{bmatrix} 0.604 & 0.604 & 0.127 \\ 0.213 & 0.213 & 0.281 \\ 0.064 & 0.064 & 0.120 \\ 0.119 & 0.119 & 0.463 \end{bmatrix}
$$

The matrix, c, of eigenvectors of the third row of matrices is given by

$$
\begin{array}{c}
 & V & E & D & O \\
M & \begin{bmatrix} 0.721 & 0.333 & 0.713 & 0.701 \\ F & 0.210 & 0.333 & 0.061 & 0.097 \\ B & 0.069 & 0.333 & 0.176 & 0.202 \end{bmatrix}
\end{array}
$$

The final composite vector of influence on well-being obtained from the product cba is given by

Mother: 0.635

Father: 0.209

Both: 0.156

It would seem that the therapy should depend on both the judgments and their considerable inconsistency involved. The individual was counseled to see more of his father to balance the parental influences.

2-8 ENERGY ALLOCATION (Saaty and Mariano, 1979)

In this example we are concerned with finding allocation weights for several large users of energy according to their overall contribution to different objectives of society. Let us assume the following conditions.

There are three large users of energy in the U.S.A.: C_1 = household users, C_2 = transportation, and C_3 = power generating plants. These comprise the third or lower level of the hierarchy. The objectives against which these energy users will be evaluated are: contribution to economic growth, contribution to environmental quality, and contribution to national security, which comprise the second level of the hierarchy. We construct the pairwise comparison matrix of these three objectives according to their impact on the overall objective of social and political advantage. We have forced consistency in this case—indicating a degree of certainty in the judgments. Thus after filling in the first row, the remaining entries were derived from it, as required by the definition of consistency.

Social and political advantage

	Economic growth	Environment	National security
Economic growth	1	5	3
M = Environmental impact	1/5	1	3/5
National security	1/3	5/3	1
$\lambda_{max} = 3.0,$	C.I. = 0.0,	C.R. = 0.0	

When the economy is compared with the environment and then with national security, according to their socio-political impact, the economy is judged to be of strong importance in the first case and of weak importance (but still more important) in the second; hence, the values 5 and 3 in the first row, respectively. The reason for a lower number when compared with national security was thought to be due to evidence that economically poor nations are known to indulge heavily in buying weapons, but of course cannot do so without building up some financial base. The numbers in the second and third rows are obtained by requiring consistency in this case. This means, for example, that in the a_{23} position, we have economy strongly favored over environment with value 5 and weakly favored over national security with value 3. Hence, the socio-political impact of the environment over national security is 3/5 and so on. In the remaining matrices of this example we do not require consistency. The priority vector derived from this matrix is given by the column vector (which we write as a row to save space): $w = (0.65, 0.13, 0.22)$. Thus, according to comparison of their socio-political impacts, the economy has the approximate value 0.65, the environment 0.13, and national security 0.22. Since as usual, the priority of the first hierarchy level (the overall socio-political objective) is 1, the weighted values of these priorities are equal to one times the above vector, which yields the vector itself.

Now the decision-maker, after a thorough study, has also made the following assessment of the relative importance of each user from the standpoint of the economy, the environment, and national security (the second hierarchy level). The matrices giving these judgments are, respectively

	Econ.	C_1	C_2	C_3		Env.	C_1	C_2	C_3
Consumers	C_1	1	3	5		C_1	1	2	7
Transport	C_2	1/3	1	2		C_2	1/2	1	5
Power	C_3	1/5	1/2	1		C_3	1/7	1/5	1

$$\lambda_{max} = 3.00 \qquad\qquad \lambda_{max} = 3.01$$
$$\text{C.I.} = 0 \qquad\qquad\quad \text{C.I.} = 0.01$$
$$\text{C.R.} = 0 \qquad\qquad\quad \text{C.R.} = 0.02$$

	N.sec.	C_1	C_2	C_3
Consumers	C_1	1	2	3
Transport	C_2	1/2	1	2
Power	C_3	1/3	1/2	1

$$\lambda_{max} = 3.01$$
$$\text{C.I.} = 0.01$$
$$\text{C.R.} = 0.02$$

As above, a priority vector is derived from each matrix. They are, respectively, the three columns of the following matrix:

$$\begin{bmatrix} 0.65 & 0.59 & 0.54 \\ 0.23 & 0.33 & 0.30 \\ 0.12 & 0.08 & 0.16 \end{bmatrix}$$

This matrix is multiplied on the right by the vector w to weight the priority vector measuring each impact with the priority of the corresponding objective. This yields the following composite priority vector of the hierarchy level of the activities C_1, C_2, and C_3, which we seek

$$\begin{bmatrix} 0.62 \\ 0.26 \\ 0.12 \end{bmatrix}$$

Thus the overall priority of activity C_1 is 0.62, that of C_2 is 0.26, and C_3 is 0.12. We have now ranked the activities on a ratio scale according to their overall impact. This answer may appear simple, but we have to show how we get it and justify its meaningfulness.

REMARK Sometimes when the weights are known from measurement such as tons of pollutants or the cost of cars, one is inclined to normalize and use them instead of constructing a judgment matrix and computing the eigenvector. This process can lead to error, particularly when the utility of relative measurements to the judge are not reflected in terms of their ratios. For example, to a rich man, one dollar or two dollars may be about the same, yet their ratio shows greater significance.

THREE

FOUNDATIONS AND EXTENSIONS

3-1 INTRODUCTION

This chapter introduces some further methodological observations. We begin with an explanation of the basic mathematical reasoning underlying our method. It leads, quite naturally, to the question why we chose a scale from 1 to 9 rather than any other of the possible scales. It will be shown that our scale is no worse than any other scale, has the advantage of simplicity, and is, appropriately, quite natural. In the remainder of the chapter we examine the process of revising judgments, give numerical calculations of all the eigenvalues and left and right eigenvectors for the wealth example, and discuss consensus in the Delphi method. Finally, we briefly discuss comparisons of triples, quadruples, and more.

3-2 PRIORITY AS AN EIGENVECTOR: RELATION TO CONSISTENCY

Let us consider the elements $C_1, \ldots, C_n$ of some level in a hierarchy. We wish to find their weights of influence, $w_1, \ldots, w_n$, on some element in the next level. As described in Chap. 1, our basic tool is a matrix of numbers, representing our judgment of pairwise comparisons. Here we show why the eigenvector with the largest eigenvalue is chosen to furnish the priorities.

We denote by a_{ij} the number indicating the strength of C_i when compared with C_j. The matrix of these numbers a_{ij} is denoted A, or

$$A = (a_{ij})$$

As noted before, $a_{ji} = 1/a_{ij}$, that is, the matrix A is *reciprocal*. If our judgment is perfect in all comparisons, then $a_{ik} = a_{ij} \cdot a_{jk}$ for all i, j, k and we call the matrix A *consistent*.

An obvious case of a consistent matrix is one in which the comparisons are based on exact measurements; that is, the weights $w_1, \ldots, w_n$ are already known. Then

$$a_{ij} = \frac{w_i}{w_j} \qquad i, j = 1, \ldots, n \tag{2-1}$$

49

and thus

$$a_{ij}a_{jk} = \frac{w_i}{w_j} \cdot \frac{w_j}{w_k} = \frac{w_i}{w_k} = a_{ik}$$

Also, of course,

$$a_{ji} = \frac{w_j}{w_i} = \frac{1}{w_i/w_j} = \frac{1}{a_{ij}}$$

Let us consider this paradigm case further. As explained in App. 1, the matrix equation

$$A \cdot x = y$$

where $x = (x_1, \ldots, x_n)$ and $y = (y_1, \ldots, y_n)$, is a shorthand notation for the set of equations

$$\sum_{j=1}^{n} a_{ij}x_i = y_i \qquad i = 1, \ldots, n$$

Now, we observe that from Eqs (2-1) we obtain

$$a_{ij} \cdot \frac{w_j}{w_i} = 1 \qquad i, j = 1, \ldots, n$$

and consequently

$$\sum_{j=1}^{n} a_{ij}w_j \frac{1}{w_i} = n \qquad i = 1, \ldots, n$$

or

$$\sum_{j=1}^{n} a_{ij}w_j = nw_i \qquad i = 1, \ldots, n$$

which is equivalent to

$$Aw = nw \qquad (2\text{-}2)$$

In matrix theory, this formula expresses the fact that w is an eigenvector of A with eigenvalue n. When written out fully this equation looks as follows

$$
A =
\begin{array}{c|cccc}
 & A_1 & A_2 & \cdots & A_n \\
\hline
A_1 & \dfrac{w_1}{w_1} & \dfrac{w_1}{w_2} & \cdots & \dfrac{w_1}{w_n} \\
A_2 & \dfrac{w_2}{w_1} & \dfrac{w_2}{w_2} & \cdots & \dfrac{w_2}{w_n} \\
\vdots & \vdots & \vdots & & \vdots \\
A_n & \dfrac{w_n}{w_1} & \dfrac{w_n}{w_2} & \cdots & \dfrac{w_n}{w_n}
\end{array}
\begin{bmatrix} w_1 \\ w_2 \\ \vdots \\ w_n \end{bmatrix}
= n
\begin{bmatrix} w_1 \\ w_2 \\ \vdots \\ w_n \end{bmatrix}
$$

Let us turn to the practical case, in which the a_{ij} are not based on exact measurements, but on subjective judgments. Thus, the a_{ij} will deviate from the "ideal" ratios w_i/w_j, and therefore Eq. (2-2) will no longer hold. Two facts of matrix theory come to our rescue.

The first one is this. If $\lambda_1, \ldots, \lambda_n$ are the numbers satisfying the equation

$$Ax = \lambda x,$$

i.e., are the eigenvalues of A, and if $a_{ii} = 1$ for all i, then

$$\sum_{i=1}^{n} \lambda_i = n$$

Therefore, if (2-2) holds, then all eigenvalues are zero, except one, which is n. Clearly, then, in the consistent case, n is the largest eigenvalue of A.

The second helpful fact is that if one changes the entries a_{ij} of a positive reciprocal matrix A by small amounts, then the eigenvalues change by small amounts.

Combining these results we find that if the diagonal of a matrix A consists of ones ($a_{ii} = 1$), and if A is consistent, then small variations of the a_{ij} keep the largest eigenvalue, $\lambda_{\max}$, close to n, and the remaining eigenvalues close to zero.

Therefore, our problem is this: if A is the matrix of pairwise comparison values, in order to find the priority vector, we must find the vector w which satisfies

$$Aw = \lambda_{\max} w$$

Since it is desirable to have a normalized solution, we alter w slightly by setting $\alpha = \sum_{i=1}^{n} w_i$ and replacing w by $(1/\alpha)w$. This ensures uniqueness, and also that $\sum_{i=1}^{n} w_i = 1$.

Observe that since small changes in a_{ij} imply a small change in $\lambda_{\max}$, the deviation of the latter from n is a measure of consistency. It enables us to evaluate the closeness of our derived scale from an underlying ratio scale which we wish to estimate. Thus, as we said in Chap. 1, we take

$$\frac{\lambda_{\max} - n}{n - 1}$$

the consistency index, as our indicator of "closeness to consistency." In general, if this number is less than 0.1, we may be satisfied with our judgments.

It is useful to repeat that reported judgments may not only violate the consistency relation, but also may not be transitive; i.e., if the relative importance of C_1 is greater than that of C_2 and the relative importance of C_2 is greater than that of C_3, then the relation of importance of C_1 need not be greater than that of C_3, a common occurrence in human judgments. An interesting illustration is afforded by tournaments regarding inconsistency or lack of transitivity of preferences. A team C_1 may lose against another team C_2 which has lost to a third team C_3; yet C_1 may have won against C_3. Thus, team behavior is inconsistent—a fact which has to be accepted in the formulation, and nothing can be done about it. Of course, our model may require transitivity internally; but the "reporting" procedure may scramble things.

May (1954) has studied the idea that intransitivity among preferences may be a natural phenomenon and not a consequence of judgmental error or aberration. He concludes that there is no way to avoid considering intransitivity as a natural phenomenon.

In an experiment 62 college students were asked to choose from three hypothetical marriage partners x, y, and z. In intelligence they ranked xyz, in looks yzx, in wealth zxy. The structure of the experiment was not explained. Subjects were confronted at different times with pairs labeled with randomly chosen letters. On each occasion x was described as very intelligent, plain looking, and well off; y as intelligent, very good looking, and poor; z as fairly intelligent, good looking, and rich. All prospects were described as acceptable in every way, none being so poor, plain, or stupid as to be automatically eliminated.

On defining group preferences by majority vote a circular pattern was indicated since x beat y by 39 to 23; y beat z by 57 to 5; and z beat x by 33 to 29.

The choices were xyz: 21; $xyzx$: 17; yzx: 12; yxz: 7; zyx: 4; xzy: 1; zxy: 0; $xzyx$: 0.

The intransitive pattern is easily explained as the result of choosing the alternative that is superior in two out of three criteria. The orderings xyz and yzx seem to have resulted from giving heavier weight to intelligence and looks, respectively. The four who chose inversely with respect to intelligence (zyx) were men and may indicate the extent of male fear of intelligent women. The seven who chose inversely with respect to wealth (yxz) must not be considered to have a wanton disregard for money. They may well have preferred y over x because of a wide disparity in looks, x over z because of a wide disparity in intelligence, and y over z because of a combination of looks and intelligence. When required to rank all three alternatives, those with intransitive patterns scattered, most choosing yzx (9) and yxz (4). Those with transitive orderings for binary choices for the most part made the obvious orderings.

In another experiment where pilots were asked to choose pairs from the set flames, red hot metal, falling, the most common choices were flames preferred to red hot metal; red hot metal preferred to falling; and falling preferred to flames.

The first two choices could probably be explained by arguing that the pilot is conditioned to recoil from hot objects; more strongly from hot objects than flames and that he is accustomed to supporting himself solidly and therefore the reaction against falling. However, this does not explain the third choice which still does not seem unreasonable.

Such experiments do not prove that human choices are intransitive but can suggest ways of designing experiments which show circularities or show only transitivity. Experiments in which components are ranked in conflicting ways can be expected to give rise to circularities. The question then is not "Are preferences transitive?" but "Under what conditions does transitivity fail?" Some people avoid this issue by asserting transitivity as part of the definition of rational behavior.

Kenneth Arrow's impossibility theorem gives a negative answer to the possibility of finding a social welfare function designed to be useful in guiding the planning authority for a society, that would also satisfy individual and social choices. It is difficult to imagine that even a single individual has a utility function that also satisfies his various choices under all the circumstances he is likely to face at any given moment. In Arrow's work, transitivity of preferences is taken as a deterministic (yes, no) basis for consistency and its violation is considered a logical disaster.

People are constantly making tradeoffs which violate transitivity but are on the whole a compromise that is acceptable because one also takes into consideration the relative importance of the criteria themselves. Clearly there are times when the individual cannot make a clear decision because the tradeoffs among several activities come out to be the same. There is no reason why not acting is any less desirable than acting if the criteria are faithfully identified and evaluated.

Although the author is not particularly sold on the absolute need for social welfare functions, he believes that the basic ideas used to prove the social impossibility theorem need to be re-examined. There cannot be an impossibility theorem for a social utility function any more than there can be for an individual utility function. The individual makes himself happy or unhappy by how well he derives his priorities and makes his compromises. He can and often does have internal conflicts with whatever choices he makes even if he is perfectly rational in expressing the intensity of his preferences.

3-3   SCALE COMPARISON

The development of the previous section is independent of the comparison scale which we employ, as long as it is a ratio scale. (We shall briefly consider difference scales in Part II.) The question is justified, however; why do we choose the values 1–9? In this section we shall attempt to satisfy the reader that this scale is, indeed, preferable to all others.

Let us begin by describing our scale in more detail, as in Table 3-1.

The names of Ernest Heinrich Weber (1795–1878), Gustav Theodor Fechner (1801–87), and Stanley Smith Stevens (1906–73) stand out as one considers the subject of stimuli and responses.

In 1846 Weber formulated his law regarding a stimulus of measurable magnitude s. (Weber found, for example, that people while holding in their hand different weights, could distinguish between a weight of 20 g and a weight of 21 g, but not if the second weight is only 20.5 g. On the other hand, while they could not distinguish between 40 g and 41 g, they could between the former weight and 42 g, and so on at higher levels.) We need to increase s by a minimum amount Δs to reach a point where our senses can just discriminate between s and $s + \Delta s$. Δs is called the just noticeable difference (jnd). The ratio $r = \Delta s / s$ does not depend on s. His law states that change in sensation is noticed when the stimulus is increased by a constant percentage of the stimulus itself. This law holds in ranges where Δs is small when compared with s, and hence in practice it fails to hold when s is either

Table 3-1

Intensity of importance	Definition	Explanation
1	Equal importance	Two activities contribute equally to the objective
3	Weak importance of one over another	Experience and judgment slightly favour one activity over another
5	Essential or strong importance	Experience and judgment strongly favor one activity over another
7	Very strong or demonstrated importance	An activity is favoured very strongly over another; its dominance demonstrated in practice
9	Absolute importance	The evidence favoring one activity over another is of the highest possible order of affirmation
2, 4, 6, 8	Intermediate values between adjacent scale values	When compromise is needed
Reciprocals of above nonzero	If activity i has one of the above nonzero numbers assigned to it when compared with activity j, then j has the reciprocal value when compared with i	A reasonable assumption
Rationals	Ratios arising from the scale	If consistency were to be forced by obtaining n numerical values to span the matrix

too small or too large. Aggregating or decomposing stimuli as needed into clusters or hierarchy levels is an effective way for extending the uses of this law.

In 1860 Fechner considered a sequence of just noticeable increasing stimuli. He denotes the first one by s_0. The next just noticeable stimulus (see Batschelet, 1973) by

$$s_1 = s_0 + \Delta s_0 = s_0 + \frac{\Delta s_0}{s_0} s_0 = s_0(1+r)$$

having used Weber's law.

Similarly

$$s_2 = s_1 + \Delta s_1 = s_1(1+r) = s_0(1+r)^2 \equiv s_0\alpha^2$$

In general

$$s_n = s_{n-1}\alpha = s_0\alpha^n \qquad (n = 0, 1, 2, \ldots)$$

Thus stimuli of noticeable differences follow sequentially in a geometric progression. Fechner felt that the corresponding sensations should follow each other in an arithmetic sequence occurring at the discrete points at which just noticeable differences occur. But the latter are obtained when we solve for n. We have

$$n = (\log s_n - \log s_0)/\log \alpha$$

and sensation is a linear function of the logarithm of the stimulus. Thus if M denotes the sensation and s the stimulus, the psychophysical law of Weber–Fechner is given by

$$M = a \log s + b, \qquad a \neq 0$$

We assume that the stimuli arise in making pairwise comparisons of relatively comparable activities. We are interested in responses whose numerical values are in the form of ratios. Thus $b = 0$, from which we must have $\log s_0 = 0$ or $s_0 = 1$, which is possible by calibrating a unit stimulus. But this results from comparing one activity with itself.

The next noticeable response is due to the stimulus

$$s_1 = s_0 \alpha = \alpha$$

This yields a response $\log \alpha / \log \alpha = 1$. The next stimulus is

$$s_2 = s_0 \alpha^2$$

which yields a response of 2. In this manner we obtain the sequence $1, 2, 3, \ldots$. For the purpose of consistency we place the activities in a cluster whose pairwise comparison stimuli give rise to responses whose numerical values are of the same order of magnitude. In practice, qualitative differences in response to stimuli are few. Roughly, there are five distinct ones as listed above with additional ones that are compromises between adjacent responses. The notion of compromise is particularly observable in the thinking judgmental process as opposed to the senses. This brings the total up to nine which is compatible with the order of magnitude assumption made earlier.

REMARK Stevens' power law extends the ideas of stimuli and response across wide ranges (as if it cuts across different hierarchic levels) estimating response as a power of the stimulus obtained from fitting curves to widely distributed data. It would appear that the power law may be an approximation to an outcome obtained by hierarchic decomposition.

Why the Upper Limit 9 is Reasonable

There are several reasons for setting an upper limit on the scale.

(1) The qualitative distinctions are meaningful in practice and have an element of precision when the items being compared are of the same order of magnitude or close together with regard to the property used to make the comparison.

(2) We note that our ability to make qualitative distinctions is well represented by five attributes: equal, weak, strong, very strong, and absolute. We can make compromises between adjacent attributes when greater precision is needed. The totality requires nine values and they may well be consecutive—the resulting scale would then be validated in practice.

(3) By way of reinforcing (2), a practical method often used to evaluate items is the

Table 3-2 Scale conversion

Scales	Equal	Betwn	Weak	Betwn	Strong	Betwn	Demon.	Betwn	Absol.
(1) 1–3	1	2	2	2	2	3	3	3	3
(2) 1–5	1	2	2	3	3	4	4	5	5
(3) 1–7	1	2	2	3	4	5	6	6	7
(4) 1–9	1	2	3	4	5	6	7	8	9
(5) 1–11	1	3	4	5	7	8	9	10	11
(6) 1–13	1	3	4	6	7	9	10	12	13
(7) 1–15	1	3	5	7	8	9	11	13	15
(8) 1–17	1	3	5	7	9	11	13	15	17
(9) 1–18	1	4	6	8	10	12	14	16	18
(10) 1–26	1	5	8	11	14	17	20	23	26
(11) 1–90	1	20	30	40	50	60	70	80	90
(12) 0.9	1	0.9 times corresponding values in 1–9 scale above							
(13) 0.7	1	0.7 times corresponding values in 1–9 scale above							
(14) 0.5	1	0.5 times corresponding values in 1–9 scale above							
(15) 0.3	1	0.3 times corresponding values in 1–9 scale above							
(16) 0.1	1	0.1 times corresponding values in 1–9 scale above							
(17) $1+0.x$	1	$1+0.x$ where x is the corresponding value in 1–9 scale							
(18) $2+0.x$	1	$2+0.x$ where x is the corresponding value in 1–9 scale							
(19) $3+0.x$	1	$3+0.x$ where x is the corresponding value in 1–9 scale							
(20) $4+0.x$	1	$4+0.x$ where x is the corresponding value in 1–9 scale							
(21) $\sqrt{x}$	1	$\sqrt{x}$ where x is the corresponding value in 1–9 scale							
(22) x^2	1	x^2 where x is the corresponding value in 1–9 scale							
(23) x^3	1	x^3 where x is the corresponding value in 1–9 scale							
(24) x^4	1	x^4 where x is the corresponding value in 1–9 scale							
(25) x^5	1	x^5 where x is the corresponding value in 1–9 scale							
(26) $2^{n/2}$	$2^0 = 1$	$2^{0.5} = 1.414$	$2^1 = 2$	$2^{1.5} = 2.828$	$2^2 = 4$	$2^{2.5} = 5.657$	$2^3 = 8$	$2^{3.5} = 11.31$	$2^4 = 16$
(27) $9^{x/8}$	1	$9^{1/8}$	$9^{2/8}$	$9^{3/8}$	$9^{4/8}$	$9^{5/8}$	$9^{6/8}$	$9^{7/8}$	9

classification of stimuli into a trichotomy of regions: rejection, indifference, acceptance. For finer classification, each of these is subdivided into a trichotomy of low, medium, and high—in all indicating nine shades of meaningful distinctions. The author's colleague Yoram Wind has indicated that marketing studies conducted by our colleague Paul Green show that one does not need more than about 7 scale points to distinguish between stimuli. Thus we need not go above 9.

(4) The psychological limit of 7 ± 2 items in a simultaneous comparison suggests that if we take $7 + 2$ items satisfying the description under (1), and if they are all slightly different from each other, we would need 9 points to distinguish these differences. (See G. A. Miller, 1956.)

Let us note that using a scale of pairwise comparison from 0 to ∞ may not be useful at all. It assumes that somehow human judgment is capable of comparing the relative dominance of any two objects, which is not the case. As we know well from experience, our ability to discriminate is highly limited in range and when there is considerable disparity between the objects or activities being compared, our guesses tend to be arbitrary and usually far from the actual. This suggests that our scales should have a finite range. In fact, the bounds should be rather close in a region which reflects our real capability at making ratio comparisons. Since unity is our standard of measurement, the upper bound should not be too far from unity, but sufficiently far to represent our range of discrimination.

Now, we will consider a wide variety of scales which we apply to particular problems for which pairwise comparisons are known qualitatively; equal, weak, strong, very strong, and absolute, with compromise judgment between each successive pair of these values. The scales appear in Table 3-2.

Next, we present the results of working out the illuminated chairs, wealth of nations, and air travel distance examples in these scales. First, the matrix of the example with qualitative values is presented (Tables 3-3–3-5). It is then followed with a listing of the eigenvector solutions corresponding to each of the scales (Tables 3a–3-5a). Adjacent to this is a column of corresponding eigenvalues. Two more columns, respectively, give the root mean square deviation and the median absolute deviation about the median. These are calculated for deviations of the corresponding row vector from the actual (known) solution vector given at the bottom. From these and many other illustrations that are less systematic for listing here, the scale 1–9 distinguishes itself. It seems to point to a strong human affinity for making correspondence between shades of feeling and the numbers 1–9. There are those who even conjecture that this has to do with the capacity of the mind, and that it is this capacity that has something to do with the number of fingers, although it is not known which is the causative factor. Under the assumption that the brain can simultaneously process 7 ± 2 factors, large matrices may be hierarchically decomposed into clusters of this size to which the scale 1–9 may still be applied, indicating its possible viability for general situations which we have only validated for small clusters.

Table 3-3 Illuminated chairs example

	C_1	C_2	C_3	C_4
C_1	E	$B(W-S)$	$B(S-D)$	D
C_2	—	E	W	$B(W-S)$
C_3	—	—	E	$B(E-W)$
C_4	—	—	—	E

E = equal, W = weak, S = strong, D = demonstrated, A = absolute, $B(.-.)$ = between values indicated in parentheses. Reciprocal values are used in the transpose position (here left vacant) when qualities are translated to numerical scale.

Table 3-3a

Eigenvector for each scale					λ_{max}	RMS	MAD
(1)	0.451	0.261	0.169	0.119	4.071	0.091	0.008
(2)	0.531	0.237	0.141	0.091	4.087	0.045	0.006
(3)	0.577	0.222	0.125	0.077	4.034	0.019	0.006
(4)	0.617	0.224	0.097	0.062	4.102	0.008	0.005
(5)	0.659	0.213	0.083	0.044	4.230	0.031	0.011
(6)	0.689	0.198	0.074	0.039	4.261	0.047	0.008
(7)	0.702	0.199	0.066	0.034	4.353	0.055	0.013
(8)	0.721	0.188	0.060	0.031	4.292	0.066	0.010
(9)	0.732	0.185	0.057	0.026	4.451	0.072	0.010
(10)	0.779	0.162	0.042	0.017	4.639	0.099	0.012
(11)	0.886	0.098	0.014	0.003	6.545	0.162	0.031
(12)	0.596	0.229	0.105	0.070	4.072	0.009	0.008
(13)	0.545	0.238	0.124	0.094	4.023	0.037	0.009
(14)	0.470	0.243	0.151	0.135	4.008	0.081	0.024
(15)	0.352	0.236	0.191	0.221	4.094	0.156	0.071
(16)	0.141	0.162	0.230	0.467	4.762	0.316	0.231
(17)	0.340	0.260	0.212	0.187	4.004	0.158	0.042
(18)	0.445	0.271	0.171	0.113	4.143	0.094	0.005
(19)	0.513	0.266	0.142	0.078	4.332	0.056	0.016
(20)	0.561	0.259	0.122	0.059	4.521	0.031	0.022
(21)	0.431	0.260	0.172	0.137	4.025	0.103	0.017
(22)	0.860	0.111	0.021	0.009	4.421	0.147	0.027
(23)	0.953	0.043	0.003	0.001	4.992	0.203	0.057
(24)	0.984	0.015	0.001	0.000	5.871	0.223	0.071
(25)	0.995	0.005	0.000	0.000	7.142	0.230	0.076
(26)	0.604	0.214	0.107	0.076	4.000	0.008	0.005
(27)	0.531	0.233	0.134	0.102	4.000	0.046	0.077
	0.608	0.219	0.111	0.062	= Actual vector solution. From inverse square law of optics		

Table 3-4 Wealth example

	U.S.	U.S.S.R.	China	France	U.K.	Japan	W. Germany
U.S.	E	$B(W-S)$	A	$B(S-D)$	$B(S-D)$	S	S
U.S.S.R.	—	E	D	S	S	W	$B(W-S)$
China	—	—	E	—	—	—	—
France	—	—	S	E	E	—	—
U.K.	—	—	S	E	E	—	—
Japan	—	—	D	W	W	E	$B(E-W)$
W. Germany	—	—	S	W	W	—	E

Table 3-4a

Eigenvector for each scale							λ_{max}	RMS	MAD
(1)	0.273	0.201	0.059	0.088	0.088	0.165	0.127	7.191	0.062	0.018
(2)	0.348	0.212	0.039	0.076	0.076	0.142	0.108	7.285	0.031	0.014
(3)	0.388	0.220	0.027	0.067	0.067	0.132	0.098	7.305	0.017	0.014
(4)	0.427	0.230	0.021	0.052	0.052	0.123	0.094	7.608	0.014	0.011
(5)	0.473	0.234	0.015	0.040	0.040	0.116	0.081	8.103	0.029	0.019
(6)	0.496	0.230	0.013	0.037	0.037	0.111	0.076	8.097	0.037	0.016
(7)	0.512	0.235	0.011	0.033	0.033	0.104	0.073	8.453	0.043	0.018
(8)	0.531	0.231	0.010	0.030	0.030	0.099	0.069	8.436	0.050	0.017
(9)	0.544	0.232	0.008	0.026	0.026	0.099	0.064	8.853	0.056	0.016
(10)	0.597	0.224	0.005	0.019	0.019	0.085	0.052	9.616	0.077	0.014
(11)	0.741	0.181	0.001	0.004	0.004	0.048	0.020	16.152	0.134	0.009
(12)	0.408	0.228	0.024	0.058	0.058	0.126	0.099	7.485	0.012	0.007
(13)	0.363	0.220	0.032	0.072	0.072	0.131	0.110	7.255	0.024	0.014
(14)	0.302	0.204	0.047	0.093	0.093	0.136	0.125	7.079	0.049	0.014
(15)	0.214	0.169	0.081	0.130	0.130	0.135	0.142	7.085	0.090	0.023
(16)	0.078	0.085	0.197	0.196	0.196	0.100	0.149	8.275	0.167	0.083
(17)	0.205	0.174	0.091	0.120	0.120	0.150	0.139	7.028	0.092	0.003
(18)	0.283	0.211	0.055	0.084	0.084	0.158	0.125	7.398	0.057	0.019
(19)	0.338	0.230	0.038	0.063	0.063	0.157	0.111	7.875	0.036	0.010
(20)	0.379	0.240	0.028	0.050	0.050	0.153	0.100	8.359	0.025	0.014
(21)	0.271	0.201	0.059	0.096	0.096	0.148	0.129	7.147	0.062	0.014
(22)	0.700	0.191	0.002	0.011	0.011	0.053	0.033	9.729	0.118	0.010
(23)	0.856	0.114	0.000	0.002	0.002	0.017	0.009	14.286	0.182	0.020
(24)	0.932	0.061	0.000	0.000	0.000	0.005	0.002	23.125	0.215	0.026
(25)	0.968	0.030	0.000	0.000	0.000	0.001	0.001	39.824	0.231	0.026
(26)	0.470	0.200	0.019	0.053	0.053	0.115	0.091	7.147	0.001	0.026
(27)	0.348	0.227	0.032	0.075	0.075	0.134	0.110	7.110	0.029	0.065
	0.413	0.225	0.043	0.069	0.055	0.104	0.091	= Actual vector solution. From GNP's 1972.		

Table 3-5 Distance example

	Cairo	Tokyo	Chicago	San Francisco	London	Montreal
Cairo	E	—	$B(D-A)$	W	W	D
Tokyo	W	E	A	W	W	A
Chicago	—	—	E	—	—	$B(E-W)$
San Francisco	—	—	$B(S-D)$	E	—	$B(S-D)$
London	—	—	S	W	E	$B(S-D)$
Montreal	—	—	—	—	—	E

Table 3-5a

Eigenvector for each scale						λ_{max}	RMS	MAD
(1) 0.234	0.296	0.083	0.150	0.175	0.062	6.258	0.043	0.039
(2) 0.247	0.320	0.058	0.150	0.180	0.045	6.224	0.027	0.015
(3) 0.253	0.334	0.045	0.151	0.183	0.035	6.190	0.019	0.008
(4) 0.262	0.397	0.033	0.116	0.164	0.027	6.454	0.019	0.010
(5) 0.265	0.437	0.027	0.098	0.154	0.019	6.870	0.036	0.011
(6) 0.267	0.443	0.024	0.099	0.152	0.016	6.848	0.038	0.011
(7) 0.265	0.483	0.020	0.080	0.138	0.014	7.074	0.057	0.017
(8) 0.266	0.482	0.017	0.082	0.140	0.012	7.106	0.056	0.015
(9) 0.264	0.506	0.016	0.073	0.131	0.010	7.494	0.067	0.019
(10) 0.259	0.550	0.011	0.058	0.116	0.007	8.109	0.088	0.024
(11) 0.210	0.707	0.002	0.019	0.061	0.001	13.727	0.159	0.048
(12) 0.259	0.380	0.037	0.124	0.169	0.030	6.354	0.013	0.010
(13) 0.251	0.340	0.047	0.143	0.178	0.042	6.171	0.018	0.013
(14) 0.236	0.286	0.062	0.168	0.187	0.062	6.042	0.044	0.019
(15) 0.202	0.210	0.091	0.201	0.190	0.107	6.092	0.086	0.042
(16) 0.113	0.084	0.156	0.227	0.154	0.266	7.261	0.178	0.144
(17) 0.203	0.227	0.117	0.165	0.178	0.110	6.022	0.082	0.070
(18) 0.233	0.321	0.085	0.131	0.172	0.065	6.349	0.039	0.044
(19) 0.247	0.371	0.066	0.110	0.163	0.045	6.779	0.024	0.024
(20) 0.253	0.414	0.053	0.094	0.153	0.033	7.214	0.032	0.023
(21) 0.229	0.282	0.083	0.153	0.181	0.073	6.111	0.049	0.040
(22) 0.254	0.591	0.004	0.048	0.101	0.003	7.993	0.106	0.030
(23) 0.198	0.736	0.000	0.015	0.050	0.000	11.180	0.172	0.049
(24) 0.138	0.837	0.000	0.004	0.022	0.000	17.124	0.219	0.061
(25) 0.089	0.901	0.000	0.001	0.009	0.000	27.862	0.250	0.075
(26) 0.257	0.385	0.029	0.138	0.166	0.025	6.156	0.015	0.009
(27) 0.248	0.342	0.044	0.151	0.175	0.039	6.097	0.019	0.029
0.278	0.381	0.032	0.132	0.177	0.019	= Actual vector solution. From actual distances		

REMARK The last scale (27) in Table 3-2, arises from the following consideration. In using the geometric mean of a judgment value estimated by several individuals (see last paragraph in this section), one may observe that the geometric mean of 2 and 8 is 4, which is one interval closer to 2 than to 8 (unlike the geometric mean of 1/3 and 3, for example, which is 2 intervals from each). Thus one is led to devise a scale for reciprocal matrices that preserves a relationship of the kind $x/y = y/z$ or $y^2 = xz$, from which we would have $\log y - \log x = \log z - \log y$. This would obtain if our nine value scale with 8 intervals is divided by starting with 1 followed by (for example) $9^{1/8}$, then by $9^{2/8}$ and so on also using the reciprocals of these values. The consistency may be thus improved but, as our examples show, not the validity.

One way to test the goodness of the consistency obtained using different scales is the following. For each order matrix construct a sample of size 100, and fill in its entries, at random, from the scales 1–5, 1–7, 1–9, 1–15, 1–20, and 1–90. Thus, for example, for the scale 1–5, the main diagonal entries are, as always, unity and for each position above the diagonal we choose, at random, any of the integers 1–5 or their reciprocals (excepting the reciprocal of 1).

The reciprocal of this entry is then given to its transpose. The same procedure is carried out for the other scales. We average $(\lambda_{\max} - n)/(n-1)$ for the 100 matrices corresponding to each value of n and for each scale. We also give the variances.

We obtain Table 3-6, useful for comparing the significance of the calculated deviation from consistency for a particular problem, with the average value obtained for the scale being used. In our case the relevant values are for the scale 1–9. In this comparison we can require the ratio to be very small, e.g., of the order of 0.1. (We have estimated the frequency distribution of $\lambda_{\max}$ based on yet another sample of size 500. For $n = 2$ it is a constant, $\lambda_{\max} = 2$; for $n = 3$ the cumulative distribution is the Weibull distribution $1 - e^{-(\lambda_{\max}/b)^c}$ where $b = 4.076$ and $c = 1.937$. For $n \geqslant 4$ we have a truncated normal distribution with means and variances of the sample as follows: $n = 4$, (6.650, 3.370); $n = 5$, (9.418, 4.424); $n = 6$, (12.313, 4.413); $n = 7$, (15.000, 4.123); $n = 8$, (17.952, 3.627); $n = 9$, (20.565, 3.327).) In practice, we use the values given in Chapter 1 for random consistency comparisons of the 1–9 scale.

We now make another interesting observation using this result. It is generally known that if λ is any of the eigenvalues of a matrix, then $|\lambda - a_{ii}| \leqslant \sum_{j \neq i} |a_{ij}|$ for some i, $i = 1, \ldots, n$.

Since for a reciprocal positive matrix $\lambda_{\max} \geqslant n$ and $a_{ii} = 1$, we may simply write

$$\lambda_{\max} \leqslant \max_i \sum_{j=1}^{n} a_{ij}$$

Now the maximum value for any a_{ij} is 9 when we use the scale 1–9. Thus $\lambda_{\max}$ is at most equal to $9(n-1)$. We also note that $(\lambda_{\max} - n)/(n-1) \leqslant 8$ and it is therefore bounded from above. In fact, one can show that $\mu = (\lambda_{\max} - n)/(n-1)$ satisfies

Table 3-6 Measure of inconsistency μ

Order of matrix	Scale	1–5	1–7	1–9	1–15	1–20	1–90
3×3	Mean	0.190	0.254	0.382	0.194	0.120	0.720
	Variance	0.024 545	0.193 822	0.266 743	0.026 226	0.006 869	0.213 737
4×4	Mean	0.520	0.592	0.946	0.820	0.934	1.490
	Variance	0.086 061	0.109 430	0.433 014	0.726 465	0.385 499	0.858 485
5×5	Mean	0.454	0.814	1.220	2.018	2.352	11.690
	Variance	0.026 549	0.087 479	0.278 788	1.024 723	2.157 268	84.438 283
6×6	Mean	0.612	0.892	1.032	2.594	3.484	16.670
	Variance	0.016 420	0.075 895	0.180 380	0.530 469	0.837 721	29.536 466
7×7	Mean	0.582	1.004	1.468	2.428	3.566	18.230
	Variance	0.036 440	0.077 964	0.120 986	0.473 147	0.867 923	19.694 040
8×8	Mean	0.620	1.030	1.402	2.578	3.654	17.280
	Variance	0.016 970	0.036 667	0.073 935	0.227 794	0.448 368	8.435 959
9×9	Mean	0.640	1.002	1.350	2.714	3.816	18.060
	Variance	0.014 949	0.031 915	0.047 980	0.180 408	0.338 731	8.551 918
10×10	Mean	0.668	1.090	1.464	2.822	3.970	19.670
	Variance	0.010 279	0.019 697	0.028 590	0.138 905	0.254 848	5.172 827
11×11	Mean	0.688	1.082	1.576	2.830	3.822	19.670
	Variance	0.010 360	0.022 703	0.046 691	0.100 505	0.209 208	4.425 352
12×12	Mean	0.704	1.096	1.476	2.785	3.948	19.730
	Variance	0.007 257	0.029 075	0.317 410	0.097 923	0.187 572	2.724 343
13×13	Mean	0.712	1.136	1.564	2.852	4.038	19.790
	Variance	0.009 552	0.022 933	0.030 610	0.070 400	0.104 904	2.955 453
14×14	Mean	0.710	1.150	1.568	2.896	4.034	19.990
	Variance	0.003 535	0.017 273	0.021 996	0.054 125	0.102 671	2.818 083
15×15	Mean	0.720	1.150	1.586	2.942	4.096	19.980
	Variance	0.004 444	0.010 808	0.021 216	0.050 339	0.113 923	2.534 949

This table is reproduced by the courtesy of Dr. R. Uppuluri of the Oak Ridge National Laboratory.

$0 \leqslant 1 - \mu/8 \leqslant 1$ which is close to unity when the consistency is high, a result confirmed by our statistical approach. What we did for each scale (instead of using difference methods), was to take the average of the last three values; i.e., for $n = 13, 14, 15$ in Table 3-6 for each scale, and use it as an approximation to the limiting value. If we denote this value by L_s for scale s, we then calculate a new table using $C \equiv L_s - \mu/L_s$ for each n and measure consistency expressed as an index between zero and unity. This leads to Table 3-7 and its associated graph of Fig. 3-1.

Now this is the consistency measured for randomly filled matrices. In general, informed judgment leads to better consistency. However, all the plots show that when the number of objects being compared exceeds 5, the value of C is less than 10 per cent and is about the same for all n.

This seems to say that among the large number of random inconsistencies which exist in relating n objects we must find the consistent framework which we

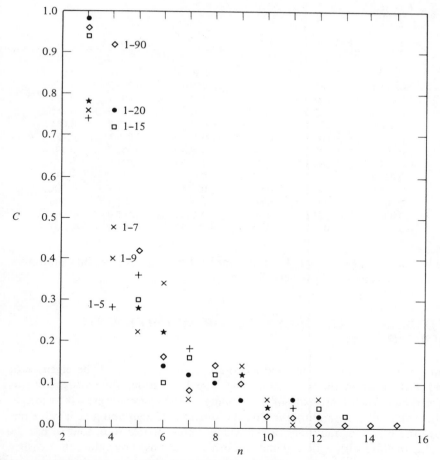

Figure 3-1 Consistency normalized using asymptotic value

seek. The chances for finding it are smaller the larger the number of objects we have to connect by a logical framework. Our chances would be better the smaller n is but again n must be large enough in order not to have automatic consistency, e.g., for $n = 2$. For larger values of n we need to use some redundancy of information to improve our validity, i.e., how well our results capture the real world.

Let us close this section with two remarks. First, if it is necessary to make very fine distinctions in pairwise comparisons, one can subdivide the 1–9 scale by treating each pair of values, 3 and 4, say, by adding to the lower one the value 0.25 for weak, 0.5 for moderate, and 0.75 for strong. In our experience, however, this has rarely been found to be of great help except when comparing only two objects. There we have used a scale from 1 to 1.5 to obtain finer shades of distinction.

Second, while taking judgments from several people it is preferable, as noted in Chap. 1, to use the geometric rather than the arithmetic mean. This is particularly clear where one person assigns the value a and the other the value $1/a$. The mean

Table 3-7 $\dfrac{L_s - \mu}{L_s}$

Scale	1–5	1–7	1–9	1–15	1–20	1–90
Order						
3	0.733 9	0.778 2	0.757 1	0.933 0	0.970 4	0.963 9
4	0.271 7	0.483 1	0.398 5	0.716 9	0.769 7	0.925 2
5	0.364 1	0.289 3	0.224 2	0.303 3	0.402 1	0.413 2
6	0.142 9	0.221 2	0.343 8	0.104 5	0.141 0	0.163 2
7	0.184 9	0.123 4	0.066 6	0.161 8	0.120 8	0.084 8
8	0.131 7	0.100 7	0.108 5	0.110 0	0.099 1	0.132 5
9	0.103 6	0.125 1	0.141 6	0.063 1	0.059 2	0.093 4
10	0.064 4	0.048 3	0.069 1	0.025 8	0.021 2	0.012 6
11	0.036 4	0.055 3	−0.002 1	0.023 0	0.057 7	0.012 6
12	0.014 0	0.043 1	0.061 5	0.038 9	0.026 6	0.009 5
13	0.002 8	0.008 1	0.005 5	0.015 4	0.004 4	0.006 5
14	0.005 6	−0.004 1	0.003 0	0.000 2	0.005 4	−0.003 5
15	−0.008 4	−0.004 1	−0.008 5	−0.015 7	−0.009 9	−0.003 0

should be 1 and not $(a + 1/a)/2$. Thus, in general, for n judgments, one multiplies their numerical values and extracts the nth root.

3-4 COMPARING THE EIGENVECTOR METHOD WITH OTHER METHODS

Several experiments were conducted to compare the accuracy of the eigenvector method with other methods in estimating a real situation. In two experiments conducted at Cornell University in the summer of 1976 people were asked to estimate the values directly and told to find the smallest element and give it value one and give the others as multiples of this value. Other people were told to use the eigenvalue method with scale 1–9 and still others could use any values they wished but the eigenvalue problem was solved with these numbers.

In a separate experiment people solved the eigenvalue problem scale 1–9 and then the same people after deriving experience from the pairwise comparisons did the direct experiments. It is likely that an expert can estimate the situation directly and may not do better on the eigenvalue scale 1–9 approach. In the social area where usually no ratio answers are available, the eigenvalue approach shows the judgment of an expert in the pairwise comparison, which is useful to have. In addition, it provides a measure of consistency which is not available in direct methods. The results were compared with the actual value and both RMS and MAD were calculated. The average value for both of these were then calculated.

From these limited experiments one learns that if people do not know what they are talking about, there is no scale that would make them look better. However, if people know something and they want a measure of it, then there is no better way of getting these judgments down than through a systematic procedure which facilitates comparisons, and is in harmony with intuition and human feelings, and is free of artificiality. If a person already knows the answer, he then has no need for any scale, and exactly because he knows the answer, using his knowledge, one cannot find out the advantages of a method used to help non-expert people who need the stimulation of an organized approach to get their ideas in proper perspective. However, his expertise may be used to see if a scaling method actually reproduces known results. Our experiments did not only compare between experts and non-experts, but also between people who were partly informed and partly diligent to apply the method well, versus people who were partly informed but less careful in providing information. We can say that for people who are knowledgeable and for all people using their senses for physical comparisons, the eigenvalue approach to ratio scaling compares very favorably with other methods we have examined. It also produces better results for people who are partly informed and attempt to scale their judgment built up logically and simply from relations between pairs. For example they may begin by arranging things on an ordinal scale. Then they can select for comparison the items of which they are sure. Among these they can start with the most dominant item and follow it by the least dominant one to get bounds on the range of their feelings. So far at least a thousand people have participated in problem solving involving applications for governments and for industries. Some have used it for their personal problems. Few applications have been in the nature of exercises.

3-5 REVISING JUDGMENTS

Assume that the consistency index is sufficiently large to warrant judgmental revision. Where should it be made? Two ways immediately present themselves. The first is to form the matrix of priority ratios w_i/w_j and consider the matrix of absolute differences $[|a_{ij}-(w_i/w_j)|]$ and attempt to revise the judgment on the element(s) or row sums with the largest such differences.

Alternatively, a more appealing idea is to form the root mean square deviation using the rows of (a_{ij}) and (w_i/w_j) and revise the judgments for the row with the largest value. The justification for this is that generally one tends to be uncertain about how an activity relates to all others rather than to a single one. The procedure can then be repeated to note improvement. What would be desirable is to have an iterative procedure which converges so that a_{ij} become w_i/w_j. The procedure consists of replacing all a_{ij} in the row in question by the corresponding w_i/w_j and recalculating the priority vector. Repetition of this process has been noted to produce convergence to the consistent case. We have worked out some examples using the row with $\max_i \sum_{j=1}^{n} |a_{ij}-w_i/w_j|$. (One need not be concerned about the fact that w_i/w_j may be greater than 9.)

The vocational training matrix which we encountered under the school selection example is given by

$$A = \begin{bmatrix} 1 & 9 & 7 \\ 1/9 & 1 & 1/5 \\ 1/7 & 5 & 1 \end{bmatrix}$$

and its vector of priorities is $(w_1, w_2, w_3) = (0.77, 0.06, 0.17)$; $\lambda_{max} = 3.21$ with consistency index 0.1. We form the matrix of the ratios of priorities corresponding to w_i/w_j. The largest absolute difference is between a_{12} and w_1/w_2. Thus we replace a_{12} by $w_1/w_2 = 14.15$ and recompute the priorities obtaining the vector (0.81, 0.04, 0.15) with $\lambda_{max} = 3.09$ and consistency 0.02. We note the continued improvement in consistency. Again, if we replace the first row which gives the largest differences from w_i/w_j we obtain the vector (0.76, 0.04, 0.20) and $\lambda_{max} = 3.023$ with consistency 0.01. Replacing the first row by the corresponding ratios, we have the vector (0.75, 0.04, 0.21) with $\lambda_{max} = 3.003$ and consistency index 0.00 indicating successive improvement in consistency. As we shall see, one can also follow a lengthy procedure of using least squares approximation by a matrix of unit rank and then obtain its eigenvector.

Another and perhaps more relevant way to revise judgments relates to selecting the largest of the ratios of a_{ij} to w_i/w_j and elaborations on that idea (see Chap. 7 for reasons).

We caution against excessive use of this process of forcing the values of judgments to improve consistency. It distorts the answer. One would rather have naturally improved judgments arising from experience.

3-6 ALL THE EIGENVALUES AND EIGENVECTORS: THE WEALTH EXAMPLE OF CHAPTER 2

In Table 3-8 we give for all eigenvalues, both left eigenvectors (these satisfy $vA = \lambda v$) and right eigenvectors (these satisfy the familiar form $Aw = \lambda w$). For $\lambda = \lambda_{max}$ a left eigenvector is dual to (i.e., the inverse of) the right eigenvector as a way of measuring the opposite of dominance with respect to a property we have been using so far in making comparisons. When we have consistency, these two principal left and right eigenvectors are exact reciprocals. This relationship also holds between principal left and right eigenvectors of all 2 by 2 and 3 by 3 reciprocal matrices.

3-7 CONSENSUS AND THE DELPHI METHOD

An important area related to taking the judgment of several people is how to obtain consensus from their judgments. The process of obtaining consensus can be used to persuade people that their interests are taken into consideration. Thus, for our purposes, consensus means improving confidence in the priority values by using several judges to bring the results in line with majority preferences.

There has been some interesting work done on the problem of reaching consensus. Kemeny and Snell (1962) whose work has been generalized by Bogart (1973) have used the axiomatic approach to develop a method for arriving at a consensus in the case of weak ordering (preferred = 1, tied = 0, not preferred = −1) of a set of objects by several people. They proved that there is a unique distance function satisfying all the axioms. It is used to derive a consensus matrix by

Table 3-8 The wealth example

Eigenvalues

7.7451	0.1157 + 2.2985i	0.1157 − 2.2985i	−0.4464 + 0.5161i	−0.4464 − 0.5161i	−0.0419 + 0.3989i	−0.0419 − 0.3989i

Right eigenvectors

7.7451	0.1157 + 2.2985i	0.1157 − 2.2985i	−0.4464 + 0.5161i	−0.4464 − 0.5161i	−0.0419 + 0.3989i	−0.0419 − 0.3989i
0.422	0.775 − 0.525i	0.775 + 0.525i	1.382 + 0.387i	1.382 + 0.387i	1.494 − 0.011i	1.494 + 0.011i
0.227	0.421 + 0.178i	0.421 − 0.178i	−0.266 + 0.757i	−0.266 − 0.757i	−0.821 − 0.374i	−0.821 + 0.374i
0.020	−0.005 − 0.045i	−0.005 + 0.045i	−0.070 − 0.032i	−0.070 + 0.032i	−0.095 + 0.038i	−0.095 − 0.038i
0.051	−0.069 − 0.011i	−0.069 + 0.011i	0.058 + 0.151i	0.058 − 0.151i	0.597 − 0.232i	0.597 + 0.232i
0.047	−0.093 − 0.011i	−0.093 + 0.011i	0.068 + 0.070i	0.068 − 0.070i	−0.123 + 0.258i	−0.123 − 0.258i
0.143	0.014 + 0.292i	0.014 − 0.292i	−0.198 − 0.217i	−0.198 + 0.217i	0.869 − 1.616i	0.869 + 1.616i
0.090	−0.042 + 0.123i	−0.042 − 0.123i	0.026 − 0.342i	0.026 + 0.342i	−0.920 − 1.295i	−0.920 + 1.295i

Left eigenvectors

7.7451	0.1157 + 2.2985i	0.1157 − 2.2985i	−0.4464 + 0.5161i	−0.4464 − 0.5161i	−0.0419 + 0.3989i	−0.0419 − 0.3989i
0.022	−0.001 − 0.047i	−0.001 + 0.047i	−0.060 − 0.036i	−0.060 + 0.036i	−0.116 − 0.188i	−0.116 + 0.188i
0.039	−0.070 − 0.036i	−0.070 + 0.036i	0.026 + 0.125i	0.026 − 0.125i	−0.092 − 0.932i	−0.092 + 0.932i
0.450	0.847 − 0.509i	0.847 + 0.509i	1.364 − 0.222i	1.364 + 0.222i	0.468 − 0.680i	0.468 + 0.680i
0.155	0.145 + 0.128i	0.145 − 0.128i	0.160 + 0.174i	0.160 − 0.174i	8.108 − 6.549i	8.108 + 6.549i
0.186	0.235 + 0.304i	0.235 − 0.304i	−0.554 + 0.206i	−0.554 − 0.206i	−8.664 − 6.397i	−8.664 + 6.397i
0.061	−0.099 − 0.056i	−0.099 + 0.056i	0.076 − 0.096i	0.076 + 0.096i	−1.115 − 1.808i	−1.115 + 1.808i
0.087	−0.057 − 0.104i	−0.057 + 0.104i	−0.012 − 0.152i	−0.012 + 0.152i	2.412 + 1.895i	2.412 − 1.895i

finding for each entry the value which minimizes the sum of the squares of the distances to each corresponding entry of the judgment matrices constructed by several people. The result may not be an integer; some practitioners round the numbers off to the nearest integer. The value obtained in this way is called the mean. The distance function is also used to derive the matrix of median values. Each entry of this matrix minimizes the sum of the distances to the corresponding entries of the judgment matrices. Although each of the mean and median appears to be a reasonable way to obtain consensus, the mean provides a way to "tie the objects" being compared whereas the median offers a way to "pick among the experts" providing the judgment. In our case the geometric mean is used.

Bogart has generalized the approach to a distance function for the collection of all partial orderings of a set, extending the previous work to semi-orders and interval orders and further to intransitive orders. After proving the uniqueness of the distance function satisfying a reasonable set of axioms he shows, among other things, the following:

(1) The mean of a collection of orderings in the set of all antisymmetric orderings satisfies the decision rule (called the powerful majority rule) that a is preferred to b if the number preferring a to b minus those preferring b to a is more than half the number of individuals providing judgment. The rule leads to a unique mean of the collection.

(2) The majority rule ordering (in which a is preferred to b if it also holds for the majority of the people providing the judgment), for a set of antisymmetric orderings is a median for the set. This median is unique unless there is a tie in the number preferring a to b and those preferring b to a.

In the present work consensus is derived along different lines. The amount of information available to provide judgments is crucial. In seeking consensus, it is preferrable that the judges interact. A well-informed person can effect substantial change in the beliefs of another person who has less information. The debate should help bring judgments closer together. Such a debate would assist in providing information to apply the method of priority assignment to the judges themselves.

Thus, our approach to consensus is to apply the method to derive priorities for the several individuals involved according to the soundness of their judgment. The factors affecting judgment may be: relative intelligence (however measured), years of experience, past record, depth of knowledge, experience in related fields, personal involvement in the issue at stake, and so on. If we have high confidence in the judgment of these people, the priority derived is used to weight the final priority result derived from the judgment of each individual and an overall weighted priority is then obtained in the usual way. On the other hand, if we have low confidence in the judgments provided by the judges, we can use the geometric mean of their individual judgments as they appear in each of the comparison matrices.

In mixed situations, a combination of the two procedures may be used, but we have not investigated the details of this problem. Another area for research is to compare the results obtained this way with those obtained using the work of other people.

How to represent group judgment in a satisfactory way when people's experiences and judgments differ, and whose opinions should be taken more seriously and why, is a major problem in social study and conflict analysis.

It seems possible that an idea developed and evaluated by one group should be handed over to another group for further debate and change in judgment. But the end result may still be wide variability in the solution. Thus bargaining and negotiation must be an intrinsic procedure for group agreement. One cannot arbitrate the priorities by using the judgments of a favored group over others. In other words, discovering a convenient and workable mathematical framework for a problem does not automatically solve its social intricacies. However, it can simplify and make clear where the most fruitful bargaining and compromising has to be done. If a social problem requires arbitration, the mediator must carefully evaluate the needs and influences of the groups before indicating where the compromises should be made. Perhaps the most promising contribution of hierarchical analysis is using it to structure the problem from the start jointly by the conflicting groups rather than by a third party, and then do the bargaining through the numerical entries.

At this point, let us briefly consider another method which depends heavily on the concept of consensus, the Delphi method.

The Delphi method is a well-known process by which problems can be analyzed, values estimated, and futures of interest to management forecasted. A rough description of the procedure is given below as a part of the comparison with hierarchical analysis.

The basic differences between Delphi and the hierarchical methods are the following.

(1) *Anonymous versus operating group discussion* In Delphi each member of the group responds anonymously to a previously prepared questionnaire to avoid disproportionate influence of strong personalities. In hierarchies the criteria and judgments are established mostly by an open group process.

(2) *Adjustment is a series of rounds versus dynamic discussion* In Delphi there must be a review of the questionnaire results, and adjustments are requested again on an anonymous basis. In hierarchies dynamic discussion is used while constructing the hierarchy and providing judgments by mutual agreement and revision of views. People attempt to present their arguments openly.

(3) *Questionnaire versus hierarchy structure as a basis for judgments* In Delphi, the design of the questionnaire implies the choice of the variables involved by the person who creates the questionnaire. In hierarchies the group decides on the variables which have any effect on the judgment to be made. Initially all variables suggested are accepted. Later in the procedure some might be ignored due to low priority assigned to them by the group.

(4) *Statistical and quantitative analysis versus qualitative analysis* The Delphi method requires numerical responses which are to be analyzed statistically as a

basis for the next round. In hierarchies the judgments involve absolute numbers from 1 to 9 reflecting qualitative judgment on pairwise comparison and used as a part of a rigorous derivation of an estimate for an underlying ratio scale. Consistency is an important criterion as a necessary condition to valid scaling of reality.

In both cases the process of analyzing the problem improves the quality of judgments, but the hierarchy method breaks down the judgment into its elementary components, and therefore better fits the human cognitive style. Another important issue here is that the group determines the important set of variables, and therefore has better confidence in the relevance of their judgments. This procedure is helpful in diminishing disagreements in an open dynamic fashion. As a short and simple procedure with highly effective results, its many practitioners have recommended its use in planning and in making forecasts as a reflection of the beliefs of the participants.

3-8 SOME EXTENSIONS

Frequent use of pairwise comparisons leads one to wonder about comparisons of triples, quadruples, etc. An example of a comparison of triples is the idea of betweenness. For example B between A and C requires all three A, B, and C to be present. If we are interested in developing a scale for a set of elements from triple or higher order comparisons we need a method of representing the comparisons to derive the scale. A simple minded way of representing such an n-tuple relation is by means of a vector whose numerical entries presumably indicate the mutual standing of n elements in the comparison.

Now it is known that with vectors of pairs we can associate numbers as follows:

It is sufficient to show that there is a (1-1) correspondence between the set E^1 of real numbers x such that $0 < x \leqslant 1$ and the set E^2 of points in the plane defined by $E^2 = \{(x, y) \mid (0 < x \leqslant 1)$ and $(0 < y \leqslant 1)\}$. Now each element x in E^1 is representable in the form $0 \cdot x_1 x_2, \ldots, x_k, \ldots$. This array may be divided into "blocks" as we shall illustrate presently. Thus the number $0.740653001\ldots$ has the successive blocks 7, then 4, then 06, then 5, then 3, then 001, etc. Each block has a digit different from zero and it is its last digit. We have the ordered pair $(0 \cdot x_1^1 x_2^1 \ldots,$ $0 \cdot x_1^2 x_2^2 \ldots)$ with $x_1^1 = 7$, $x_1^2 = 4$, $x_2^1 = 06$, $x_2^2 = 5$, $x_3^1 = 3$, $x_3^2 = 001$, etc. which gives $(0.7063, 0.45001)$ in which the blocks are assigned alternately to the two coordinates of a point in E^2. This reversible process gives a (1-1) correspondence between elements in the unit interval and points in the unit square with zero corresponding to $(0, 0)$.

It is clear that the process (though ambiguous) may be extended to a vector of 3 components, by taking the first entry along with the number in E^1 associated with the vector of the next two entries, and then again associating a new number in E^1 with the resulting pair and so on for vectors of n components. Thus we can conceptually associate numbers (though non-unique) with vectors. For a particular problem one needs a good way to make the selection.

One may also generalize the pairwise comparison eigenvalue approach to the use of complex numbers. The process would correspond to comparing objects according to two independent attributes simultaneously. The consistent case remains $Aw = nw$ with n being the largest eigenvalue of A, and the consistency relation $a_{jk} = a_{ik}/a_{ij}$ also survives. Small perturbations in the coefficients may now produce a small complex perturbation in n, yielding a λ_{max} that is a complex number, and of course the solution would in general be complex. Normalizing to unity by straight addition is no longer meaningful. It may be necessary to use the Euclidean norm of $(a_1, a_2) = a_1 + ia_2$ which is $(a_1^2 + a_2^2)^{1/2}$. The generalization may be carried to quaternions, i.e., numbers of the form

$$a_1 + ia_2 + ja_3 + ka_4$$

and to octaves or octonions involving eight of the imaginary arguments. It is known that one cannot go beyond these numbers since identities of the form

$$(a_1^2 + \cdots + a_8^2)(b_1^2 + \cdots + b_8^2) = c_1^2 + \cdots + c_8^2$$

are only possible for sums of 1, 2, 4, and 8 squares (Van Der Waerden).

FOUR

HIERARCHIES AND PRIORITIES: A FORMAL APPROACH

4-1 INTRODUCTION

Because of its crucial relevance to applications, despite its partly abstract content, we have included this chapter in the early part of the book. The illustrative examples given earlier adequately demonstrate the idea of how to compose weights in a hierarchy. The nontechnical reader can ignore the early more mathematical discussion of the chapter and read the remaining sections which give deeper insight into the important role that hierarchies play in human thought.

We begin by giving a formal definition of a hierarchy and the priority structures. This is followed by a discussion of clustering and its efficiency, standardizing measurement, and the consistency of a hierarchy. Also, a graph theoretic interpretation of the concept of priority is presented. The reader, whose knowledge of matrix theory and graph theory is sketchy, may be well-advised to first consult the two appendices on these subjects.

4-2 HIERARCHIES AND PRIORITIES

As the examples and graphical representations of hierarchies as given in Part One, suggest, we may consider a hierarchy a special type of ordered set, or a particular case of a graph. We have chosen the first interpretation as the basis of our formal definition, and the second as an illustration. No doubt, the roles could be reversed.

First we need to introduce the concept of a lattice which we will use in the definition of a hierarchy.

Definition 4-1 An ordered set is any set S with a binary relation $\leqslant$ which satisfies the reflexive, antisymmetric, and transitive laws:

> Reflexive: For all x, $x \leqslant x$.
> Antisymmetric: If $x \leqslant y$ and $y \leqslant x$, then $x = y$.
> Transitive: If $x \leqslant y$ and $y \leqslant z$, then $x \leqslant z$.

For any relation $x \leqslant y$ (read, y includes x) of this type, we may define $x < y$ to mean that $x \leqslant y$ and $x \neq y$. y is said to cover (dominate) x if $x < y$ and if $x < t < y$ is possible for no t.

Ordered sets with a finite number of elements can be conveniently represented by a directed graph. Each element of the system is represented by a vertex so that an arc is directed from a to b if $b < a$.

Definition 4-2 A simply or totally ordered set (also called a chain) is an ordered set with the additional property that if x, $y \in S$ then either $x \leqslant y$ or $y \leqslant x$.

Definition 4-3 A subset E of an ordered set S is said to be bounded from above if there is an element $s \in S$ such that $x \leqslant s$ for every $x \in E$. The element s is called an *upper bound* of E. We say E has a supremum or least upper bound in S if E has upper bounds and if the set of upper bounds U has an element u_1 such that $u_1 \leqslant u$ for all $u \in U$. The element u_1 is unique and is called the supremum of E in S. The symbol sup is used to represent a supremum. (For finite sets largest elements and upper bounds are the same.)

Similar definitions may be given for sets bounded from below, a *lower bound* and *infimum*. The symbol inf is used.

There are many ways of defining a hierarchy. The one which suits our needs best here is the following:

We use the notation $x^- = \{y | x$ covers $y\}$ and $x^+ = \{y | y$ covers $x\}$, for any element x in an ordered set.

Definition 4-4 Let H be a finite partially ordered set with largest element b.

H is a *hierarchy* if it satisfies the conditions

(1) There is a partition of H into sets L_k, $k = 1, \ldots, h$ where $L_1 = \{b\}$.
(2) $x \in L_k$ implies $x^- \subset L_{k+1}$ $k = 1, \ldots, h-1$.
(3) $x \in L_k$ implies $x^+ \subset L_{k-1}$ $k = 2, \ldots, h$.

For each $x \in H$, there is a suitable weighting function (whose nature depends on the phenomenon being hierarchically structured):

$$w_x : x^- \to [0, 1] \quad \text{such that} \quad \sum_{y \in x} w_x(y) = 1$$

The sets L_i are the *levels* of the hierarchy, and the function w_x is the *priority function* of the element in one level with respect to the objective x. We observe that even if $x^- \neq L_{k+1}$ (for some level L_k), w_x may be defined for all of L_k by setting it equal to zero for all elements in L_{k+1} not in x^-.

The weighting function, we feel, is a significant contribution towards the application of the Analytic Hierarchy Process.

Definition 4-5 A hierarchy is *complete* if, for all $x \in L_k$ $x^+ = L_{k-1}$, for $k = 2, \ldots, h$.

We can state the central question:

BASIC PROBLEM Given any element $x \in L_\alpha$, and subset $S \subset L_\beta$, $(\alpha < \beta)$, how do we define a function $w_{x,S} : S \to [0, 1]$ which reflects the properties of the priority functions w_y on the levels L_k, $k = \alpha, \ldots, \beta - 1$. Specifically, what is the function $w_{b,L_h} : L_h \to [0, 1]$?

In less technical terms, this can be paraphrased thus:

Given a social (or economic) system with a major objective b, and the set L_h of basic activities, such that the system can be modeled as a hierarchy with largest element b and lowest level L_h. What are the priorities of the elements of L_h with respect to b?

From the standpoint of optimization, to allocate a resource among the elements any interdependence must also be considered. Analytically, interdependence may take the form of input–output relations such as, for example, the interflow of products between industries. A high priority industry may depend on flow of material from a low priority industry. In an optimization framework, the priority of the elements enables one to define the objective function to be maximized, and other hierarchies supply information regarding constraints, e.g., input–output relations.

We shall now present our method to solve the basic problem. Assume that $Y = \{y_1, \ldots, y_{m_k}\} \in L_k$ and that $X = \{x_1, \ldots, x_{m_{k+1}}\} \in L_{k+1}$. (Observe that according to the remark following Definition 4-4, we may assume that $Y = L_k$, $X = L_{k+1}$.) Also assume that there is an element $z \in L_{k-1}$, such that $y \subset z^-$. We then consider the priority functions

$$w_z : Y \to [0, 1] \quad \text{and} \quad w_y : X \to [0, 1] \qquad j = 1, \ldots, n_k$$

We construct the "priority function of the elements in X with respect to z," denoted $w, w : X \to [0, 1]$, by

$$w(x_i) = \sum_{j=1}^{n_k} w_{y_j}(x_i) w_z(y_j), \qquad i = 1, \ldots, n_{k+1}$$

It is obvious that this is no more than the process of weighting the influence of the element y_j on the priority of x_i by multiplying it with the importance of y_i with respect to z.

The algorithms involved will be simplified if one combines the $w_{y_j}(x_i)$ into a matrix B by setting $b_{ij} = w_{y_j}(x_i)$. If we further set $W_i = w(x_i)$ and $W'_j = w_z(y_j)$, then the above formula becomes

$$W_i = \sum_{j=1}^{n} b_{ij} W'_j \qquad i = 1, \ldots, n_{k+1}$$

Thus, we may speak of the *priority vector w* and, indeed of the *priority matrix B* of the $(k+1)$st level; this gives the final formulation

$$W = BW'$$

The foregoing composition of priorities has involved weighting and adding. This requires independence among the criteria in each level, otherwise one element may get some priority with respect to an attribute, and additional priority for the overlap of this attribute with another attribute giving rise to double counting. In simple terms, a set of attributes or criteria are said to be independent if it is possible to make tradeoffs between any pair without regard to the influence of the others. In other words criteria are independent if there is no interaction among them. There are formal definitions of independence and good elaborate methods for testing for independence using judgments of participants (see, for example, Keeney and Raiffa, 1976). Behind this informal discussion of independence there are rigorous and also time consuming methods for verifying independence. In practice people prefer to depend on their intuitive interpretation of non-interaction than to perform a series of tests. In a test, with each attribute is associated a set of "levels", e.g., for learning, one has grade levels A, B, C, D, etc. One conducts preference in judgment among these for a certain individual. This preference may be ordinal or cardinal. If there are attributes other than learning one must fix each at some base level before doing this preference comparison of A, B, C, D. Then one varies the preference of the level of one other attribute and does the preference comparison among the different levels of learning A, B, C, D. One continues to do this by varying all the levels of the second attribute. If the preferences among A, B, C, D stay the same, then learning is said to be conditionally independent of the second attribute. It is conditional because the other attributes are fixed at a certain level. If there are several attributes the process is continued. For additivity, two activities must be independent and satisfy a cancellation condition. For three, each pair must be independent and other conditions must be satisfied, etc. We now repeat the basic idea in a simple set theoretic framework and present a principle.

Principle of Hierarchical Composition: Additivity of Weighting

Given two finite sets S and T. Let S be a set of independent properties (for examples of dependence see Chap. 7) and let T be a set of objects which have the properties as characteristics. Assume that a numerical weight, priority, or index of relative importance, $w_j > 0$, $j = 1, \ldots, n$, is associated with each $s_j \in S$, such that $\sum_{j=1}^{n} w_j = 1$. Let $w_{ij} > 0$, $i = 1, \ldots, m$, with $\sum_{i=1}^{m} w_{ij} = 1$, be weights associated with $t_i \in T$, $i = 1, \ldots, m$, relative to s_j. Then the convex combination of w_{ij}, $j = 1, \ldots, n$,

$$\sum_{j=1}^{n} w_{ij} w_j \qquad i = 1, \ldots, m$$

gives the numerical priority or relative importance of t_i with respect to S. Note that the principle generalizes to a chain of sets. An axiomatization of the principle of hierarchical composition would be useful.

REMARK "Hierarchical measurement" is a weighting process of "linear" variables associated with each level with nonlinear coefficients that are products and sums of variables associated with higher levels. Note that linearity here simply means multiplying numbers directly without raising them to powers or forming functions of them. The actual value itself is a complex (nonlinear) measure of priority.

The following is a first step towards validating the above principle as it shows that ordinal preferences are preserved under composition.

Definition 4-6 Suppose that for each subgoal or activity e_j in L_k there is an ordinal scale o_j over the activities e_α ($\alpha = 1, \ldots, n_{k+1}$) in L_{k+1}. Define a partial order over L_{k+1} by: $e_\alpha \geqslant e_\beta$ if and only if for $j = 1, \ldots, n_k$, $o_{\alpha j} \geqslant o_{\beta j}$.
It is easy to prove:

Theorem 4-1 Let $(w_{1j}, \ldots, w_{n_{k+1}j})$ be the priority vector for L_{k+1} with respect to e_j, and suppose it preserves the order of the $o_{\alpha j}$. Let $W_1, \ldots, W_{n_{k+1}}$ be the (composite) priority vector for L_{k+1}. Then $e_\alpha \geqslant e_\beta$ implies $W_\alpha \geqslant W_\beta$.
Thus hierarchical composition preserves ordinal preference.
The following is easy to prove.

Theorem 4-2 Let H be a complete hierarchy with largest element b and h levels. Let B_k be the priority matrix of the kth level, $k = 2, \ldots, h$. If W' is the priority vector of the pth level with respect to some element z in the $(p-1)$st level, then the priority vector W of the qth level ($p < q$) with respect to z is given by

$$W = B_q B_{q-1} \cdots B_{p+1} W'$$

Thus, the priority vector of the lowest level with respect to the element b is given by

$$W = B_h B_{h-1} \cdots B_2 W'$$

If L_1 has a single element, as usual, W' is just a scalar; if more, a vector.
The following observation holds for a complete hierarchy, but it is also useful in general. The priority of an element in a level is the sum of its priorities in each of the comparison subsets to which it belongs; sometimes each of these is weighted by the fraction of elements of the level which belong to that subset and by the priority of that subset. The resulting set of priorities of the elements in the level is then normalized by dividing by its sum. The priority of a subset in a level is equal to the priority of the dominating element in the next level.
Note that composition of weights in a hierarchy yields multilinear expressions of the form

$$\sum_{i_1, \cdots, i_p} x_1^{i_1} x_2^{i_2} \cdots x_p^{i_p}$$

where i_j indicates the jth level of the hierarchy and the x_j is the priority of an element in that level. There seems to be a good opportunity to investigate the relationship obtained by composition to covariant tensors and their algebraic properties.

More concretely we have the covariant tensor

$$w_i^h = \sum_{i_2,\cdots,i_{h-1}=1}^{N_{h-1},\cdots,N_1} w_{i_1 i_2}^h w_{i_2 i_3}^{h-1} \cdots w_{i_{h-2} i_{h-1}}^2 w_{i_{h-1}}^1 \qquad i_1 \equiv i$$

for the priority of the ith element in the hth level of the hierarchy. The composite vector W^h for the entire hth level is represented by the covariant hypertensor (a vector with tensor components). Similarly, the left eigenvector approach to a hierarchy gives rise to a contravariant hypertensor.

The classical problem of relating space (geometry) and time to subjective thought (see Russell, 1945, p. 468) can perhaps be examined by showing that the functions of mathematical analysis (and hence also the laws of physics) are derivable as truncated series from the above tensors by composition in an appropriate hierarchy. The foregoing is reminiscent of the theorem in dimensional analysis that any physical variable is proportional to the product of powers of primary variables.

4-3 DECOMPOSITION AND AGGREGATION OR CLUSTERING

There are essentially two fundamental ways in which the idea of a hierarchy can be used.

The first is by now clear: it has to do with modeling the real world hierarchically.

The second is probably even more fundamental than the first and points to the real power of hierarchies in nature. It is to break things down into large groupings or clusters and then break each of these into smaller clusters and so on. The object would then be to obtain the priorities of all the elements by means of clustering. This is by far a more efficient process than treating all the elements together. Thus, it is immaterial whether we think of hierarchies as intrinsic in nature as some have maintained, or whether we simply use them because of our limited capacity to process information. In either case, they are a very efficient way of looking at complex problems.

A useful way to deal with a larger number of elements which fall in a level of a hierarchy is to group them into clusters according to their relative importance. Thus, one would have one cluster of the most important (most similar, or closest) elements, another of those of moderate importance, and another of those of low importance. Then one compares in pairwise fashion the relative impact of the clusters on the relevant criteria of the next upper level. The clustering may differ from criterion to criterion. After this analysis of clusters, the elements in each cluster are then compared pairwise according to their relative importance in that cluster. If there are too many, again they may be put into clusters. In this way each element, since it belongs to several clusters, would receive several weights from the different clusters. There is no alternative to this process of clustering and decomposition, particularly if one desires to maintain high consistency. Knowing this for a fact, one need not be intimidated with the size of a problem as he knows what can be done. We have carried out this process very successfully in many instances. It is easy to show mathematically that clustering should produce the same results as an overall approach would.

A Distance Hierarchy

The example of distances between cities will now be structured into a hierarchy.

If we group the cities into clusters according to their falling in nearly equivalent distances from Philadelphia, we have three classes compared in the following matrix.

Philadelphia	Chicago Montreal	London San Francisco	Cairo Tokyo	Eigenvector
{ Chicago { Montreal	1	1/7	1/9	0.056
{ London { San Francisco	7	1	1/4	0.26
{ Cairo { Tokyo	9	4	1	0.68

$$\lambda_{max} = 3.15, \quad \text{C.I.} = 0.08, \quad \text{C.R.} = 0.14$$

If we now compare the cities in each cluster separately according to their relative distance from Philadelphia, we have on using for the 2 by 2 case the scale $1 + \varepsilon$:

Philadelphia	Chicago	Montreal	Eigen-vector
Chicago	1	2	0.67
Montreal	1/2	1	0.33

$$\lambda_{max} = 2, \quad \text{C.I.} = 0, \quad \text{C.R.} = 0$$

Philadelphia	Cairo	Tokyo	Eigen-vector
Cairo	1	1/1.5	0.4
Tokyo	1.5	1	0.6

$$\lambda_{max} = 2, \quad \text{C.I.} = 0, \quad \text{C.R.} = 0$$

Philadelphia	San Francisco	London	Eigen-vector
San Francisco	1	1/1.3	0.43
London	1.3	1	0.57

$$\lambda_{max} = 2, \quad \text{C.I.} = 0, \quad \text{C.R.} = 0$$

Now we multiply the first eigenvector by 0.056, the second by 0.26 and the third by 0.68 to obtain the overall relative distance vector.

	Cairo	Tokyo	Chicago	San Francisco	London	Montreal
Recall that the actual	0.27	0.41	0.037	0.11	0.15	0.019
result is:	0.278	0.361	0.032	0.132	0.177	0.019

The Wealth Example as a Cluster

The comparison of the worth of seven nations was made by means of clustering the nations into three groups: $A = $ (U.S.), $B = $ (U.S.S.R.), and $C = $ (U.K., France, Japan, West Germany). The clusters were first compared, yielding the matrix

	A	B	C	Eigenvector
A	1	2	1	0.4
B	1/2	1	1/2	0.2
C	1	2	1	0.4

$\lambda_{max} = 3.00,$ C.I. $= 0.0,$ C.R. $= 0.0$

The elements of C were compared among themselves in the following matrix

	U.K.	France	Japan	West Germany	Eigenvector
U.K.	1	1	1/3	1/2	0.14
France	1	1	1/3	1/2	0.14
Japan	3	3	1	2	0.45
W. Germany	2	2	1/2	1	0.26

$\lambda_{max} = 4.01,$ C.I. $= 0.003,$ C.R. $= 0.01$

The estimated relative wealth obtained this way is given by

U.S.	U.S.S.R.	U.K.	France	Japan	W. Germany
0.4	0.2	0.056	0.056	0.18	0.10

Let us assume that we have a set of n elements. If we wish to compare the elements in pairs to obtain a ratio scale ranking by solving the eigenvalue problem, $(n^2 - n)/2$ judgments would be necessary. Suppose now that 7 is the maximum number of elements which can be compared with any reasonable (psychological) assurance of consistency. Then m must be first decomposed into equivalence classes of seven clusters or subsets, each of these decomposed in turn to seven new clusters and so on down generating levels of a hierarchy until we obtain a final decomposition, each of whose sets has no more than seven of the original elements. Let $\{x\}$ denote the smallest integer greater than or equal to x. We have

Theorem 4-3 The maximum number of comparisons obtained from the decomposition of a set of $n > 1$ elements into a hierarchy of clusters (under the assumption that no more than seven elements are compared simultaneously), is bounded by $(7/2)(7^{\{\log n/\log 7\}} - 1)$ and this bound is sharp.

PROOF We have the following for the *number of comparisons* in each level where we must have in the hth or last level at most seven elements in each cluster.

$$
\begin{array}{ll}
1 & 0 \\[2mm]
2 & \dfrac{7^2-7}{2} \\[4mm]
3 & 7 \times \dfrac{7^2-7}{2} \\[2mm]
& \vdots \\[2mm]
h & 7^{h-2} \times \dfrac{7^2-7}{2}
\end{array}
$$

where $7^{h-2} \times 7 = n, h = \{\log n/\log 7\}+1, h > 2$.
The sum of these comparisons is

$$
21 \times \frac{7^{h-1}-1}{7-1} \;=\; \frac{7}{2}\,(7^{\{\log n/\log 7\}}-1)
$$

To show that the bound is sharp it is sufficient to put $n = 7^m$.

REMARK It looks as if the Saint Ives conundrum finds its solution in hierarchies.

The efficiency of a hierarchy may be defined to be the ratio of the number of direct pairwise comparisons required for the entire set of n elements involved in the hierarchy, as compared with the number of pairwise comparisons resulting from clustering as described above.

Theorem 4-4 The efficiency of a hierarchy is of the order of $n/7$.

PROOF To prove the theorem we must compare $(n^2-n)/2$ with

$$
\frac{7}{2}\,(7^{\{\log n/\log 7\}}-1)
$$

Let $n = 7^{m+\varepsilon} \qquad 0 \leqslant \varepsilon < 1$
Then we clearly have

$$
7^{2m+2\varepsilon} - 7^{m+\varepsilon}/7 \cdot (7^m-1) \geqslant 7^{m+\varepsilon}/7 = n/7
$$

Thus $n/7$ is equal to the efficiency.

One might naturally ask why we do not use 2 in place of 7 for even greater efficiency. We note that in using a hierarchy we seek both consistency and good correspondence to reality. The former is greater the smaller the size of each matrix; the latter is greater the larger the size of the matrix due to the use of redundant information. Thus we have a tradeoff. Actually, we have shown, using the consistency index, that the number 7 is a good practical bound on n, a last outpost, so far as consistency is concerned.

Suppose we have a set of 98 elements to which we want to assign priority. We decompose the problem into seven sets, each having on the average 14 elements. Now we cannot compare 14 elements, so we decompose each of these sets into two sets, each having no more than seven elements. We then compare the elements among themselves.

To look at the efficiency of this process closely we note that if it were possible to compare 98 elements among themselves, we would require $[(98)^2 - 98]/2 = 4,753$ comparisons. On the other hand, if we divide them into seven clusters of 14 elements each, then do pairwise comparisons of the seven clusters, we need $(7^2 - 7)/2 = 21$ comparisons. Each cluster can now be divided into two clusters each with seven elements. Comparing two clusters falling under each of the 14 element clusters requires one comparison, but there are seven of these, hence, we require seven comparisons on this level; then we need $14 \times 21 = 294$ comparisons on the lowest level. The total number of comparisons in this hierarchical decomposition is $21 + 7 + 294 = 322$ as compared with 4,753 comparisons without clustering. Indeed the theorem is satisfied since $322 \ll 4,753/7$.

Clustering a complex problem into hierarchical form has two advantages.

(1) Great efficiency in making pairwise comparisons.
(2) Greater consistency under the assumption of a limited capacity of the mind to compare more than 7 ± 2 elements simultaneously.

The efficiency of a hierarchy has been illustrated by H. Simon with an example of two men assembling watches, one by constructing modular or component parts from elementary parts and using them to construct higher order parts and so on, and the other by assembling the entire watch piece by piece from beginning to end. If the first man is interrupted, he only has to start reassembling a small module, but if the second man is interrupted, he has to start reassembling the watch from the beginning. If the watch has 1,000 components and the components at each level have 10 parts, the first man will, of course, have to make the components and then from there make subassemblies in a total of 111 operations. If p is the probability of an interruption while a part is being added to an incomplete assembly, then the probability that the first man completes a piece without interruption is $(1-p)^{10}$ and that for the second is $(1-p)^{1000}$. For the first man, an interruption would cost the time required to assemble five parts. The cost to the second man will, on the average, be the time needed to assemble $1/p$ parts, which is approximately the expected number of parts without interruption. If $p = 0.01$ (a chance in a hundred that either man would be interrupted in adding any one part), the cost to the first man is 5 and to the second man 100. The first man will assemble 111 components while the second would make just one component. However, the first man will complete an assembly in $(1-0.01)^{-10} = 10/9$ attempts whereas the second man will complete an assembly in $e^{10} = (1-0.01)^{-1000} + 1/44 \times 10^6$ attempts. Thus the efficiency of the first man to that of the second man is given by

$$\frac{100/0.99^{1000}}{111\{[(1/0.99^{10})-1]5+10\}} = 2,000$$

In man-made systems, the task of managing a complex enterprise is, in general, considerably simplified when it is broken down into subsystems or levels that are individually more tractable, i.e., a manager having a limited span of management. The steps of solving a large-scale problem are simplified and efficiently accomplished when they are modularized, e.g., by taking n sets of m variables each rather than by taking mn variables simultaneously.

4-4 STANDARDIZING THE MEASUREMENT OF ELEMENTS IN A LARGE CLASS

The elements are first ordered according to relative comparability and grouped into classes. In each class the measure on the elements is of the same order of magnitude. If two classes differ by more than one order of magnitude, an attempt is made to breakdown or decompose the elements in the class receiving the higher measurement into smaller elements. Otherwise the elements in the smaller class are aggregated to form one large element of the higher class. If neither of these alternatives is possible, additional elements are brought into the comparison process that are intermediate between the two classes to enable transition from one class to another.

In order to standardize the measurement between classes we use the largest element in the class of smaller weight elements also as the smallest element in the next larger class. One can also use the smallest element in the next class as the largest element in the smaller weights in order to help improve the accuracy. In this manner the weight of the element used in both classes can be used to uniformize or standardize the weights of both, yielding a single class with all its elements properly weighted. The procedure is then carried on up through all the classes, and in this manner we have a measure introduced on a large number of elements in a set.

4-5 CONSISTENCY OF A HIERARCHY

We have generalized the measurement of consistency to an entire hierarchy. What we do is to multiply the index of consistency obtained from a pairwise comparison matrix by the priority of the property with respect to which the comparison is made and add all the results for the entire hierarchy. This is then compared with the corresponding index obtained by taking randomly generated indices, weighting them by the priorities and adding. The ratio should be in the neighborhood of 0.10

in order not to cause concern for improvements with the actual operation and in the judgments. This has been applied to two examples.

Applying the indices to the school selection example, we have

First level priority vector: (0.32, 0.14, 0.03, 0.13, 0.23, 0.14)

First level C.I.: C.I. $= (7.49-6)/5 = 0.298$

2nd level vector of C.I.'s: (0.025, 0, 0, 0.105, 0, 0.025)

Hence

$$M = 0.298 + (0.32, 0.14, 0.03, 0.13, 0.24, 0.14) \begin{bmatrix} 0.025 \\ 0.0 \\ 0.0 \\ 0.105 \\ 0.0 \\ 0.025 \end{bmatrix} = 0.323$$

and using the corresponding R.I.'s we have

$$\overline{M} = 1.24 + (0.32, 0.14, 0.03, 0.13, 0.24, 0.14) \begin{bmatrix} 0.58 \\ 0.58 \\ 0.58 \\ 0.58 \\ 0.58 \\ 0.58 \end{bmatrix} = 1.82$$

The consistency ratio of the hierarchy (C.R.H.) is therefore $M/\overline{M} = 0.18$; which is not very good, because it reflects the high inconsistency arising from ($\lambda_{\max} = 7.49$ for $n = 6$).

For another example we have the following numbers.

First level priority vector: (0.16, 0.19, 0.19, 0.05, 0.12, 0.30)

First level C.I.: 0.07

Second level vector of C.I.'s for 3×3 matrices: (0.01, 0.01, 0.28, 0.025, 0.0, 0.105)

Hence

$$M = 0.07 + (0.16, 0.19, 0.19, 0.05, 0.12, 0.30) \begin{bmatrix} 0.01 \\ 0.01 \\ 0.28 \\ 0.025 \\ 0.0 \\ 0.105 \end{bmatrix} = 0.159$$

and $\overline{M} = 1.24 + 0.58 = 1.82.$

The C.R.H. is $M/\overline{M} = 0.09$ and is more acceptable than in the previous example.

4-6 GRAPH THEORETIC INTERPRETATION OF PRIORITIES

The following interpretation uses graph theory to lend geometric insight into the meaningfulness of the relations among the activities or objectives of a hierarchy level. See Appendix Two for a brief introduction to graphs.

How can we be sure that the "more favored" activity in the pairwise comparison matrix obtains a greater priority value? Although we examine this question in an algebraic setting, it can also be intuitively appreciated through ideas from graph theory.

Definition 4-7 Let the nodes of a directed graph G be denoted by $1, 2, \ldots, n$. With every directed arc x_{ij} from node i to node j, we associate a nonnegative number, $0 < q_{ij} < 1$, called the *intensity* of the arc. (Loops and multiple arcs are allowed.)

Definition 4-8 A *walk* in a directed graph is an alternating sequence of nodes and arcs such that each node is the target of the arc in the sequence preceding it and the source of the arc following it. Both endpoints of each arc are in the sequence. The *length* of a walk is the number of arcs in its sequence. A walk of length k will be called a "k-walk."

Definition 4-9 The *intensity of a walk* of length k from node i to node j is the product of the intensities of the arcs in the walk.

Definition 4-10 The *total intensity* of all k-walks from node i to node j is the sum of the intensities of the walks.

REMARK Note that for the total intensity of 1-walks, one takes the sum of the intensities of all 1-walks from i to j. These are simply the arcs connecting i and j. All intensities along i, j arc are assumed equal. Thus, the total intensity from i to j is given by $t_{ij} = p_{ij}q_{ij}$ where p_{ij} is the number of arcs from i to j and q_{ij} is the intensity of each arc.

Definition 4-11 Given a directed graph D, the *intensity-incidence* matrix $U = (u_{ij})$ is defined as the matrix whose entries are given by $u_{ij} = t_{ij}$ for all i and j.

The following example is presented to clarify the concepts given above. In Fig. 4-1, the number beside each arc indicates its intensity.

The intensity-incidence matrix U associated with this graph is given by

$$U = \begin{bmatrix} 1 & 3/2 & 2 \\ 2/3 & 1 & 3 \\ 3 & 2 & 1 \end{bmatrix}$$

The total intensity of 1-walks from i to j is given by the (i, j) entry of this

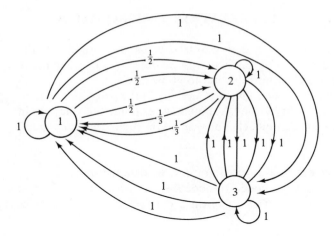

Figure 4-1

matrix. The total intensity of a walk of length 2 from node 1 to node 3, for example, is equal to the sum of the following three quantities, with the associated walk indicated on the right. (Note that each arc between the first two nodes is taken once with every arc between the two nodes.)

$$3[(1/2 \times 1)+(1/2 \times 1)+(1/2 \times 1)]: 1, x_{12}, 2, x_{23}, 3$$
$$2(1 \times 1): 1, x_{11}, 1, x_{13}, 3$$
$$2(1 \times 1): 1, x_{13}, 3, x_{33}, 3$$

The sum of these quantities is equal to 17/2. This is the entry in the (1, 3) position of the matrix U^2. In this manner one can show that for every i and j, the total intensity of 2-walks from node i to node j is the (i, j) entry of the matrix

$$U^2 = \begin{bmatrix} 8 & 7 & 17/2 \\ 31/3 & 8 & 22/3 \\ 22/3 & 17/2 & 13 \end{bmatrix}$$

This result may be generalized according to the following easily-proved theorem.

Theorem 4-5 The (i, j) entry, $u_{ij}(k)$, of U^k is the total intensity of k-walks from node i to node j.

COROLLARY If $q_{ij} = 1$ for all i and j, then the (i, j) entry in U^k gives the number of k-walks from i to j.

The Concept of Dominance with Respect to a Property: The Converse Problem

In the foregoing, we went from a graph to its corresponding matrix to study the idea of the intensity of k-walks. The converse problem of interpreting the powers of a matrix as a method of enumerating intensity of walks is important for our problem.

We associate with each of the n activities in our pairwise comparison procedure a node of a directed graph D. In that case, the intensity-incidence matrix U is the same as the judgment matrices discussed in Chap. 1. The numerator p_{ij} of the (i, j) entry of this matrix (assumed to be in relatively prime fractional form) represents the number of arcs directed from vertex i to vertex j. The intensity of each arc from i to j is the same, and is equal to the reciprocal q_{ij} of the denominator of the entry. This is a natural way of defining the associated graph since for $q_{ij} = 1$, it reduces to the ordinary vertex matrix whose kth power gives the number of walks of length k.

The entry in the (i, j) position of the matrix A may be interpreted as the direct dominance or intensity of importance of activity i with respect to activity j. It signifies the relative contribution that activity i makes towards the fulfillment of a certain objective as compared with the contribution made by activity j. The normalized row sums of A give the level of contribution of the corresponding activities relative to all other activities. The normalized row sums of A^2 provide this index of relative importance of dominance by considering all 2-walks thus giving indirect comparison between pairs through a single intermediate vertex. Hence, an activity's level of importance is enhanced or reduced depending on its interdependence with other activities. In general, the net effect of dominance between activities is obtained by taking the limiting value of the row sum of A^k, the kth power of A. When normalized by the sum of these row sums, each number serves as an overall index of relative dominance or priority among the activities.

Formally, the concept of relative dominance of activity i over activity j in k-steps may now be explained in terms of the total intensity of all k-walks from node i to node j. Relative dominance of an activity i over another activity j, directly and indirectly through intermediate activities, in k-steps is given by the (i, j) entry of the matrix A^k. Because of the presence of a loop at each vertex, it turns out that each entry of A^k is a sum of all walks of length less than or equal to k. How many times each walk is included is related to its length and to the number of permutations of its loops to obtain the desired walk length. A loop by itself contributes unit intensity to the walk. Thus, the total intensity of a walk is unchanged by going around the loop several times. It is important to note that the limiting result is identical to the one we derived by different considerations previously.

Theorem 4-6 Let $A = (a_{ij})$ be the $n \times n$ comparison matrix. The (i, j) entry, $a_{ij}(k)$, of the matrix A^k gives the *relative dominance (or importance) of activity i over activity j in k-steps.*

PROOF This follows directly from the above correspondence and the last theorem.

Definition 4-12 An index of dominance, $w_i(k)$, of activity i over all other activities *in k-steps* is defined to be

$$w_i(k) = \frac{\sum\limits_{j=1}^{n} a_{ij}(k)}{\sum\limits_{i=1}^{n} \sum\limits_{j=1}^{n} a_{ij}(k)}$$

Thus, $w_i(k)$ is the ith row sum of A^k divided by the sum of the rows.

Definition 4-13 *A total index of dominance*, w_i, of activity i over all other activities is defined by

$$w_i = \lim_{k \to \infty} w_i(k) = \lim_{k \to \infty} \frac{\sum\limits_{j=1}^{n} a_{ij}(k)}{\sum\limits_{i=1}^{n} \sum\limits_{j=1}^{n} a_{ij}(k)}$$

Definition 4-14 The priority index associated with activity i is its total index of dominance w_i.

TWO

APPLICATIONS

Marginal priorities—Dynamic priorities—Input–output interdependence—Resource allocation—Planning: public, private—Conflict resolution—Energy—

Our program has been to reach decision-makers by first describing the AHP, then showing some of its deeper and varied uses, and finally, for the scientist and mathematician, giving some of the basic theory. In this part we sometimes repeat ourselves by illustrating areas of applications despite the fact that the method seems the same. However, for the most part the applications are intended to highlight the possibility of using the AHP as a simple and reliable method for dealing with real-world problems alongside or frequently instead of some of the existing methods. A theme which keeps recurring is: if decomposition and synthesis are fundamental brain operations which do take place along the lines suggested here, then there may be some social, scientific, and even mathematical problems that may gain insight by this type of formalization.

Our applications produce priorities for activities satisfying certain objectives which themselves must satisfy other constraints as higher objectives of the hierarchy. We have been dealing with a relative form of optimization (without the use of a metric). This type of research is being continued. In Chapter 5 we deal with formally oriented applications whereas in Chapter 6 the applications cover a variety of real-life situations, and the formal framework for two point boundary planning and conflict resolution is presented.

PREDICTION, DYNAMIC PRIORITIES, INPUT–OUTPUT INTERDEPENDENCE, AND RESOURCE ALLOCATION

5-1 INTRODUCTION

As is the case with any new idea, our method and the underlying theory have many branches which are not yet fully developed. In this chapter we present several other facets of the eigenvector method (five in all) which have attained practical and theoretical value, although much remains to be explored in depth.

The first of these areas is the calculation of expected values in the framework of a prediction problem. The second is to illustrate the use of marginal priorities. The third topic we treat here is that of dynamic priorities where the judgments themselves are functions of time and the eigenvector up to the four by four case is explicitly calculated in terms of the coefficients. A sketch of a proof that in the three by three case the left eigenvector is the reciprocal of the right eigenvector appears in Chapter 7. We then illustrate the ideas with an example. This procedure may be generalized to a hierarchy decomposed into clusters and elements whose numbers in each level is at most four. There is no theoretical difficulty in decomposing any hierarchy this way. The fourth topic deals with computing a table of national input–output coefficients and thus also illustrates how to develop priorities when there is interdependence among the activities. The table was generated by expert econometricians through elaborate techniques, and is given here for comparison purposes. It will be seen that the results are close and our approach may be used to make a first cut estimate of input–output tables. The final useful application deals with resource allocation by using a benefit hierarchy and a cost hierarchy and goes on to give other examples to illustrate the effectiveness of the AHP in this important field of application. Finally, we mention in passing some results of research done on probabilistic judgments and their interpretation. This may be useful in doing statistical analysis of judgments obtained from many people.

5-2 EXPECTED VALUES BY THE AHP: PREDICTION

The following example is used as an illustration, not as conclusive evidence of the fact that people's judgments can produce results in close agreement with scientific projections made by experts based on a number of factors.

Two sets of people participated in an hierarchical approach to estimate the family size. (One group considered the subject from World War II to the early 1970's and the other looked ahead to the 1980's.) The first group developed the following hierarchy of levels and factors in each level.

Level 1. The average number of children in a U.S. family.
Level 2. Years of education, income, size of present family, religion, and intensity of work for the mother.
Level 3. High, medium, low for each factor in level 2.
Level 4. The expected number of children from 1 to 5 in a family.
The result was that five factors dominated according to the priority of their contribution to family size between World War II and the early 1970's. They were: low years of education, low income, high income, medium years of education, and high religion. Their priorities were then normalized.

We now note that a high priority factor, which affects the size of a family such as high income, may not occur with the frequency that medium income or high religion occur in the population. Thus, we must estimate the relative frequency of occurrence of these factors in the population using pairwise comparisons, obtain the eigenvector, and multiply the corresponding components of the two eigenvectors, the original and the population oriented one, and then normalize over the factors of the new vector to obtain a net relative priority for each high priority factor according to its distribution in the population. Finally, the eigenvectors for the dominance of the number of children according to each of the five factors were weighted each by their corresponding component of the renormalized vector. The result was as follows

Number of children	1	2	3	4	5
Priority	0.087	0.191	0.282	0.292	0.150

The expected number of children is

$$0.087 \times 1 + 0.191 \times 2 + 0.282 \times 3 + 0.292 \times 4 + 0.150 \times 5 = 3.23$$

Later it was determined that demographer's projections for the average number of children born to women who themselves were born in the period 1923–27 was 3.10 and for those born in the period 1928–32 was 3.14, both sets mothering children in the period after World War II.

The second set of people looking ahead to the average family size used the following factors; availability of birth controls and abortion, working mother, older age at motherhood, education of mother, cost of raising children, and social pressure. The eigenvectors of those factors did not require demographic smoothing; they were considered to be homogenously distributed. There was no consideration of high, medium, or low values of the factors. Prioritization of the number of children with respect to these five factors resulted in the following eigenvector,

Number of children	0	1	2	3	4
Priority	0.028	0.174	0.495	0.239	0.064

leading to 2.14 as the expected number which compares with 2.11 as projected by some demographers for the 1980's.

In a corporate application of the method to estimate sales increase despite the impact of inflation, recession, and rise in energy cost, the three criteria were first prioritized. Then sales increases were divided into the ranges 0–5 percent, 6–10 percent, 11–15 percent, and 15–20 percent. These four ranges were used as elements to be compared in separate matrices according to their likelihood of occurrence under each of the three criteria. The average rate of increase was calculated as we did with family size. The mean can be used to calculate the variance.

5-3 MARGINAL PRIORITIES

So far in our study of prioritization we have compared activities with respect to criteria on the assumption that a criterion could be thought of in some average form. For example, when we compared schools according to friends we were not concerned with the possibility that the number of friends may be small or large, for then the desirability of the schools may be different.

There are two ways to cope with this problem. The first is to parameterize the number of friends along lines we just indicated, e.g., no friends, a few friends, more than a few, many, and so on. But this approach has a certain amount of fuzziness attached to it, since the number does not seem to have direct bearing on the property of friendliness and how much of it one may be scaling. One individual may have a greater or a lesser capacity for being a friend than another.

A more useful approach is to compare the schools according to their desirability if the criterion of friends were increased or decreased by one more (a unit!) friend. This type of marginal analysis may be carried out in several iterations. The result is a set of eigenvectors which yields a law for the variation of the desirability of each school with respect to the number of friends, or amount of friendliness one may also be seeking. For many problems this would more faithfully represent the dynamics of a problem, since a marginal increase in the property could affect the criteria differently, depending on the level of saturation (analogous to the derivative of a function, whose value generally differs from point to point). The approach may be generalized to an entire hierarchy, but the computations would be demanding and tedious.

The eigenvalue method may be used to develop an eigenvector measure for marginal changes in the properties being considered. These, of course, need not coincide with the eigenvector which represents the dominance of the properties. The following should be taken as an illustrative example rather than as a precise representation of a problem. Let us first do the usual dominance analysis matrix with its eigenvector, and follow it by the marginal analysis matrix with its eigenvector.

We have as an example a highway construction man who was unemployed and who has just got a job. His preferences are illustrated over the following properties involved.

	A	B	C	D	E	F
A	1	6	5	3	7	9
B	0.17	1	0.25	0.2	4	3
C	0.2	4	1	0.33	3	4
D	0.33	5	3	1	6	7
E	0.14	0.25	0.33	0.17	1	0.2
F	0.11	0.33	0.25	0.14	5	1

$\lambda_{max} = 6.79$,   C.I. = 0.16,   C.R. = 0.13

A: Money
B: Team work participation
C: Good working conditions
D: Shorter hours
E: Variety of tasks
F: Autonomy

The largest eigenvalue of this matrix is equal to 6.79. The eigenvector is (0.448, 0.076, 0.135, 0.257, 0.031, 0.052). This indicates that money is by far the most important property of the job, followed by short hours, good team work, and so on.

The entries of the following marginal comparison matrix are estimated by answering the question, "Having gotten the job, how much more does the man prefer an incremental change in a property over an incremental change in another property?"

	A	B	C	D	E	F
A	1	0.14	0.2	0.333	3	6
B	7	1	3	3	5	7
C	5	0.333	1	3	3	3
D	3	0.333	0.333	1	5	5
E	0.333	0.2	0.333	0.2	1	4
F	0.17	0.14	0.333	0.2	0.25	1

$\lambda_{max} = 6.87$,   C.I. = 0.17,   C.R. = 0.14

The largest eigenvalue of this matrix is 6.87. The eigenvector is (0.093, 0.409, 0.236, 0.166, 0.062, 0.034). In this case he favors a marginal improvement in teamwork participation, followed by good working conditions, then by short working hours, and so on.

This kind of analysis should enable him to look at the job not simply from the standpoint of its initial merits, but from the potential capabilities of the management to make the kind of marginal improvement which he values most highly.

5-4 DYNAMIC JUDGMENTS AND THE EQUATION: $A(t)w(t) = \lambda_{\max}(t)w(t)$

The question often arises in regard to the use of the Analytic Hierarchy Process: What would one do if the judgments were to change? A simple answer to that problem is that one should solve the new problem. But this is not what people usually have in mind. Presumably what they would like is a parameterized eigenvector solution as a function of time in order to make the implementation compatible, not just with what people think now, but what they are likely to think later on. Thus one would like an analytic solution of the eigenvalue problem $A(t)w(t) = \lambda_{\max}(t)w(t)$.

Judgments by their very nature may be expected to vary according to different situations. If they follow a known trend corresponding to a particular parameter, then one could adjust the judgments to follow the changes in the parameter. For example, a combat pilot may have a number of strategies to choose from depending upon the speed of his aircraft, his distance from an enemy aircraft or on the amount of fuel in the tanks. The importance of one strategy over another would then be a function of speed or distance or amount of fuel. One way to solve this problem is to repeatedly fix the value of the time parameter and then use curve fitting for the different values obtained for each of the eigenvector components.

An elegant approach would be to decompose the hierarchy into clusters whose number does not exceed four in a cluster of comparisons, obtain the solution for $\lambda_{\max}$ as a function of the coefficients by solving a quadratic, a cubic, or a quartic as the need may be, and then solve the eigenvalue problem explicitly in terms of the coefficients and also in terms of $\lambda_{\max}$. One could then apply the hierarchical composition principle to obtain the overall weighting as a time-dependent function.

It is well known according to Galois theory, that by using simple quadrature $n = 4$ is the highest order matrix for which we can obtain solutions for $\lambda_{\max}$ in closed form. As we said before, if one insists on using higher order matrices one should enter static numerical judgments provided for different periods of time and solve the corresponding problem.

For the pairwise comparison judgments one may attempt to fit one of the functions given in Table 5-1 to the changing judgments. These functions have been left in parametric form so that the parameter may be set for the particular comparison, hopefully adhering to the 1–9 scale we have been using in the discrete case as a limit on the range of values (or any other convenient scale used in the discrete case). These functions reflect our intuitive feeling about change in trend: constant, linear, logarithmic, and exponential, rising to a maximum and declining, or falling to a minimum and rising, oscillating, and finally, allowing for catastrophic change.

Table 5-1 Dynamic judgments

Time-dependent importance intensity	Description	Explanation
α	Constant for all t, $1 \leqslant \alpha \leqslant 9$ an integer	No change in relative standing
$a_1 t + a_2$	Linear relation in t, increasing or decreasing to a point and then a constant value thereafter. Note that reciprocal is a hyperbola	Steady increase in value of one activity over another
$b_1 \log (t+1) + b_2$	Logarithmic growth up to a certain point and constant thereafter	Rapid increase (decrease) followed by slow increase (decrease)
$c_1 e^{c_2 t} + c_3$	Exponential growth (or decay if c_2 is negative) to a certain point and constant thereafter (note reciprocal of case c_2 is negative is the the logistic S-curve)	Slow increase (decrease) followed by rapid increase (decrease)
$d_1 t^2 + d_2 t + d_3$	A parabola giving a maximum or minimum (depending on d_1 being negative or positive) with a constant value thereafter. (May be modified for skewness to the right or left)	Increase (decrease) to maximum (minimum) and then decrease (increase)
$e_1 t^n \sin (t + e_2) + e_3$	Oscillatory	Oscillates depending on $n > 0$ ($n \leqslant 0$) with decreasing (increasing) amplitude
Catastrophies	Discontinuities indicated	Violent change in intensity

Quadratic Case

For this case $\lambda_{\max}(t) = 2$ and our time-dependent eigenvalue problem is given by

$$\begin{bmatrix} 1 & a(t) \\ 1/a(t) & 1 \end{bmatrix} \begin{bmatrix} w_1(t) \\ w_2(t) \end{bmatrix} = 2 \begin{bmatrix} w_1(t) \\ w_2(t) \end{bmatrix}$$

From which we have

$$w_1(t) + a(t)\, w_2(t) = 2w_1(t)$$
$$w_1(t)/a(t) + w_2(t) = 2w_2(t)$$

The first equation yields

$$w_1(t) = a(t)w_2(t)$$

which is also what we can obtain from the second equation. These two equations cannot be independent, otherwise the determinant of $A(t)$ would not be zero and we would not have a nonzero solution. Thus, we can fix $w_2(t)$ arbitrarily, e.g., put

$w_2(t) = 1$ from which we have $w_1(t) = a(t)$. The normalized right eigenvector has the form $\{a(t)/[a(t)+1], 1/[a(t)+1]\}$. The normalized left eigenvector is the componentwise reciprocal of this given by $\{1/a(t)[a(t)+1], 1/[a(t)+1]\}$.

Cubic Case

In a straightforward fashion, Morris (1979), by solving a cubic equation, showed that λ_{max} for the three by three case with $a_{ji} = 1/a_{ij}$ is given by

$$\lambda_{max} = (a_{13}/a_{12}a_{23})^{1/3} + (a_{12}a_{23}/a_{13})^{1/3} + 1$$

Note that λ_{max} is always $\geqslant 3$ (we have proved that in general $\lambda_{max} \geqslant n$).

The system of equations corresponding to this problem is given by

$$w_1(t) + a_{12}w_2(t) + a_{13}w_3(t) = \lambda_{max}(t)w_1(t)$$
$$w_1(t)/a_{12} + w_2(t) + a_{23}w_3(t) = \lambda_{max}(t)w_2(t)$$
$$w_1(t)/a_{13} + w_2(t)/a_{23} + w_3(t) = \lambda_{max}(t)w_3(t)$$

Put $w_1 = 1$. The first equation becomes

$$a_{12}w_2 + a_{13}w_3 = -(1-\lambda)$$

and the second

$$(1-\lambda)w_2 + a_{23}w_3 = -\frac{1}{a_{12}}$$

We now solve for w_2 and w_3. We have

$$w_2 = \frac{(\lambda-1)a_{23} + (a_{13}/a_{12})}{\Delta}$$

$$w_3 = \frac{-1 + (1-\lambda)^2}{\Delta}$$

where

$$\Delta = a_{12}a_{23} + a_{13}(\lambda-1)$$

In order to normalize the components we form

$$w_1 + w_2 + w_3 = \frac{a_{12}a_{23} + a_{13}(\lambda-1) + (\lambda-1)a_{23} + (a_{13}/a_{12}) - 1 + (1-\lambda)^2}{\Delta} \equiv \frac{D}{\Delta}$$

Thus, finally

$$w_1 = \frac{\Delta}{D}$$

$$w_2 = \frac{(\lambda-1)a_{23} + (a_{13}/a_{12})}{D}$$

$$w_3 = \frac{-1 + (1-\lambda)^2}{D}$$

For the left eigenvector which is the elementwise reciprocal of the above we have:

$$v_1 = \frac{-1+(1-\lambda)^2}{E}$$

$$v_2 = \frac{a_{12}(\lambda-1)+a_{13}/a_{23}}{E}$$

$$v_3 = \frac{\Delta}{E}$$

where

$$E = -1+(1-\lambda)^2+a_{12}(\lambda-1)+a_{13}/a_{23}+a_{12}a_{23}+a_{13}(\lambda-1)$$

Quartic Case

Consider the four by four matrix with reciprocal entries, all functions of time t

$$A = \begin{bmatrix} 1 & a & b & c \\ \dfrac{1}{a} & 1 & d & e \\ \dfrac{1}{b} & \dfrac{1}{d} & 1 & f \\ \dfrac{1}{c} & \dfrac{1}{e} & \dfrac{1}{f} & i \end{bmatrix}$$

Note that all the coefficients may be functions of a parameter t. The characteristic equation of this matrix is

$$\lambda^4-4\lambda^3-(B-8)\lambda+(B+C-5) = 0$$

where

$$B = \left(\frac{df}{e}+\frac{e}{df}\right)+\left(\frac{ae}{c}+\frac{c}{ae}\right)+\left(\frac{ad}{b}+\frac{b}{ad}\right)+\left(\frac{bf}{c}+\frac{c}{bf}\right)$$

$$C = 3-\left(\frac{adf}{c}+\frac{c}{adf}\right)-\left(\frac{ae}{bf}+\frac{bf}{ae}\right)-\left(\frac{cd}{be}+\frac{be}{cd}\right)$$

We consider reduction of the quartic as follows, We write

$$(\lambda^2-2\lambda)^2 = (B-8)\lambda-(B+C-5)+4\lambda^2$$

Adding

$$(\lambda^2-2\lambda)r+\tfrac{1}{4}r^2$$

(where r is a parameter) to both sides we have

$$(\lambda^2 - 2\lambda + \tfrac{1}{2}r)^2 = (r+4)\lambda^2 + (B-8-2r)\lambda + \tfrac{1}{4}r^2 - (B+C-5)$$

The right-hand side is a perfect square of a linear function in λ if and only if its discriminant is zero, i.e.

$$\begin{aligned} \Delta &= [(B-8)-2r]^2 - 4[\tfrac{1}{4}r^2 - (B+C-5)](r+4) \\ &= -r^3 + 4(C+3)r + (-16 + B^2 + 16C) = 0 \end{aligned}$$

which is called the resolvent cubic equation of the quartic.
Whenever r is a root of this equation we have $\Delta = 0$.
   We have

$$(\lambda^2 - 2\lambda + \tfrac{1}{2}r)^2 = (r+4)\left[\lambda + \frac{B-2(r+4)}{2(r+4)}\right]^2$$

$$= (r+4)\left[\lambda - 1 + \frac{B}{2(r+4)}\right]^2$$

from which we get, using the largest value of r

$$\lambda_{max} = \frac{2+\sqrt{r+4}}{2} + \sqrt{\frac{8-r}{4}} + \frac{B}{2\sqrt{r+4}}$$

Now let us look at the solution of the cubic. The resolvant cubic may be put in the form

$$r^3 + pr + q = 0$$

where

$$p = -4(C+3)$$

and

$$q = 16 - B^2 - 16C$$

Using the transformation

$$r = z - \frac{p}{3z}$$

the resolvent is transformed to

$$z^3 - \frac{p^3}{27z^3} + q = 0$$

or

$$z^6 + qz^3 - \frac{p^3}{27} = 0$$

and this equation is a quadratic in z^3.
   So the solutions are

$$z^3 = -\frac{q}{2} \pm \sqrt{R}$$

where $R = (p/3)^3 + (q/2)^2$. Let

$$T_1 = \sqrt[3]{-\frac{q}{2} + \sqrt{R}}, \qquad T_2 = \sqrt[3]{-\frac{q}{2} - \sqrt{R}}$$

Now the cube roots of unity are

$$1, \qquad w = -\tfrac{1}{2} + \tfrac{1}{2}\sqrt{3}\,i, \qquad w^2 = -\tfrac{1}{2} - \tfrac{1}{2}\sqrt{3}\,i$$

We obtain the following six solutions

$$T_1, \qquad wT_1, \qquad w^2T_1, \qquad T_2, \qquad wT_2, \qquad w^2T_2$$

to the equation

$$z^6 + qz^3 - \frac{p^3}{27} = 0$$

It is known that the roots of the reduced cubic equation $r^3 + pr + q = 0$ are given by

$$r_1 = T_1 + T_2$$
$$r_2 = wT_1 + w^2T_2$$
$$r_3 = w^2T_1 + wT_2$$

Therefore

$$r_1 = \left[-8 + \frac{B^2}{2} + 8C + \sqrt{\left[-\frac{4}{3}(C+3) \right]^3 + \left(8 - \frac{B^2}{2} - 8C \right)^2} \,\right]^{1/3}$$

$$+ \left[\left(-8 + \frac{B^2}{2} + 8C \right) - \sqrt{\left[-\frac{4}{3}(C+3) \right]^3 + \left(8 - \frac{B^2}{2} - 8C \right)^2} \,\right]^{1/3}$$

$$r_2 = (-\tfrac{1}{2} + \tfrac{1}{2}\sqrt{3}\,i)T_1 + (-\tfrac{1}{2} - \tfrac{1}{2}\sqrt{3}\,i)T_2 = -\tfrac{1}{2}(T_1 + T_2) + \frac{\sqrt{3}}{2}(T_1 - T_2)i$$

$$r_3 = (-\tfrac{1}{2} - \tfrac{1}{2}\sqrt{3}\,i)T_1 + (-\tfrac{1}{2} + \tfrac{1}{2}\sqrt{3}\,i)T_2 = -\tfrac{1}{2}(T_1 + T_2) - \frac{\sqrt{3}}{2}(T_1 - T_2)i$$

When $T_1 = T_2$, $R = 0$ and $r_2 = r_3 = (-q/2)^{1/3}$ is real. Also, $r_1 = 2(-q/2)^{1/3}$. In addition, since complex roots occur in conjugate pairs, r_1 is always a real root of the resolvent cubic. This follows from the fact that $p \geqslant 0$. To see this we note that C has three terms of the form $x + 1/x$. The minimum value of such a term is 2. Hence, $C \leqslant -3$ and $p = -4(C+3) \geqslant 0$. Thus $r = r_1$ is always real. In addition, $r \geqslant 0$ since $q \leqslant 0$. This follows from

$$B^2 + 16C \geqslant 16$$
$$B^2 \geqslant 16(1 - C)$$

Now the minimum of $16(1 - C)$ is 64.

Similarly the minimum value of B^2 is 64. Thus $q \leqslant 0$.

Now, the first term in r_1 is positive. The second term is always dominated by the first term. Thus, $r \equiv r_1 \geqslant 0$ is what we use in the expression for $\lambda_{\max}$ above.

The solution of the system $Aw = \lambda_{\max}w$ which in expanded form is given by

$$(1-\lambda)w_1 + aw_2 + bw_3 + cw_4 = 0$$

$$\frac{1}{a}w_1 + (1-\lambda)w_2 + dw_3 + ew_4 = 0$$

$$\frac{1}{b}w_1 + \frac{1}{d}w_2 + (1-\lambda)w_3 + fw_4 = 0$$

$$\frac{1}{c}w_1 + \frac{1}{e}w_2 + \frac{1}{f}w_3 + (1-\lambda)w_4 = 0$$

when normalized, is

$$w_1 = \frac{\overline{w}_1}{Q}, \qquad w_2 = \frac{\overline{w}_2}{Q}, \qquad w_3 = \frac{\overline{w}_3}{Q}, \qquad w_4 = \frac{\overline{w}_4}{Q}$$

where

$$Q = (\lambda-1)^3 + (c+f+e)(\lambda-1)^2 + \left[(ae-3) + (b+d)f + \left(\frac{1}{a}+\frac{1}{b}\right)c + \frac{e}{d}\right](\lambda-1)$$

$$+ \left[(adf-a-c-e-f) + \left(\frac{be}{d}+\frac{bf}{a}\right) + \frac{cd+ae}{b} + \frac{c-b}{ad}\right]$$

$$\overline{w}_1 = c(\lambda-1)^2 + (ae+bf)(\lambda-1) + \left(adf + \frac{be}{d} - c\right)$$

$$\overline{w}_2 = e(\lambda-1)^2 + \left(df + \frac{c}{a}\right)(\lambda-1) + \left(\frac{bf}{a} + \frac{cd}{b} - e\right)$$

$$\overline{w}_3 = f(\lambda-1)^2 + \left(\frac{e}{d} + \frac{c}{b}\right)(\lambda-1) + \left(\frac{c}{ad} + \frac{ae}{b} - f\right)$$

$$\overline{w}_4 = (\lambda-1)^3 - 3(\lambda-1) - \left(\frac{ad}{b} + \frac{b}{ad}\right)$$

REMARK It is easy to see from this solution that if any coefficient is increased (decreased) in a given row of the pairwise comparison matrix the value of the eigenvector component corresponding to that row is increased (decreased) relative to the remaining components. This property holds in general for a reciprocal matrix.

To end this section let us consider the simple case of a family consisting of a father, a mother, and a child. Obviously the amount of time the child spends at home will depend on his age. The infant would spend the same amount of time as the mother and then, as he grows older, he will progressively spend less time at home as compared to the time spent by the mother. We assume that the mother does not go out to work.

If we were to compare the length of time spent at home by mother and child

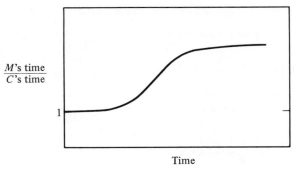

Figure 5-1

and plot this relation as a function of time (i.e., as the child grows older), we would get the type of curve shown in Fig. 5-1.

Thus the curve begins with mother and child spending the same amount of time, then the ratio of mother's to child's time increases until it levels off by the time the child is in his mid-teens.

Comparison of father to child times yields a relationship which is a mirror image of the above—reflected about a horizontal axis halfway up the curve. This is illustrated in Fig. 5-2. The relative length of time spent by father and mother would not vary too much and could be expected to be fairly constant.

If we were to make a pairwise comparison of the different lengths of time spent at home by the different members of the family, we would get a sequence of comparison matrices each corresponding to a particular period of time.

Consider the time period corresponding to the child's age 0–4 years. If we were to exclude, say, eight hours of the night, we would expect the mother and child to spend about two to three times the length of time the father spends at home. The mother and child would of course spend the same amount of time.

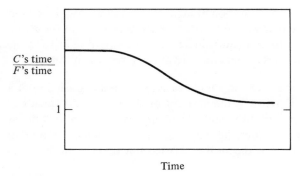

Figure 5-2

This would give rise to the following matrix

$$
\begin{array}{c c c c}
 & F & M & C \\
\begin{array}{c} F \\ M \\ C \end{array} &
\left[\begin{array}{c c c}
1 & 1/2.5 & 1/2.5 \\
2.5 & 1 & 1 \\
2.5 & 1 & 1
\end{array}\right]
\end{array}
$$

$$\lambda_{\max} = 3.0, \qquad \text{C.I.} = 0.0, \qquad \text{C.R.} = 0.0$$

This yields the following eigenvector for their relative times at home

$$
\begin{aligned}
F &: \quad 0.167 \\
M &: \quad 0.417 \\
C &: \quad 0.417
\end{aligned}
$$

which is a reasonable reflection of the proportions of time they each spend at home.

Around the age of four the child begins school, so there is a sudden change in the relative proportions of time spent at home by mother and child and by father and child.

We can express the varying proportions in a single matrix using a time-dependent expression for these proportions we have

$$
\begin{array}{c c c c}
 & F & M & C \\
\begin{array}{c} F \\ M \\ C \end{array} &
\left[\begin{array}{c c c}
1 & 1/2 & 1/(3-\ln t/2) \\
2 & 1 & 0.4+\ln t/2 \\
3-\ln t/2 & 1/(0.4+\ln t/2) & 1
\end{array}\right]
\end{array}
$$

where t denotes the time ranging between 4 and 16 years.

This matrix, along with the previous one, gives rise to the curves in Figs 5-3–5-5 which depict the corresponding pairwise comparisons as time varies from zero to 16 years.

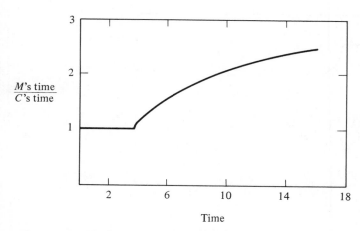

Figure 5-3 Mother and child: age 0–16 years

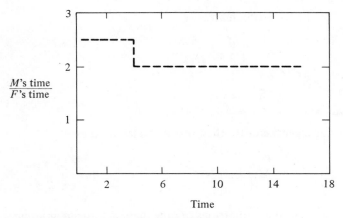

Figure 5-4 Father and mother: age 0–16 years

The solution of the maximum eigenvalue problem corresponding to these pairwise comparison curves for $(4 \leqslant t \leqslant 16)$ is

$$\lambda = 1 + \left[\frac{2}{(3 - \ln t/2)(0.4 + \ln t/2)} \right]^{1/3} + \left[\frac{(3 - \ln t/2)(0.4 + \ln t/2)}{2} \right]^{1/3}$$

The corresponding eigenvector is given by

$$\Delta/D$$

$$\left[(\lambda - 1)(0.4 + \ln t/2) + \frac{2}{3 - \ln t/2} \right] / D$$

$$[-1 + (1 - \lambda)^2]/D$$

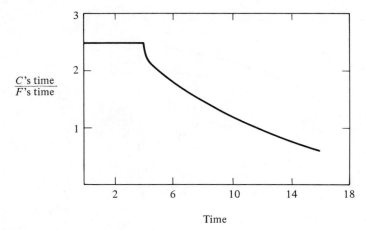

Figure 5-5 Father and child: age 0–16 years

where

$$\Delta = 0.5(0.4 + \ln t/2) + \frac{\lambda - 1}{3 - \ln t/2}$$

$$D = (\lambda - 0.5)(0.4 + \ln t/2) + \frac{\lambda + 1}{3 - \ln t/2} - 1 + (1 - \lambda)^2$$

As the child finishes school, he begins spending even less time at home than the father. The proportions once again become fairly constant and are reflected in the following (consistent) pairwise comparison matrix

$$
\begin{array}{c@{\quad}c@{\quad}c@{\quad}c}
 & F & M & C \\
\begin{array}{c} F \\ M \\ C \end{array} &
\left[\begin{array}{ccc}
1 & 0.5 & 1.25 \\
2 & 1 & 2.5 \\
0.80 & 0.4 & 1
\end{array}\right]
\end{array}
$$

$$\lambda_{max} = 3.0, \qquad \text{C.I.} = 0.0, \qquad \text{C.R.} = 0.0$$

whose eigenvector solution is given by

$$
\begin{aligned}
F: &\quad 0.263 \\
M: &\quad 0.526 \\
C: &\quad 0.211
\end{aligned}
$$

Plotting these results together for $0 \leqslant t \leqslant 4$, $4 \leqslant t \leqslant 16$, and $16 \leqslant t$ gives a realistic representation of the relative time, with respect to all others, which each spends at home (see Fig. 5-6).

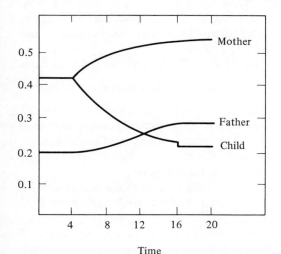

Time

Figure 5-6 Relative proportion of time spent at home

5-5 MEASURING DEPENDENCE BETWEEN ACTIVITIES; INPUT–OUTPUT; APPLICATION TO THE SUDAN

For brevity, in our study of dependence we focus on input–output type of relations. Input–output matrices in economics are obtained in general as follows.

Given N sectors (of an economy) $A_1, A_2, \ldots, A_N$, and given a matrix S whose s_{ij} entry indicates the output from sector i which becomes an input to sector j. The output from sector i to final (consumer) demand we denote by Y_i. We have

$$\sum_{j=1}^{N} s_{ij} = S_i \quad \begin{array}{l} \text{total intermediate output of sector } i \\ \text{(domestic needs from other sectors)} \end{array}$$

$$S_i + Y_i = O_i \quad \text{total output of sector } i$$

The technological coefficients are obtained as follows

$$\frac{s_{ij}}{S_i + Y_i} = w_{ij} \quad \text{(contribution of sector } i \text{ to produce a unit of output } j\text{)}$$

$$\frac{s_{ij}}{S_i + Y_i} = \frac{s_{ij}}{S_i} \cdot \frac{S_i}{S_i + Y_i} = \frac{s_{ij} S_i}{S_i O_i}$$

To obtain the matrix of technological coefficients by the AHP we must estimate s_{ij}/S_i and S_i/O_i. Let us see what these represent. $S_i/(S_i + Y_i)$ represents the proportion of the total output of section i allocated to domestic consumption. The total output is estimated, for $i = 1, \ldots, N$, by means of the AHP by asking the following question: How strong is one sector compared to another when allocating outputs to domestic needs? If this question cannot be answered directly, domestic needs may be hierarchically decomposed into production, demand, labor, capital, and cost and the sectors are prioritized separately with respect to each criterion, and after prioritizing these criteria according to their impact on production, composition is used to obtain an overall measure of importance for the sectors. Let us denote the estimates of (S_i/O_i) by x_i.

Again s_{ij}/S_i represents the proportion of the total intermediate output from sector i allocated to sector j. We have $\sum_{j=1}^{N} s_{ij}/S_i = 1$. We construct a matrix of pairwise comparisons among the sectors as they relate to sector i. We answer the following question. How strong is the dependence of one sector in comparison with another in receiving output from sector i? The result is a matrix of pairwise comparisons which yields a column eigenvector of weights. When this is done for each sector we obtain a matrix W whose columns are these eigenvectors.

Finally, we take the product elementwise of each column of the matrix W with the column vector $x = (x_1, x_2, \ldots, x_N)$ to obtain the estimates of the technological coefficients, i.e., the input–output matrix.

The most important fact we have to take into consideration when the matrix of technological coefficients is estimated by means of the hierarchical approach, is the proportion of total intermediate outputs for each sector in relation to the total

output. This proportion was estimated in this example by extensive study of the literature on the Sudanese economy available at the time (Saaty and Vargas, 1979).
We have considered the following six sectors.

(1) Agriculture (AGR)
(2) Public utilities (PU)
(3) Manufacturing and mining (M&M)
(4) Transportation and distribution (T&D)
(5) Construction (CONS)
(6) Services (SERV)

The Sudan is considered mainly as an agricultural country. At the time the econometric models were constructed (1973) and the input–output analysis was done, the data used were from the year 1961. The major problem of the Sudan was the lack of an adequate transport system. To make the same order of magnitude comparison with Agriculture and Transportation (another major activity), the other sectors were grouped into an aggregate. We have

$$\text{Aggregate} \atop \text{(AGG)} \left\{ \begin{array}{l} \text{Public utilities} \\ \text{Manufacturing and mining} \\ \text{Construction} \\ \text{Services} \end{array} \right.$$

The question to be asked to form the matrices of pairwise comparisons is: Given two sectors, i and j, which sector allocates more of its outputs to satisfy domestic needs (total intermediate outputs)? We first compare the elements in the aggregate, then separately compare the aggregate with agriculture and transport and use the resulting weight of the aggregate to compose the relevant weights from the four sectors in the aggregate itself. To save space we have not written out justifications of the judgments, which are available in a separate study.

	Satisfaction of domestic needs	PU	M&M	CONS	SERV	Eigenvector
AGG:	PU	1	1/2	1/2	1/3	0.127 2
	M&M	2	1	1	1	0.280 4
	CONS	2	1	1	1	0.280 4
	SERV	3	1	1	1	0.312 0

$$\lambda_{max} = 4.02, \quad \text{C.I.} = 0.007, \quad \text{C.R.} = 0.007$$

Satisfaction of domestic needs	AGR	T&D	AGG	Eigenvector
AGR	1	1/2	2	0.310 8
T&D	2	1	2	0.493 4
AGG	1/2	1/2	1	0.194 8

$\lambda_{max} = 3.05,$ C.I. = 0.025,   C.R. = 0.04

We have for the relative importance of the sectors:

Sectors	Final weights $S_i/(S_i + Y_i)$	Estimates of $Y_i/(S_i + Y_i)$
1	0.310 8	0.689 2
2	0.024 8	0.975 2
3	0.054 6	0.945 4
4	0.493 4	0.506 6
5	0.054 6	0.945 4
6	0.060 8	0.939 2

Now we identify the relationships among the sectors. They are given by the rows of Table 5-2.

Table 5-2

I.O.	AGR	PU	M&M	T&D	CONS	SERV
AGR	X		X	X	X	
PU	X		X	X		X
M&M	X			X	X	X
T&D	X	X	X		X	X
CONS						X
SERV		X	X	X	X	X

Given a certain sector i we ask: for any two sectors, h and k, to which sector are more products from sector i allocated? The following matrices answer this question for each sector.

Agriculture

The main crop in the Sudan is cotton. Cotton is exported and also allocated to the manufacturing sector. Thus agriculture, transportation and distribution, and construction do not receive a large amount of agricultural products. A new aggregate is formed. (Note that only four sectors are considered under agriculture.)

$$\text{Aggregate} \atop (AGG) \begin{cases} \text{Agriculture} \\ \text{Transport and distribution} \\ \text{Construction} \end{cases}$$

As we pointed out above, the main problem in the Sudan is lack of transportation. We aggregated the two sectors which do not consume substantial quantities from agriculture, AGR and T&D, because, although the main crop after cotton is wheat, the agricultural sector allocates most of its output (i.e., wood) to construction. Transportation is being developed by means of loans from Arab oil countries and the World Bank. Thus, we also aggregated agriculture and transportation to form a subaggregate.

	Input from agriculture	AGR	T&D	Eigenvector
SUBAGG:	AGR	1	9	0.900 0
	T&D	1/9	1	0.100 0

$\lambda_{max} = 2.0$, C.I. = 0.0, C.R. = 0.0

	Input from agriculture	SUBAGG	CONS	Eigenvector
AGG:	SUBAGG	1	1/9	0.100 0
	CONS	9	1	0.900 0

$\lambda_{max} = 2.0$, C.I. = 0.0, C.R. = 0.0

	Input from agriculture	AGG	M&M	Eigenvector
	AGG	1	1/3	0.25
	M&M	3	1	0.65

$\lambda_{max} = 2.0$, C.I. = 0.0, C.R. = 0.0

Sectors	Final weights
1	0.022 5
2	0.000 0
3	0.750 0
4	0.002 5
5	0.225 0
6	0.000 0

Note: The weights of AGR and T&D are obtained as follows.

$$\begin{matrix} \text{AGR} \\ \text{T\&D} \end{matrix} \begin{bmatrix} 0.9 \\ 0.1 \end{bmatrix} \times (0.1) \times (0.25) = \begin{bmatrix} 0.022\ 5 \\ 0.002\ 5 \end{bmatrix}$$

The weight of construction is obtained by multiplying (0.9) by (0.25) = 0.225.

Public Utilities

Input from PU	AGR	M&M	T&D	SERV	Eigenvector
AGR	1	1/9	1/7	1/5	0.041 0
M&M	9	1	2	5	0.524 2
T&D	7	1/2	1	3	0.303 0
SERV	5	1/5	1/3	1	0.131 8

$\lambda_{max} = 4.12$, C.I. = 0.04, C.R. = 0.04

Manufacturing and Mining

Input from M&M	AGR	T&D	CONS	SERV	Eigenvector
AGR	1	1/2	1/9	1	0.075 8
T&D	2	1	1/5	3	0.162 8
CONS	9	5	1	9	0.694 1
SERV	1	1/3	1/9	1	0.068 1

$\lambda_{max} = 4.03$, C.I. = 0.01, C.R. = 0.01

Transportation and Distribution

Input from T&D	AGR	PU	M&M	CONS	SERV	Eigenvector
AGR	1	1/3	1/2	1/2	7	0.140 0
PU	3	1	1	2	9	0.343 4
M&M	2	1	1	1	7	0.259 6
CONS	2	1/2	1	1	7	0.226 0
SERV	1/7	1/9	1/7	1/7	1	0.031 0

$\lambda_{max} = 5.11$, C.I. = 0.03, C.R. = 0.03

Construction

Construction only gives its products to services. Thus we associate the value 1 with services.

Services in the Sudan are very poor. We have assumed that the allocation of service outputs to services, and to construction, are so negligible that these two could be aggregated. We have

$$\text{Aggregate (AGG)} \begin{cases} \text{Construction} \\ \text{Services} \end{cases}$$

Input from services	CONS	SERV	Eigenvector
AGG: CONS	1	9	0.900 0
SERV	1/9	1	0.100 0

$\lambda_{max} = 2.0$, C.I. = 0.0, C.R. = 0.0

Services

Input from services	PU	M&M	T&D	AGG	Eigenvector
PU	1	1/2	1/2	3	0.193 0
M&M	2	1	1	5	0.368 0
T&D	2	1	1	5	0.368 0
AGG	1/3	1/5	1/5	1	0.070 4

$$\lambda_{max} = 4.004, \quad \text{C.I.} = 0.001, \quad \text{C.R.} = 0.001$$

The weights of construction and services are obtained by multiplying 0.070 4, the weight of the aggregate by 0.9, 0.1, respectively.

Sectors	Final weights
1	0.000 0
2	0.193 0
3	0.368 0
4	0.368 0
5	0.063 4
6	0.007 0

The matrix whose rows are the foregoing eigenvectors gives the distribution of total intermediate outputs to the sectors. It is given by Table 5-3.

Table 5-3

	Producers	AGR	PU	M&M	T&D	CONS	SERV
Shares of	→ ↓						
the total	AGR	0.022 5	0	0.750 0	0.002 5	0.225 0	0
intermediate	PU	0.041 0	0	0.524 2	0.303 0	0	0.131 8
outputs	M&M	0.075 0	0	0	0.162 8	0.684 1	0.068 1
	T&D	0.140 0	0.343 4	0.259 6	0	0.226 0	0.031 0
	CONS	0	0	0	0	0	1
	SERV	0	0.193 0	0.368 3	0.368 3	0.063 4	0.007 0

At the beginning we computed how strongly the sectors allocate outputs to domestic needs. The vector of weights was

$$
\begin{matrix}
\text{AGR} \\ \text{PU} \\ \text{M\&M} \\ \text{T\&D} \\ \text{CONS} \\ \text{SERV}
\end{matrix}
\begin{bmatrix}
0.310\ 8 \\ 0.024\ 8 \\ 0.054\ 6 \\ 0.493\ 4 \\ 0.054\ 6 \\ 0.060\ 8
\end{bmatrix}
$$

Thus we multiply each column of the above matrix by this vector (element-wise multiplication), e.g., for the first column we have

$$\begin{bmatrix} 0.022\ 5 \times 0.310\ 8 \\ 0.041\ 0 \times 0.024\ 8 \\ 0.075\ 0 \times 0.054\ 6 \\ 0.140\ 0 \times 0.493\ 4 \\ 0 \quad\ \times 0.054\ 6 \\ 0 \quad\ \times 0.060\ 8 \end{bmatrix} = \begin{bmatrix} 0.007\ 0 \\ 0.000\ 9 \\ 0.004\ 1 \\ 0.069\ 1 \\ 0 \\ 0 \end{bmatrix}$$

The weighted matrix is then given by Table 5-4.

If we compare the matrix of Table 5-4 with the input–output matrix obtained by traditional methods (Table 5-5), we see that there are few differences.

Table 5-4

	AGR	PU	M&M	T&D	CONS	SERV
AGR	0.007 0	0	0.233 1	0.000 8	0.069 9	0
PU	0.000 9	0	0.013 0	0.007 5	0	0.003 3
M&M	0.004 1	0	0	0.008 9	0.037 9	0.003 7
T&D	0.069 1	0.169 4	0.128 1	0	0.111 5	0.015 3
CONS	0	0	0	0	0	0.054 6
SERV	0	0.011 7	0.022 4	0.022 4	0.003 9	0.000 4

Table 5-5

	AGR	PU	M&M	T&D	CONS	SERV
AGR	0.007 37	0	0.219 53	0.000 42	0.067 21	0
PU	0.000 24	0	0.011 59	0.006 18	0	0.002 83
M&M	0.003 93	0	0	0.008 57	0.042 16	0.003 22
T&D	0.069 93	0.145 36	0.125 74	0	0.098 79	0.006 41
CONS	0	0	0	0	0	0.054 02
SERV	0	0.010 30	0.025 49	0.024 22	0.005 20	0.000 21

The factors involved in this problem were purely economic. This suggests extending this type of analysis to study social systems and particularly to introduce social factors in the resource allocation problem (a problem briefly mentioned by V. Leontief, the founder of input–output analysis) when the activities are interrelated. As of this writing, a project has been undertaken to carry out this research in the social domain.

To introduce the concept of interdependence priority as a single number, we first observe that activities may be interdependent from the standpoint of some of the properties represented in the hierarchy, but not all. For example, in production, activities may depend on each other in the flow of physical material but not on their particular contributions to the economy, defense, or welfare.

The interdependence priority numbers are computed as follows. Each row of an input–output-type matrix is again weighted elementwise by the independence weight of the corresponding recipient activity. The reason for this is that if we were to sum over each row to obtain how much material flows from an activity to all other activities as an indication of the priority of their dependence on it, we must weight the amount received by the importance of the receiving activity. Otherwise a low priority activity supplying a great amount of material to another low priority activity would receive a high priority. Of course the receiver may in turn supply material to a high priority activity. To take into consideration all such second and higher order interactions, we must raise the resulting matrix to higher and higher powers and for the priorities we need to take the normalized sum of the rows of the limiting matrix. But we know that this result can be obtained by solving the largest eigenvalue problem, taking care that we work with irreducible primitive submatrices of the original matrix if necessary. Application of the foregoing to the input–output matrix of the Sudan by multiplying its rows elementwise by the independence priorities and obtaining the principal eigenvector yields: (0.14, 0.10, 0.11, 0.33, 0.06, 0.26) for the interdependence priority of the sectors with transportation receiving the lion's share (as all sectors depend on it) and services the next highest. Both agriculture and transport are eventual consumers of services. This should be compared with the independence priority vector (0.31, 0.03, 0.06, 0.49, 0.05, 0.06) which is significantly different. These two vectors have different meanings for decision making. Note that we could have taken the normalized row sums of the weighted input–output matrix as estimates of the interdependence priorities. This is given by (0.16, 0.07, 0.05, 0.50, 0.11, 0.12), not a satisfactory estimate.

5-6 RESOURCE ALLOCATION

In general terms, resource allocation is a transformation of a system from one state to another. For example, building a bridge transforms the state of transportation. The resource may take the form of materials, energy, time, or human effort, or a combination of them. Money is usually used to estimate the various amounts needed of each of these kinds of resources. By the laws of physics we cannot get something for nothing, i.e., effort is needed to change the state of a system. The resource must be found.

To allocate a resource we need to look deeper into what is needed and how it should be allocated. A simple illustration would be to allocate the resource to several alternatives. To do this, we must prioritize the alternatives according to their benefits and costs. Thus we need to look at the alternatives in terms of what purposes they fulfill and how strongly and also in terms of what it would cost to bring about these alternatives. It may be that two alternatives together may accrue a greater benefit to cost ratio than a single one.

To calculate the benefits of alternatives we need to consider a hierarchy of objectives and attributes of alternatives and the alternatives themselves to judge how much they each contribute to the fulfillment of the objectives. There is usually uncertainty in estimating the impact of the alternatives. Thus we need a level in the hierarchy to represent uncertainty. This level must be followed by a representation of known and unknown technological factors associated with bringing about the outcomes. In this manner we can obtain an estimate of the priorities of the alternatives subject to uncertainty.

The next step is to consider a hierarchy for the cost of bringing about the alternatives. Here the question to be asked is which alternative is likely to present what type of problem and what has to be done to solve such a problem? Again an estimate of the problem and what it takes to solve it is often in the realm of the uncertain. Occasionally a prefeasibility study is needed to identify and look into both cost and benefit problems before constructing the hierarchies.

There are several kinds of allocations followed in practice. The first is whether resources should be allocated to a given project or not. Here the alternatives, doing the project or not doing it, are compared in the lowest levels of the benefits and costs hierarchies. Comparison of the benefit to cost ratios would determine what to do.

If there is doubt as to whether implementing a project is worth investing the resources, the alternatives to consider in the benefits and costs hierarchies are the project as one alternative and generating and saving the resource for future need as another alternative. There may be several alternatives to prioritize and the problem may be to allocate a measurable resource proportionately to their benefits. This is usually the case with research projects which require a continuous flow of resources over a long period. The question in this type of hierarchy is: which research area is likely to encounter serious difficulties to satisfy basic "virtues" represented in the hierarchy (subject to uncertainties). At other times we may wish to allocate a resource to projects to maximize their benefit to cost ratios. There are also times when the priorities serve as indicators of which project should receive funds and which should not. In a large number of cases where resources such as money are scarce, the financial cost of an alternative is used to represent its cost priority. We have made this kind of application in the Sudan Transport Study. A still more complex type of allocation involves interdependence among the activities and allocation must be made subject to interdependence constraints. This type of allocation would avoid penalizing a high priority activity by not making enough resources available to a lower priority activity on which it depends.

There are three types of allocation problems of a resource of total amount X.

(1) *Total funding* If we start with new projects which must be completed in the allocation period, we calculate their benefits b_i and costs c_i and relabel so that we can identify the projects according to the relation

$$b_1/c_1 \geqslant b_2/c_2 \geqslant \cdots \geqslant b_n/c_n$$

and allocate the resource in decreasing order until it is depleted.

(2) *Partial funding* In case several projects must be started and monitored over several allocation periods, one allocates according to

$$\sum_{i=1}^{n} (b_i/c_i)x_i = \max$$

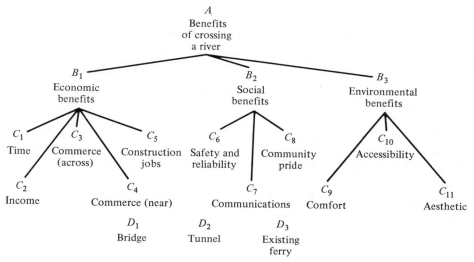

Figure 5-7

subject to

$$\sum_{i=1}^{n} x_i = X$$

and to

$$x_i \geqslant \frac{c_i}{X}$$

Thus we do not support a project which gets less than the relative value of its cost to the total resource available.

(3) For projects that are already in progress one may allocate according to their remaining (marginal) priority to cost ratio.

REMARK It is clear that in some instances benefit to cost ratio is not what we want because some things will get implemented with low benefit but very low cost that are not needed. Therefore, requirements must first be set before applying benefit/cost analysis to the contenders.

Example 5-6-1 Benefits and Costs in Crossing a River

A governmental agency (such as the New York Port Authority) which has jurisdiction over the building of bridges, tunnels, etc. in a certain area must decide on whether to build or not to build a tunnel and/or a bridge across a river presently served by a privately owned ferry.

The factors which affect both the benefits and costs of crossing a river are given in two hierarchies, see Figs 5-7 and 5-8. These factors fall into three categories: economic, social, and environmental. The decision is made in terms of the ratios of benefits to costs.

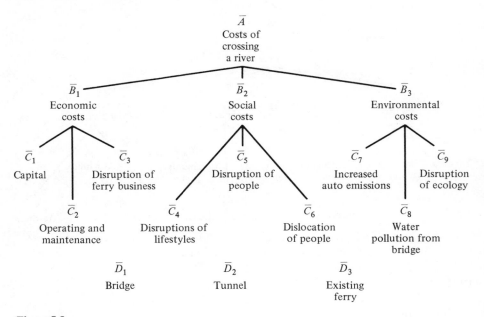

Figure 5-8

Benefits The economic factors affecting the choice consist of the benefit derived from the time saved in using a new bridge or tunnel rather than using the existing ferry. The increased traffic from outside the area could bring in toll revenue which can add to the general income of the local government. The rise in commerce caused by this increased flow of traffic is seen as being beneficial to the community in general. Additionally, the traffic will aid the commerce nearby (such as gas stations, restaurants, etc.). There is also economic benefit from the construction jobs generated. If they were the only ones to consider, most of these factors could be calculated quantitatively. The associated cost could also be computed quantitatively and a benefit/cost ratio could be used to make the decision. But we have to consider social and environmental factors which do not translate in any reasonable way to dollars.

The social benefits of the project are viewed to represent the benefits which the society as a whole will derive from the presence of a bridge or tunnel. They would provide greater safety and reliability than the ferry. They would also contribute to a greater number of trips across to visit relatives, friends, museums, etc. Finally, they could generate community pride not present to the same degree in using the ferry.

Environmental factors are viewed in terms of their contribution to individual personal benefits. Personal benefits differ from benefits to society, in that they are less abstract. The environmental factors of interest to an individual are the comfort of using the bridge, tunnel, or ferry, the ease of accessibility of one over the others, and the aesthetics affecting the choice of alternative for crossing the river.

Costs As with benefits, the costs of crossing a river also involve economic, social, and environmental factors. The three economic costs considered were the capital costs of the alternatives, the operating and maintenance costs associated with the three projects, and the economic consequence of not having a ferry boat business.

The social costs again represent costs to society. The degree to which lifestyles are disrupted using the alternatives to cross the river was thought to be important. The congestion of traffic differs between the various modes of crossings and is also deemed an important cost. The final social cost is the effect on society of the dislocation of people from their homes according to the alternative chosen.

Environmental costs differ from environmental benefits in that they represent possible harm done to the ecosystem by the various alternates. The various ways of crossing the river add to the amount of auto emissions in the area. Additionally, pollution of the water and the general disruption of the ecology were thought to contribute to environmental costs.

Results In the calculation of both benefits and costs, economic factors outweighed the other factors. The benefits derived from the commerce across the bridge, the added safety and reliability, and quick accessibility of crossing the river all received high priorities.

As for costs, the capital required, the dislocation of people from their homes, and the amount of auto emissions all received high priorities.

The composite benefits and costs are as follows.

	Bridge	Tunnel	Ferry
Benefits (b_i)	0.57	0.36	0.07
Costs (c_i)	0.36	0.58	0.05

The criterion used in benefit/cost analysis is to find $\max_i b_i/c_i$, that is, choose the project with largest benefit to cost ratio.

For this example we have

Bridge	Tunnel	Ferry
$\dfrac{b_1}{c_1} = 1.58$	$\dfrac{b_2}{c_2} = 0.62$	$\dfrac{b_3}{c_3} = 1.28$

The criterion favors the construction of a bridge across the river. Note that this has taken into consideration the capital requirements.

Judgment matrices for benefits

A	B_1	B_2	B_3	Eig
B_1	1	3	6	0.67
B_2	1/3	1	2	0.22
B_3	1/6	1/2	1	0.11
	C.I. = 0			

B_1	C_1	C_2	C_3	C_4	C_5	Eig
C_1	1	1/3	1/7	1/5	1/6	0.04
C_2	3	1	1/4	1/2	1/2	0.09
C_3	7	4	1	7	5	0.54
C_4	5	2	1/7	1	1/5	0.11
C_5	6	2	1/5	5	1	0.23
	C.I. = 0.14					

B_2	C_6	C_7	C_8	Eig
C_6	1	6	9	0.76
C_7	1/6	1	4	0.18
C_8	1/9	1/4	1	0.06
	C.I. = 0.05			

B_3	C_9	C_{10}	C_{11}	Eig
C_9	1	1/4	6	0 25
C_{10}	4	1	8	0.69
C_{11}	1/6	1/8	1	0.06
	C.I. = 0.07			

C_1	D_1	D_2	D_3	Eig
D_1	1	2	7	0.58
D_2	1/2	1	6	0.35
D_3	1/7	1/6	1	0.07
	C.I. = 0.02			

C_2	D_1	D_2	D_3	Eig
D_1	1	1/2	8	0.36
D_2	2	1	9	0.59
D_3	1/8	1/9	1	0.05
	C.I. = 0.02			

C_3	D_1	D_2	D_3	Eig
D_1	1	4	8	0.69
D_2	1/4	1	6	0.25
D_3	1/8	1/6	1	0.06
	C.I. = 0.07			

C_4	D_1	D_2	D_3	Eig
D_1	1	1	6	0.46
D_2	1	1	6	0.46
D_3	1/6	1/6	1	0.08
	C.I. = 0			

C_5	D_1	D_2	D_3	Eig
D_1	1	1/4	9	0.27
D_2	4	1	9	0.27
D_3	1/9	1/9	1	0.05
	C.I. = 0.11			

C_6	D_1	D_2	D_3	Eig
D_1	1	4	7	0.68
D_2	1/4	1	6	0.68
D_3	1/7	1/6	1	0.06
	C.I. = 0.09			

C_7	D_1	D_2	D_3	Eig
D_1	1	1	5	0.46
D_2	1	1	5	0.46
D_3	1/5	1/5	1	0.09
	C.I. = 0			

C_8	D_1	D_2	D_3	Eig
D_1	1	5	3	0.64
D_2	1/5	1	1/3	0.11
D_3	1/3	3	1	0.26
	C.I. = 0.02			

C_9	D_1	D_2	D_3	Eig
D_1	1	5	8	0.73
D_2	1/5	1	5	0.21
D_3	1/8	1/5	1	0.06
	C.I. = 0.07			

C_{10}	D_1	D_2	D_3	Eig
D_1	1	3	7	0.64
D_2	1/3	1	6	0.29
D_3	1/7	1/6	1	0.07
	C.I. = 0.05			

C_{11}	D_1	D_2	D_3	Eig
D_1	1	6	1/5	0.27
D_2	1/6	1	1/3	0.10
D_3	5	3	1	0.63
	C.I. = 0.31			

Total benefits hierarchy C.R.H. < 0.1 (good). (Poor consistency in the last matrix does not affect final result because of low priority of C_{11}.)

Example 5-6-2 Project Implementation and Deferral

Suppose that the prioritization procedure yielded the following priority vector (second column) for a set of projects based on a hierarchical analysis of their impacts and suppose the cost for constructing these projects are given by (third column):

Judgment matrices for costs

$\bar{A}$	$\bar{B}_1$	$\bar{B}_2$	$\bar{B}_3$	Eig
$\bar{B}_1$	1	5	7	0.74
$\bar{B}_2$	1/5	1	2	0.17
$\bar{B}_3$	1/7	1/2	1	0.09

C.I. = 0.01

$\bar{B}_1$	$\bar{C}_1$	$\bar{C}_2$	$\bar{C}_3$	Eig
$\bar{C}_1$	1	7	9	0.77
$\bar{C}_2$	1/7	1	5	0.17
$\bar{C}_3$	1/9	1/5	1	0.06

C.I. = 0.1

$\bar{B}_2$	$\bar{C}_4$	$\bar{C}_5$	$\bar{C}_6$	Eig
$\bar{C}_4$	1	1/3	1/5	0.11
$\bar{C}_5$	3	1	1/5	0.26
$\bar{C}_6$	5	3	1	0.64

C.I. = 0.02

$\bar{B}_3$	$\bar{C}_7$	$\bar{C}_8$	$\bar{C}_9$	Eig
$\bar{C}_7$	1	3	4	0.62
$\bar{C}_8$	1/3	1	1/3	0.13
$\bar{C}_9$	1/4	3	1	0.25

C.I. = 0.11

$\bar{C}_1$	$\bar{D}_1$	$\bar{D}_2$	$\bar{D}_3$	Eig
$\bar{D}_1$	1	1/3	8	0.30
$\bar{D}_2$	3	1	9	0.65
$\bar{D}_3$	1/8	1/9	1	0.05

C.I. = 0.05

$\bar{C}_2$	$\bar{D}_1$	$\bar{D}_2$	$\bar{D}_3$	Eig
$\bar{D}_1$	1	1/3	8	0.30
$\bar{D}_2$	3	1	9	0.65
$\bar{D}_3$	1/8	1/9	1	0.05

C.I. = 0.05

$\bar{C}_3$	$\bar{D}_1$	$\bar{D}_2$	$\bar{D}_3$	Eig
$\bar{D}_1$	1	1	9	0.47
$\bar{D}_2$	1	1	9	0.47
$\bar{D}_3$	1/9	1/9	1	0.05

C.I. = 0

$\bar{C}_4$	$\bar{D}_1$	$\bar{D}_2$	$\bar{D}_3$	Eig
$\bar{D}_1$	1	4	9	0.69
$\bar{D}_2$	1/4	1	8	0.26
$\bar{D}_3$	1/9	1/8	1	0.05

C.I. = 0.09

$\bar{C}_5$	$\bar{D}_1$	$\bar{D}_2$	$\bar{D}_3$	Eig
$\bar{D}_1$	1	1	9	0.47
$\bar{D}_2$	1	1	9	0.47
$\bar{D}_3$	1/9	1/9	1	0.05

C.I. = 0

$\bar{C}_6$	$\bar{D}_1$	$\bar{D}_2$	$\bar{D}_3$	Eig
$\bar{D}_1$	1	1	9	0.47
$\bar{D}_2$	1	1	9	0.47
$\bar{D}_3$	1/9	1/9	1	0.05

C.I. = 0

$\bar{C}_7$	$\bar{D}_1$	$\bar{D}_2$	$\bar{D}_3$	Eig
$\bar{D}_1$	1	3	8	0.65
$\bar{D}_2$	1/3	1	6	0.29
$\bar{D}_3$	1/8	1/6	1	0.06

C.I. = 0.04

$\bar{C}_8$	$\bar{D}_1$	$\bar{D}_2$	$\bar{D}_3$	Eig
$\bar{D}_1$	1	3	7	0.65
$\bar{D}_2$	1/3	1	5	0.28
$\bar{D}_3$	1/7	1/5	1	0.07

C.I. = 0.03

$\bar{C}_9$	$\bar{D}_1$	$\bar{D}_2$	$\bar{D}_3$	Eig
$\bar{D}_1$	1	1/6	7	0.21
$\bar{D}_2$	6	1	8	0.73
$\bar{D}_3$	1/7	1/8	1	0.05

C.I. = 0.16

Total cost hierarchy C.R.H. < 0.1 (good).

Projects	Priorities	Costs in $	Priority to cost ratio	Priority of implementation
A	0.21	10,000	0.21×10^{-4}	3
B	0.07	100	$7 \quad \times 10^{-4}$	1
C	0.42	70,000	0.06×10^{-4}	4
D	0.30	6,000	0.50×10^{-4}	2

The fourth column gives the priority to cost ratio and the fifth indicates the suggested priority order of implementation corresponding to this ratio if the resources are unlimited and it is desired to proceed with the projects one at a time. Note that the lowest priority project B has the highest index, but D which has relatively high priority has the second highest index. This allocation need not take into consideration the presence of constraints if those constraints can themselves be included in the process of prioritizing the projects. If the resources are limited, e.g., to \$72,000, and if partial implementation of a project is not a useful undertaking, resource allocation can be critical. Project C has high priority, but unless it is possible to borrow money, it may be deferred until there is adequate return from the other projects.

Example 5-6-3 Allocation Subject to Constraints

What is a rational basis for allocating fuel to meet demand for energy given that fuel supply is limited? This is the problem we wish to address here.

It is clear that if the shortage is small, a correspondingly small cutback may be made in delivering fuel to consumers generally without adverse effects. Thus, a percentage cut at low levels of scarcity should not entail major difficulties.

Now suppose that the shortage is sufficiently large that a corresponding amount of cutback would harm a consumer. For example, certain industries require a threshold amount of energy below which they cannot operate. In that case either the industry would have to rearrange and perhaps reduce its production activity if possible, or it may be forced to close down. Alternatively, fuel allocation may have to take into consideration the fact that some activities are essential to society and would have to get their required share of fuel while others may have to shut down. Thus, the problem is a matter of priority assignment and interdependence. Priority considerations are needed to decide which activities should have precedence. On the other hand, interdependence considerations are needed to insure that highest priority activities which receive some inputs from lower priority activities are not penalized indirectly by not making adequate fuel available to the lower priority activities on which they depend.

Our goal would be to develop an objective function whose coefficients are priorities of the activities concerned and whose variables are the amount of fuel to be allocated to the corresponding activities. We would then maximize this objective function subject to input–output constraints indicating interdependence among the activities.

Thus, the general allocation model requires the maximization of productivity according to priority (where the objective function has priority coefficients rather than cost coefficients), subject to an allocation constraint of a limited resource and to input–output constraints. It has the form: find $x_i \geqslant 0$ such that Max $\sum\limits_{i=1}^{n} w_i x_i$

subject to

$$\sum_{i=1}^{m} \gamma_i x_i \leqslant R \tag{5-1}$$

where

$$\gamma_i x_i \leqslant R_i \qquad (i = 1, 2, \ldots, m) \tag{5-2}$$

and

$$\sum_{j=1}^{m} a_{ij} x_j + y_i \leqslant x_i \qquad (i = 1, \ldots, m) \tag{5-3}$$

where all variables and coefficients are nonnegative, and where x_i is the level of output of activity i, (appropriately measured in dollars, for instance); y_i is the total amount of output of activity i that goes into final consumption (i.e., is not consumed by other activities for further production), and a_{ij} is the dollar input required from activity i for every dollar output of activity j.

Also, w_i is the priority of the ith activity, R is the total amount of resources available for allocation, R_i is the amount required by the ith activity ($\Sigma R_i \geqslant R$) and γ_i is the amount of resource that is required by the ith activity per unit of output.

Note that the first and second constraints are concerned with resource allocation. The additional constraints in (5-3) indicate the structural interdependence of the activities. Through the use of parametric programming, the space of priorities w_i is tessellated with convex cells. With each cell is associated a vertex of the constraint polyhedron corresponding to a solution of the problem. Thus, small changes in w_i generally do not lead to dramatic changes in the solution. It is interesting to note that the dual problem involves minimization of an objective function whose coefficients are y_i (the final consumer products). It follows that variations in w_i permit investigating this impact on consumer products y_i. In particular, one may be able to determine a more implementable solution corresponding to changes in priorities. Thus, priorities need not be taken for granted.

For the energy demand allocation problem to industries, let the priorities of three industries C_1, C_2, C_3 according to their contribution to the economy, national defense, and environmental protection, be $w_1 = 0.55$, $w_2 = 0.24$, $w_3 = 0.21$, respectively. Let us assume that we are given the following hypothetical input–output or interdependence matrix.

$$
\begin{array}{cccc}
 & C_1 & C_2 & C_3 \\
\begin{array}{c} C_1 \\ C_2 \\ C_3 \end{array} &
\left[\begin{array}{ccc}
1.097\ 30 & 0.226\ 80 & 0.190\ 20 \\
0.079\ 90 & 1.065\ 70 & 0.060\ 10 \\
0.039\ 50 & 0.332\ 10 & 1.207\ 10
\end{array}\right]
\end{array}
$$

In this example, we have not used the input–output constraints directly. Instead, we multiply the coefficient in the (i, j) position of the above matrix by w_i and w_j (w_i gives the priority of producing activity C_i and w_j gives the priority of the consuming activity C_j), thus deriving a new matrix of coefficients, each weighted according to the priorities of both producer and consumer. The sum is then taken over each row. This gives the vector

$$
\beta = \begin{bmatrix} 0.386\ 59 \\ 0.072\ 80 \\ 0.075\ 23 \end{bmatrix}
$$

Suppose that the energy requirements R_i (in trillion Btu) of the three users are as follows:

Activity (C_i)	Energy requirements (R_i)	R_i/Total
C_1	4,616	0.308 93
C_2	7,029	0.470 42
C_3	3,297	0.220 65
Total	14,942	

Also assume that the total energy available has been cut back to a level of $R = 12,000$ Btu. We have the following linear programming problem.
Maximize

$$z = 0.386\ 59z_1 + 0.072\ 80z_2 + 0.075\ 23z_3$$

whose coefficients are the corresponding elements of the vector β, subject to

$$0 \leqslant z_1 \leqslant 0.384\ 67$$
$$0 \leqslant z_2 \leqslant 0.585\ 75$$
$$0 \leqslant z_3 \leqslant 0.274\ 75$$

in which the quantities on the right are, respectively, R_i/R, $i = 1, 2, 3$ and subject to

$$z_1 + z_2 + z_3 = 1$$

The optimal allocation is given by

$$z_1 = 0.384\ 67$$
$$z_2 = 0.340\ 58$$
$$z_3 = 0.274\ 75$$

Thus only C_2 is not given its full requirement since $0.470\ 42 > 0.340\ 58$.

The decision-maker may use this allocation as an indicator only of which activities are to be rationed, and compare it with other information to be used in the allocation.

We have applied the ideas of this example in a real-life electricity rationing problem indicating the cutback of electricity (partial or complete) for the activities (see Saaty and Mariano, 1979).

5-7 PROBABILITY JUDGMENTS

We have undertaken an analysis of the eigenvector solution as the judgments are allowed to vary probabilistically. It turns out that a gamma distribution is a convenient way of representing this variation in judgments. As a result, in the solution of the consistent case the eigenvector components subject to the normalization constraint have a Dirichlet distribution. It is difficult to specify the distribution for the general reciprocal case. However, results are available for matrices of order 3.

PLANNING, CONFLICT RESOLUTION, AND OTHER APPLICATIONS

6-1 INTRODUCTION

In this chapter, we shall give a select collection of applications. Several of these applications derive from actual decision-making situations. Others are given for variety, particularly to show how the method can be adapted for vastly different purposes. All are severely abbreviated to save space and include more examples. The Sudan Study alone has 1,700 pages.

To save space, we shall not attempt to define carefully the elements in every hierarchy. However, the examples are usually sufficiently clear that the reader will obtain an adequate understanding of the nature of the problem and the hierarchical representation it received. In addition, we have included only a few matrices to illustrate an idea or to give him an opportunity to compare his judgments in some of these examples, and to help him become involved in the process.

In the analysis of most of these applications, different contingencies can occur, each with some risk. Therefore, in estimating likely outcomes it is useful to list in the second level of the hierarchy the various contingencies in order to obtain a balanced assessment of which future is most likely to occur. For many problems, the use of planning scenarios in the second level is one way of taking care of contingency planning. This we have done in the extensive application we made in designing the Sudan Transport System for 1985.

We begin the chapter with two applications, one concerned with prioritizing resources and the other with world influence. We then move on to a discussion of planning and conflict resolution illustrating the systematic use of the AHP in these areas.

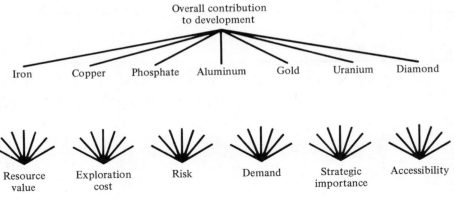

Figure 6-1

6-2 INTEGRATED FINDINGS OF RESOURCE PRIORITIES FOR A DEVELOPING NATION

The AHP has been applied to develop an overall estimate of priorities, both for the seven most important minerals found in a developing country and for six criteria associated with them. This has been done so that future as well as present potentials may be considered in shaping a mineral exploration strategy.

The hierarchy has a structure depicted in Fig. 6-1.

Our definitions of the criteria are as follows: *Resource value*—This is the potential monetary value of the particular mineral if developed in the country in proportion to what has been projected for the entire region of the continent. Within this region, areas exist for which mineral production has been documented. Calculations of the potential in the country are based upon this material. The lag in time between mine production and data summaries makes valid the possibility that present discoveries and ore extraction may be higher. *Exploration cost*—This is the estimated cost for mineral exploration by air and ground crews including drilling, laboratory analysis, and backup facilities. *Risk*—This is a measure of the potential success for finding the mineral deposit and in the quantity projected. Risk is low as the price and demand go up. *Demand*—A measure of the projected world supply and demand. Is the mineral in abundant supply and low demand or is it in low supply and high demand? *Strategic considerations*—This judgment is based upon two factors.

(1) The role which a mineral could play to advantage in terms of worldwide energy resource development or political leverage. Iron ore, for example, is considered strategic as a vital resource. Uranium, on the other hand, which has not yet been explored, should be regarded as a strategic resource to the region as a whole but not necessarily for the nation.

(2) The possibility that the country could become an alternative supplier of a material considered strategic to the United States or other developed countries.

Accessibility—An accessible mineral is one whose source is near a transportation route. An inaccessible one is in a desolate area, the cost of development of which may be uneconomical.

The question posed was: How strongly dominant is one mineral relative to another with respect to industrial/economic development based on reserve estimates? Then the six criteria were compared according to their importance with regard to each of the seven minerals. The question here was (for each mineral): How strongly more important is one criterion over another in the development of the mineral?

All priorities are given in the Tables 6-1–6-3.

Table 6-1 Mineral priorities

Iron	0.40	Aluminum	0.04
Copper	0.26	Gold	0.04
Phosphate	0.15	Diamond	0.02
Uranium	0.09		

Table 6-2 Criteria priorities

	Iron	Copper	Phosphate	Uranium	Aluminum	Gold	Diamond
Resource value	0.44	0.41	0.44	0.34	0.33	0.18	0.13
Exploration cost	0.05	0.15	0.08	0.03	0.11	0.21	0.15
Risk	0.05	0.03	0.07	0.05	0.34	0.26	0.50
Demand	0.13	0.20	0.23	0.15	0.07	0.07	0.04
Strategic importance	0.26	0.16	0.11	0.29	0.04	0.03	0.04
Accessibility	0.07	0.05	0.07	0.14	0.11	0.25	0.14

Table 6-3 Composite weights for all criteria

	Total	Iron	Copper	Phosphate	Uranium	Aluminum	Gold	Diamond
Resource value	0.40	0.18	0.11	0.07	0.03	0.01	0.007	0.002
Exploration cost	0.09	0.02	0.04	0.01	0.003	0.004	0.008	0.003
Risk	0.08	0.02	0.008	0.01	0.004	0.014	0.01	0.01
Demand	0.16	0.05	0.05	0.034	0.014	0.003	0.003	0.001
Strategic importance	0.19	0.10	0.04	0.017	0.03	0.002	0.001	0.003
Accessibility	0.08	0.03	0.013	0.01	0.013	0.004	0.01	0.003

Let us interpret these results. The existing estimates indicate that iron and copper together constitute two thirds of the projected future impact produced by minerals on the economy. The role of phosphates is to increase to a noteworthy 15 percent level. The influence of each of the remaining minerals seems to be individually negligible, but together they comprise an aggregate influence on the economy of about 20 percent.

Now let us examine the criteria. The relative resource value of the first four minerals is higher than for any other criterion. In the case of aluminum, gold, and diamonds it turns out that the risk involved is higher than the resource value, which is to be expected since there has been little attempt to look into the degree of availability of these minerals. For example, the value of diamonds at 0.13 is about one-fourth the loss from risk whose value is 0.50. In addition, the demand for these minerals as seen at present may not be great. The projected relative demand for phosphate is seen to be the greatest of all the minerals because of its value to agriculture, the most intense activity in the world.

The composite set of weights show that the overall benefit of the resources: their value, their strategic importance and accessibility by far offset the negative criteria of exploration cost and risk by a factor of 67 to 17 or approximately 4 to 1. In practical terms this says what is known qualitatively, that the nation must do all it can to identify its resource potentialities and its economic future based on projected variability in demand and mineral price and its availability elsewhere in the world.

The projected resource value essentially lies in iron, then copper, then uranium. The exploration cost is low for all minerals compared to their value, and is highest for copper then iron then phosphate. The risk loss is highest for iron and lowest for copper. The projected demand is about equal for iron and copper with phosphate as a runner-up. The strategic importance of iron is by far the greatest for the nation. Copper is a low second. Accessibility is the greatest for iron with copper, uranium, and phosphate following.

It is safe to ignore the extraction of the other minerals at this time.

6-3 A MEASURE OF WORLD INFLUENCE

It is not unusual to think and write about power without adequate definition. A look at the Oxford English Dictionary shows why. Power is such a rich concept that even for special use it would carry more meaning than may be intended. Power is closely identified with the ability to do something (Bell and Wagner, 1969). Influence is the capacity to sway others to obtain favorable results in the pursuit of objectives. Influence greatly benefits from the potential use of certain forms of power to achieve ends.

Wagner (in Bell and Wagner) indicates that the difficulty to define power is related to a lack of agreement in politics as to who has power and how much. Klaus Knorr makes a strong distinction between putative power (the capability to make effective threats) and actualized power (actually achieved influence). Both concepts catch a part of reality. Examples of both kinds are easily perceived in military power, economic power, racial power, political power, healing power, purchasing power, etc. Herbert Simon (see Bell and Wagner) sees in his definition of power an asymmetrical relation between influencer and influencee and makes the principal conclusion regarding the measurement of power that one should admit many other kinds of units besides cardinal numbers.

Robert Dahl (in Bell and Wagner) makes the interesting observation that "the main problem is not to determine the existence of power but to make comparisons." This is precisely what we do here. Of some relevance to our presentation is the following observation:

J. G. Stoessinger writes that "... the image of the world situation that top policy makers have constructed and accepted as objective in their own minds is more important than any other image, including the correct one." Our concept of influence (Saaty and Khouja, 1976) has an analogy with a mix of Knorr's definition of power. Influence derives from demonstrated past actions and from an imputed capability to make an effective contribution to solve a problem given the opportunity to do so.

Below we develop an overall index of power for seven nations as it is derived from separate indices based on five attributes with respect to which the nations are individually compared. The attributes are themselves compared with regard to their perceived impact on world influence, and the result is used to weight each of the previous five indices and then composed to obtain the overall power index.

Our measure of influence derives from the following factors relating to each nation: (1) human resources, (2) economic strength (which we call wealth), (3) technology, (4) trade, and (5) military strength. Other factors such as politics, social stability, culture, and communication were not included, although they can be added without difficulty.

By the influence of a nation through its human resources, we mean its potential capability to mobilize its population to carry out missions affecting the rest of the world whether in producing essential products such as foodstuffs, machines, medicines, or more generally ideas of importance that would contribute to solving major world problems.

By economic influence, we mean the total production of goods and services of a nation, particularly as it reflects in its standard of living, its ability to sustain growth and to support and develop new ideas and new technologies and in a capacity to provide economic aid to other nations.

Technology is the level of scientific and technical progress achieved by a nation including organizational and managerial capability, with a capacity to sustain a notable pace of technological development.

Trade is the value, pattern, and structure of exports and imports undertaken by the nation with the rest of the world, including the degree of concentration enjoyed with respect to its trade relations with other countries.

Military strength is the amount of weapons (especially nuclear weapons) and manpower, the degree of mobility and the strength of alliances which a nation has.

The seven nations (studied in 1973) were the United States (U.S.A.), the Soviet Union (U.S.S.R.), China, France, the United Kingdom (U.K.), Japan and West

Germany. Now we have a hierarchy at whose lowest level are the seven nations, dominated by a level consisting of the five objectives described above, which in turn are dominated by a single element level "world influence". The hierarchy of this table has the form shown in Fig. 6-2.

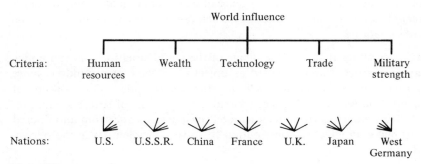

Figure 6-2

The pairwise comparison matrix for the contribution of the seven nations to world influence through their wealth has been discussed in Chap. 2. The four other matrices and the matrix of the criteria will not be given here (see Saaty and Khouja, 1976). The final eigenvectors and the composite weights are shown in Tables 6-4 and 6-5.

Table 6-4 Normalized eigenvectors corresponding to five criteria

	Human resources	Wealth	Trade	Technology	Military strength	Priorities of criteria	
U.S.A.	0.339	0.429	0.332	0.458	0.443	Human	
U.S.S.R.	0.123	0.231	0.042	0.068	0.304	resources	0.043
China	0.057	0.021	0.020	0.018	0.070	Wealth	0.393
France	0.134	0.053	0.089	0.109	0.072	Trade	0.228
U.K.	0.116	0.053	0.070	0.109	0.068	Technology	0.136
Japan	0.116	0.119	0.239	0.119	0.021	Military	
West Germany	0.155	0.095	0.209	0.119	0.021	strength	0.199
$\lambda_{max} =$	7.023	7.608	7.968	7.424	7.576		5.187
C.I. $=$	0.003	0.101	0.161	0.071	0.096		0.047
C.R. $=$	0.002	0.077	0.122	0.054	0.073		0.042

Table 6-5 Weighted result as relative measure of world influence (1973)

U.S.A.	U.S.S.R.	China	France	U.K.	Japan	West Germany
0.409	0.175	0.032	0.076	0.070	0.127	0.112

We now compare the previous results with some experimental work on power and its measurement done by Shinn. Assuming that perceptions are necessarily important determinates of human action, Shinn used a power function model (see Stevens, 1957) to derive a single index for measuring power. He attempted to capture perceptions of national power P held by students in two international politics courses by asking questions and arranging the answers and using magnitude estimation. He expressed power by a single expression in terms of the size of the nation's population, the level of its economic development in terms of its GNP and the resources it devotes to military purposes. He obtained

$$P = 0.37(\text{Pop.})^{0.41}(\text{GNP})^{0.62}(\text{Mil.})^{0.28}$$

Shinn notes that this expression serves well to account for just over 96 percent of the observed variation in the data (of averages taken over all subjects) assuming that variation between individuals is due to random measurement error.

Table 6-6 supplies information on the population (in millions), GNP, and military expenditures (in billions of dollars) which was introduced in Shinn's formula. The results obtained were normalized to obtain a relative index of power to be compared with the corresponding relative index obtained from the human resources, wealth, and military strength factors through the eigenvalue method.

Table 6-6

Country	Pop.	GNP	Mil.	Normalized index using Shinn's formula	Normalized eigenvector power index
U.S.A.	210	1,167	85.2	0.435	0.426
U.S.S.R.	242	635	65.8	0.294	0.246
China	800	120	4.5	0.081	0.039
France	50	196	8.5	0.042	0.064
U.K.	46	154	8.7	0.035	0.062
Japan	105	294	3.5	0.057	0.088
W. Germany	59	257	11.1	0.057	0.076

It is worth noting that although Shinn considers the size of a population always an asset in measuring power, we may not. For example, the very large Chinese population is a liability as it is now difficult to feed and to mobilize effectively in the pursuit of goals. This observation, along with the fact that military expenditures do not allow for power discrepancy through nuclear weapons may explain some of the deviations between the two results. It is doubtful that Japan and Germany and even England and France, would be ranked below China today on a power scale. In any case, the figures in both scales fall in the same ball park. Of course, they can both be equally bad, but the fact that they were obtained independently at different times and by different methods makes their closeness strikingly interesting.

6-4 TWO-POINT BOUNDARY VALUE PROCESSES: FORWARD AND BACKWARD PLANNING

Planning is a dynamic and purposeful activity concerned with steering a system from a likely outcome to a desired outcome. The likely or projected outcome is the resultant scenario or state of the system determined by the existing state and the actors who pursue their objectives, policies, and individual outcomes. Estimating the likely future is called the *forward planning process*. It is a descriptive process of what can happen. The desired outcome is brought about by applying policies to influence actors to remove obstacles in the way of this outcome. This is the *backward planning process*. It is a normative or prescriptive process. The effectiveness of change in objectives or new policies is tested in the forward process to see if the resultant future is brought closer to the desired future. If not, objectives and policies and even the desired future are altered for greater success in the projected outcome. There is repeated iteration of forward projection and backward policy improvization. It is in this manner that the two-point boundary process fixed at the likely and desired futures is carried out.

The same procedure can be used to produce stable outcomes in a conflict. Conflict resolution is concerned with improving each party's position from an existing to a more desired state. Iterations must consider the availability of policies to each party and bounds on these policies in a simultaneous fashion.

Although planning for a process over which one has control should use the iterations we just described, other aspects of planning may simply involve exploration of the forward or the backward processes. After a brief discussion of scenarios we shall illustrate the forward, the backward, and the joint forward–backward processes through applications we have made of them.

A scenario is a portrayal of the particular idea or subject being emphasized (e.g., a transport system) with an "adequate" account of its interaction with environmental, social, political, technological, and economic factors. It follows that a faithful scenario analysis must examine, in considerable depth, projections of all these factors in order to arrive at a convincing description of the state of the particular subject under various possible assumptions. In some of these approaches to scenario construction, one must guard against free use of uninhibited or undisciplined imagination and avoid falling into a science fiction type of prognostication.

There are two general types of scenarios. They are as follows.

(1) *Exploratory Scenario* The idea here is to explore in a set of trend-seeking scenarios, alternative futures, examining events that are logically necessary for a possible future by parameterizing the principal components of the system under study. Its starting point is the present. Limiting scenarios are constructed in conjunction with trend-seeking scenarios to constrain the possible futures through parametric variations and by careful examination of the hypotheses of evolution from the present. The Exploratory Scenario is often used as a technique to force the imagination, stimulate discussion, and attract the attention of

decision-makers to specific issues. The trend-seeking scenario does not make use of references to theory and methodology. Its practitioners, although they take its conclusions with a grain of salt, argue that so far as making errors in predicting the future, they are in good company with all the other methods.

(2) *Anticipatory Scenario* This approach is concerned with the conceptualization of feasible and desirable futures. Unlike the exploratory scenario which proceeds from the present to the future, anticipatory scenarios follow the inverse path by starting with the future and work backwards to the present to discover what alternatives and actions (trajectory corrections) are necessary to attain these futures. There are two types of Anticipatory Scenarios: The *normative scenario*, which determines at the start a set of given objectives to be realized and defines a path for their realization (one version is to idealize the objectives and find technologically feasible means with viable descriptions to reach them); and the *contrast scenario* which is characterized by a sketch of the desirable and feasible future which is on the boundary of the anticipatory scenario. Each contrast scenario emphasizes sharply a particular range of assumptions whose totality comprises the convex hull of the possible futures. Normative or contrast scenarios are synthesized into a composite scenario which retains the properties of each of the scenarios with appropriate mix or emphasis. Since the future is shaped by a variety of forces or interests, each seeking the fulfillment of its particular objectives, the synthesis of a wide ranging set of scenarios into a composite scenario must take into consideration the actors who influence the future, their objectives and the particular policies they will pursue in each scenario to fulfill their objectives. Thus, the normative process of constructing the composite scenario must reflect the priority of the actors according to importance to bring about a certain degree of fulfillment of the building blocks of each scenario.

A major technical problem in scenario construction is how to construct a composite scenario from a large set of scenarios which defines the "cone" of the future.

Some of the most important components of scenario construction are the following:

(1) Definition of the general system and of external and internal constraints and identification of subsystems.

(2) Hierarchical structuring of subsystems and identification of regulating components.

(3) Definition of the states of the system and modeling its historical development.

(4) Scenario treatment of the historical analysis highlighting the system's evolution and its impacts on characteristics of the society together with examination of the internal dynamics of the model.

(5) Definition of the objectives of the scenario with a discussion of their values.

(6) Choice of the types of scenario to be used.

(7) Development of a data base of past, present, and future information.

(8) Identification of the structural components, factors which offset equilibrium, evolutionary tendencies of the system.
(9) Description of the tensions inherent in the functional mechanisms.
(10) Analysis of the regulators of the system and of its coherence.
(11) Critique and revision of the previous analysis, refinement of the scenario by examining constraints, disequilibrium, tensions, forces, contradiction, intervention of the regulators, and statement of the contradictions which affect the survival of the system.
(12) Produce an improved scenario.

Probably, the best answer to the question of validation of the scenario approach is that it is a unique aid in forecasting the future. Its conclusions should be amenable to reasonable interpretation. The results derived from it for implementation should be categorized into urgency classes and only the most urgent projects implemented first and after a period, the planning process is then revised or iterated.

6-5 FUTURE OF HIGHER EDUCATION IN THE UNITED STATES (1985–2000): FORWARD PROCESS

This description is based on an experiment conducted by twenty-eight college level teachers, mostly from the mathematical sciences, under the leadership of the author at an NSF Chautauqua type course in Operation Research and the Systems Approach in February 1976. The problem was to construct seven weighted scenarios and a composite scenario which would describe the future of higher education in the United States during the period 1985–2000 (Saaty and Rogers, 1976).

Figure 6-3 presents the hierarchical structure of the factors, actors, and their motivating objectives which the group saw as the influences which would affect the form that higher education will take between 1985 and 2000. No strict definitions of the various terms will be given although during the development (which took approximately nine hours) comments were made on the intended meanings.

Seven scenarios are offered.

(1) (PROJ) 1985-Projection of the present status quo (slight perturbation of present).
(2) (VOTEC) Vocational-technical oriented (skill orientation).
(3) (ALL) Education for all (subsidized education).
(4) (ELITE) Elitism (for those with money or exceptional talent).
(5) (APUB) All public (government owned).
(6) (TECH) Technology based (little use of classroom—use of media, computers).
(7) (PT) Part-time teaching—no research orientation.

The characteristics which were considered and which were calibrated so as to give profiles of the various scenarios are given in Table 6-7. The calibration numbers are integers between -5 and 5 (this scale was changed later to a -8 to 8 scale to

133

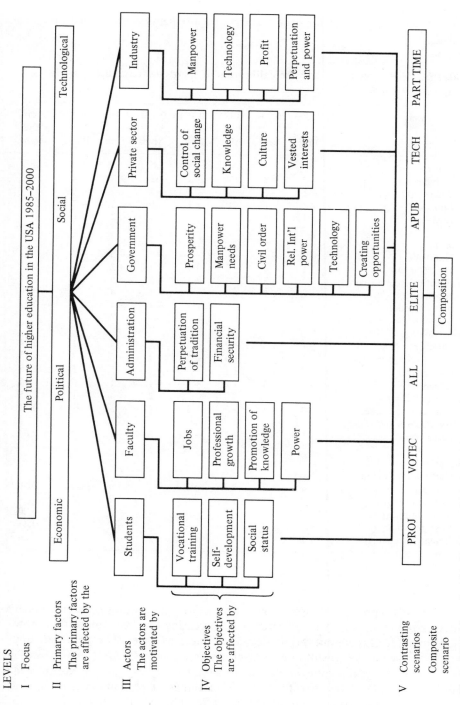

Figure 6-3 A hierarchy of influences on higher education

correspond to the 1–9 ratio scale). These measurements were arrived at by consensus.

Table 6-7 Seven scenarios and the calibration of their characteristics.
Scale: $-5 \leftrightarrow +5$

| Scenario weights | 0.096 | 0.259 | 0.191 | 0.174 | 0.122 | 0.068 | 0.081 | Com- |
| | 1 | 2 | 3 | 4 | 5 | 6 | 7 | posite |
Characteristics	Proj	Votec	All	Elite	Apub	Tech	PT	weight
Students								
1. Number	−2	+2	+4	−3	−1	+2	−2	0.42
2. Type (I.Q.)	−1	−2	−3	+3	−1	−2	−1	1.0
3. Function	+1	−1	0	+1	0	−2	+2	0.03
4. Jobs	+1	+4	−3	+4	+1	−2	+1	1.32
Faculty								
1. Number	−2	+2	+4	−3	−1	−5	−4	−0.22
2. Type (Ph.D.)	+1	0	−2	+3	+1	+2	−3	0.25
3. Function (role on campus)	−2	−3	−2	+1	−2	−5	−5	−2.12
4. Job security	−2	+1	+2	−3	−1	−4	−4	−0.79
5. Acad. freedom	0	−2	0	+2	−1	−4	−5	−0.97
Institution								
1. Number	−1	+2	+2	−3	−1	−4	−1	−0.19
2. Type (acad./non-acad.)	−1	−4	−3	+3	−1	−3	−3	−1.75
3. Governance	+2	+4	+1	−2	+2	5	5	2.06
4. Efficiency	+2	+3	−2	+4	−1	−1	0	1.09
5. Accessibility	0	+2	+5	−3	+2	+4	+1	1.55
6. Culture–entertainment	0	−2	+3	+3	+1	−3	−1	0.41
7. Available $ and other								
resources	−1	+2	+2	−2	0	−1	−3	0.64
Education								
1. Curriculum (lifelong								
learning)	1	−2	+2	+3	+1	+0	−1	0.50
2. Length of study	0	−3	+2	0	+1	+2	0	−0.14
3. Value of a degree	−1	0	−2	+4	−1	−2	−2	−0.20
4. Cost per student	+3	+3	+3	+4	+2	−1	−1	2.43
5. Research by faculty	+1	−1	−1	+3	+1	−3	−4	0.24

Zero (0) represents things as they now are (in the group's opinion). Positive integers represent the various degrees of "increasingness" or "more than now". Negative integers represent various degrees of "decreasingness" or "less than now". For example, under Institution—Governance we see a 5 for scenario 6. This means that the group thought that there would be a very large measure of administrative control (relative to the state of things at present) in a technology-based higher education system in 1985 and after. On the other hand, if scenario 2

(Education for all) were to prevail, then the value of a degree (Education–Value of a degree) would diminish considerably (-2) compared to how it is valued today. The row "Scenario weight" and the column "Composite weight" should be ignored for the moment but will be filled in the course of the discussion.

We first developed a matrix of pairwise comparisons of the factors relative influence on higher education.

The next step was to find the importance of the actors relative to their impact on the factors which affect higher education. This is done by multiplying the matrix of eigenvectors of the actors with respect to each factor in level II on the right by the eigenvector obtained for level II.

$$
\begin{array}{c}
 \\
S \\
F \\
A \\
G \\
P \\
I
\end{array}
\begin{array}{cccc}
\text{ECON} & \text{POL} & \text{SOC} & \text{TECH} \\
\begin{bmatrix}
0.04 & 0.04 & 0.10 & 0.02 \\
0.02 & 0.04 & 0.07 & 0.10 \\
0.06 & 0.03 & 0.04 & 0.03 \\
0.47 & 0.49 & 0.41 & 0.23 \\
0.12 & 0.12 & 0.12 & 0.16 \\
0.28 & 0.27 & 0.26 & 0.44
\end{bmatrix}
\end{array}
\begin{bmatrix}
0.55 \\
0.11 \\
0.24 \\
0.21
\end{bmatrix}
\begin{array}{c}
E \\
P \\
S \\
T
\end{array}
=
\begin{bmatrix}
0.05 \\
0.05 \\
0.05 \\
0.46 \\
0.14 \\
0.34
\end{bmatrix}
\begin{array}{c}
S \\
F \\
A \\
G \\
P \\
I
\end{array}
$$

Since Government and Industry account for 80 percent ($=0.46+0.34$) of the impact on the four primary factors which affect higher education, it was decided to use only these two actors to obtain the weights for the scenarios. Should one decide to use more actors, the computations follow the same procedure shown below, but the amount of work is increased.

Now we want to find the important objectives of the two actors; government and industry. To do this, we multiply the eigenvector for objectives by the respective actor weight which was just calculated.

$$
\text{For Government: } 0.46
\begin{bmatrix}
0.20 \\
0.52 \\
0.09 \\
0.11 \\
0.05 \\
0.03
\end{bmatrix}
=
\begin{bmatrix}
0.09 \\
0.24 \\
0.04 \\
0.05 \\
0.01 \\
0.01
\end{bmatrix}
\begin{array}{l}
\text{Prosperity} \\
\text{Civil order} \\
\text{Manpower} \\
\text{Rel. Int'l Power} \\
\text{Technology} \\
\text{Creating oppor.}
\end{array}
$$

$$
\text{For Industry: } 0.34
\begin{bmatrix}
0.04 \\
0.08 \\
0.33 \\
0.55
\end{bmatrix}
=
\begin{bmatrix}
0.01 \\
0.03 \\
0.11 \\
0.19
\end{bmatrix}
\begin{array}{l}
\text{Manpower} \\
\text{Technology} \\
\text{Profit} \\
\text{Perpetuation and Power}
\end{array}
$$

From this we see that the most influential objectives are prosperity and civil order for Government and profit and perpetuation and power for Industry. Using these four objectives and normalizing their weights we get the weight vector:

$$\begin{bmatrix} 0.11 \\ 0.38 \\ 0.17 \\ 0.30 \end{bmatrix} \begin{matrix} \text{Prosperity} \\ \text{Civil order} \\ \text{Profit} \\ \text{Perpetuation and power} \end{matrix}$$

This vector will be used to get our scenario weights.

The scenarios were weighted with respect to the four objectives. To obtain the scenario weights, we multiply the matrix of eigenvectors of the scenarios by the weight vector for the objectives: prosperity, civil order, profit, and perpetuation and power. This product yields the scenario composite weights.

Scenario	PROS	C.ORD	PROF	P & P			Scenario
1	0.129	0.125	0.067	0.062	0.14	0.096	1
2	0.329	0.180	0.309	0.306		0.259	2
3	0.275	0.369	0.028	0.026	0.38	0.191	3
4	0.041	0.033	0.331	0.330	=	0.174	4
5	0.149	0.177	0.048	0.085	0.17	0.122	5
6	0.032	0.050	0.129	0.075		0.068	6
7	0.045	0.065	0.089	0.115	0.30	0.081	7

Next we use these weights in Table 6-7 for "scenario weights" to compose the values of the variables yielding the right column of Table 6-7 as we said earlier that we would be doing.

We note that the second scenario has the greatest weight 0.259. This can be interpreted as the scenario most heavily favored by the group. A description of this scenario could be as follows.

"Higher education in the United States in 1985 and beyond will be vocational–technical oriented. There will be more students who will be less bright (as measured by I.Q.) and who will be a little less active in influencing the institution, but they will have no problem in getting jobs upon graduation.

"There will be more faculty of about the same intellectual level as today, but they will have considerably less to say about the governing of the university. Their job security will be a little better than it is now, but there will be less academic freedom. As for the institutions, there will be more of them, but with much less academic orientation. The administration will control things to a much greater degree and the efficiency (less student attrition) will be considerably higher. The schools will be more accessible, but their cultural and entertainment roles will decrease somewhat. The availability of dollar and other resources will be greater than at present.

"Finally, the type of curriculum will be more vocationally (skill) oriented with less of the learning experience which benefits one for a lifetime. The length of time it takes to complete a degree program will be considerably less and the value of a degree will not be any more or less than at present. The per student cost will rise quite a bit. There will be a little less research going on."

We now obtain the composite scenario: a single scenario obtained by finding composite scale measurement for each of the characteristics. The composite scale measurement for a characteristic is obtained by forming the sum of the products of scenario weight by the corresponding characteristic measurement, for example, for the number of students we have

$$(-2) \ (0.096) + (2) \ (0.259) + (4) \ (0.191) + (-3) \ (0.174) + (-1) \ (0.122) +$$
$$(2) \ (0.068) + (-2) \ (0.081) = 0.420$$

This measurement is found in Table 6-7 in the last column on the right. Similarly for the other characteristics. An interpretation of the composite scenario from the values of its characteristics might be:

"Higher Education in the United States in 1985 and beyond will witness not much, if any, increase in total enrollment. The student will exhibit slightly lower performance levels as measured by the type of standardized tests we have today. Students will play about the same role as they do today in setting university educational policy. Their chances for jobs upon graduation will be a little better than at present.

"The Faculty characteristics will be about the same as today regarding numbers, Ph.D. holders, and job security. However, faculty will play considerably less of a role in campus affairs while possessing a little more academic freedom.

"The number of institutions of higher education will not change much, if at all. They will be definitely less academically oriented with the administration exhibiting more control. There will be some increase in efficiency (less student attrition). Accessibility will be greater, but their cultural and entertainment roles will be about the same as today. There will be practically no increase in dollar resources.

"The lifelong learning qualities of the curriculum will not undergo much change, nor will the length of study, the value of a degree. Costs will continue to increase significantly. The amount of faculty research will be at a lower level."

In the course of the study it was suggested that different results might be obtained by eliminating the level of factors and weighting the actors according to their direct impact on higher education. This produced the following eigenvectors.

Actors:	S	F	A	G	P	I
Weights:	0.09	0.04	0.05	0.44	0.09	0.28

These are in close agreement with the ones obtained by keeping the level of factors. In search of a way to make the faculty have greater importance, it was suggested that another primary factor, ideology, be included in the second level. This again did not change the results significantly and it was decided to keep ideology out.

The question sometimes arises as to who will rank the actors according to their power and how can anyone be entrusted to do it. If the actors themselves participate in the evaluation, each will want a high priority. We believe that this problem can be alleviated or solved by inserting a level in the hierarchy between the actors and the overall objectives which should consist of criteria reflecting a variety of aspects of the conflict so that no actor can brazenly claim superiority on all of them without considerable evidence and justification to stymie counter arguments. If this is done well, then it may be easy for an outside party to rank the actors according to their abilities and threats to solve their conflict.

6-6 SUDAN TRANSPORT STUDY—BACKWARD PROCESS

The Sudan, with a population of 18 million is the largest country in area in Africa (about a million square miles). It is irrigated by the White and Blue Niles, which together with considerable rain south of the capital Khartoum, where the two rivers meet give rise to one of the most agriculturally fertile vast lands left in the world. It is estimated that with nearly 120 million acres for growing food and 80 million acres for cattle feed the Sudan could feed several hundred million people. Thus, many funding agencies such as the World Bank and the oil rich countries have focused on its development. But exporting agricultural goods requires a wide transport network inside the country. Of course this network is not all required at once. Different parts need to be implemented at different times.

The author was project director of a study (Saaty, 1977d) to develop a transport network projected for the late 1980's in the Sudan. This study involves estimates of the economic rate of growth, done by econometric experts, and a canvas of known natural resources. Patterns of production and consumption of food and goods under assumed different rates of growth were also determined and used to estimate the movement patterns from the regions to the Sudan's major export outlet on the Red Sea, Port Sudan. The projects of the network were then prioritized according to their contribution to the development of the regions through which they passed. They were considered separately for each region and their priorities were aggregated later. Now the regions in turn were prioritized according to their impact on the potential (feasible and desirable) future scenarios of the Sudan. These scenarios represent the outcome of development that each of the different forces shaping the future is implicitly striving to produce in the Sudan. They were: the status quo, representing the present state of affairs extended into the future; agriculture for export which brings back capital for development, and for raising the standard of living in what is now one of the poorest countries in the world; balanced regional growth in which for political and social reasons the regions are developed in a balanced way rather than pushing agricultural development in some, thus raising their style and standard of life, while the others lag behind and may cause internal instability; and, finally, Arab African Interface scenario, in which the Sudan serves as an interface between Arab resources and influence and the African countries, thereby profiting from this role. These scenarios were developed in considerable depth in the study over a period of several months. The Sudan, after the British left, fought a major civil war between North and South to keep the South from forming a new state. The result of this 16 year war was considerable destruction of the South and the death of 1/2 million people. The South does not play a major role in agricultural development but is a significant political entity of over 3 million, and also controls the White Nile, which originates in Uganda. Thus, development for purely economic reasons was considered inadequate for the overall future stability of the Sudan. Projects were assigned to connect the North with the South and with other regions in this vast country to help it stay intact. Intensive economic development in the North could offend the South about the distribution of resources. Thus the future is a composite outcome of these four scenarios. The people who participated in the prioritization were high level Sudanese officials, young professionals and several experts who did the Sudan Transport Study. The total study comprised 1,700 manuscript pages. Here we give the reader a very abbreviated version of the priority setting process. The results of the study have proved to be of great value for resource allocation. Nearly 6 billion dollars have been earmarked for the development of the Sudan and a good deal of this investment will go to transport as guided by the study. The fact that the projects were ranked by priority rather than by cost has made it possible to follow the study even in an era of severe world-wide inflation where dollar figures rapidly become meaningless.

Pairwise comparison of the four scenarios according to their feasibility and desirability by 1985 (revision of the plan could separate these two criteria) gave rise to the matrix and its corresponding eigenvector of weights presented in Table 6-8.

Table 6-8 Priorities of the scenarios

		I	II	III	IV
Status quo	I	1	1/7	1/5	1/3
Agricultural export	II	7	1	5	5
Balanced regional growth	III	5	1/5	1	5
Arab–African regional expansion	IV	3	1/5	1/5	1

$\lambda_{max} = 4.39$, C.I. $= 0.13$, C.R. $= 0.14$

The priorities of the scenarios in the order they are listed are

$$(0.05, 0.61, 0.25, 0.09)$$

The figure shows the perceived importance of each scenario relative to the other scenarios as well as the final priority ratings assigned to each. As can be seen, Scenario II dominates, with Scenario III next in importance. Since the future is likely to be not one or the other, but rather a composition of these scenarios—with emphasis indicated by the priorities—this information was used to construct a composite scenario of the Sudan of 1985.

The importance of transport in the projected development implies a large investment in capital goods for the rail system, such as rolling stock and communication equipment. An extensive portion of the main line would have been double-tracked, and a new western spur line constructed.

The road system would be well developed, extensively, and all-weather roads would connect the major cities, and the highway to Port Sudan would be in operation. Many feeder roads to the railway will have been built throughout the agricultural areas. In general, it would have been found possible to implement the transport objective of both Scenarios II and III as far as the highway system is concerned.

The Nile waterway would have been improved and would be navigated by a modern fleet, backed up by excellent maintenance and docking facilities. The airway system would accommodate Scenario II, with an operating air freight export service. Most air traffic and all international traffic would use the Khartoum airport. The secondary port at Suakin would have been opened and connected to the rail and road systems.

Priorities of Regions and Projects

The Sudan has 12 regions (whose individual economic and geographic identity more or less justifies political division into distinct entities). The regions were compared pairwise in separate matrices according to their impact on each of the scenarios. They comprise the third hierarchy level. The resulting eigenvectors are used as the columns of a matrix which, when multiplied by the eigenvector of weights or priorities of the scenarios, gave a weighted average for the impact of the regions. Now the projects, the fourth level of the hierarchy, were compared pairwise in 12 matrices according to their impact on the regions to which they physically belonged. A project may belong to several regions, and this had to be considered. The resulting matrix of eigenvectors was again weighted by the vector of regional weights to obtain a measure of the overall impact of each project on the future.

The priorities of the projects could have been done separately according to economic, social and political impacts. However, these attributes were considered jointly in the judgment debate. A number of refinements of the approach along these lines are possible for future revisions of the plan.

The results of prioritization not only showed the relative importance of the regions (see Table 6-9) for possible investment purposes, but also those of the projects as to which of the three phases of implementation they should belong: the first phase—to remove bottlenecks; the second phase—to open up the agricultural areas and ship goods to the outside world; and the third phase—to encourage balanced regional growth and transport between regions whose contribution to the Composite Scenario is not as visibly urgent as those of other regions, and, hence, will probably receive less of the overall investment.

Table 6-9 Priority weights of regions (percent)

Bahr El Ghazal	Blue Nile	Darfur	East Equatoria	Gezira	Kassala	Khartoum	Kordofan	Northern	Red Sea	Upper Nile	West Equatoria
3.14	6.55	5.37	1.70	12.41	5.25	21.40	5.96	2.94	22.54	3.37	9.39

Table 6-10 provides a sample of the recommendations for project implementation. A useful column, not included here, measures the cost-benefit of each project. It is obtained by dividing the priority of each project by its cost. The result is a ranking of the projects according to their overall feasibility and desirability.

(1974 Price Level in LS 1,000,000—1 LS = $2.50) (6 per cent growth rate)

Projects	Distance (km)	Priority	4.3 L	4.3 H	6.0 L	6.0 H	7.3 L	7.3 H	Cost A	Cost B	Cost C	Recommended class	Flow	Main reason Other	Committed (Financing in progress)	Cost Total	Cost Foreign currency	Cost Local currency
Rail																		
Port Sudan–Haiya	203	4.724	A	B	A	B	A	B	9.10	7.10	—	A	X			9.10	4.55	4.55
Haiya–Atbara	271	3.455	B	B	B	B	A	B	12.20	9.50	—	B	X			9.50	6.30	3.20
Atbara–Khartoum	313	8.443	B	B	B	B	A	B	14.10	11.00	—	B	X			11.00	7.30	3.70
El Rahad–Babanusa	363	1.005	B	B	B	B	B	B	—	12.70	—	B	X			12.70	8.50	4.20
Fleet (6 % GNP)																40.90	40.90	—
Maintenance facilities																2.00	1.00	1.00
Sub-total																85.20	68.55	16.65
Road																		
Wad Medani–Gedaref	231	2.840	A	A	A	A	A	A	23.90	—	—	A	X		X	23.90	16.70	7.20
Gedaref–Kassala	218	0.872	A	A	A	A	A	A	14.20	—	—	A	X		X	14.20	9.90	4.30
Kassala–Haiya–Port Sudan	625	2.229	A	A	A	A	A	A	50.00	—	—	A	X		X	50.00	35.00	15.00
Wad Medani–Sennar	100	0.526	A	A	A	A	A	A	14.90	—	—	A	X		X	14.90	10.40	4.50
Sennar–Kosti	110	0.345	A	A	A	A	A	A	7.20	—	—	A	X		X	7.20	5.00	2.20
Sennar–Es Suki	47	0.546	A	A	A	A	A	A	7.00	—	—	A	X			7.00	4.90	2.10
Ed Dubeibat–Kadugli	137	1.253	C	C	C	C	B	C	—	12.30	8.80	B	X		X	12.30	7.40	4.90
Kadugli–Talodi	100	0.266	—	—	—	B	—	C	—	6.60	—	—						
Nyala–Kass–Zalingei	210	0.951	B	C	B	C	B	C	—	11.30	7.40	B	X			11.30	6.80	4.50
Jebel Al Aulia–Kosti*	300	1.567	B	B	B	B	A	B	44.70	29.70	—	—	X	High cost, alternative provided				
Juba–Nimuli	190	0.329	C	C	C	C	B	C	—	8.70	5.30	C	X			5.30	1.60	3.70
Juba–Amadi–Rumbek–Wau	725	0.494	C	C	C	C	C	C	—	—	20.30	C	X	Together with alternative, high priority		20.30	6.10	14.20
Fleet																20.80	20.80	
Sub-total																187.20	124.60	62.60

* The priority rating of this project is based mostly on potential rather than present development. In view of its high cost relative to other road projects, it has been omitted. It is recommended that it be given urgent consideration in the following planning period.

Implementation will proceed by focusing on the highest ranked projects constrained by the total amount of resources available for investment.

Note that a project, such as a road, may be implemented with different grades of sophistication and the cost of each of these was estimated. It was now far easier to see what needed to be implemented and what could simply be improved or upgraded, and what gaps had to be filled by new projects.

We found that at a 7.3 percent growth rate, which we assumed first, everything seemed to be needed: many rail lines would have to be double-tracked and ballasted, roads proliferated everywhere, etc. The cost was so high that the Sudan would be committing its future for 100 years to pay for it, even if funds had been available, which they were not.

We went back to the 4.3 percent, the present growth rate, and found that most of the current facilities with the prevailing level of efficiency would be crammed to their limit. Obviously, a compromise with a rational justification for growth had to be made somewhere between these two extremes. When we examined the 6 percent GNP growth rate, found feasible by the econometric analysis, it provided excellent guidelines for those projects which were found to be needed at 4.3 percent and remained invariant with high priority at 7.3 percent. These were mostly the projects we recommended for implementation.

6-7 COMBINED FORWARD–BACKWARD PROCESS

Electric Power Utility

The following discussion focuses on planning for the future of an electric power utility. A forward–backward planning process is used to account for interactions among the various actors who have influence over the utility's future, the objectives of each actor, possible future scenarios, problems inherent in achieving desired scenarios, and decision variables or policies under the control of the electric power utility.

Forward process   The forward process provides a description of the environment in which the electric utility must operate. It is illustrated in Fig. 6-4 together with the basic (noncomposite) priorities of the factors represented in the hierarchy.

We note that the objectives of the management of the utility are a high rate of return to protect capital market access, a high base load to insure system reliability, and low excess capacity to avoid high capital carrying costs for unused equipment. The other actors' objectives are reasonably self-explanatory. The scope of this discussion precludes an in-depth description of the other objectives.

The fourth level of the forward process hierarchy contains the possible future scenarios for the electric utility. The first is business as usual, which means that the utility would pursue the status quo, short term policies implying no effort to plan for long run diversification or service reliability. The second scenario is to maintain and plan for moderate electric business growth while diversifying with retained earn-

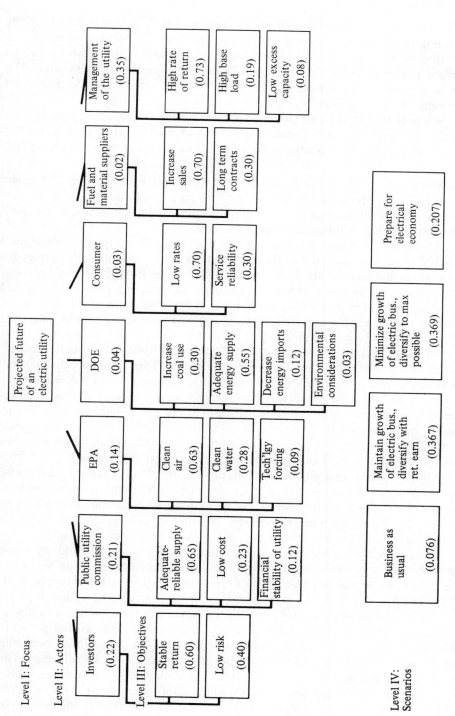

Figure 6-4 Process hierarchy

ings. The third scenario advocates minimizing electric business growth while pursuing an aggressive diversification policy. The difference between scenarios two and three is that the former maintains electric growth with moderate diversification while the latter de-emphasizes electric growth with aggressive diversification. The fourth scenario is to pursue and plan for high electric growth rates leading to an economy which relies heavily on electricity as an energy source.

We note that the second and third scenarios have almost equal priority with the first and fourth getting relatively low values. A brief interpretation is that the most probable scenario outcome will be either scenario two or three, *ceteris paribus*.

Backward process Given the description of the environment and the insight gained from the forward process, the backward process is used as a prescriptive mechanism to determine which policies the electric utility should pursue to attain a "desired" scenario outcome. A different hierarchy is formulated as shown in Fig. 6-5.

The first level is now the desired future of the electric utility. The second level contains the desired scenarios of the electric utility which coincidentally (it does not always happen this way) are the two probable outcomes from the forward process. The third level contains problems associated with achieving each of the desired scenarios. An elaboration of the problems is beyond the scope of this discussion. Most of them are self-explanatory. The fourth level contains the most influential actors in terms of their ability to affect the future of the electric utility. They were chosen on the basis of the weighting obtained in the forward process. In this case, all actors with a weight of 0.10 or less were not included. Therefore, only the management of the utility, the state PUC, the investors, and the EPA were considered.

The fifth level is the basic reason for the backward process. This level contains the decision variables or policies under control of the utility. They include: (1) pursuit of stable returns to investors, (2) assurance of supply reliability to electric customers, (3) pursuit of a high rate of return on invested capital, (4) assuring low risk investments, and (5) an aggressive energy conservation campaign.

The next step is to apply the AHP to this hierarchy in the same manner as we did in the forward process. The objective is to obtain a composite priority vector for the policies on the fifth level. These weights show which policies ought to be pursued by the utility most aggressively in order to achieve its most desired scenario outcome. The results of applying this procedure appear in Fig. 6-5.

In this case the third scenario of de-emphasis on electric growth and aggressive diversification was chosen as the most desired outcome. The composite weights of the policies to be pursued are: investor stable return, 0.16; reliable supply, 0.24; high rate of return, 0.26; low risk investment, 0.10; energy conservation, 0.24.

An interpretation of the fifth level composite vector is of interest. In order to achieve the desired scenario, the electric utility must pursue policies that provide a reliable energy or electric supply, a high rate of return on capital investment, and energy conservation. Each of these exhibits weights which are almost equal. The other two policies have low priority weights and should be given weak emphasis.

In the second forward process (Fig. 6-6) the actors whose priorities were below 0.05 in the first forward process have been removed. The relative importance of

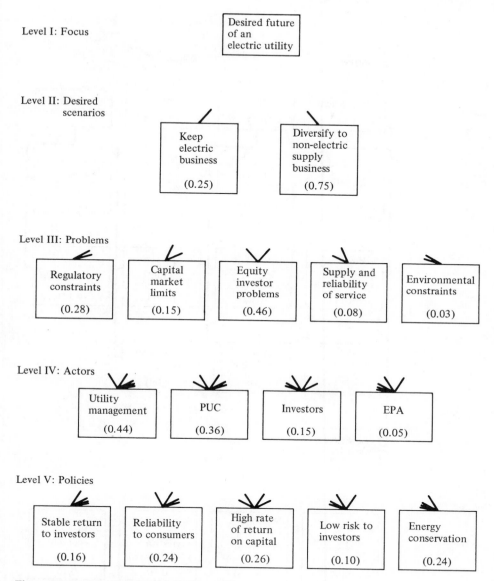

Figure 6-5 Backward process hierarchy

each actor changes also, since the situation now is that the electric utility is pursuing aggressive diversification. The following table shows that change.

	Management	PUC	EPA	Investors
First forward	0.38	0.26	0.15	0.23
Second forward	0.54	0.13	0.04	0.24

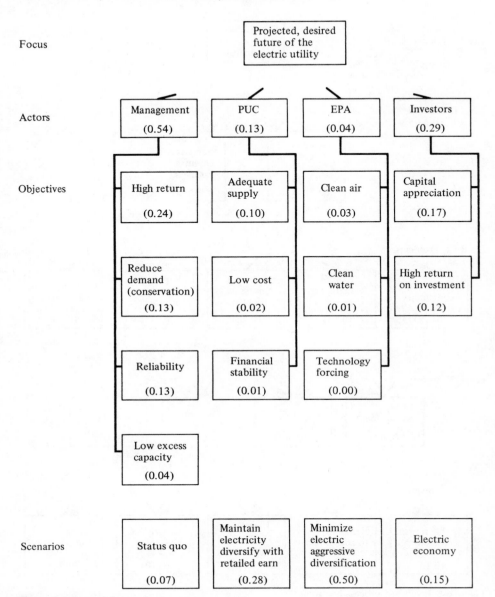

Figure 6-6 Second forward process

There is a shift in priority from the EPA and PUC to the management of the utility.

The objectives of management to better reflect the pursuit of the desired scenario are determined from the backward process. The PUC objectives show the change of the utility management in reaching the desired scenario. Investors' objectives also change for the same reasons. The priorities were then recalculated for the actors and their objectives in the second forward process shown in Fig. 6-6.

Conclusion The implementation of the strategy suggested in the backward process produces results consistent with the objectives of the management when tested in the second forward process. The shift seems to be primarily between the two favored scenarios and the development of an electric economy.

The exercise gives insight to the management as to the tradeoffs necessary to reach its desired goals. The process should be repeated to sharpen the strategy to be followed.

Corporate Planning

The purpose of this application, done for a large corporation with the participation of its planning staff, was to identify potential problem areas. The object was to decide which areas and which outside actors could be affected by corporate policies to bring about a more desired future than there would be without special directed effort.

The planning was studied in terms of:

(1) *The projected future* What will be the corporation's future if the planning policies of the company remain as they are now and other, mainly external, actors and forces continue unchanged?
(2) *The desired future* What changes in policies are needed to achieve a desired future as constrasted with the current projected future?

For the *Projected Future* hierarchy, the levels represented the following in descending order of importance.

(*a*) The actors who will affect the future of the corporation: evaluate their relative importance.
(*b*) The policies/objectives of each important actor that will affect their planning behavior: evaluate their relative importance to the corresponding actor.
(*c*) The alternative scenarios of corporate futures that are related to actor policies: evaluate the relative likelihood of each scenario.

For the *Desired Future* hierarchy the identified levels were as follows.

(*a*) The scenarios desired by the directors: evaluate their relative desirability.
(*b*) The problems and obstacles that must be overcome to achieve one or more of the scenarios: evaluate the relative importance of each problem.
(*c*) The actors who control the solution of each problem: assess the relative importance of these actors.
(*d*) The policies/objectives of each actor which affect his behavior in regard to the problems: evaluate the relative importance of each policy/objective.

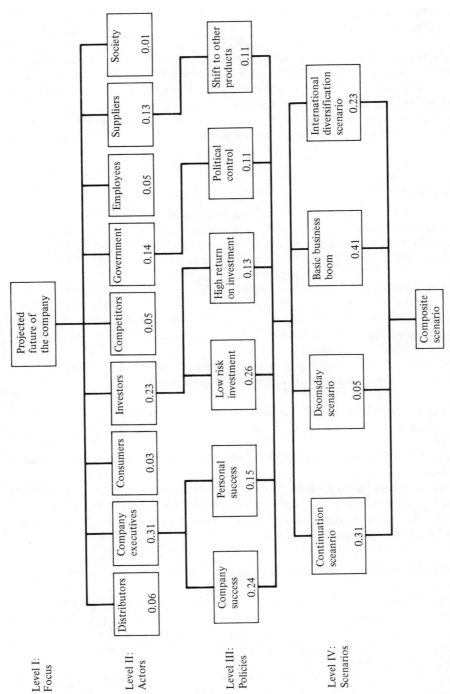

Level I:
Focus

Level II:
Actors

Level III:
Policies

Level IV:
Scenarios

Figure 6-7

(*e*) The counter-policies of the corporation to favorably influence the behavior of actors to solve the problems in order to maximize the achievement of the desired futures: evaluate the relative importance of each counter-policy.

Results The structure of the Projected Future is illustrated in Fig. 6-7. Each scenario is structured by identifying a group of relevant factors and assigning a value to each of them. The weight of each scenario is obtained based on its compatibility with the policies of the actors. The final weight of each scenario is calculated to be: Boom—0.41; Continuation—0.31; International Diversification—0.23; Doomsday—0.05.

The structure of the Desired Future is illustrated in Fig. 6-8. The major policies and their final normalized weights were found to be: Investors/Low risk—0.24; Government/Political control—0.20; Competitors/Discourage competition—0.15; Directors/Company success—0.13; Investors/High return—0.12; Competition/Increase market share—0.09; Directors/Personal success—0.07.

The projected future suggests a successful concentration by the company on the development of the business area that has made it successful in the past. Some efforts for international diversification will take place, but this will be driven more by the failure of domestic markets to develop rapidly than by the attractiveness of internationalization. The projected future indicates a distinct possibility that the domestic market will not provide an acceptable growth rate, primarily because of either supplier or government actions.

The actors most significant to the company's projected future are (in order of importance) the company's own vice-presidents, the major financial investors in the company, the government, and raw material suppliers. Product consumers were not considered to be particularly significant in the projected future, implying that purchasing habits would not change unless there were new actions by the company itself.

The policy and objectives of the key company managers were oriented first toward company success and then personal success, implying that the development of existing functional areas has a high priority as long as that leads to acceptable growth for the company as a whole. Financial investors were thought to be motivated primarily by risk minimization and secondarily by maximization of investment return. The government desired political control, development, and revenue in that order. Suppliers were assumed to seek profit return and were not particularly loyal to the customers who purchased their products; hence, risks of supply availability existed.

International expansion was seen as a much more desirable future. The major problems relevant to achieving the desired future were: (1) competition in domestic and international markets, (2) the risk involved in investing in new products and markets, and (3) the political and social problems. For the desired future, the supply of raw material and organizational development were judged to be less significant than other problems.

The most significant actors that would affect the outcome of the desired future are (in order of importance): the government, investors, competitors, and the

150

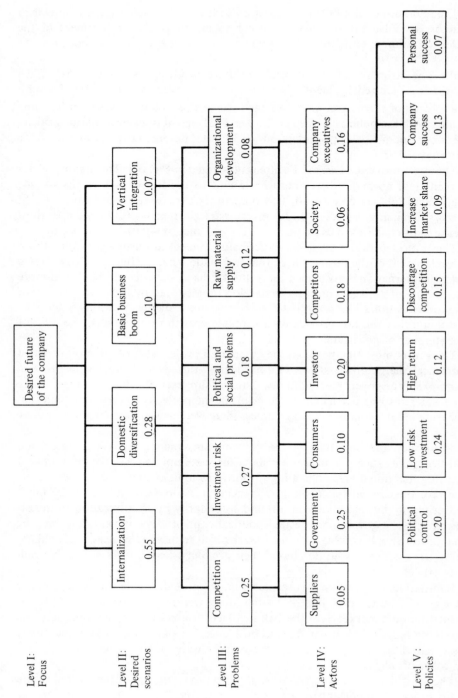

Level I :
Focus

Level II:
Desired
scenarios

Level III:
Problems

Level IV:
Actors

Level V :
Policies

Figure 6-8

company's management. It is significant that the government appeared to be the key actor in creating desired change. Also, the company's own management, which was the most influential actor in the forward process, is much less important here.

Counter policies by company management were discussed briefly because of time limitations. However, the findings were that there is urgent need for (1) further knowledge, analysis, and understanding of the behavior of key external stakeholders, (2) a method for evaluating risk and returns on alternative new growth strategies, and (3) developing methods for exerting greater influence over external factors that have a major impact on those future courses which the company might desire to pursue.

6-8 CONFLICT ANALYSIS

Health Care Management

The prevailing mode of operations in health care systems has led to skyrocketing costs. The health care system has important differences from industrial systems. In industry, management obtains organizational support through concrete goals, formal authority, and task independence and performance measures. In health care systems, goals tend to be abstract, authority diffuse, interdependence low, and measures few and controversial. In short, the organizational problems in health care management result in a high degree of conflict between the various hospital tasks. Goals are often incompatible and the tasks are quite differentiated. Thus, there is a need for integrating mechanisms to reduce the conflict. One new proposal receiving much attention is the team concept that attempts to integrate hospital functions. Instead of individuals performing separate appointed tasks, patient care will be the result of interdependent tasks.

Our hierarchy recognizes the high degree of conflict of interests between physicians, hospital administration, board of trustees, support personnel, and prospective patients. Two alternatives to the current health care management system are considered: the team concept and the status quo with administrative controls. These two scenarios will be evaluated to determine the relative preference of the actors and, thus their influence to achieve cost containment. Hence, by reducing internal conflict at a private health care institution, the hierarchical analysis should indicate (1) the relative power of the actors in the hospital to influence cost containment; (2) the effect of the two scenarios upon the objectives of the actors; (3) the nature and degree of conflicts between each group's objectives; (4) which alternative is most likely to occur, and (5) the general recommendation to make to hospitals about the kind of decisions needed.

To save space, we shall not describe the details of the elements in the hierarchy. They and their priorities appear in Fig. 6-9. However, it may be useful to elaborate on the bottom or fourth level. It represents two organizational policies. The status quo policy would involve no fundamental change to the current organizational arrangements. The cost containment mechanisms are purely administrative in

152

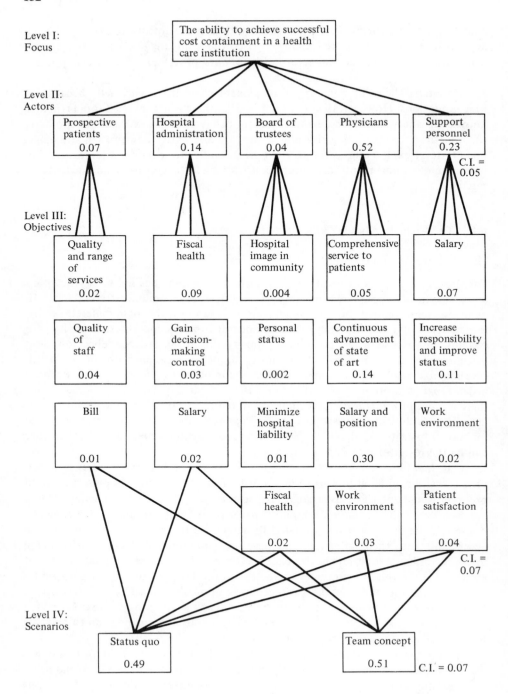

Level I:
Focus

The ability to achieve successful cost containment in a health care institution

Level II:
Actors

Prospective patients
0.07

Hospital administration
0.14

Board of trustees
0.04

Physicians
0.52

Support personnel
0.23

C.I. = 0.05

Level III:
Objectives

Quality and range of services
0.02

Fiscal health
0.09

Hospital image in community
0.004

Comprehensive service to patients
0.05

Salary
0.07

Quality of staff
0.04

Gain decision-making control
0.03

Personal status
0.002

Continuous advancement of state of art
0.14

Increase responsibility and improve status
0.11

Bill
0.01

Salary
0.02

Minimize hospital liability
0.01

Salary and position
0.30

Work environment
0.02

Fiscal health
0.02

Work environment
0.03

Patient satisfaction
0.04

C.I. = 0.07

Level IV:
Scenarios

Status quo
0.49

Team concept
0.51

C.I. = 0.07

Figure 6-9 The hierarchy and the composite eigenvectors

nature, with possible changes only in restrictions on rate increases and budgets. The second policy represents a changed organizational concept in the hospital. The team concept is a new management policy including both economic and clinical dimensions of patient care management. In the process, physicians and support personnel, will be linked more closely to the hospital administration in the management task. The emphasis will be on justifying diagnostic and treatment methodologies in terms of their cost effectiveness. Being responsible for a more well-defined population as well as a more well-defined (and circumscribed) amount of money, hospital administrators will need to know more about the economic implication of operating decisions. Those decisions will not be clinical decisions nor administrative decisions, but joint decisions of a health care *team*.

The results of the initial forward process show that the team concept does not exhibit a definite advantage over the status quo as a favored approach to contain costs in a health care institution. This is a consequence of the conflicting objectives between two participating groups of actors—the physicians and the remaining four actors, resulting in a standoff between these two outcomes. The physicians favor remaining in de facto control of the hospital (and their objectives) via the status quo, while the other groups support change via the team concept, to gain more control in the hospital and, consequently, better cost containment.

However, it is important to note that the question of salary objectives (and also position, in the case of the physicians), some 37 percent of the total overall weighting, was equally divided, indicating separation of individual salaries with respect to the improvement of cost containment. Thus, health care institution employee salaries will not change with the choice of organizational structure and is hence not a decisive factor.

Modifications were made in the structure of the hierarchy to focus on the conflicting parties and try to produce a more conclusive result, i.e., obtain greater emphasis on one of the two outcomes although the team concept outcome would be more desirable for all.

A backward process was applied, initially eliminating both the insignificantly weighted objectives (below an individual weighting of 0.01), and the objectives which were indifferent to an organizational change—such as salaries. Then a second forward process was carried out to test the effect of these changes.

The conclusions from the first forward process have resulted in focussing on seven basic objectives, common, in part, to all the actors. They represent a reduced grouping of the most germane and sensitive issues relative to the two opposing groups. Three of these objectives, the main concern of the physicians, are now also considered, in part, by all the actors. Because of the central position of the physician in the current structure of the hospital, all the actors consider as important the satisfaction of doctors and the patients with the doctor's treatment. The remaining four objectives relate to the block of non-physicians. The justification for grouping them together in a common block is due to the similarity of the actors in their basic concerns in a hospital. For each of them, the team concept is a favored approach in attaining their highest weighted objectives. Thus, they have concentrated their original interests on these four areas to achieve their goals. The physicians, however, do not consider the team approach at all relevant to their role in the institution and, consequently, are not interested in any of the objectives presented by the non-physician block.

The second forward process hierarchy (Fig. 6-10) includes the following seven objectives: (1) physicians: service satisfaction; (2) physicians: state of the art; (3) physicians: working environment; (4) other actors: fiscal health; (5) other actors: decision power; (6) other actors: service satisfaction; and (7) other actors: working environment. These were prioritized for each of the actors and N.C. (i.e., not considered) was entered for the eigenvector coefficient wherever the corresponding objective does not apply to the actor. The overwhelming weight of the physicians and their relative resistance to change has resulted in a switch to a more favored view of the status quo in the second forward process. The physicians are not willing to change their objectives, and hence the team concept is not likely to emerge (creating better opportunity for cost containment). The existing trends will continue unless the impasse is broken by a change in the basic structure of the institution which affects the relative weighting of the physicians, such as in the health management organizations.

Table 6-11

Level 1	Level 2	wt	Level 3	comp. wt	Level 4	comp. wt.
Power of actors	Actors		Actor objectives Sphere of influence	0.32* (0.36)	Political structures across actors	
	Britain	0.45	Good relations	0.09* (0.11)		
			Power sharing	0.04	United Ireland	0.15
					Integrated parlia-	
			No link with Dublin	0.20* (0.25)	ment	0.15
			Separate state	0.02		
	Allegiants	0.31	No Irish Nationalists in Government	0.06* (0.07)	Assembly without a council from	
			British connection	0.02	Dublin (minority	
			Economic well-being	0.02	participation)	0.13
			Power sharing	0.05* (0.07)	Assembly with	
	Moderates	0.07	Irish dimension	0.01	a council from	
			Economic well-being	0.01	Dublin (minority	
					participation)	0.16
			Union Ulster-Ireland	0.02		
	I.R.A.	0.14	Drive out British	0.12* (0.15)	Dominion without a link to Dublin	0.25
			Stability	0.01		
			Union Ulster-Ireland	0.002	Dominion with a	
	Dublin	0.03	Re-election	0.01	link to Dublin	0.16
			British markets	0.01		

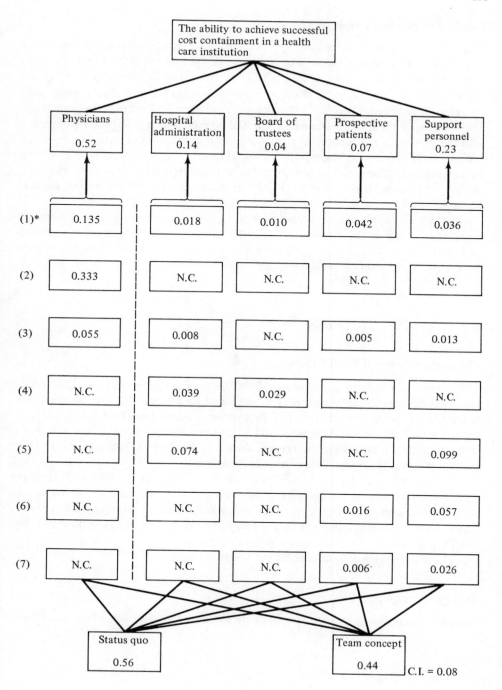

Figure 6-10 The backward/forward process—The revised hierarchy

Conflict in Northern Ireland

The AHP was applied to the conflict in Northern Ireland to yield a stable solution in the form of Dominion status. The hierarchy of the forward process has the levels and the corresponding weights shown in Table 6-11. The objectives were weighted with respect to their actors and the composite weights were obtained. Only high priority objectives marked by asterisks were retained for subsequent weighting. Dublin as an actor was eliminated since it had no contending high priority objective and the powers of the remaining parties were renormalized and used to weight the six surviving objectives. The composite weights were then renormalized as shown in parentheses. The political structures were compared with respect to the high priority objectives. It is seen that Dominion status has the widest overall acceptability.

In order to apply the backward process, it is first necessary to find the desired outcome for each of the parties to the conflict, and to evaluate their reactions to all of the outcomes. The remainder of the analysis is tedious and the references should be consulted. (Alexander and Saaty, 1977.)

6-9 ENERGY EXAMPLES

Optimum Choice of Coal Plants

The problem of optimum choice of a Coal Using Energy System (CUESS) technology for a given community may be regarded as a hierarchy with three major criteria. One is concerned with energy resource utilization (ERU) efficiency, a second with environmental impacts, and a third one with economics. Each of these criteria involves a number of subcriteria shown in the charts (Figs. 6-11–6-13). (No breakdown is given under the economics criterion.)

For example, under ERU efficiency we have four levels. The first level is concerned with season, topography, geography, etc. The second level is concerned with various energy requirements of a community such as heating and cooling, lighting, etc. The third level is concerned with the method of energy supply and the fourth with the type of plant which generates this energy.

The chart for environmental effects is self-explanatory.

Energy Storage Systems

Four advanced energy storage systems were evaluated on the basis of six feasibility

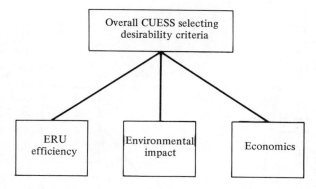

Figure 6-11

criteria. The storage systems are: S_1—compressed air storage; S_2—underground pumped hydro storage; S_3—electric batteries; S_4—hydrogen energy storage.

The six criteria are: I—environmental feasibility; II—economic feasibility; III—societal feasibility; IV—siting flexibility; V—construction lead time; VI—compatibility with power system.

The comparison matrix of the six criteria and its eigenvector are:

	I	II	III	IV	V	VI	Eigenvector
I	1	1/5	2	1/3	1/2	2	0.09
II	5	1	7	2	3	7	0.42
III	1/2	1/7	1	1/5	1/2	1	0.05
IV	3	1/2	5	1	2	5	0.25
V	2	1/3	2	1/2	1	3	0.14
VI	1/2	1/7	1	1/5	1/3	1	0.05

$$\lambda_{max} = 6.05, \quad \text{C.I.} = 0.01, \quad \text{C.R.} = 0.01$$

We have the following ranking for the storage systems: $S_1 = 0.26$; $S_2 = 0.14$; $S_3 = 0.36$; $S_4 = 0.24$. This suggests that S_3, the Electric Battery Storage System is the best of the four systems.

158

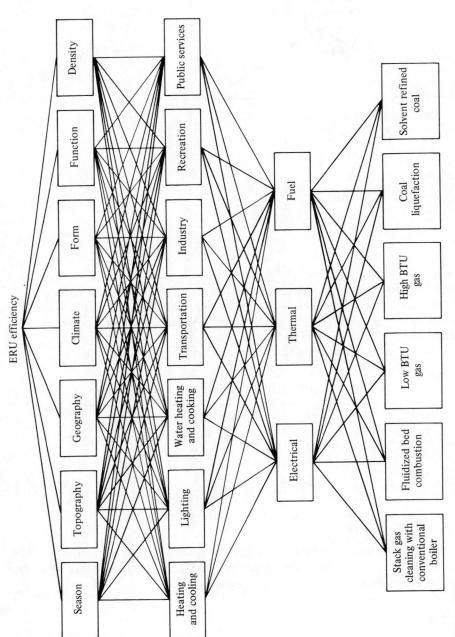

Figure 6-12

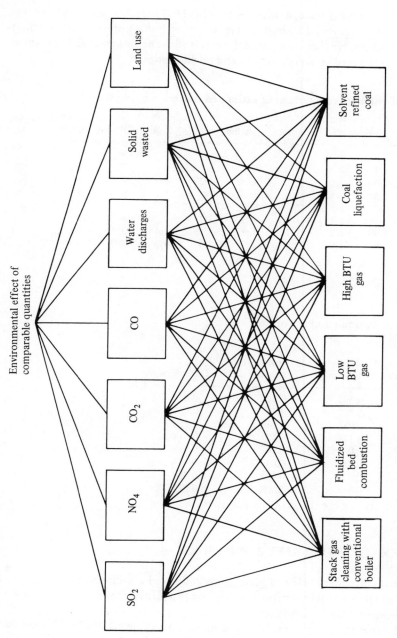

Figure 6-1. Hierarchy interrelationships for environmental impacts

Estimating the Annual KWH Consumption of Home Appliances

In this example, using 1–9 scale, a student attempted to estimate the relative kilowatt hours of electricity consumed by each of the following home appliances by comparing it with the others. He then compared the result with their normalized real values taken out of a standard reference on electric consumption.

The matrix of pairwise comparison of estimated annual consumption

	Range	Refrigerator	T.V. color	Dishwasher	T.V. b&w	Iron	Radio	Hairdryer
Range	1	3	6	3	7	7	9	9
Refrigerator	1/3	1	4	5	5	5	7	9
T.V. color	1/6	1/4	1	1	1/2	4	4	8
Dishwasher	1/3	1/5	1	1	2	3	9	9
T.V. b&w	1/7	1/5	2	1/2	1	3	3	7
Iron	1/7	1/5	1/4	1/3	1/3	1	4	9
Radio	1/9	1/7	1/4	1/9	1/3	1/4	1	7
Hairdryer	1/9	1/9	1/8	1/9	1/7	1/9	1/7	1

$$\lambda_{max} = 9.256, \quad \text{C.I.} = 0.18, \quad \text{C.R.} = 0.13$$

The results are summarized as follows.

Home appliances	Weights using 1–9 scale	Normalized actual weights	Difference
Range	0.362	0.348	0.014
Refrigerator	0.252	0.215	0.037
T.V. color	0.088	0.148	−0.060
Dishwasher	0.118	0.107	0.011
T.V. b&w	0.083	0.101	−0.018
Iron	0.053	0.042	0.011
Radio	0.030	0.025	0.005
Hairdryer	0.014	0.003	0.011

$$\text{RMS} = 0.027, \quad \text{MAD} = 0.0045$$

6-10 BEVERAGE CONTAINER PROBLEM

Seven types of containers made of glass, bimetallic, and aluminum cans to be used by the beverage industry were evaluated based on four criteria: energy-consumption, cost, environmental waste, and customer convenience.

The container types were: (1) refillable glass, no recycle (GRNR); (2) refillable glass, recycle (GRR); (3) throwaway glass, no recycle (GTNR); (4) throwaway glass, recycle (GTR); (5) bimetallic can, no recycle (BMNR); (6) aluminum can, no recycle (ALNR); (7) aluminum can, recycle (ALR).

The judgmental matrix of the pairwise comparison of the four objective factors was:

	Energy	Cost	Environmental waste	Customer convenience
Energy	1	5	3	9
Cost	1/5	1	1/4	8
Environmental waste	1/3	4	1	9
Customer convenience	1/9	1/8	1/9	1

$$\lambda_{max} = 4.38, \quad \text{C.I.} = 0.13, \quad \text{C.R.} = 0.14$$

The containers were then compared with respect to each criterion. The composite weight vector is given by

GRNR	GRR	GTNR	GTR	BMNR	ALNR	ALR
0.318 31	0.318 31	0.095 29	0.103 03	0.106 83	0.027 37	0.030 86

It is interesting to note that the above results were consistent when, instead of the judgmental data of pairwise comparison, the actual data based on published literature pertaining to energy, cost, and environmental waste were used. The matrices for the fourth criterion—customer convenience and the weighting matrix of the objective criterion—were taken as in the above case.

This yielded the following priorities:

GRNR	GRR	GTNR	GRT	BMNR	ALNR	ALR
0.32	0.302 29	0.093 35	0.093 18	0.083 94	0.052 24	0.055 0

by way of validation, which is close to the previous vector.

It needs to be pointed out that the quantitative factors had minimum and maximum values attached to them which served as indicators for the range of values of the 1–9 scale used together with an idea of the strength of utility. In any case, glass containers are favored in the analysis corresponding to their increased use in practice.

6-11 APPLICATION TO THE CHOICE OF A DEMOCRATIC NOMINEE

An individual faced with the problem of judging a political candidate's qualifications is often internally divided between assessing a number of attributes. One deeply affected by the Watergate scandals may place a premium on integrity and honesty. If unemployed, he is likely to weight more heavily a candidate's domestic economic policies. If he is preoccupied with the security and welfare of an oppressed foreign people (take your choice!), international relations may get greater attention in his evaluation. But what if he is sensitive in some degree to all these considerations? It is obvious that he must decide how to balance these—and others—criteria.

Our first concern is the choice of issues relevant to candidacy. Candidates' position on these issues form criteria for evaluation. The set of issues can be arbitrary, but some are undoubtedly more widely accepted as important to political outcomes than others.

To delineate a realistic set of issues, we borrowed the expertise of a Democratic Congressman sufficiently sensitive to the criteria of his constituency. Eight issues emerged as shown in Table 6-12.

Table 6-12 Political issues functioning as criteria for the choice of a democratic nominee

Charisma	Personal leadership qualities inspiring enthusiasm and support
Glamor	Charm, allure, personal attractiveness; associations with other attractive people
Experience	Past officeholding relevant to the Presidency; preparation for the Presidency
Economic policy	Coherence and clarity of a national economic policy
Ability to manage international relations	Coherence and clarity of foreign policy plus ability to deal with foreign leaders
Personal integrity	Quality of moral standards, trustworthiness
Past performance	Quality of role fulfillment—independent of what the role was—in previous public offices; public record
Honesty	Lawfulness in public life, law-abidingness

These issues were compared pairwise according to their relative dominance in contributing to the overall success to Presidential candidacy.

Integrity is most important with four almost equal runners-up: experience, past performance, economic policy, and honesty. Charisma, international relations and—especially—glamor appear comparably insignificant. The Congressman's judgments had high consistency (consistency index 0.07, which is small for that order matrix). (See Saaty and Bennett, 1977a.)

Several candidates were selected and compared with respect to these criteria to obtain their relative priority weights.

6-12 PROMOTION AND TENURE QUESTION

Each year across the country committees pour over the credentials of candidates for promotion and tenure. Here is the hierarchy which has been used in practice to provide a basis for judgment. Although the criteria used may be the same for assistant, associate, and full professorship the judgments used should differ and become more demanding for a professor for significance and quality. One then obtains the overall priorities for the criteria as evaluated by the committee to set the standards.

Now each candidate is evaluated by the same criteria and the resulting candidate's eigenvector compared with the standards committee eigenvector obtained above. Root mean square deviation and MAD can be used to decide on how significant the difference is. (See Fig. 6-14.)

6-13 OPTIMUM LAND USE

In an application to land use the following criteria were used to derive priorities for different pieces of land: wildlife, recreation, mining, economic development, timber. The land was first divided into clusters of several pieces in each and then these were disaggregated and compared.

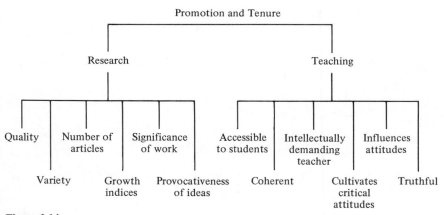

Figure 6-14

THREE

THEORY

**Reciprocal matrices—Feedback systems—
Brief comparison with other work**

We now take up the formalism of the subject, defining and characterizing hierarchies and nonlinear networks, and investigating the properties of a reciprocal matrix of pairwise comparisons and the stability of its maximum eigenvalue and the corresponding eigenvector. Chapter 7 deals with Perron–Frobenius theory and the properties of consistent and of reciprocal matrices. In Chapter 8 we present Warfield's method of structuring a system and then give our theory of priorities generalized to systems. In Chapter 9 we give a brief discussion of scaling and utility theory, including the work by Thurstone and the least squares procedure. Appendix One gives a brief elementary introduction to matrices.

POSITIVE RECIPROCAL MATRICES AND THEIR EIGENVALUES

7-1 INTRODUCTION

In a previous chapter, we defined a priority function, and the priority vector w, in a hierarchy H. As the reader knows, the manner in which this priority is found is of central importance to our method. One begins with a matrix A of real numbers, representing the pairwise comparison of the importance of the elements of one level in H with respect to one element of the next higher level, finds the largest eigenvalue $\lambda_{\max}$, and determines the solution of the equation

$$Aw = \lambda_{\max} w$$

Therefore, our interest is guided to the study of square matrices $A = (a_{ij})$, such that

$$a_{ij} > 0 \qquad i, j = 1, \ldots, n$$

and

$$a_{ji} = \frac{1}{a_{ij}} \qquad i, j = 1, \ldots, n$$

i.e., positive, reciprocal, square matrices. Of particular importance are those matrices which have not only the above properties, but are also consistent, which means that the following cardinal relationship holds:

$$a_{ik} = a_{ij} a_{jk} \qquad i, j, k = 1, \ldots, n$$

In this chapter, we shall develop those parts of matrix theory which prove the mathematical properties of our method. (See Appendix One for definitions.)

We shall begin systematically by introducing first concepts first. This requires that we introduce the idea of an irreducible matrix. We also use this opportunity to put in the section other relevant material used elsewhere in the book. We then give the fundamental Perron–Frobenius theorem for nonnegative irreducible matrices which assures the existence of a unique solution to our eigenvalue problem. Since our reciprocal matrices are positive, we concentrate on positive matrices and the theorem of Perron and its proof. Next we prove that the eigenvector solution can be obtained as the limiting sum of the rows of A^k where A is primitive. This is then followed by a brief description of how the eigenvector is computed in practice. Following that is a discussion of the consistency of a reciprocal matrix in terms of its principal eigenvalue and its deviation from n (the order of A), the insensitivity of this eigenvalue to small perturbations in A, together with a study of consistent matrices.

Next we turn our attention to characterizing reciprocal matrices and their right and left eigenvectors. We then study the important idea that small perturbations of the entries of a reciprocal matrix entail small perturbations in its principal eigenvector components. Also in that section we give a formula due to Vargas for the size of perturbation that each component of the eigenvector undergoes as a function of the perturbations of the matrix.

7-2 IRREDUCIBLE MATRICES

Our reciprocal pairwise comparison matrices have no zeros, and hence are always irreducible. We shall need the concept of irreducibility when we deal with a general system in Chap. 7. Since a certain amount of generality, i.e., dealing with irreducible instead of merely positive matrices, is needed for our later work, we have stated and proved some of the theorems of this chapter under such a more relaxed assumption.

Definition 7-1 A square matrix is *irreducible* (by permutations) if it cannot be decomposed into the form $\begin{bmatrix} A_1 & 0 \\ A_2 & A_3 \end{bmatrix}$ where A_1 and A_3 are square matrices and 0 is the zero matrix. Otherwise the matrix is said to be *reducible*.

The following matrix is reducible

$$A = \begin{bmatrix} -2 & 0 & 1 \\ 1 & 3 & 4 \\ 3 & 0 & 2 \end{bmatrix}$$

In the graph corresponding to this matrix, there is an arc from the first to the first and third vertices and similarly from the third to the first and third vertices, but one cannot go from there to the second vertex. From the second vertex one can go to all three vertices.

Thus the first and third vertices form an irreducible component and the second is connected to them. It is obvious that by interchanging the second and third columns and second and third rows, the above matrix can be put in the form

$$A = \begin{bmatrix} -2 & 1 & 0 \\ 3 & 2 & 0 \\ 1 & 4 & 3 \end{bmatrix} = \begin{bmatrix} A_1 & 0 \\ A_2 & A_3 \end{bmatrix}$$

where A_1 and A_3 are square matrices and where A_1 is irreducible.

The following theorem gives the equivalence of the matrix property of irreducibility and the strong connectedness of the directed graph of the matrix.

Theorem 7-1 An $n \times n$ complex matrix A is irreducible if and only if its directed graph $D(A)$ is strongly connected.

The proof of this theorem is rather obvious. Any power of a reducible matrix A is also reducible and hence has a block of zeros in the upper right corner. Therefore there is no path between the vertices corresponding to A_1 and those corresponding to A_2 and A_3. Conversely, if the graph is not strongly connected, then there is a block of vertices which cannot be reached, and by appropriate permutations the corresponding matrix can be reduced to the above form.

Theorem 7-2 A square matrix A is either irreducible or can be reduced by a permutation of indices to a block diagonal matrix of irreducible matrices, and other block matrices, having the normal form

$$
\begin{bmatrix}
A_1 & 0 & \cdots & 0 & 0 & \cdots & 0 \\
0 & A_2 & \cdots & 0 & 0 & \cdots & 0 \\
\vdots & \vdots & & \vdots & \vdots & & \vdots \\
0 & 0 & \cdots & A_k & 0 & \cdots & 0 \\
A_{k+1,1} & A_{k+2,2} & \cdots & A_{k+1,k} & A_{k+1} & \cdots & 0 \\
\vdots & \vdots & \cdots & \vdots & \vdots & \cdots & \vdots \\
A_{m1} & A_{m2} & \cdots & A_{mk} & A_{m,k+1} & \cdots & A_m
\end{bmatrix}
$$

At least one of the matrices with double subscript in each row in which they appear, is nonzero. (See Gale, Gantmacher.)

The proof of the theorem proceeds by assuming that if the matrix is reducible and is represented in the form given by the definition of a reducible matrix, then if either of its diagonal blocks is reducible it can again be represented in that form. In turn, if either of its diagonal blocks is reducible, it again is represented according to the standard form of a reducible matrix. After appropriate permutation of indices the result is a matrix all of whose elements above the diagonal blocks are zero; all the diagonal blocks are irreducible. In addition by a suitable permutation of indices all rows whose diagonal blocks are the only nonzero matrices may be arranged to fall as indicated above.

Note that each of the "isolated" blocks $A_1, \ldots, A_k$ is reachable, in the graph-theoretic sense, from nodes corresponding to the double-indexed rows, but not conversely. Note also that all the double-indexed matrices in each column may be simply written as a row of blocks $R_1, R_2, \ldots, R_k, Q$ where Q is, of course, no longer irreducible. The above form is unique to within permutations of the block indices.

We could just as well have ended with a transpose form in which the blocks $R_1, R_2, \ldots, R_k, Q$ form the last column of our matrix. Actually, it is this form that we shall be using later, as we look at our "stochastic" priority matrices.

The process of constructing the normal form of a priority matrix is straightforward. One starts with any element and fills in its column the nonzero priority impacts (as component of an eigenvector) of all those elements which have an impact on it. Each of these is in turn entered in the adjacent columns, entering the nonzero priority impacts of all other elements on them. The process is continued until there are no new elements which impact on this set. One must make sure of this, element by element. This yields a block for an irreducible set. The process is repeated by starting with another element for the next block, etc.

7-3 EXISTENCE AND UNIQUENESS OF PRINCIPAL EIGENVECTORS

We said earlier that the general existence and uniqueness theorem for the solution of a matrix eigenvalue problem for a nonnegative irreducible matrix (more general than a positive reciprocal matrix) will be given first. This is actually the theorem proved by Frobenius, who generalized Perron's results for a positive matrix. This is then followed by a discussion and proof of Perron's theorem. The proof of Frobenius' theorem may be found in Gantmacher (1960).

Theorem 7-3 (Perron–Frobenius) Let $A \geqslant 0$ be irreducible. Then

(1) A has a real positive simple (i.e., not multiple) eigenvalue λ_{max} which is not exceeded in modulus by any other eigenvalue of A. (Some may be complex.)
(2) The eigenvector of A corresponding to the eigenvalue λ_{max}, has positive components, and is essentially (to within multiplication by a constant) unique.
(3) The number λ_{max} (sometimes called the Perron root of A) is given by

$$\lambda_{max} = \max_{x \geqslant 0} \min_{1 \leqslant i \leqslant n} \frac{(Ax)_i}{x_i} = \min_{x \geqslant 0} \max_{1 \leqslant i \leqslant n} \frac{(Ax)_i}{x_i}; \quad x \geqslant 0 \text{ arbitrary}$$

COROLLARY Let $A \geqslant 0$ be irreducible, and let $x \geqslant 0$ arbitrary. Then the Perron root of A satisfies

$$\min_{1 \leqslant i \leqslant n} \frac{(Ax)_i}{x_i} \leqslant \lambda_{max} \leqslant \max_{1 \leqslant i \leqslant n} \frac{(Ax)_i}{x_i}$$

Theorem 7-4 (Perron) The statement of this theorem is the same as that above, except that $A > 0$ (consequently irreducible), and the modulus of λ_{max} actually dominates the moduli of all other eigenvalues.

Let us proceed to prove several useful facts about positive n by n matrices (see Cogan, et al., 1959) which includes a sketch of the proof of Perron's theorem. The order of these facts is as follows: Let A be a positive n by n matrix, and λ_{max} its largest eigenvalue.

(1) λ_{max} is bounded from above by the maximum row sum, and from below by the minimum row sum.

Thus if A is a stochastic matrix, i.e., if its row sums are unity, then $\lambda_{max} = 1$.

(2) For a stochastic matrix A

$$\lim_{k \to \infty} A^k = ev$$

where v is a positive row vector, $v = (v_1, v_2, \ldots, v_n)$, $\sum_{i=1}^{n} v_i = 1$, and $e = (1, 1, \ldots, 1)^T$.

(3) For a positive matrix A there is a positive constant λ, a nonzero row vector v, and a nonzero column vector w such that

$$\lim_{k \to \infty} \frac{A^k}{\lambda^k} = wv$$

(4) λ is the largest eigenvalue of A. It is called the *principal eigenvalue*, and w and v are *principal eigenvectors*, unique to within a multiplicative constant.

(5) w is orthogonal to all nonprincipal column eigenvectors, and v is orthogonal to all nonprincipal row eigenvectors.

(6) If λ_1 is the largest eigenvalue of A, if $\lambda_i \neq \lambda_j$; $i \neq j$, $i, j = 1, \ldots, n$, and if w_i is the right eigenvector corresponding to λ_i, then

$$\lim_{k \to \infty} \frac{A^k e}{e^T A^k e} = cw_1$$

When stated in this form, this important theorem is very easy to prove. As for its generalization

(7) We generalize the proof to the case where $A \geqslant 0$, $A^p > 0$, for some integer $p \geqslant 1$, without the remaining assumptions.

Theorem 7-5

$$(1) \begin{cases} \min_{j} \sum_{i=1}^{n} a_{ij} \leqslant \lambda_{max} \leqslant \max_{j} \sum_{i=1}^{n} a_{ij} \\ \\ \min_{i} \sum_{j=1}^{n} a_{ij} \leqslant \lambda_{max} \leqslant \max_{i} \sum_{j=1}^{n} a_{ij} \end{cases}$$

The inequality holds when the sums are not all the same

(2) $\lambda_{max} = \lim_{k \to \infty} [\text{trace } (A^k)]^{1/k}$

(3) $\lambda_{max} = \max_{u>0} \min_{i} \dfrac{\sum_{j=1}^{n} a_{ij} u_j}{u_i} = \min_{u>0} \max_{i} \dfrac{\sum_{j=1}^{n} a_{ij} u_j}{u_i}$

(4) $\lambda_{max} = \max_{u>0} \min_{j} \dfrac{\sum_{i=1}^{n} a_{ij} u_i}{u_j} = \min_{u>0} \max_{j} \dfrac{\sum_{i=1}^{n} a_{ij} u_i}{u_j}$

PROOF The row sums of A are given by the components of Ae. Let the largest row sum be M and the smallest m. Then $me \leqslant Ae \leqslant Me$ and equality holds only if $m = M$.

From

$$vA = \lambda_{\max}v$$

we have

$$vAe = \lambda_{\max}ve$$
$$vme \leqslant \lambda_{\max}ve \leqslant vMe$$

If we divide by the positive number ve we have $m \leqslant \lambda_{\max} \leqslant M$ and either equality holds if $m = M$. Similarly for column sums. We have the proof of (2) from

$$\lim_{k \to \infty} \left[\operatorname{trace} \frac{1}{\lambda^k} A^k \right]^{1/k} = 1 = \frac{1}{\lambda} \lim_{k \to \infty} [\operatorname{trace} A^k]^{1/k}$$

or from $\lambda_1^n + \cdots + \lambda_n^k = \operatorname{trace} A^k$, let $\lambda_1 = \lambda_{\max}$ then

$$\lambda_1 \left[1 + \left(\frac{\lambda_2}{\lambda_1} \right)^k + \cdots + \left(\frac{\lambda_n}{\lambda_1} \right)^k \right]^{1/k} = [\operatorname{trace} A^k]^{1/k}$$

as $k \to \infty$, $\lambda_1 \to [\operatorname{trace} A^k]$. The remainder of the proof will not be given here.

Theorem 7-6 If A is a positive n by n matrix, each of whose rows sums to unity, then there is a positive row vector v, with $\sum_{i=1}^{n} v_i = 1$, such that $\lim_{m \to \infty} A^m = ev$ where $e = (1, 1, \ldots, 1)^T$.

PROOF Let y_0 be any column n-vector. Define $y_m = A^m y_0$ and let a_m and b_m be the maximum and minimum components of y_m, respectively. Let α be the minimum entry in A. Since $y_{m+1} = Ay_m$ a component of y_{m+1} is obtained by multiplying a row of A with y_m, and hence we have the following bounds on an arbitrary component c of y_{m+1}

$$(1-\alpha)b_m + \alpha a_m \leqslant c \leqslant \alpha b_m + (1-\alpha)a_m$$

This also holds for the largest and smallest components of y_{m+1} yielding

$$a_{m+1} \leqslant \alpha b_m + (1-\alpha)a_m$$

(thus a_m is monotone increasing) and

$$(1-\alpha)b_m + \alpha a_m \leqslant b_{m+1}$$

(thus b_m is monotone decreasing) or

$$-b_{m+1} \leqslant -(1-\alpha)b_m - \alpha a_m$$

and

$$a_{m+1} - b_{m+1} \leqslant (1-2\alpha)(a_m - b_m)$$

from which by induction we have

$$a_m - b_m \leqslant (1-2\alpha)^m (a_0 - b_0)$$

which tends to zero. Thus a_m and b_m tend to a common limit, and hence all the components approach this limit, i.e., $\lim_{m \to \infty} y_m = Ce$ with $b_0 \leqslant C \leqslant a_0$. (The two equalities must hold simultaneously.) Let $y_0 = (y_0^1, y_0^2, \ldots, y_0^n)$ with $y_0^i = 1$, $y_0^j = 0, j \neq i$. Then y_m is the ith column of A^m, and as we have already established $y_m \to (c_i, \ldots, c_i)^T \equiv v^T$ since $b_0 = 0$, $c_i > b_0 = 0$. Thus $\lim_{m \to \infty} A^m = ev$.

Note that since all rows of A^m sum to unity, it follows that $\sum_{i=1}^{n} v_i = 1$.

Theorem 7-7 If A is a positive $n \times n$ matrix then

$$\lim_{k \to \infty} \frac{A^k}{\lambda^k} = wv$$

where λ is a positive constant, v a nonzero row vector, and w a nonzero column vector.

SKETCH OF PROOF Let $S = \{x | x = (x_1, \ldots, x_n), x_i \geqslant 0, i = 1, \ldots, n, \sum_{i=1}^{n} x_i = 1;$ i.e. $fx = 1\}$ and let $Ax = y$ with $x, y \in S$, A continuous, i.e. $A(x+y) = Ax$ as $y \to 0$. Then Brouwer's fixed point theorem asserts that there is an $x_0 \in S$ such that $Ax_0 = x_0$. Since a matrix defines a linear transformation, i.e., $A(x+y) = Ax + Ay$, $y \to 0$ implies $Ay \to 0$ and A is continuous.

Consider the transformation

$$Tx = \left[\frac{1}{fAx}\right] Ax$$

This transformation is positive. Since $fx = 1$, x has a nonzero component and hence $Ax > 0$ and $fAx > 0$. Now

$$fTx = \left[\frac{1}{fAx}\right] fAx = 1$$

and T transforms S into S. Since A is continuous by Brouwer's fixed point theorem (a continuous mapping of the closed unit n-sphere into itself has a fixed point), there is a fixed point w such that

$$\left[\frac{1}{f(Aw)}\right] Aw = w$$

Since the left side is positive, w is positive and $f(Aw) > 0$. Thus $Aw = \lambda w$, $\lambda > 0$, $w > 0$. Finally, let D be a diagonal matrix with $d_{ii} = w_i$ and $d_{ij} = 0$, $i \neq j$. Since $w > 0$, D has an inverse D^{-1}, again diagonal, with diagonal entries $1/w_i$. Thus $w = De$ and

$$\left[D^{-1}\left(\frac{1}{\lambda}\right)AD\right]e = \left[D^{-1}\left(\frac{1}{\lambda}\right)A\right]w = D^{-1}w = e$$

It follows that the row sums of $[D^{-1}(1/\lambda)AD]$ are all equal to unity. From the theory of stochastic matrices, there is a row vector v^* such that,

$$ev^* = \lim_{k \to \infty} \left[D^{-1}\left(\frac{1}{\lambda}\right) A D \right]^k = \lim_{k \to \infty} D^{-1}\left(\frac{1}{\lambda^k}\right) A^k D$$

(i.e., the rows of the limiting matrix are all the same) from which we have

$$\lim_{k \to \infty} \frac{1}{\lambda^k} A^k = Dev^* D^{-1} = wv^* D^{-1} \equiv wv$$

Theorem 7-8   The vectors v and w are eigenvectors of A, both with eigenvalue λ.

PROOF

$$\frac{1}{\lambda} Awv = \frac{1}{\lambda} A \lim_{k \to \infty} \left(\frac{1}{\lambda}\right)^k A^k = \lim_{k \to \infty} \left(\frac{1}{\lambda}\right)^{k+1} A^{k+1} = wv$$

from which we have $Awv = \lambda wv$ and $Awve = \lambda wve$ and, since ve is a constant, $Aw = \lambda w$. Similarly $vA = \lambda v$.

Corollary   The vectors v and w are positive.

PROOF   From $Aw = \lambda w$ we have $(1/\lambda)Aw = w$. Since λ is positive and A is positive and w is nonnegative (with some nonzero components) every component to the left is positive and hence w is positive; similarly for v.

Theorem 7-9   All eigenvectors corresponding to the eigenvalue λ are constant multiples of w and v.

PROOF   If $Au = \lambda u$, then $A^k u = \lambda^k u$, and $(1/\lambda)^k A^k u = u$ for all k. Letting $k \to \infty$ we have $wvu = u$. Since vu is some number α, we have $\alpha w = u$. Similarly for row vectors.

Theorem 7-10   The modulus of any other eigenvalue h of A satisfies the inequality $|h| < |\lambda|$.

PROOF   If $Au = hu$, then $A^k u = h^k u$, and $(1/\lambda)^k A^k u = (h/\lambda)^k u$. Taking the limit as $k \to \infty$, we have

$$wvu = \lim_{k \to \infty} \left[\frac{h}{\lambda}\right]^k u$$

and the right side must exist, which can only happen for $h = \lambda$ or $|h| < |\lambda|$, yielding a zero limiting value.

The eigenvalue λ is the principal eigenvalue of A which we denote by $\lambda_{\max}$, and v and w are the principal eigenvectors of A.

Corollary   The principal row and column eigenvectors v (and w) are orthogonal to all nonprincipal column and row eigenvectors of A.

PROOF Consider the result $wvu = 0$ in the proof of the previous theorem. Since $w > 0$ we have $vu = 0$, and therefore v is orthogonal to the column vector u. A similar argument can be used to show that w is orthogonal to all nonprincipal row eigenvectors of A.

Corollary $vw = 1$.

PROOF In the proof of the theorem, let $u = w$ then $h = \lambda$ and $wvw = w$. Since vw is a number we must have $vw = 1$.

REMARK vw is the trace of the matrix wv, and hence this trace is always equal to unity.

REMARK The system $\sum_{j=1}^{n} a_{ij}x_j = b_i, i = 1, \ldots, n$ where $a_{ij} \geqslant 0, a_{ii} > 0$ has a non-negative solution $x_j \geqslant 0, j = 1, \ldots, n$ if the upper left-corner principal minors of $|A|$, $A = (a_{ij})$ are positive, i.e., if

$$a_{11} > 0, \quad \begin{vmatrix} a_{11} & a_{12} \\ a_{21} & a_{22} \end{vmatrix} > 0, \quad \begin{vmatrix} a_{11} & a_{12} & a_{13} \\ a_{21} & a_{22} & a_{23} \\ a_{31} & a_{32} & a_{33} \end{vmatrix} > 0, \ldots, |A| > 0$$

Theorem 7-11 (Wielandt) If A is a nonnegative irreducible matrix, then the value of λ_{max} increases as any element a_{ij} increases.

PROOF Let A be nonnegative, and define $B(\rho) = \rho I - A$, where ρ is a real valued parameter (Nikaido, 1970). Let M be the set of all ρ for which the system $B(\rho)$ has a nonnegative solution, i.e., the inverse matrix $(\rho I - A)^{-1}$ exists and is nonnegative. The set M is nonempty for $x > 0$ and is such that for sufficiently large ρ, $\rho x > Ax$, i.e., $\rho x - Ax > 0$ and this condition assures the existence of a nonnegative solution, and is equivalent to the above principal minor condition. Since M depends on A we denote it by M(A).

Let $A' \geqslant A'' \geqslant 0$. Then M($A'$) $\subset$ M(A''). To see this, note that if $\rho \in$ M(A') then $(\rho I - A')x > 0$ for some $x \geqslant 0$ and since $\rho I - A'' \geqslant \rho I - A'$, $(\rho I - A'') > 0$ for the same x and hence the system with A'' has a nonnegative solution and $\rho \in$ M(A''). Now the maximum eigenvalue λ_{max} of $A > 0$ is the inf ρ for which $(\rho I - A)^{-1}$ exists, i.e., it is the first value for which $|\rho I - A| = 0$ and hence all other eigenvalues must be no greater than λ_{max}. In any case we have

$$\lambda_{max}(A') = \inf_{\rho \in M(A')} \rho \geqslant \lambda_{max}(A'')$$

Thus λ_{max} is a monotone function of A.

We now show the significant result that the eigenvector corresponding to λ_{max} is the normalized row sums of the limiting matrix of just the kth power A^k of A, and not of the sums of all powers of A.

Theorem 7-12

$$\lim_{k \to \infty} \frac{A^k e}{e^T A^k e} = c w_1$$

where $A > 0$, w_1 is its principal eigenvector corresponding to the maximum eigenvalue λ_1, $\lambda_i \neq \lambda_j$ for all i and j, and w_i is the right eigenvector corresponding to λ_i and c is a constant.

PROOF $e = a_1 w_1 + \cdots + a_n w_n$ where a_i, $i = 1, \ldots, n$ are constants.

$$A^k e = a_1 \lambda_1^k w_1 + \cdots + a_n \lambda_n^k w_n = \lambda_1^k \left[a_1 w_1 + a_2 \left(\frac{\lambda_2}{\lambda_1} \right)^k w_2 + \cdots + a_n \left(\frac{\lambda_n}{\lambda_1} \right)^k w_n \right]$$

$$e^T A^k e = \lambda_1^k \left[b_1 + b_2 \left(\frac{\lambda_2}{\lambda_1} \right)^k + \cdots + b_n \left(\frac{\lambda_n}{\lambda_1} \right)^k \right]; \qquad b_i = a_i e^T w_i$$

Since $w_1 > 0$, $b_1 \neq 0$. The theorem follows.

Next we generalize this theorem.

Definition 7-2 A nonnegative irreducible matrix A is *primitive* if and only if there is an integer $m \geqslant 1$ such that $A^m > 0$. Otherwise it is called *imprimitive*. The graph of a primitive matrix has a path of length $\geqslant m$ between any two vertices.

From the work of Frobenius (1912), Perron (1907), and Wielandt (1950) we have that a nonnegative irreducible matrix A is primitive, if and only if A has a unique characteristic root of maximum modulus, and if this root has multiplicity 1.

Theorem 7-13 For a primitive matrix A

$$\lim_{k \to \infty} \frac{A^k e}{\|A^k\|} = c w, \qquad \|A^k\| \equiv e^T A e$$

where c is a constant and w is the eigenvector corresponding to $\lambda_{\max} \equiv \lambda_1$.

PROOF Assume that $A > 0$. Consider the Jordan canonical form B of A. Then for some nonsingular matrix N

$$NAN^{-1} = \begin{bmatrix} \lambda_1 & & & & 0 \\ & B_2 & & & \\ & & \cdot & & \\ & & & \cdot & \\ 0 & & & & B_r \end{bmatrix} = B$$

where B_i, $i = 2, \ldots, r$ is the $m_i \times m_i$ Jordan block form defined by

$$B_i = \begin{bmatrix} \lambda_i & & & & & \\ 1 & \lambda_i & & & 0 & \\ & 1 & \lambda_i & & & \\ & & 1 & \cdot & & \\ 0 & & & \cdot & & \\ & & & & \cdot & \\ & & & & \lambda_i & \\ & & & & 1 & \lambda_i \end{bmatrix}$$

where $\lambda_2, \ldots, \lambda_r$ are distinct eigenvalues with multiplicities $m_2, \ldots, m_r$, respectively, and $1 + \sum\limits_{i=2}^{r} m_i = n$, the dimension of A. We choose the appropriate basis vectors for each subspace of the Jordan form

$$V_1$$
$$V_{21}, V_{22}, \ldots, V_{2m_2}$$
$$V_{31}, V_{32}, \ldots, V_{3m_3}$$
$$\vdots \qquad \vdots$$
$$V_{r1}, V_{r2}, \ldots, V_{rm_r}$$

and we have

$$AV_1 = \lambda_1 V_1$$
$$AV_{i1} = \lambda_i V_{i1} + V_{i2}$$
$$AV_{i2} = \lambda_i V_{i2} + V_{i3}$$
$$AV_{im_i} = \lambda_i V_{im_i}$$

Note that

$$B_i = \lambda_i I + u$$

where

$$u = \begin{bmatrix} 0 & & & & \\ 1 & 0 & & 0 & \\ & 1 & \cdot & & \\ & & \cdot & \cdot & \\ 0 & & \cdot & \cdot & \\ & & & \cdot & \cdot \\ & & & & 1 & 0 \end{bmatrix}$$

and

$$B_i^k = \lambda_i^k I + \binom{k}{1} \lambda_i^{k-1} u + \binom{k}{2} \lambda_i^{k-2} u^2 + \cdots + u^k$$

where u^k is the zero matrix if $k \geqslant n$, and if $k < n$ the diagonal of ones in u shifts downwards by one for each additional power of u. For example

$$u^2 = \begin{bmatrix} 0 & 0 & \cdots & 0 & 0 & 0 \\ 0 & 0 & \cdots & 0 & 0 & 0 \\ 1 & 0 & \cdots & 0 & 0 & 0 \\ 0 & 1 & \cdots & 0 & 0 & 0 \\ 0 & 0 & \cdots & 1 & 0 & 0 \end{bmatrix}$$

Now let

$$e = a_1 V_1 + a_{21} V_{21} + a_{22} V_{22} + \cdots + a_{2m_2} V_{2m_2} + a_{31} V_{31} + \cdots + a_{rm_r} V_{rm_r}$$

$$A^k e = a_1 \lambda_1^k V_1 + \sum_{i=2}^{r} \sum_{j=1}^{m_r} \sum_{l=0}^{j} a_{ij} \begin{bmatrix} k \\ j-l \end{bmatrix} \lambda_i^{k-l} V_{ij}$$

$$\|A^k\| = c_1 \lambda_1^k + p_{2,k} \lambda_2^k + p_{2,k-1} \lambda_2^{k-1} + \cdots + p_{2,1} \lambda_2 + \cdots$$
$$+ p_{rk} \lambda_r^k + \cdots + p_{r1} \lambda_r + c_2$$

where the p_{ij} are polynomials in k and c_1, c_2 are constants independent of k.

The expression $\dfrac{A^k e}{\|A^k\|}$ will have a term

$$\frac{a_1 \lambda_1^k V_1}{c_1 \lambda_1^k + p_{2,k} \lambda_2^k + p_{2,k-1} \lambda_2^{k-1} + \cdots + c_2}$$

the limit of which as $k \to \infty$ is $(a_1/c_1) V_1$, since λ_1 is the unique largest eigenvalue.

A typical term $(i > 2)$

$$\frac{a_{il} \begin{bmatrix} k \\ j-l \end{bmatrix} \lambda_i^{k-l} V_{ij}}{c_1 \lambda_1^k + \cdots + p_{ik} \lambda_i^k + \cdots + c_2}$$

would approach 0 as $k \to \infty$ (since λ_1 dominates all other λ's). On putting $e = (a_1/c_1)$ and $V_1 = w$, we have the theorem proved for $A > 0$.

REMARK Note that $c = 0$ if and only if $a_1 = 0$. We can show that $a_1 \neq 0$ whenever all a_{ij} in the expansion of e and all V_i are real and positive. We observe that a small perturbation in e would make $a_1 \neq 0$, and the result remains the same.

Now to prove the theorem for $A \geqslant 0$ we note that because $a_{ii} > 0$ there exists a positive integer m such that $A^m > 0$ (i.e., by going around loops it is possible to eventually obtain paths of any desired length between an arbitrary pair of vertices of the corresponding graph). The above proof applies to A^m and its largest eigenvector $w(A^m)$. Indeed, since A is a bounded linear operator (and therefore continuous on $E^n \to E^n$) we have

$$\lim_{k \to \infty} \frac{A^{mk+i}\text{e}}{\|A^{mk+i}\|} = cw(A)^m \qquad 0 \leqslant i < m$$

It is trivial to show that $w(A^m)$ is the desired nonnegative eigenvector of A.

This completes the proof.

REMARK The following nonnegative matrix is irreducible (its graph is strongly connected since every pair of vertices has a path connecting them).

$$A = \begin{bmatrix} 0 & 2 & 0 \\ 0 & 0 & 4 \\ 1 & 0 & 0 \end{bmatrix}$$

This matrix does not satisfy the theorem because it is imprimitive as it has 2 as the only eigenvalue of multiplicity 3. To see this, note the following
$Ae = (2, 4, 1)^T$; normalizing yields $x_1 = (\frac{2}{7}, \frac{4}{7}, \frac{1}{7})^T$; $Ax_1 = (\frac{8}{7}, \frac{4}{7}, \frac{2}{7})^T$; normalizing yields $x_2 = (\frac{4}{7}, \frac{2}{7}, \frac{1}{7})^T$; $Ax_2 = (\frac{4}{7}, \frac{4}{7}, \frac{4}{7})^T$; normalizing yields $x_3 = (\frac{1}{3}, \frac{1}{3}, \frac{1}{3})^T$; $Ax_3 = (\frac{2}{3}, \frac{4}{3}, \frac{1}{3})^T$ and normalizing yields $x_4 = (\frac{2}{7}, \frac{4}{7}, \frac{1}{7})^T$ which is the same as x_1 thus cycling without convergence.

7-4 COMPUTATION OF THE EIGENVECTOR

The actual computation of the principal eigenvector is based on the last theorem above. It says that the normalized row sums of the limiting power of a primitive matrix (and hence also for a positive matrix) gives the desired eigenvector. Thus a short computational way to obtain this vector is to raise the matrix to powers that are successively squared each time. The row sums are calculated and normalized. The computer is instructed to stop when the difference between these sums in two consecutive calculations is smaller than a prescribed value.

7-5 CONSISTENCY

Reciprocal nonnegative matrices may have complex eigenvalues. Hence, they have no simple generic characterization. However, we note that since the maximum eigenvalue lies between the largest and the smallest row sums, a matrix whose columns are identical has an eigenvalue which is equal to the sum of any of its columns. Also we shall see that a small perturbation leaves the maximum eigenvalue close to its value, and that the remaining eigenvalues are perturbed away from zero, and their sum is real.

The choice of perturbation most appropriate for describing the effect of inconsistency on the eigenvector depends on what is thought to be the psychological process involved in pairwise comparisons of a set of data. We assume that all perturbations of interest can be reduced to the general form $a_{ij} = (w_i/w_j)\varepsilon_{ij}$. Consistency occurs when $\varepsilon_{ij} = 1$. For example

$$\frac{w_i}{w_j} + \alpha_{ij} = \frac{w_i}{w_j}\left[1 + \frac{w_j}{w_i}\alpha_{ij}\right]$$

Let us now develop a few elementary but essential results about consistent matrices. We start with the relation

$$\lambda_{\max} = \sum_{j=1}^{n} a_{ij}\frac{w_j}{w_i}$$

which is the ith component of $Aw = \lambda_{\max}w$, and define

$$\mu = -\frac{1}{n-1}\sum_{i=2}^{n}\lambda_i$$

Then

$$\sum_{i=1}^{n}\lambda_i = n \text{ implies that } \mu = \frac{\lambda_{\max}-n}{n-1}; \lambda_{\max} \equiv \lambda_1$$

and since

$$\lambda_{\max} - 1 = \sum_{j \ne i} a_{ij}\frac{w_j}{w_i}$$

we find that

$$n\lambda_{\max} - n = \sum_{1 \le i < j \le n}\left[a_{ij}\frac{w_j}{w_i} + a_{ji}\frac{w_i}{w_j}\right]$$

and therefore

$$\mu = \frac{\lambda_{\max}-n}{n-1} = \frac{1}{n-1} - \frac{n}{n-1} + \frac{1}{n(n-1)}\sum_{1 \le i < j \le n}\left[a_{ij}\frac{w_j}{w_i} + a_{ji}\frac{w_i}{w_j}\right]$$

Substituting, $a_{ij} = (w_i/w_j)\varepsilon_{ij}$, $\varepsilon_{ij} > 0$ we arrive at the equation

$$\mu = -1 + \frac{1}{n(n-1)}\sum_{1 \le i < j \le n}\left[\varepsilon_{ij} + \frac{1}{\varepsilon_{ij}}\right]$$

We observe that as $\varepsilon_{ij} \to 1$, i.e., as consistency is approached, $\mu \to 0$. Also, μ is convex in the ε_{ij}, since $\varepsilon_{ij} + 1/\varepsilon_{ij}$ is convex (and has its minimum at $\varepsilon_{ij} = 1$), and since the sum of convex functions is convex. Thus, μ is small or large depending on ε_{ij} being near to or far from unity, respectively (i.e., near to or far from consistency). Finally, if we write $\varepsilon_{ij} = 1 + \delta_{ij}$, with $\delta_{i_j} > -1$ we have

$$\mu = \frac{1}{n(n-1)}\sum_{1 \le i < j \le n}\left[\delta_{ij}^2 - \frac{\delta_{ij}^3}{1+\delta_{ij}}\right]$$

Theorem 7-14 $\lambda_{\max} \geqslant n$.

PROOF

$$\frac{\lambda_{\max} - n}{n-1} = \frac{1}{n(n-1)} \sum_{1 \leqslant i < j \leqslant n} \frac{\delta_{ij}^2}{1 + \delta_{ij}}$$

which is $\geqslant 0$, since $a_{ij} = (w_i/w_j)(1 + \delta_{ij})$ with $\delta_{ij} > -1$.

Theorem 7-15 A positive, reciprocal matrix is consistent if and only if $\lambda_{\max} = n$.

PROOF If A is consistent then $\delta_{ij} = 0$ and $\lambda_{\max} = n$.

Conversely, using the result above, we conclude from $\lambda_{\max} = n$ that $\delta_{ij} = 0$ for each choice of i and j, and hence, that A is consistent.

As we saw, we wish μ to be near zero, or, $\lambda_{\max}$ to be near to its lower bound n, and thus to approach consistency. It is interesting to see that $(\lambda_{\max} - n/n - 1)$ is related to the statistical root mean square error. Indeed, let us assume that $|\delta_{ij}| < 1$ (and hence that $(\delta_{ij}^3/1 + \delta_{ij})$ is small compared with δ_{ij}^2). This is a reasonable assumption for an unbiased judge, who is limited by the "natural" greatest lower bound -1 on δ_{ij} (since a_{ij} must be greater than zero), and who would tend to estimate symmetrically about zero in the interval $(-1, 1)$. Now, $\mu \to 0$ as $\delta_{ij} \to 0$. Multiplication by 2 gives the variance of the δ_{ij}. Thus, 2μ is this variance.

Small perturbations of the entries in a positive reciprocal matrix imply small perturbations in the eigenvalues from their original value. This observation is not true for general positive matrices. We prove this fact for $\lambda_{\max}$.

Theorem 7-16 Let $\delta = \max_{i,j} \delta_{ij}$ then

$$\lambda_{\max} - n < \frac{1}{n} \sum_{1 \leqslant i < j \leqslant n} \delta_{ij}^2 \leqslant \frac{(n-1)}{2} \delta^2$$

PROOF *Obvious*

Thus if the perturbation (or judgmental error) is small and the number of elements being compared is also <u>small</u> (e.g., less than 10) then the departure of $\lambda_{\max}$ from n is also small. Again we note that to remain near consistency we need to keep n small. For example, $\delta = 0.1$, $n = 7$ give $\lambda_{\max} - n < 0.04$ and $\delta = 0.9$, $n = 7$ give $\lambda_{\max} - n < 2.43$.

REMARK The nonnegative matrix $A = (a_{ij})$ with $a_{i,i+1} = 1$, $a_{ij} = 0$ otherwise, has all its eigenvalues zero, but the same matrix with a_{n1} replaced by ε, where $\varepsilon > 0$ is small, has the maximum eigenvalue $\lambda_{\max} = \varepsilon^{1/n}$ which tends to unity with increasing n. Thus, although $\lambda_{\max}$ changes continuously with the coefficient ε, its value becomes large even for small ε (communicated to me by Alan Laub of MIT).

Vargas (1978) has observed that from $a_{ij}a_{jk} = a_{ik}$, we have, on using the reciprocal property $a_{ji} = 1/a_{ij}$, that $a_{ij}a_{jk}a_{ki} = 1$. Thus consistency for a reciprocal matrix means that all cycles of length three have unit intensity.

Assuming $|\delta_{ij}| < 1$, and considering triangular cycles we have

$$a_{ij}a_{jk}a_{ki} = (1+\delta_{ij})(1+\delta_{jk})(1-\delta_{ik}) \simeq 1+\delta_{ij}+\delta_{jk}-\delta_{ik}$$

and, since $\lambda_{\max} = \sum_{j=1}^{n} \varepsilon_{ij}$, we have

$$\sum_{i,j,k} a_{ij}a_{jk}a_{ki} = n^2\lambda_{\max}$$

For $i \ne j, j \ne k, i \ne k$, this sum becomes $n^2(\lambda_{\max}-n)+n(n-1)(n-2)$, since by putting $a_{pp} = 1$, $a_{pq} = a_{qp}^{-1}$, we have $n^2+2n(n-1)$ terms whose value is unity. Averaging over the number of terms, i.e., $n(n-1)(n-2)$, the result is $(n/n-2)$ $(\lambda_{\max}-n/n-1)+1$ valid for $n \geqslant 3$. In any case it is $\lambda_{\max}-n$ that is of interest to us as it also appears in these global considerations of consistency.

Suppose now, that we wish to develop a test of a hypothesis of consistency. Perfect consistency may be stated as the null hypothesis:

$$H_0: \mu = 0$$

and we test it against its one-sided alternative.

$$H_1: \mu > 0$$

The appropriate test statistic is

$$m = \frac{\tilde{\lambda}_{\max}-n}{n-1}$$

where $\tilde{\lambda}_{\max}$ is the maximum observed eigenvalue of the matrix whose elements, a_{ij}, contain random error. Developing a statistical measure for consistency requires finding the distribution of the statistic m. While its specific form is beyond the scope of this chapter, we observe that m follows a nonnegative probability distribution whose variance is twice its mean $\bar{x}$, and appears to be quite similar to the Chi-square distribution, if we assume that all δ_{ij} are $N(0, \sigma^2)$ on $(-1, 1)$.

For our purpose, without knowing the distribution, we use the conventional ratio $(\bar{x}-\mu_0)/(\sqrt{2\bar{x}})$ with $\mu_0 = 0$, i.e., we use $\sqrt{\bar{x}/2}$ in a qualitative test to confirm the null hypothesis when the test statistic is, say, $\leqslant 1$. Thus when $\bar{x} > 2$, it is possible that inconsistency is indicated.

A better method for testing the statistic m is the one we have been using by comparing C.I. with R.I.

REMARK Note that for $A = (a_{ij})$, $W = (w_i/w_j)$, we have

$$(A - W)w = (\lambda_{\max} - n)w$$

which shows that the approximation to (a_{ij}) by (w_i/w_j) is the better, the closer $\lambda_{\max}$ is to n.

Returning to the representation

$$a_{ij} = \frac{w_i}{w_j}+\frac{w_i}{w_j}\delta_{ij}$$

we find that

$$\delta_{ij}^2 = \left[a_{ij} \frac{w_j}{w_i} - 1 \right]^2$$

Thus replacing the a_{ij} by w_i/w_j yields $\delta_{ij}^2 = 0$, and hence decreases the value of $2(\lambda_{max} - n)/(n-1)$.

Thus, whenever $|\delta_{ij}| < 1$, approximating any a_{ij} by w_i/w_j will bring us closer to consistency. (See the discussion of least squares given later.)

Theorem 7-17 If a positive matrix A is consistent, then each row is a positive multiple of any given row.

PROOF Without loss of generality, let us assume that each row is a positive multiple of the ith row. The relation $a_{jk} = a_{ik}/a_{ij}$ implies that by fixing j and putting $k = 1, 2, \ldots, n$ the jth row is equal to the ith row, multiplied by the positive constant $(1/a_{ij})$.

REMARK Obviously the converse of this theorem is false. A matrix of unit rank need not be consistent. For example, the following matrix

$$\begin{bmatrix} 1 & 2 \\ 2 & 4 \end{bmatrix}$$

a_{21} is not equal to a_{11}/a_{12}.
Thus, a consistent matrix has the following general form

$$\begin{bmatrix} \dfrac{a_{i1}}{a_{i1}} & \dfrac{a_{i2}}{a_{i1}} & \cdots & \dfrac{a_{in}}{a_{i1}} \\[2mm] \dfrac{a_{i1}}{a_{i2}} & \dfrac{a_{i2}}{a_{i2}} & \cdots & \dfrac{a_{in}}{a_{i2}} \\[2mm] \vdots & \vdots & \vdots\vdots\vdots & \vdots \\[2mm] a_{i1} & a_{i2} & \cdots & a_{in} \\[2mm] \vdots & \vdots & \vdots\vdots\vdots & \vdots \\[2mm] \dfrac{a_{i1}}{a_{in}} & \dfrac{a_{i2}}{a_{in}} & \cdots & \dfrac{a_{in}}{a_{in}} \end{bmatrix}$$

with $a_{ii} = 1$.
Since the matrix $A = (w_i/w_j)$ has the form of the transpose of the above matrix, it is consistent.

Theorem 7-18 If A is positive and consistent, then $a_{ii} = 1$ and $a_{ij} = 1/a_{ji}$.

PROOF The definition implies that $a_{ii} = a_{ii}a_{ii}$, and hence $a_{ii} = 1$ for all i. Also, $a_{ii} = a_{ij}a_{ji}$ implies $a_{ij} = a_{ii}/a_{ji} = 1/a_{ji}$.

Theorem 7-19 A positive matrix A is consistent if and only if it has unit rank and its principal diagonal entries are equal to unity.

PROOF If A is consistent than $a_{ii} = 1$. Also

$$a_{ij} = \frac{a_{1j}}{a_{1i}} = \frac{1}{a_{1i}}(a_{1j})$$

and the ith row is $1/a_{1i}$ times the first row and hence the rank of A is unity. Conversely, if the rank of A is unity and $a_{ii} = 1$ for all i, then each row is a constant multiple of the first row, i.e.,

$$a_{ij} = c_i a_{1j}, \; a_{jk} = c_j a_{1k}, \; a_{ik} = c_i a_{1k}, \; a_{jj} = c_j a_{1j}$$

$$a_{ij} a_{jk} = c_i c_j a_{1j} a_{1k} = c_i c_j a_{1j} \frac{a_{ik}}{c_i} = c_j a_{1j} a_{ik} = a_{jj} a_{ik} = a_{ik}$$

and A is consistent.

In line with our earlier discussion of graphs we have the following.

Definition 7-3 The intensity of judgments associated with a path from i to j called the path intensity is equal to the products of the intensities associated with the arcs of that path.

The following theorem may help remove some doubts one may have regarding path intensities and consistency. Recall that a spanning tree on n vertices has $n-1$ edges. It is a connected graph which includes all the vertices and has no cycles. Thus there is a unique path between any pair of vertices.

Theorem 7-20 A necessary and sufficient condition that there is a unique positive consistent matrix derived by path intensities from an arbitrary assignment of pairwise comparison judgments and their reciprocals to activities is that the activities (as vertices) and their connecting judgments (as arcs) form a spanning tree.

PROOF *Necessity* If the activities form a cycle there is a non-unique representation of the path between two vertices in the cycle yielding two different values for the same entry. All activities must be represented in the tree otherwise judgments would have to be provided to connect isolated activities, and their judgments would be arbitrary. This would violate the uniqueness of the matrix.

Sufficiency. For each arc of the spanning tree we use the unique path intensity to compose the intensities between activities i and j. This defines a matrix $A = (a_{ij})$.

To prove that A is consistent, we consider any row, e.g., the ith. For any pair of vertices j and k we must show that a_{jk} defined by the product of arcs in

Figure 7-1

the path jk is given by a_{ik}/a_{ij} where a_{ik} and a_{ij} are the corresponding products of arc intensities on paths connecting i to k and i to j.

There are two cases to consider.

(1) i lies on the path between j and k. In that case $a_{jk} = a_{ji}a_{ik} = a_{ik}/a_{ij}$.
(2) i does not lie between j and k, then

  (a) i, j and k form a path in which case the path defining a_{jk} is given by a_{ik}/a_{ij} if j is between i and k and by the reciprocal of a_{ij}/a_{ik}, i.e. a_{ik}/a_{ij}, if k is between i and j since the path must go from j to k and not from k to j.
  (b) i, j, k form a fork at m (see Fig. 7-1). Then $a_{jk} = a_{jm}a_{mk} = a_{jm}a_{mi}a_{im}a_{mk}$
  $= a_{ji}a_{ik} = a_{ik}/a_{ij}$.

Theorem 7-21 If A is consistent then $A^k = n^{k-1}A$.

PROOF From Sylvester's theorem we have

$$f(A) = \sum_{i=1}^{n} f(\lambda_i) \frac{\prod_{j \neq i} (A - \lambda_j I)}{\prod_{j \neq i} (\lambda_i - \lambda_j)}$$

This gives the same result for $f(A) = A^k$ as the modified form (for multiple eigenvalues) when the multiple eigenvalue is zero. We obtain on putting $f(A) = A$ first and $f(A) = A^k$ second, both with $\lambda_1 = n$, $\lambda_j = 0$, $j \neq 1$:

$$A^{n-1} = n^{n-2}A, \qquad A^k = n^{k-n-1}A^{n-1}$$

respectively. Substituting for A^{n-1} from the first result into the second gives $A^k = n^{k-1}A$.

Theorem 7-22 Any column of the matrix $A = (w_i/w_j)$ is a solution of the eigenvalue problem $Aw = nw$, $w = (w_1, \ldots, w_n)$.

PROOF Since any column of the matrix is given by

$$\left[\frac{w_1}{w_j}, \frac{w_2}{w_j}, \ldots, \frac{w_n}{w_j} \right]^T$$

it is simply a constant multiple of w and hence is a solution of the problem.

The last theorem implies the one preceding it, since, if we denote the columns of A by $(a_1, a_2, \ldots a_n)$, then $A \cdot A = (a_1, a_2, \ldots, a_n)^2 = (na_1, na_2, \ldots na_n) = nA$.

Theorem 7-23 Any row of the matrix $A = (w_i/w_j)$ is a solution of $vA = nv$.

PROOF Obvious.

Corollary The right and left eigenvectors, w and v, have reciprocal entries to within a constant multiplier. (They are what we call *dual* vectors.)

Let us define the *norm* of the matrix A by $\|A\| \equiv e^T A e$ (i.e., it is the sum of all entries of A), where as in page 176,

$$e = \begin{bmatrix} 1 \\ 1 \\ \vdots \\ 1 \end{bmatrix}$$

We know that for a primitive matrix A

$$\lim_{k \to \infty} (A^k e / \|A^k\|) = c w_{\max}$$

where c is a constant and $w_{\max}$ is the normalized principal eigenvector of A. The following is a simplified version of this theorem for a consistent matrix.

Theorem 7-24 If A is a positive consistent n by n matrix then $Ae = Cw$ where $C > 0$ is a constant, and w satisfies $Aw = nw$.

PROOF The vector Ae is the sum of the rows of A, and it is, obviously, a constant multiple of any column. It is therefore a solution of the eigenvalue problem.

ALTERNATE PROOF It is easy to show that "A has unit rank" if and only if there exist vectors x and y such that $A = xy^T$. Hence

$$Aw = (y, w)x = nw, \qquad (y, w) = y_1 w_1 + \cdots + y_n w_n$$

and hence

$$Ae = (y, e)\mathbf{x} = (y, e) \frac{n}{(y, w)} w \equiv Cw$$

Corollary 1 If $A = w_i/w_j$ then $Cw_i = w_i \sum_{i=1}^{n} w_i$

Corollary 2

$$\frac{A^k e}{e^T A^k e} = \frac{n^{k-1} Ae}{n^{k-1} e^T A e} = \frac{Ae}{e^T A e} = C(w_1, \ldots, w_n), \quad C > 0$$

The following theorem shows that, in the case of consistent matrices, the eigenvector components vary monotonically with changes in single entries.

Theorem 7-25 (Monotonicity Theorem) Let $A = (a_{ij})$ be a positive consistent matrix with principal eigenvector $w = (w_1, \ldots, w_n)$. Replace a single entry a_{xy} by $a_{xy} + \varepsilon > 0$ and, using row x, construct a new consistent matrix $A^* = (a_{ij}^*)$. Let $w^* = (w_1^*, \ldots, w_n^*)$ be the principal eigenvector of A^*. Then $w_x^* > w_x$.

PROOF Since both A and A^* are consistent, any normalized column gives the principal eigenvector. Consider the column containing $1/a_{xy}$ in A, and the corresponding column containing $1/a_{xy} + \varepsilon$ in A^*. The two columns are identical, except for this single entry. However, the sum of the column entries in A^* is less than the sum of the column entries in A. Thus, normalizing by this column yields a larger ratio for all those entries that remain the same in both matrices. This is particularly true for w_x^*, therefore $w_x^* > w_x$.

Later we shall generalize this theorem to reciprocal matrices of order 2, 3, and 4.

Theorem 7-26 If A is a positive, consistent matrix and A' is obtained from A by deleting the ith row and ith column, then A' is consistent and its corresponding eigenvector is obtained from that of A by putting $w_i = 0$, and normalizing the components.

PROOF Given any row of A, e.g., the first, we have $a_{ij} = a_{1j}/a_{1i}, j = 1, \ldots, n$, and the ith row of A depends on the ith column entry in its first row. A similar consequence follows from $a_{jk} = a_{1k}/a_{1j}$. Thus, no entry in A' depends on the ith row or ith column of A and hence A' is also consistent. Since their entries coincide except in the ith row and ith column of A and since the solution of an eigenvalue problem with a consistent matrix is obtained from any normalized column, the theorem follows.

REMARK In the general case, if $A = (a_{ij})$ is a matrix constructed from pairwise comparisons, and $A' = (a_{ij}')$ with $a_{ij}' = a_{ij}, i, j = 1, \ldots, n, i \neq k, j \neq k$, $a_{ij}' = 0, i = k$ or $j = k$, and if the normalized eigenvector solutions of $Aw = \lambda_{max}w$ and $A'w' = \lambda_{max}w'$ are w and w', respectively, then $w_k' = 0$, but $w_\alpha'/w_\beta' \neq w_\alpha/w_\beta$, for all α and β. In other words, leaving out one activity of a pairwise comparison matrix does not distribute its weight proportionately among the other activities.

The following theorem shows that seeking order type of relationship between a_{ij} and w_i/w_j involves all of A, and its powers, in a complicated fashion.

Theorem 7-27 For a primitive matrix A we have

$$a_{ij} \geqslant a_{kl} \quad \text{if and only if} \quad \frac{w_i}{w_j} \geqslant \frac{w_k}{w_l}$$

whenever

$$\lim_{m \to \infty} \frac{\sum\limits_{p \neq j} a_{ip}(A^m e)_p}{(A^m e)_j} \geqslant \lim_{m \to \infty} \frac{\sum\limits_{q \neq l} a_{kq}(A^m e)_q}{(A^m e)_l}$$

holds. (A pth subscript on a vector indicates use of its pth entry.)

PROOF In a typical case

$$\sum_{j=1}^{n} a_{ij} w_j = \lambda w_i$$

from which we have

$$a_{ij} = \frac{\lambda w_i}{w_j} - \frac{1}{w_j} \sum_{p \neq j} a_{ip} w_p$$

and

$$a_{kl} = \frac{\lambda w_k}{w_l} - \frac{1}{w_l} \sum_{q \neq l} a_{kq} w_q$$

Thus

$$a_{ij} \geqslant a_{kl}$$

if and only if

$$\frac{\lambda w_i}{w_j} \geqslant \frac{\lambda w_k}{w_l} + \frac{1}{w_j} \sum_{p \neq j} a_{ip} w_p - \frac{1}{w_l} \sum_{q \neq l} a_{kq} w_q$$

Thus, the theorem is true whenever the following inequality holds

$$\frac{1}{w_j} \sum_{p \neq j} a_{ip} w_p \geqslant \frac{1}{w_l} \sum_{q \neq l} a_{kq} w_q$$

Using the theorem on the limit of a primitive matrix we replace every w_s by

$$\lim_{m \to \infty} \frac{(A^m e)_s}{e^T A^m e}$$

yielding the proof.

We now turn to an important extension of the previous results. Let us assume that our mind works, in fact, with pairwise comparisons, but that the a_{ij} are not estimates of w_i/w_j but of some function of the latter, $a_{ij}(w_i/w_j)$. For example, Stevens (see Churchman and Ratoosh, 1959) observed that a_{ij} as perceived for prothetic phenomena (the process of adding excitation to excitation) takes the form $(w_i/w_j)^a$ where a lies somewhere between 0.3 (in the case of loudness estimation) and 4 (in the case of electric shock estimation. Others are: brightness, 0.33 to 0.50, length 1.1, duration 1.15, numerousness 1.34, heaviness 1.45, and velocity 1.77. For metathetic phenomena (the process of substituting excitation for excitation), Stevens points out that the power law need not apply, i.e., that $a = 1$ for thought processes.

These observations indicate that it is of interest to study the general form of the solution $g_i(w_i)$, $i = 1, \ldots, n$, of an eigenvalue problem, where we assume a consistency condition of the form

$$f(a_{ij})f(a_{jk}) = f(a_{ik})$$

for which the matrix also has unit rank. Our main result is as follows.

Theorem 7-28 (Eigenvalue Power Law) If the matrix $A = [a_{ij}(w_i/w_j)]$ of order n satisfies the generalized consistency condition, then the eigenvalue problem

$$\sum_{j=1}^{n} a_{ij}(w_i/w_j)g_j(w_j) = ng_i(w_i) \qquad i = 1, \ldots, n$$

has the eigenvector solution $(w_1^a, \ldots, w_n^a) \equiv [g_1(w_1), \ldots, g_n(w_n)]$.

PROOF The relation

$$a_{ij}(w_i/w_j) = g_i(w_i)/g_j(w_j)$$

is satisfied by the solution $g_i(w_i)$, $i = 1, \ldots, n$, of the eigenvalue problem. If we substitute it into the consistency condition, we have

$$f[g_i(w_i)/g_j(w_j)]\, f[g_j(w_j)/g_k(w_k)] = f[g_i(w_i)/g_k(w_k) \cdot g_j(w_j)/g_j(w_j)]$$

Or, if we put $x = g_i(w_i)/g_j(w_j)$, $y = g_j(w_j)/g_k(w_k)$, we have $f(x)f(y) = f(xy)$. This functional equation has the general solution

$$f(x) = x^a$$

Thus, generalizing the consistency condition for A, we find that a generalization of the corresponding eigenvalue problem (with $\lambda_{max} = n$) is solvable, if we replace a_{ij} by a constant power a of its argument. But we know that when $a = 1$, $a_{ij} = w_i/w_j$; thus, in general, $a_{ij} = (w_i/w_j)^a$ which implies that

$$g_i(w_i)/g_j(w_j) = (w_i/w_j)^a \qquad i, j = 1, \ldots, n$$

and, hence

$$g_i(w_i) = w_i^a = g(w_i) \qquad i = 1, \ldots, n$$

This theorem shows that the solution of a pairwise comparison eigenvalue problem satisfying consistency produces estimates of a power of the underlying scale rather than the scale itself. In applications where knowledge rather than our senses are used to obtain the data, one would expect the power to be equal to unity, and hence we have an estimate of the underlying scale itself. This observation may be useful in social applications.

REMARK Note that we have a many-to-one correspondence between pairwise comparison matrices and eigenvectors. This is fortunate as it allows one to make tradeoffs between attributes and still obtain the same eigenvector for an answer. Therefore, we can obtain the same result from a variety of points of view, and thus choose those matrices which we favor. Otherwise, the universe of experiences would be reduced to a small set of attributes with fixed relative scale values. Relations and their intensity would be deterministic and individual choice would be nonexistent. Of course, this would not introduce conflict. But variety with conflict is richer than determinism. The technical question is: given an eigenvector and all matrices which give rise to it, can one go from one of them to any other by making small perturbations in the entries? In particular, is it possible to go from the matrix of ratios to any other by small perturbations? Another question is: consider two eigenvectors that are small perturbations of each other. Do there exist small perturbations which carry one class of corresponding matrices to the other?

7-6 RECIPROCAL MATRICES

We now investigate some of the properties of positive, reciprocal matrices.

Theorem 7-29 The eigenvalues of a positive reciprocal matrix satisfy the following equation:

$$\sum_{\substack{j,k \\ j \neq k}} \lambda_j \lambda_k = 0$$

PROOF We know that

$$\lambda_1 + \cdots + \lambda_n = \text{trace}(A) = n$$

and

$$\lambda_1^2 + \cdots + \lambda_n^2 = \text{trace}(A^2) = n^2$$

Since λ_i^2 is an eigenvalue of A^2.

Thus

$$n^2 = (\lambda_1 + \cdots + \lambda_n)^2 = \sum_{i=1}^{n} \lambda_1^2 + \sum_{\substack{j,k \\ j \neq k}} \lambda_j \lambda_k$$

which implies that the second term on the right is zero.

Theorem 7-30 Let $A = (a_{ij})$ be an $n \times n$ matrix of positive entries with $a_{ji} = a_{ij}^{-1}$. A is consistent if and only if $\lambda_{\max} = n$.

PROOF From

$$\lambda = \sum_{j=1}^{n} a_{ij} w_j w_i^{-1}$$

we obtain

$$n\lambda - n = \sum_{\substack{i,j=1 \\ i \neq j}}^{n} a_{ij} w_j w_i^{-1} = \sum_{1 \leq i < j \leq n} (a_{ij} w_j w_i^{-1} + w_i w_j^{-1}/a_{ij})$$

It is obvious that $a_{ij} = w_i/w_j$ yields $\lambda = n$, and also $\lambda_{\max} = n$, since the sum of the eigenvalues is equal to n, the trace of A.

To prove the converse, note that in the foregoing expression we have only two terms involving a_{ij}. They are $a_{ij}w_jw_i^{-1}$ and $(w_iw_j^{-1})/(a_{ij})$. Their sum takes the form $y + 1/y$.

To see that n is the minimum value of $\lambda_{\max}$ attained uniquely at $a_{ij} = w_i/w_j$ we note that for all these terms we have $y + 1/y \geqslant 2$. Equality is uniquely obtained on putting $y = 1$, i.e., $a_{ij} = w_i/w_j$. Thus, when $\lambda_{\max} = n$ we have

$$n^2 - n \geqslant \sum_{\substack{i,j=1 \\ i \neq j}}^{n} 2 = n^2 - n$$

from which it follows that $a_{ij} = w_i/w_j$ holds.

If A is not consistent, then we would expect that in some cases $a_{ij} \geqslant a_{kl}$ need not imply $w_i/w_j \geqslant w_k/w_l$. However, since the $w_i, i = 1, \ldots, n$ are determined by the values of an entire row, we would expect the following.

Theorem 7-31 *Preservation of Ordinal Consistency* If $(o_1, \ldots, o_n)$ is an ordinal scale on the activities $C_1, \ldots, C_n$, where $o_i \geqslant o_k$ implies $a_{ij} \geqslant a_{kj}, j = 1, \ldots, n$, then $o_i \geqslant o_k$ implies $w_i \geqslant w_k$.

PROOF Indeed, we have from $Aw = \lambda_{\max}w$, that

$$\lambda_{\max}w_i = \sum_{j=1}^{n} a_{ij}w_j \geqslant \sum_{j=1}^{n} a_{kj}w_j = \lambda_{\max}w_k$$

and $w_i \geqslant w_k$.

Theorem 7-32 Every positive reciprocal 2×2 matrix is consistent.

PROOF Obvious

Theorem 7-33 The normalized left eigenvector components of a reciprocal positive 3 by 3 matrix are the reciprocals of the normalized right eigenvector components.

The proof requires use of the following equality in the expressions for w and v given in Chap. 5 under dynamic priorities for $n = 3$.

$$-(1-\lambda)^3 = \frac{a_{13}^2 + a_{12}^2 a_{23}^2}{a_{12}a_{13}a_{23}} + 3(\lambda - 1)$$

The normalized reciprocal relationship between the left and right eigenvector components no longer holds for $n = 4$ as seen by the following counter-example.

$$A = \begin{bmatrix} 1 & 1/2 & 1/100 & 2 \\ 2 & 1 & 1/3 & 10 \\ 100 & 3 & 1 & 6 \\ 1/2 & 1/10 & 1/6 & 1 \end{bmatrix}$$

$$\lambda_{\max} = 5.73$$
$$w = (0.031, 0.142, 0.793, 0.034)$$
$$v = (0.506, 0.075, 0.020, 0.399)$$

The reciprocal of w normalized is given by

$$(0.461, 0.102, 0.108, 0.419)$$

Thus $n = 4$ is the first case where the solution depends on the consistency of observations and their validity, rather than on the structure of the pairwise comparison matrix. (We also have counterexamples for $n = 5, 6, 7$.)

One is tempted to conjecture that the reciprocal property between principal left and right eigenvector components holds if and only if the matrix is consistent for $n \geqslant 4$.

Johnson–Wang–Beine Observation

Johnson, Wang, and Beine (1979) have observed that since left and right eigenvectors are not reciprocals of each other for $n \geqslant 4$, the solution should benefit somehow by incorporating both left and right eigenvectors. This observation is both philosophically and mathematically interesting. There does not seem to be a natural way for our mind to synthesize its dominance and anti-dominance or recessiveness measures to obtain unified interpretation of reality. Although it is possible to construct iterative schemes to incorporate both left and right eigenvectors into a single measure, such a measure needs a simple natural interpretation.

We have been using benefit/cost analysis to incorporate two opposing concepts within the AHP framework. This seems to be an effective way for dealing with the two sides of human experience.

7-7 SENSITIVITY OF THE EIGENVECTOR

The question often arises, how sensitive the priorities given by the eigenvector components are to slight changes in the judgment values. Clearly, it is desirable that the priorities do not fluctuate widely with small changes in judgment. There are essentially three ways to test this sensitivity: (1) by finding a mathematical estimate of the fluctuation; (2) by deriving answers based on a large number of computer runs appropriately designed to test the sensitivity; (3) by a combination of the two, particularly when it is not possible to carry out the full demonstration analytically.

We have already pointed out, in the case of consistency, that λ_{max} is equal to the trace of the matrix which consists of unit entries. In this case one would expect the eigenvector corresponding to the perturbed matrix to undergo an overall change by an amount inversely proportional to the size of the matrix.

In general, the eigenvalues of a matrix lie between its largest and smallest row sums. Changing the value of an entry in the matrix changes the corresponding row sum and has a tendency to change λ_{max} by an equal amount. However, since a change in the eigenvector should also be influenced by the size of the matrix, we expect that the larger the matrix, the smaller the change in each component.

We begin the analytical treatment of this question by considering a matrix A with the characteristic equation. (See Wilkinson, 1965.)

$$\det(A - \lambda I) = \lambda^n + a_1 \lambda^{n-1} + \cdots + a_n = 0$$

Now, let $A + \varepsilon B$ be the matrix obtained by introducing a small perturbation in A. The corresponding characteristic equation is

$$\det(A + \varepsilon B - \lambda I) = \lambda^n + a_1(\varepsilon)\lambda^{n-1} + \cdots + a_n(\varepsilon) = 0$$

where $a_k(\varepsilon)$ is a polynomial in ε of degree $(n-k)$, such that $a_k(\varepsilon) \to a_k$ as $\varepsilon \to 0$.

Let λ_1 be the maximum simple eigenvalue corresponding to the characteristic equation of A. Wilkinson (1965) proved that for small ε, there exists an eigenvalue of $A + \varepsilon B$ which can be expressed as the sum of a convergent power series, i.e.,

$$\lambda_1(\varepsilon) = \lambda_1 + k_1 \varepsilon + k_2 \varepsilon^2 + \cdots$$

Let w_1 denote the eigenvector of A corresponding to λ_1 and let $w_1(\varepsilon)$ be the eigenvector of $A + \varepsilon B$ corresponding to $\lambda_1(\varepsilon)$. The elements of $w_1(\varepsilon)$ are polynomials in $\lambda(\varepsilon)$ and ε, and, since the power series for $\lambda_1(\varepsilon)$ is convergent for small ε, each element of $w_1(\varepsilon)$ can be represented as a convergent power series in ε. We may write

$$w_1(\varepsilon) = w_1 + \varepsilon z_1 + \varepsilon^2 z_2 + \cdots$$

If the matrix A has linear elementary divisors, then there exist complete sets of right and left eigenvectors $w_1, w_2, \ldots, w_n$ and $v_1, v_2, \ldots, v_n$, respectively, such that

$$v_i^T w_j = 0 \qquad i \neq j$$

Note that w_j and v_j are the jth eigenvectors (right and left), and not the jth components of the vectors.

The vectors z_i can be expressed in terms of the w_j as

$$z_i = \sum_{j=1}^{n} s_{ij} w_j$$

which, when substituted in the formula for $w_1(\varepsilon)$, gives

$$w_1(\varepsilon) = w_1 + \sum_{i=2}^{n} \sum_{j=1}^{n} t_{ij} \varepsilon^j w_i$$

where the t_{ij} are obtained by dividing the s_{ij} by the coefficient of w_1.

The first order perturbations of the eigenvalues are given by the coefficient k_1 of $\lambda_1(\varepsilon)$.

We now derive the expression for the first order perturbations of the corresponding eigenvectors.

Normalizing the vectors w_j and v_j by using the euclidean metric we have

$$|v_j^T| \, |w_j| = 1$$

We know that

$$(A + \varepsilon B) w_1(\varepsilon) = \lambda_1(\varepsilon) w_1(\varepsilon)$$

If we substitute the expressions for $\lambda_1(\varepsilon)$ and $w_1(\varepsilon)$ obtained above and use $Aw_1 = \lambda_1 w_1$, we have

$$\sum_{j=2}^{n} (\lambda_j - \lambda_1)t_{j1}w_j + Bw_1 = k_1 w_1$$

Multiplying across by v_j^T and simplifying, we obtain

$$k_1 = v_1^T Bw_1/v_1^T w_1 \qquad \text{for } j = 1$$

and

$$t_{j1} = (v_j^T Bw_1/(\lambda_1 - \lambda_j)v_1^T w_j) \qquad \text{for } j \neq 1$$

where, as noted above, k_1 is the first order perturbation of λ_1 and

$$|k_1| = (v_1^T Bw_1/v_1^T w_1) \leqslant [B]/v_1^T w_1$$

where $[B]$ is the sum of the elements of B.

Thus for sufficiently small ε the sensitivity of λ_1 depends primarily on $v_1^T w_1$. $v_1^T w_1$ might be arbitrarily small.

The first order perturbation of w_1 is given by

$$\Delta w_1 = \varepsilon \sum_{j=2}^{n} t_{j1}w_j$$

$$= \sum_{j=2}^{n} (v_j^T Bw_1/(\lambda_1 - \lambda_j)v_j^T w_j)w_j$$

$$= \sum_{j=2}^{n} (v_j^T(\Delta A)w_1/(\lambda_1 - \lambda_j)v_j^T w_j)w_j \quad \text{where} \quad \Delta A \equiv \varepsilon B$$

The eigenvector w_1 will be very sensitive to perturbations in A if λ_1 is close to any of the other eigenvalues. When λ_1 is well separated from the other eigenvalues and none of the $v_i^T w_i$ is small, the eigenvector w_1 corresponding to the eigenvalue λ_1 will be comparatively insensitive to perturbations in A. This is the case, for example, with skew-symmetric matrices ($a_{ji} = -a_{ij}$).

The $v_i^T w_i$ are interdependent in a way which precludes the possibility that just one $1/v_i^T w_i$ $i = 1, 2, \ldots, n$ is large. Thus if one of them is arbitrarily large, they are all arbitrarily large.

However, we want them to be small, i.e., near unity. To see this let

$$w_i = \sum_j c_{ij}v_j \qquad \text{and} \qquad v_j = \sum_j d_{ij}w_j$$

where $|w_i| = |v_i| = 1$, $i = 1, 2, \ldots, n$. It is easy to verify by substitution that

$$c_{ij} = w_j^T w_i/v_j^T w_j$$

and

$$d_{ij} = v_j^T v_i/v_j^T w_j$$

Then

$$v_i^T w_i = \sum_j d_{ij}w_j^T \sum_j c_{ij}v_j$$

$$= \sum_j (w_j^T w_i)(v_j^T v_i)/v_j^T w_j$$

for $i = j$

$$w_i^T w_i = v_i^T v_i = 1$$

and

$$v_i^T w_i = (v_i^T w_i)^{-1} + \sum_{j \neq i} (w_j^T w_i)(v_j^T v_i)(v_j^T w_j)^{-1}$$

Since

$$w_j^T w_i = \cos \theta_{ij} \quad \text{and} \quad v_j^T v_i = \cos \phi_{ij}$$

we have

$$|(v_i^T w_i)^{-1}| \leqslant |(v_i^T w_i)| + \sum_{j=i} |(v_j^T w_j)^{-1}|$$

$$\leqslant 1 + \sum_{j=i} |(v_j^T w_j)^{-1}|$$

which must be true for all $i = 1, 2, \ldots, n$. This proves that all the $v_i^T w_i$ must be of the same order.

We now show that for consistent matrices $(v_1^T w_1)^{-1}$ cannot be arbitrarily large. We have in the case of consistency

$$v_1^T = (1/w_{11}, \ldots, 1/w_{1n}) / \sum_{i=1}^{n} 1/w_{1i}$$

$$w_1^T = (w_{11}, \ldots, w_{1n})$$

Therefore

$$(v_1^T w_1)^{-1} = \left[(1/w_{11}, \ldots, 1/w_{1n})(w_{11}, \ldots, w_{1n})^T / \sum_{i=1}^{n} 1/w_{1i} \right]^{-1}$$

$$= \left[n / \sum_{i=1}^{n} 1/w_{1i} \right]^{-1} > n$$

since $n / \sum_{i=1}^{n} 1/w_{1i} < \sum_{i=1}^{n} w_{1i}/n$.

Now $(v_1^T w_1)^{-1}$ is minimized when all w_{1i} are equal since $\sum_{i=1}^{n} w_{1i} = 1$.

In practice, to keep $(v_1^T w_1)^{-1}$ near its minimum we must deal with relatively comparable activities so that no single w_{1i} is too small.

To improve consistency the number n must not be too large. On the other hand, if we are to make full use of the available information and produce results which are valid in practice, n should also not be too small.

If, for example, we reject the values $v_1^T w_1 \leqslant 0.1$, then we must have $n \leqslant 9$.

Under the assumption that the number of activities being compared is small and that they are relatively comparable, i.e., their weights differ by a multiple of their number, we can show that none of the components of w_1 is arbitrarily small and none of those of v_1 is arbitrarily small, and hence the scalar product of the two normalized vectors cannot be arbitrarily small.

With large inconsistency one cannot guarantee that none of the w_{1i} is arbitrarily small. Thus, near-consistency is a sufficient condition for stability. Note also that we need to keep the number of elements relatively small, so that the values of all the w_{1i} are of the same order.

The foregoing suggests that reciprocal matrices are the archtypical matrices which produce stable eigenvectors on small perturbations of the consistent case. It provides the *significant observation* that: to assure the stability of an estimate of an underlying ratio scale from pairwise comparisons, the mind must deal with a small number of elements that are relatively comparable. Social scientists experimentally arrived at this result long ago. They have observed that the number of elements should be 7 ± 2, but have not adequately recognized the need for the relative comparability requirement (Miller, 1956.)

Another useful observation is that if we assume "objects of the same magnitude" to differ by no more than a factor of 10, the scale used in the pairwise comparisons of comparable objects should have values somewhere between one and ten, otherwise we would compare things that are widely disparate in magnitude. This would produce relatively small values for some of the w_{1i}, thus disturbing the stability of the scale, i.e., the eigenvector would vary wildly, even if the judgmental values in the comparison matrix are only slightly changed.

Vargas' Formula

To determine how large the perturbation of an eigenvector would be if the original matrix is perturbed by a certain amount, my student, Luis Vargas (1979), has shown in his dissertation that if a reciprocal matrix A is perturbed by a reciprocal matrix P, using elementwise (Hadamard) multiplication (we write $A \circ P$), then the resulting matrix is reciprocal, the value of the perturbation Δw of the principal eigenvector w of A is given by

$$\Delta w = (\langle y, w \rangle^{-1} y - 1) \circ w$$

where $\langle \ , \ \rangle$ is the inner product of two vectors, and $y \circ w$ is the vector of elementwise multiplication of y by w. The vector y is the principal eigenvector of the matrix $E^* = E \circ P$ where E is obtained by dividing elementwise the entries of A with the corresponding entries of $W = (w_i/w_j)$.

Example 7-1

In developing the chair brightness example in Chap. 2, we had from the inverse square law of optics for the relative brightness of the chairs (0.6077, 0.2188, 0.1108, 0.0623). The matrix A below consists of the ratios of these values, and the matrix P is the first optics matrix given in Chap. 2 which is a perturbation of A. we have

$$A = \begin{bmatrix} 1 & 2.7 & 5.4 & 9.76 \\ 0.36 & 1 & 1.97 & 3.51 \\ 0.18 & 0.51 & 1 & 1.78 \\ 0.10 & 0.28 & 0.56 & 1 \end{bmatrix} \qquad P = \begin{bmatrix} 1 & 5 & 6 & 7 \\ 0.2 & 1 & 4 & 6 \\ 0.17 & 0.25 & 1 & 4 \\ 0.14 & 0.17 & 0.25 & 1 \end{bmatrix}$$

The eigenvector of A is given by $w = (0.6079, 0.2188, 0.1108, 0.0623)$, and $\lambda_{\max} = 4$. The eigenvector of P is given by $w^* = (0.6187, 0.2353, 0.1009, 0.04507)$ and $\lambda_{\max} = 4.391$. The perturbation matrix E is obtained by dividing A elementwise by P.

$$E = \begin{bmatrix} 1 & 1.80 & 1.09 & 0.71 \\ 0.56 & 1 & 2.03 & 1.71 \\ 0.91 & 0.49 & 1 & 2.25 \\ 1.39 & 0.58 & 0.44 & 1 \end{bmatrix}$$

The eigenvector of E is $y = (0.2730, 0.2885, 0.2444, 0.1941)$ and $\lambda_{\max} = 4.391$, the same as that of P. Finally, $\Delta w = (0.01076, 0.01651, -0.00985, -0.01722)$. It is easy to verify that $w + \Delta w = w^*$.

EIGHT

PRIORITIES IN SYSTEMS WITH FEEDBACK

8-1 INTRODUCTION

So far we have modeled our problems hierarchically from higher to lower levels or conversely and developed a theory for measuring the priority of elements in the different levels of the hierarchy with respect to elements in higher levels, and with respect to the overall purpose of the hierarchy.

We now turn to problems of systems in which the levels can no longer be labeled higher or lower. This is because a level may both dominate and be dominated, directly or indirectly, by other levels. Such systems are known as *systems with feedback*. They may be represented by a network where the nodes correspond to the levels or components. The elements in a node (or level) may influence some or all the elements of any other node. Our problem is to study priorities in such systems. We shall be mainly interested in systems in which all the elements in a node are taken together with respect to each element of another node—the counterpart of a complete hierarchy between levels.

At first look one wonders why we need to look at more complex entities than hierarchies since the latter provide a reasonable representation for the functions of a system. One may easily conceive of a situation too complex to be represented hierarchically; the simplicity offered by the hierarchy may be deceptive. Many social science problems fall into this category. For example, recent work in organization theory suggests forms of organizations already in practice that are not hierarchical. An individual can do many or all tasks in the various components of a production system (see Herbst, 1976).

We have analyzed some conflict problems both by means of a hierarchy and also, by a simple network in the form of a loop. Such a simple network is called a *holarchy*. The results were surprisingly close, thus demonstrating that both methods can lead to the same results at least in simple cases.

In the next section we study a method based on graph theoretic concepts for structuring a set of elements put together in a brainstorming session, or obtained in some other way, into a system with levels. There are other methods, which we do not study here, for grouping elements in the same cluster or level depending on the closeness of their measurement (see Johnson, 1967). However, for our purposes this would be putting the cart before the horse as we need to identify and group the elements prior to conducting measurement.

In Sec. 8-3 we examine the concept of priority measurement in feedback systems, and then introduce the supermatrix in Sec. 8-4 for carrying out such measurement. We show that hierarchical composition is a special case of this approach. In Sec. 8-5 we define impact and absolute priorities and their limiting values and give conditions for their existence and methods to obtain them for various types of systems. In Sec. 8-6 we give two examples illustrating some of these ideas.

8-2 REACHABILITY MATRIX IN STRUCTURING SYSTEMS

Suppose there is a set of elements to be considered in a contextual relation. The set of elements to be modeled may have been generated by deductive logic, causal observation, empirical data, brainstorming, or any combination of these sources. A very important part of this method resides in the fact that a redefinition of the original set of elements is a normal and important part of the process. The partial or full description of the system may take one of two different, but related, forms: (1) a binary matrix; (2) a directed graph (or network) for a geometric representation of relations. (See Malone, 1975; Waller, 1976; Warfield, 1973.)

Let us assume that a set of elements H has been identified. By means of the binary relation "is subordinated to" we can fill in the matrix B. A "yes" answer is associated with one and a "no" answer with zero. The way in which we decide to give a "yes" or "no" answer depends on the available data, judgment, or both. Thus, the binary matrix $B = \{b_{ij}\}$ is defined in the following way

$$b_{ij} = \left\{ \begin{matrix} 1 & \text{if } i \text{ is subordinated to } j \\ 0 & \text{otherwise} \end{matrix} \right\}$$

Once the matrix has been filled out, a transitivity check should be made to discover violations of that condition. If a transitivity violation is discovered, the elements involved must be examined to discover and correct the violation.

Having generated or been given B, we form the binary matrix $(I+B)$, where I is the identity matrix. It is possible to show that there is a smallest integer k such that

$$(I+B)^{k-1} \leqslant (I+B)^k = (I+B)^{k+1}$$

i.e., each element in the matrix $(I+B)^{k-1}$ is less than or equal to the corresponding element in the matrix $(I+B)^k$, and corresponding elements are equal in matrices $(I+B)^k$ and $(I+B)^{k+1}$.

The matrix in the right side of the above relation is called a reachability matrix.

Definition 8-1 The reachability matrix of a directed graph is defined as a binary matrix in which the entries are 1 if an element is reachable from another by a path, and 0 otherwise.

The use of a reachability matrix induces a partition of H into a set of levels and also induces a partition of each level into subsets, not necessarily disjoint.

Definition 8-2 An element h_j is said to be reachable from element h_i if a path can be traced on the directed graph from h_i to h_j.

Definition 8-3 An element h_j is called an antecedent of h_i if it is possible to reach h_i from h_j.

One can find from H two kinds of sets: a reachability set and a set of antecedent elements called an antecedent set. We denote these by $R(h_i)$ and $A(h_i)$, respectively.

$R(h_i)$ is the reachability set of the element $h_i \in H$, consisting of all elements of H lying on paths which originate at h_i. Thus

$$R(h_i) = \{h_i \in H \mid \text{the entry } (i, j) \text{ in } (I + B)^k \text{ is } 1\}$$

$A(h_i)$ is the antecedent set of the element $h_i \in H$ consisting of all elements of H lying on paths that include h_i but do not originate at h_i. Thus

$$A(h_i) = \{h_j \in H \mid \text{the entry } (j, i) \text{ in } (I + B)^k \text{ is } 1\}$$

The set of those elements h_i for which we have $A(h_i) = A(h_i) \cap R(h_i)$ are not reachable from any of the remaining elements of H, and hence can be denoted as a level of a hierarchy.

To build all levels, it is only necessary to apply the following iterative procedure:

(1) Form a table with entries: h_i, $R(h_i)$, $A(h_i)$, and $R(h_i) \cap A(h_i)$.
(2) Find the elements in the table which satisfy the condition

$$A(h_i) = R(h_i) \cap A(h_i)$$

These elements form the first level.
(3) Delete this set from the table and apply the second step, and so on.

This process, useful as it is, does not, for all contextual relations, usually lead to a hierarchy as we have defined it above. However, it leads to a network, thus:

The first level may not have only one element.
All elements in the first level are not necessarily connected only with elements in the second level.
Intermediate levels may have only one element.

Example 8-1

$$B = \begin{bmatrix} 0 & 0 & 0 & 0 & 1 & 0 & 0 \\ 1 & 1 & 1 & 0 & 0 & 0 & 0 \\ 1 & 0 & 1 & 0 & 0 & 0 & 0 \\ 1 & 0 & 0 & 1 & 0 & 0 & 0 \\ 0 & 1 & 1 & 1 & 1 & 0 & 0 \\ 0 & 1 & 1 & 1 & 0 & 1 & 0 \\ 0 & 1 & 1 & 1 & 0 & 0 & 1 \end{bmatrix}$$

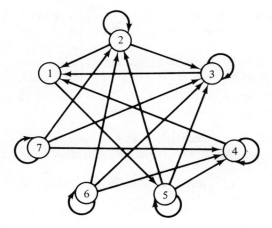

Figure 8-1

Form $(I+B)$ and the reachability matrix is

$$(I+B)^3 = \begin{bmatrix} 1 & 1 & 1 & 1 & 1 & 0 & 0 \\ 1 & 1 & 1 & 1 & 1 & 0 & 0 \\ 1 & 1 & 1 & 1 & 1 & 0 & 0 \\ 1 & 1 & 1 & 1 & 1 & 0 & 0 \\ 1 & 1 & 1 & 1 & 1 & 0 & 0 \\ 1 & 1 & 1 & 1 & 1 & 1 & 0 \\ 1 & 1 & 1 & 1 & 1 & 0 & 1 \end{bmatrix}$$

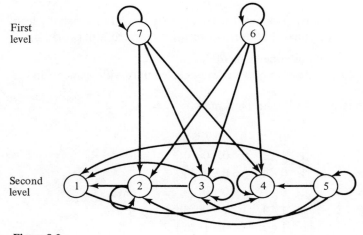

First level

Second level

Figure 8-2

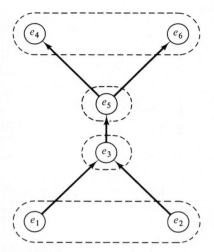

Figure 8-3

h_i	$R(h_i)$	$A(h_i)$	$A(h_i) \cap R(h_i)$
$i = 1, 2, 3, 4, 5$	1, 2, 3, 4, 5	1, 2, 3, 4, 5, 6, 7	1, 2, 3, 4, 5
h_6	1, 2, 3, 4, 5, 6	6	6
h_7	1, 2, 3, 4, 5, 7	7	7

Since $A(h_6)$ and $A(h_7)$ coincide with $A(h_6) \cap R(h_6)$ and $A(h_7) \cap R(h_7)$, respectively, the first is composed of the elements h_6 and h_7, i.e.,

First level: (h_6, h_7)

Deleting h_6 and h_7 from the table yields for the second level: $(h_1, h_2, h_3, h_4, h_5)$ whose table is easy to generate. Thus, we may write

$$H = \{1, 2, 3, 4, 5, 6, 7\} = \{6, 7, \quad 1, 2, 3, 4, 5\}$$

See Figs 8-1 and 8-2 for the network before and after the method is applied.

Applying the foregoing technique, we obtain what others have called a hierarchy but what we call a network with the two levels: (1) {6, 7}, and (2) {1, 2, 3, 4, 5}. This is also illustrated in Fig. 8-2.

Example 8-2 The following network of Fig. 8-3 is the result of applying the method to the matrix B.

$$B = \begin{array}{c} \\ e_1 \\ e_2 \\ e_3 \\ e_4 \\ e_5 \\ e_6 \end{array} \begin{array}{cccccc} e_1 & e_2 & e_3 & e_4 & e_5 & e_6 \\ \left[\begin{array}{cccccc} 0 & 0 & 1 & 0 & 0 & 0 \\ 0 & 0 & 1 & 0 & 0 & 0 \\ 0 & 0 & 0 & 0 & 1 & 0 \\ 0 & 0 & 0 & 0 & 0 & 0 \\ 0 & 0 & 0 & 1 & 0 & 1 \\ 0 & 0 & 0 & 0 & 0 & 0 \end{array}\right] \end{array}$$

To see this, we have

$$(I+B)^4 = \begin{bmatrix} 1 & 0 & 1 & 1 & 1 & 1 \\ 0 & 1 & 1 & 1 & 1 & 1 \\ 0 & 0 & 1 & 1 & 1 & 1 \\ 0 & 0 & 0 & 1 & 0 & 0 \\ 0 & 0 & 0 & 0 & 1 & 1 \\ 0 & 0 & 0 & 0 & 0 & 1 \end{bmatrix}$$

This is the reachability matrix since $(I+B)^5 = (I+B)^4$.

e_i	$R(e_i)$	$A(e_i)$	$R(e_i) \cap A(e_i)$
1	1, 3, 4, 5, 6	1	1
2	2, 3, 4, 5, 6	2	2
3	3, 4, 5, 6	1, 2, 3	3
4	4	1, 2, 3, 4, 5	4
5	4, 5, 6	1, 2, 3, 5	5
6	6	1, 2, 3, 5, 6	6

Thus, the first level is given by $\{e_1, e_2\}$ because $A(e_i) = A(e_i) \cap R(e_i)$, $i = 1, 2$.

e_i	$R(e_i)$	$A(e_i)$	$R(e_i) A(e_i)$
3	3, 4, 5, 6	3	3
4	3, 4	3, 4, 5	4
5	4, 5, 6	3, 5	5
6	6	3, 5, 6	6

The second level is given by $\{e_3\}$, the third level is given by $\{e_5\}$, and the fourth level is given by $\{e_4, e_6\}$.

8-3 PRIORITY MEASUREMENT IN FEEDBACK SYSTEMS

We now give a generalization of the Analytic Hierarchy Process to systems with feedback. These can be represented by a directed network.

In order to describe the kind of network we are dealing with, it is worth remembering that priority measurement of the elements in one level of a hierarchy with respect to the elements of an adjacent level gives rise to a directed bipartite graph. A hierarchy, all of whose bipartite graphs are complete, is known as a complete hierarchy. This is a special case of the general incomplete hierarchy with which we have also dealt. The bipartite graph describes the connections between all the elements of one level (a lower or subservient level, with respect to the elements of an adjacent—higher or dominant—level). If we simply wish to indicate which level

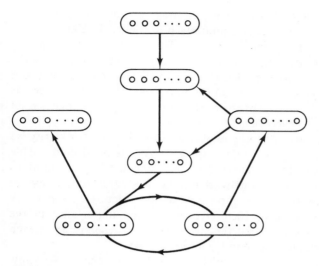

Figure 8-4

dominates which other level, it is sufficient to draw a single arc from the lower to the higher level. Thus a hierarchy may be represented by a chain or more precisely a path since there is direction on the arcs.

Now for a system, interaction between two components, just as in the case of levels of a hierarchy, may be characterized by a bipartite graph which may or may not be complete. Again for simplicity, we may simply use an arc to show the order of dominance between components. Here it may be feasible to draw arcs between two components going in opposite directions. It is even possible, in the case of interdependence to draw a loop at a component. This is also possible for a hierarchy. In any case the result of this simplified representation of the components of a system with respect to prioritization is a directed network. An illustration of such a network is given in Fig. 8-4. We need this representation for the construction of the supermatrix. Raising this matrix to powers gives priorities along paths of prescribed lengths in this representation.

We shall introduce a supermatrix to serve as a unifying framework for the study of priorities in hierarchies and in systems. A general composition principle for priorities in systems is developed of which our previous principle of hierarchical composition is shown to be a special case.

For a system with feedback, the notion of composition of priorities among components requires particular attention. In this case we do not usually have a top level as a frame of reference to carry out composition sequentially from level to level. The elements of the system can interact along more than a single path. In order for the measurement of priorities to be meaningful, there needs to be uniformity in how to consider all the paths. The priorities of any component of a system with respect to any other may be measured in a non-unique way along the paths and cycles which connect them. For example, along a cycle, priorities may be measured by going around the cycle only once, or twice, or more. It is useful to know, for a system, a set of ultimate, i.e., limiting, priorities of its elements as a whole. It may be necessary to do the latter when the elements do not cluster neatly into components. In that case we have a measure of the relative priorities of all the elements in the system with respect to each element of that system, leading to a stochastic matrix (a matrix whose columns sum to unity and all of whose elements are nonnegative). The columns are eigenvectors of pairwise comparison matrices of all the elements with respect to each element of the system.

The method of the supermatrix can be applied to this case, but for clarity we shall deal with the case where the system is decomposable. A system is decomposable if its elements can be aggregated into independent components whose interactions are represented by the arcs of a directed network (see Feraro, 1973). In this case we derive the priorities between adjacent components as in a hierarchy, separately develop priorities for the components themselves as to their importance in the system, and use these priorities to weight the eigenvectors corresponding to each component, thus again obtaining a column stochastic matrix.

Our study of systems with priorities parallels that of Markov chains. We show the correspondence between the two in order to adapt Markov chain results for systems. To save space, we shall be very brief and the work will be condensed. With the aid of a computer it is relatively easy to obtain estimates of limiting priorities by raising the supermatrix to high powers. However, this gives the right answer only if certain conditions are satisfied. For the general case, Markov chains provide an elegant theoretical prescription for what to do.

Terminology of correspondence between

Systems with priorities	Markov chains
System	System
Component (with one or more elements)	State
Impact or influence at time k	Transition at time k
Priority	Probability
Impact from a component	Transitions into a state
Impact priority (from the ith to the jth component)	Conditional transition probability
Composite priority	Absolute probability

8-4 THE SUPERMATRIX—GENERAL COMPOSITION OF PRIORITIES

Consider a system which has been decomposed into N clusters or components $C_1, C_2, \ldots, C_N$. Let the elements in component C_k be denoted by $e_{k1}, e_{k2}, \ldots, e_{kn_k}$ where n_k is their number. Our earlier discussion of impact between adjacent levels of a hierarchy enables us to construct the following type of matrix of impact measurement between the elements in corresponding components. Here we have assumed that every pair of components interact. If this is not the case somewhere, then the corresponding entry is zero.

The supermatrix plays a fundamental role in our subsequent development of priorities for systems. However, we first show how hierarchical composition may be derived by raising the supermatrix to powers.

As we explained earlier, we could construct pairwise comparison matrices to measure the priority of all the elements in the system with respect to each other as if there were no clustering of the elements into components. For example, we may be comparing industries and their impact on, or contribution to, every other industry. However, we prefer the component cluster approach for reasons of consistency as it is easier to give pairwise comparison judgments on a small set of elements. Thus we assume that we have the priority eigenvectors of the elements in a component with respect to the elements in another component (which may be the component itself). When this comparison makes no sense we use zeros for the eigenvector.

The supermatrix corresponding to the interaction between the components of a system may be displayed as follows.

$$
W = \begin{array}{c} \\ C_1 \\ \\ \\ C_2 \\ \\ \\ \vdots \\ \\ C_N \\ \\ \end{array}
\begin{array}{c}
e_{11} \\ e_{12} \\ \vdots \\ e_{1n_1} \\ e_{21} \\ e_{22} \\ \vdots \\ e_{2n_2} \\ \vdots \\ e_{N1} \\ e_{N2} \\ \vdots \\ e_{Nn_N}
\end{array}
\begin{bmatrix}
W_{11} & W_{12} & \cdots & W_{1N} \\
\\
W_{21} & W_{22} & \cdots & W_{2N} \\
\\
\vdots & \vdots & \vdots\vdots\vdots & \vdots \\
\\
W_{N1} & W_{N2} & \cdots & W_{NN}
\end{bmatrix}
$$

$$
\begin{array}{cccc}
C_1 & C_2 & \cdots & C_N \\
e_{11}e_{12}\cdots e_{1n_1} & e_{21}e_{22}\cdots e_{2n_2} & & e_{N1}e_{N2}\cdots e_{Nn_N}
\end{array}
$$

where the i, j block is given by

$$
W_{ij} = \begin{bmatrix}
w_{i1}^{(j1)} & w_{i1}^{(j2)} & \cdots & w_{i1}^{(jn_j)} \\
w_{i2}^{(j1)} & w_{i2}^{(j2)} & \cdots & w_{i2}^{(jn_j)} \\
\vdots & \vdots & \vdots\vdots\vdots & \vdots \\
w_{in_i}^{(j1)} & w_{in_i}^{(j2)} & \cdots & w_{in_i}^{(jn_j)}
\end{bmatrix}
$$

each of whose columns is an eigenvector which represents the impact of all the elements in the ith component on each of the elements in the jth component.

The supermatrix W is not stochastic (although each of its blocks is) unless we assume that its components have also been weighted according to the importance of their contribution to the system. See the examples at the end of the chapter for how to do this. The resulting priorities of the components can then be used to weight their corresponding elements in W which would transform W into a stochastic matrix. Hereafter, whenever we refer to W we assume that it has been weighted to a stochastic matrix.

It is useful to mention the following facts.

Theorem 8-1 A nonnegative matrix A is stochastic if and only if the vector $(1, 1, \ldots, 1)$ is a solution of $xA = x$ where unity is the principal eigenvalue of A. (See Gantmacher, 1960.)

Theorem 8-2 An n by n matrix A is irreducible if and only if its directed graph is strongly connected.

Theorem 8-3 A connected graph is strongly connected if and only if every arc belongs to at least one cycle.

Theorem 8-4 A matrix A is reducible if and only if at least one of the principal minors of order $n-1$ of the matrix $(\lambda_{\max} I - A)$ is zero.

Theorem 8-5 If A is a nonnegative irreducible matrix of order n we have $(I+A)^{n-1} > 0$.

(This says that if a graph is strongly connected and we add loops at every vertex the resulting matrix is primitive, i.e., any vertex is reachable from any other by a path of fixed length.)

Theorem 8-6 A strongly connected graph (with $n \geqslant 2$ vertices) with vertex matrix A is primitive if and only if the greatest common divisor of the lengths of all simple cycles is unity.

Theorem 8-7 A primitive (column) stochastic matrix A has the property that $\lim A^k$ has identical columns w (the unique equilibrium probability vector) and hence $w = Aw$ has a unique solution; in addition, for any initial probability vector $w^{(0)}$ ($w_i^{(0)} \geqslant 0$, $\sum w_i^{(0)} = 1$), $A^k w^{(0)} \to w$.

This is the key theorem for calculating priorities when the matrix is primitive.

The supermatrix of a hierarchy has the following form

$$W = \begin{bmatrix} 0 & 0 & 0 & \cdot & \cdot & \cdot & 0 & 0 \\ W_{21} & 0 & 0 & \cdot & \cdot & \cdot & 0 & 0 \\ 0 & W_{32} & 0 & \cdot & \cdot & \cdot & 0 & 0 \\ \cdot & \cdot & \cdot & \cdot & \cdot & & \cdot & \cdot \\ \cdot & \cdot & \cdot & \cdot & \cdot & & \cdot & \cdot \\ \cdot & \cdot & \cdot & \cdot & \cdot & W_{n-1,n-2} & \cdot & \cdot \\ 0 & 0 & 0 & \cdot & \cdot & \cdot & W_{n,n-1} & I \end{bmatrix}$$

This matrix has the stable form

$$W^k = \begin{bmatrix} 0 & 0 & \cdots & 0 & 0 & 0 \\ 0 & 0 & \cdots & 0 & 0 & 0 \\ \vdots & \vdots & \vdots\vdots & \vdots & \vdots & \vdots \\ 0 & 0 & \cdots & 0 & 0 & 0 \\ W_{n,n-1}W_{n-1,n-2}\cdots W_{32}W_{21} & W_{n,n-1}W_{n-1,n-2}\cdots W_{32} & \cdots & W_{n,n-1}W_{n-1,n-2} & W_{n,n-1} & I \end{bmatrix}$$

for all $k \geqslant n-1$. Each coefficient in the last row gives the composite priority impact of the last component on each of the remaining components. Note that the principle of hierarchical composition appears in the $(n, 1)$ position as the impact of the nth component on the first. The nth component drives the hierarchy and is the counterpart of an absorbing state in a Markov chain. It is a component of elements which diffuse or are a source of priority impacts. The essence of the above is summarized by the *Principle of Hierarchical Composition:*

The composite vector of a hierarchy of n levels is the entry in the $(n, 1)$ position of W^{k-1}, $k \geqslant n-1$.

Now let us look briefly at what happens to cycles. Here repeated powers of a regular set of components reveals lack of stability. For example for a three component cycle we have

$$W = \begin{bmatrix} 0 & W_{12} & 0 \\ 0 & 0 & W_{23} \\ W_{31} & 0 & 0 \end{bmatrix}; \quad W^2 = \begin{bmatrix} 0 & 0 & W_{12}W_{23} \\ W_{23}W_{31} & 0 & 0 \\ 0 & W_{31}W_{12} & 0 \end{bmatrix}$$

$$W^3 = \begin{bmatrix} W_{12}W_{23}W_{31} & 0 & 0 \\ 0 & W_{23}W_{31}W_{12} & 0 \\ 0 & 0 & W_{31}W_{12}W_{23} \end{bmatrix}$$

$$W^{3k} = \begin{bmatrix} (W_{12}W_{23}W_{31})^k & 0 & 0 \\ 0 & (W_{23}W_{31}W_{12})^k & 0 \\ 0 & 0 & (W_{31}W_{12}W_{23})^k \end{bmatrix}$$

$$W^{3k+1} = \begin{bmatrix} 0 & (W_{12}W_{23}W_{31})^k W_{12} & 0 \\ 0 & 0 & (W_{23}W_{31}W_{12})^k W_{23} \\ (W_{31}W_{12}W_{23})^k W_{31} & 0 & 0 \end{bmatrix}$$

$$W^{3k+2} =$$
$$\begin{bmatrix} 0 & 0 & (W_{12}W_{23}W_{31})^k W_{12}W_{23} \\ (W_{23}W_{31}W_{12})^k W_{23}W_{31} & 0 & 0 \\ 0 & (W_{31}W_{12}W_{23})^k W_{31}W_{12} & 0 \end{bmatrix}$$

Since the product of stochastic matrices is stochastic and the limit of powers of a stochastic matrix, all of whose elements are positive is a matrix with identical columns, multiplying this limiting matrix on the right by any stochastic matrix leaves the former invariant. The result of a cycle is that in the limit along different subsequences of powers of W, the impact of each component on every other component (including the component itself) is given by the same expression, i.e., by its limiting priority with respect to its neighboring component.

Starting with the ith component of a cycle we index adjacent components successively by $i, i_1, i_2, \ldots, i_n, i$. The following is in accordance with our intuitive expectations.

In a simple cycle of components, the limiting impact priority of the ith component is given by the eigenvector solution of the problem $W_{ii_1}x = x$. To see this, we note from the previous remark that we have for the impact of the ith component (by ignoring the stochastic matrices on the right as they do not affect the result)

$$\lim_{k \to \infty} (W_{ii_1}W_{i_1 i_2} \cdots W_{i_n i})^k = \lim_{k \to \infty} W_{ii_1}^k W_{i_1 i_2}^k \cdots W_{i_n i}^k$$

$$= \lim_{k \to \infty} W_{ii_1}^k$$

which is a stochastic matrix with identical columns. Thus in the limit the priority of a component in a cycle is given by the eigenvector corresponding to the largest eigenvalue (which is unity for a stochastic matrix) of its impact matrix.

8-5 IMPACT AND ABSOLUTE PRIORITIES

We are interested in two types of priorities. Those that give the influence or impact of one element on any other element in the system are known as the impact priorities. We are also interested in the absolute priority of any element regardless of which elements it influences. Generally we seek limiting values of these two kinds of priorities. Calculation of these priorities shows where existing trends might lead if there is no change in preferences which affects the priorities. By experimenting with the process of modifying priorities and noting their limiting trends, we may be able to steer a system towards a more desired outcome.

Now for the formal definitions. If w_{ij} is the impact priority of the ith element on the jth element in the system then (see Feller, 1950; Isaacson and Madsen, 1976; and Rosenblatt, 1962)

$$w_{ij}^{(1)} = w_{ij}$$

$$w_{ij}^{(2)} = \sum_m w_{im} w_{mj}$$

$$w_{ij}^{(k+1)} = \sum_m w_{im} w_{mj}^{(k)}$$

$$w_{ij}^{(h+k)} = \sum_m w_{im}^{(h)} w_{mj}^{(k)}$$

The sum of the impact priorities along all possible paths from a given element gives the priority of an element. This amounts to raising the matrix W to powers. (The last expression is equivalent to $W^{h+k} = W^h W^k$.)

Given that the initial priority of the ith element is $w_i^{(0)}$, we have the following absolute priority of the jth element in paths of length $k \neq 0$

$$w_j^{(k)} = \sum_i w_i^{(0)} w_{ij}^{(k)}$$

The problem is to find the limiting impact priority (LIP) matrix W^∞ and the limiting absolute priority (LAP) vector w^∞ as $k \to \infty$. (For a priority system we may also be interested in determining priorities for finite values of k. That does not present problems of existence as does the limiting case.) Of particular interest is to determine when the LAP priority is independent of the initial priorities $w_i^{(0)}$. Such independence is called the *ergodicity* of the system.

The following is a classification of elements useful in characterizing a system. The reader may wish to go on to the actual discussion of existence and construction of LIP and LAP solutions.

The element j can be reached from the element i if for some integer $k \geqslant 1$, $w_{ij}^{(k)} > 0$ where $W^k = (w_{ij}^{(k)})$. Here W^k gives the k-*reach* of each element. A subset of elements C of a system is *closed* (opposite definition to that for Markov chains) if $W_{ji}^{(k)} = 0$ whenever i is in C and j is not in C. It follows that no element in C can be reached from any element not in C. The subset C is minimal if it contains no proper closed subset of elements. A set of elements which forms a minimal closed subset corresponds to an irreducible matrix. If the matrix of an entire system or subsystem is irreducible, the system or subsystem itself is called irreducible. A system is called decomposable if it has two or more closed sets.

If we *initially* start with the jth element for some fixed j and denote its first impact on itself in a path of length $k \geqslant 1$ by $f_j^{(k)}$, we have $f_j^{(1)} = w_{jj}^{(1)}, f_j^{(2)} = w_{jj}^{(2)} - f_j^{(1)} w_{jj}^{(1)} \dots f_j^{(k)} = w_{jj}^{(k)} - f_j^{(1)} w_{jj}^{(k-1)} - \dots - f_j^{(k-1)} w_{jj}^{(1)}$ and

$$f_j = \sum_{k=1}^{\infty} f_j^{(k)}$$

gives the cumulative impact of j on itself. The *mean* impact (of j on itself) is given by

$$u_j = \sum_{k=0}^{\infty} k f_j^{(k)}$$

According to priority influence we have (the new terms introduced below are essential, as we are not dealing with time transitions)

(1) If $f_j = 1$, j is called an *enduring* (recurrent) element. Thus an element is enduring if the sum of its impact priorities on itself in a single step (by a loop) in two steps (through a cycle involving one other element), in three steps involving two other elements, etc. is equal to unity. (2) If $f_j < 1$, j is called *transitory* (transient). An element j that is either enduring or transitory is called *cyclic* (periodic) with cyclicity c if u_j has values $c, 2c, 3c, \ldots$ where c is the greatest integer *greater than* unity with this property ($w_{ij}^{(k)} = 0$ where k is not divisible by c). An enduring element j for which u_j is infinite is called *fading* (null). An enduring element j that is neither cyclic nor fading (i.e., $u_j < \infty$) is called *sustaining* (ergodic).

For either a transitory or a fading element j, $w_{ij}^{(k)} \to 0$ for every i. If one element in an irreducible subsystem is cyclic with cyclicity c, all the elements in that subsystem are cyclic with cyclicity c. It is known that if j is a sustaining element, then as $k \to \infty$, $w_{jj}^{(k)} \to 1/u_j$; j is a fading element if this number is zero and sustaining if it is positive. Either all the elements of an irreducible subsystem are all transitory or all enduring and the system itself is called transitory or enduring, respectively.

REMARK The following expression always exists whether a system is irreducible or not. In the former case its values are known and are as indicated

$$\lim_{m \to \infty} \sum_{k=0}^{m-1} w_{ij}^{(k)} = \begin{cases} 0 & \text{if } i \text{ and } j \text{ are transitory} \\ 1/u_j & \text{if } i \text{ and } j \text{ are enduring} \end{cases}$$

All finite systems of elements must have at least one sustaining element which generates a closed irreducible subset of elements. Since the enduring elements of a finite system are all sustaining the block (or component) thus generated is called sustaining.

If j is cyclic with cyclicity $c > 1$ then

$$w_{jj}^{(k)} = 0$$

if k is not a multiple of c and

$$w_{jj}^{(m)} \to \frac{c}{u_j}$$

as $m \to \infty$; $k = mc$, m positive and c the largest integer for which $k = mc$ holds.

We had said earlier that reducibility and primitivity play an important role in proving the existence of LIP and LAP. We now give a few basic facts relating these concepts which will be useful in the ensuing discussion.

A nonnegative irreducible matrix is primitive if it has a unique principal eigenvalue. If the matrix has another eigenvalue with the same modulus as the principal eigenvalue, it is called imprimitive.

If the principal eigenvalue has multiplicity greater than unity (equal to unity), but there are no other eigenvalues of the same modulus as the principal eigenvalue then the matrix is called proper (regular).

A primitive matrix is always regular and hence proper but not conversely, e.g., the identity matrix which has unity as an eigenvalue of multiplicity equal to the order of the matrix. A matrix is proper if and only if in the normal form, the isolated blocks are primitive. For a regular matrix the number of isolated blocks is unity.

We note that if all the entries of W are positive, we have a primitive matrix and the theorem on stochastic primitive matrices applies, both LIP and LAP exist. LIP and LAP are the same and are given by the solution of the eigenvalue problem $Ww = w$. Actually w is any column of $\lim_{k \to \infty} W^k$. The same result is true if W is a primitive matrix.

In general the nonnegative matrix W may have some zeros. In that case it is either an irreducible or a reducible matrix. If it is irreducible then it is either primitive in which case the above discussion applies, or it is imprimitive. In the latter case it has a number s of eigenvalues (called the index of imprimitivity) that are not equal to unity whose moduli are equal to unity. This number plays an important role in the solution of the general case from which we can also obtain the solution to this case. It is sufficient to point out here that $W, W_1^2, \ldots, W^{s-1}$ are all not proper and multiples of these matrices tend toward periodic repetition. The system is cyclic with cyclicity s.

REMARK The system is acyclic, cyclic, irreducible, reducible, depending on whether the corresponding matrix W is primitive, imprimitive, irreducible, reducible.

If W is nonnegative and reducible then it is reduced to the normal form. If the isolated blocks are primitive (they are said to correspond to essential components and the residual matrices correspond to inessential components). The system is by definition called proper and LIP and LAP exist (see Gantmacher, 1960, p. 112).

IMPORTANT REMARK When our column stochastic matrix is reducible its essential components drive the system since they are "sources" or impact-priority-diffusing components as opposed to "sinks" or transition-probability-absorbing states of a Markov chain. In any diagram, except for loops, arrows initiate from and none terminate at such components.

The solution for LIP is given by

$$W^\infty \equiv \lim_{k \to \infty} W^k = \frac{(I-W)^{-1}\Psi(1)}{\Psi'(1)}$$

where $\Psi(\lambda)$ is the minimum polynomial of W and $\Psi'(\lambda)$ is its first derivative with respect to λ. Each column of W^∞ is a characteristic vector of W corresponding to $\lambda_{max} = 1$. If $\lambda_{max} = 1$ is simple, i.e., W is regular, $\Psi(\lambda)$ may be replaced by $\Delta(\lambda)$ the characteristic polynomial of W. LAP is obtained as

$$w^\infty = W^\infty w^{(0)}$$

if W is proper, and as the eigenvector solution of

$$Ww^\infty = w^\infty$$

if W is regular.

REMARK One can show that the matrices of W^∞ corresponding to essential components are positive and those to priority impacts from essential to inessential components are also positive (these are given by the product $(I-Q)^{-1} (R_1, R_2, \ldots, R_k)^T$ of the normal form; see Chap. 7.) Only impacts from inessential to inessential or from inessential to essential components are zero.

Finally, if not all isolated blocks are primitive then each has an index of imprimitivity as we pointed out earlier. We consider the least common multiple of these which is the cyclicity c of the system. Using the powers of W, LIP is given by

$$\tilde{W} = \frac{1}{c}(I + W + \cdots W^{c-1})(W^c)^\infty$$

$$= \frac{1}{c}(1 - W^c)(1 - W)^{-1}(W^c)^\infty$$

and LAP is given by

$$w = \tilde{W}w^{(0)}$$

Both $\tilde{W}$ and w are called the mean LIP and mean LAP, respectively.

If there is a single isolated block, then the mean LAP are independent of the initial priorities and are uniquely determined by the solution of

$$Ww = w$$

This is precisely the case of an irreducible imprimitive system.

8-6 EXAMPLES

The two examples below are given for two reasons: the first is to show how the supermatrix works, and the second is to show how the method may be applied in the social sciences. Of course, to formulate the questions for judgment takes a good deal of background preparation by experts in the field to present the relevant factors, and to be sure that there is no confusion or overlap in concepts being compared. As we shall see, interpretation of increasing powers of W have practical importance.

In both cases, the problem is identified very briefly, together with a diagram representing the system and its connections. Pairwise comparison matrices of which there are 68 for the elements and 1 for the components in the first example, and 33 for the elements and 4 for the components in the second example, are not given except for these last 4.

The supermatrix is then developed in two stages. First the blocks of eigenvectors are filled. After developing priorities for the components and using their weights in the matrix, the final column stochastic supermatrix is obtained. It is important to note that the column sums must be precisely one, otherwise there might be divergence to infinity or convergence to zero.

How to weight the components is an important subject. In general, each block in a column corresponding to a component in the supermatrix is weighted by the respective eigenvector coefficient arising from the pairwise comparison matrix involving those components (with nonzero block entries in that column of blocks) which have an impact on the column component in question. (In the diagrams these components have arrows directed from them to the given column component.)

In both examples we are interested in approximations to LIP by raising W to large powers. In this age of the computer my students (N. Bahmani, who worked on the first example, and D. Chalson and S. Parker who worked on the second), preferred to use it to raise the matrix to large powers than to use the formulas for W^∞ given in the theory of Sec. 8-5.

In the first example, we give the unweighted supermatrix. It corresponds to a complete graph on the components of the system. Hence it is positive and a fortiori primitive. For LIP all the columns of W^∞ are the same and the LAP vector is any of these columns. It is sufficient to give an approximation to LAP from W^{100}. For the convenience of the reader, we have placed this solution vector next to the initial definitions of the factors and components.

In the second example we give the blocks of the supermatrix before weighting. This is followed by the pairwise comparison matrices of the components and then by the supermatrix W resulting from weighting each block as described above. We finally give W^{89} as an approximation to W^∞.

We note that in our work on terrorism with J. P. Bennett, we have shown that a properly constructed hierarchy can give results close to those of a system with feedback.

Child Upbringing Example

Our first example is about child upbringing. A child comes under the influence of a number of forces in his early years. We would like to establish priorities for these influences. As there is feedback in the interaction of these forces, the problem can be represented as a network. The main groupings of the sources of influence and their relevant characteristics are as shown in Table 8-1.

Table 8-1

Components		Factors		Priorities (from the lap approximation)
C_1	Father (Fa)	W	Work	0.024
		R_f	Recreation	0.022
		Re_f	Religion	0.019
		Ed	Education	0.044
		RWC	Relationship with wife and children	0.020
C_2	Mother (Mo)	H	Home	0.024
		R_m	Recreation	0.026
		RE_m	Religion	0.027
		PI	Professional interest	0.025
		TC	Take care of children	0.028
		RHC	Relationship with husband and children	0.021
C_3	Children (Ch)	RP	Relationship with parent	0.013
		S	School	0.020
		PL	Play	0.012
		PE	Parent education	0.026
C_4	Outside (OT)	So	School	0.120
		PR	Peer	0.074
		ME	Mass media	0.090
		C	Culture	0.360

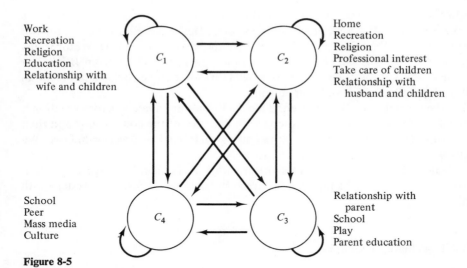

Work
Recreation
Religion
Education
Relationship with
    wife and children

Home
Recreation
Religion
Professional interest
Take care of children
Relationship with
    husband and children

School
Peer
Mass media
Culture

Relationship with
    parent
School
Play
Parent education

Figure 8-5

The judgments for the pairwise comparison matrices were provided by a group of students who were particularly interested in the subject. It is noteworthy that these students were from overseas and that their judgments may differ from those which would have been given by a group of Americans. It does not seem reasonable to dwell on the interpretation of the results, other than to point out that according to this the dominant factors, which include culture and school lie in the "Outside" component.

The network of interactions is illustrated in Fig. 8-5.

Steel Industry Example

In this example we consider the components of the steel trading system and their factors to look for changes in priority from the present. The factors and components are shown in Fig. 8-6, page 222.

Efficiency is measured by production performance and is closely related to modern technology.

Surplus production: Japan has produced large amounts in excess of its consumption and hence can sell steel cheaply.

Unused capacity results from declining demand. To keep the labor force employed and destroy competition the product may be sold at lower than cost price.

Government attitude is against inflation caused by steel price rises lobbied for by industry.

Government trade policy expresses reluctance to protect domestic industry.

Price of capital: low interest rates to steel industry in foreign countries and high interest rates in the U.S. causing indirect rise in other costs.

The unweighted supermatrix is given in Table 8-3.

In order to weight the supermatrix (to make it column-stochastic) we weight the components according to their impact on each column of blocks. Thus the row components with nonzero entries for their blocks in that column block are compared according to their impact on the component of that column block. Then each block is weighted by the eigenvector coefficient corresponding to the component in that row. This process gives rise to the following four pairwise comparison matrices.

		M	S	F	D	Eigenvector
Block	M	1	0.125	0.167	0.333	0.047
column	S	8	1	3	6	0.568
M	F	6	0.333	1	5	0.293
	D	3	0.167	0.200	1	0.092

		S	P	Eigenvector
Block	S	1	0.333	0.250
column	P	3	1	0.750
S				

		S	U	F	Eigenvector
Block	S	1	0.143	0.333	0.081
column	U	7	1	5	0.731
U	F	3	0.20	1	0.188

		U	F	Eigenvector
Block	U	1	4	0.8
column	F	0.25	1	0.2
F				

Weighting the supermatrix by the above weights we have the following column stochastic matrix of Table 8-4 and its 89th power of Table 8-5.

Raising the matrix to powers gives the long-term relative influences of the elements on each other. What we can first say is that price and demand are the driving factors in the steel industry. We note as the matrix is raised to higher powers, that the importance of the price of capital on U.S. market share rises (shown in matrices not all included here) from 0 to 0.43, thus making it expensive to invest in the domestic steel industry, indicating a threat to its future expansion or even survival. The importance of unused capacity decreases to 0 as do all transitory elements in the system.

Another more obvious conclusion is that the influence of demand within the steel industry does not change over the long run. Capital prices have the greatest overall effect on the model. As expected, the price of capital would increase in priority when compared with other input prices because the cost of capital has a large influence on the other input prices. This is what actually happens in the long run, but in the short run other elements have a larger influence on relative priorities.

Table 8-2 The unweighted supermatrix for the child upbringing example

		C_1					C_2						C_3				C_4			
		W	R	RE	ED	RWC	H	R	RE	PI	TC	RHC	RP	S	PL	PE	SO	PR	ME	C
C_1	W	0.222	0.209	0.212	0.208	0.257	0.224	0.224	0.150	0.228	0.198	0.213	0.198	0.170	0.123	0.372	0.246	0.149	0.157	0.143
	R	0.095	0.125	0.140	0.170	0.220	0.151	0.224	0.150	0.170	0.232	0.111	0.111	0.144	0.324	0.148	0.150	0.186	0.142	0.178
	RE	0.100	0.145	0.147	0.100	0.110	0.172	0.149	0.344	0.172	0.174	0.122	0.110	0.127	0.132	0.089	0.126	0.130	0.142	0.161
	ED	0.462	0.396	0.374	0.382	0.194	0.229	0.254	0.161	0.260	0.198	0.245	0.260	0.401	0.303	0.297	0.353	0.375	0.423	0.357
	RWC	0.121	0.125	0.127	0.140	0.219	0.224	0.149	0.105	0.170	0.198	0.309	0.314	0.158	0.118	0.094	0.125	0.160	0.136	0.161
C_2	H	0.216	0.185	0.144	0.142	0.145	0.195	0.195	0.220	0.168	0.283	0.200	0.257	0.249	0.148	0.116	0.203	0.131	0.164	0.110
	R	0.105	0.190	0.144	0.162	0.111	0.130	0.137	0.122	0.102	0.122	0.113	0.115	0.124	0.174	0.219	0.132	0.207	0.213	0.198
	RE	0.122	0.148	0.260	0.129	0.127	0.155	0.088	0.122	0.113	0.103	0.113	0.103	0.124	0.111	0.109	0.129	0.145	0.147	0.282
	PI	0.278	0.170	0.144	0.283	0.163	0.135	0.143	0.189	0.178	0.140	0.161	0.139	0.142	0.156	0.268	0.210	0.168	0.147	0.124
	TC	0.140	0.146	0.143	0.142	0.226	0.215	0.239	0.192	0.246	0.221	0.253	0.244	0.249	0.300	0.178	0.165	0.188	0.164	0.176
	RHC	0.139	0.161	0.165	0.142	0.225	0.170	0.198	0.155	0.193	0.131	0.160	0.142	0.112	0.111	0.110	0.161	0.162	0.165	0.110
C_3	RP	0.132	0.141	0.250	0.087	0.204	0.278	0.167	0.250	0.183	0.247	0.333	0.236	0.140	0.143	0.166	0.177	0.167	0.147	0.160
	S	0.151	0.140	0.250	0.246	0.246	0.163	0.167	0.250	0.282	0.209	0.167	0.200	0.103	0.270	0.410	0.195	0.333	0.390	0.354
	PL	0132	0.263	0.250	0.133	0.204	0.163	0.333	0.250	0.164	0.198	0.167	0.095	0.117	0.162	0.103	0.195	0.167	0.159	0.131
	PE	0.585	0.456	0.250	0.534	0.346	0.396	0.333	0.250	0.371	0.346	0.333	0.469	0.340	0.425	0.321	0.433	0.333	0.304	0.355
C_4	SO	0.290	0.151	0.135	0.209	0.186	0.220	0.165	0.140	0.343	0.162	0.200	0.186	0.225	0.140	0.262	0.341	0.220	0.177	0.161
	PR	0.108	0.240	0.129	0.095	0.166	0.121	0.200	0.131	0.150	0.162	0.200	0.156	0.124	0.263	0.140	0.109	0.121	0.114	0.080
	ME	0.101	0.085	0.129	0.103	0.156	0.121	0.140	0.140	0.110	0.151	0.200	0.166	0.135	0.140	0.140	0.118	0.121	0.188	0.143
	C	0.501	0.424	0.607	0.593	0.492	0.538	0.495	0.589	0.397	0.525	0.400	0.492	0.516	0.457	0.458	0.532	0.538	0.521	0.616

Table 8-3 The unweighted supermatrix for the steel industry example

		M		S			U		F				P				D
		M_a	M_f	S_u	S_e	S_p	U_a	U_p	F_s	F_e	F_c	F_p	P_k	P_e	P'	P_r	D
M	M_a	0.5	0.5	0			0		0				0				0
	M_f	0.5	0.5														
S	S_u	0.09	0.09	0.43	0.64	0.08	0.58	0.73	0				0				0
	S_e	0.09	0.09	0.43	0.10	0.23	0.11	0.10									
	S_p	0.82	0.82	0.14	0.26	0.69	0.31	0.17									
U	U_a	0		0			0.9	0.17	0.1	0.1	0.1	0.1	0				0
	U_p						0.1	0.83	0.9	0.9	0.9	0.9					
F	F_s	0.28	0.28	0			0.21	0.31	0.06	0.39	0.26	0.32	0				0
	F_e	0.06	0.06				0.43	0.08	0.18	0.07	0.56	0.13					
	F_c	0.06	0.06				0.05	0.08	0.20	0.39	0.07	0.50					
	F_p	0.60	0.60				0.21	0.53	0.56	0.15	0.11	0.05					
P	P_r	0		0.05	0.05	0.06	0		0				0.12	0.12	0.04	0.04	0
	P_e			0.57	0.31	0.56							0.06	0.06	0.16	0.16	
	P'			0.28	0.11	0.26							0.26	0.26	0.57	0.23	
	P_k			0.10	0.53	0.12							0.56	0.56	0.23	0.57	
D	D	1	1	0			0		0				0				1

Table 8-4 The weighted supermatrix

	M	M	S	S	S	U	U	F	F	F	F	P	P	P	P	D
M	0.03	0.03	0.00	0.00	0.00	0.00	0.00	0.00	0.00	0.00	0.00	0.00	0.00	0.00	0.00	0.00
	0.03	0.03	0.00	0.00	0.00	0.00	0.00	0.00	0.00	0.00	0.00	0.00	0.00	0.00	0.00	0.00
S	0.05	0.05	0.11	0.16	0.02	0.06	0.05	0.00	0.00	0.00	0.00	0.00	0.00	0.00	0.00	0.00
	0.05	0.05	0.11	0.03	0.06	0.01	0.01	0.00	0.00	0.00	0.00	0.00	0.00	0.00	0.00	0.00
	0.47	0.47	0.04	0.06	0.17	0.01	0.03	0.00	0.00	0.00	0.00	0.00	0.00	0.00	0.00	0.00
U	0.00	0.00	0.00	0.00	0.00	0.12	0.66	0.08	0.08	0.08	0.08	0.00	0.00	0.00	0.00	0.00
	0.00	0.00	0.00	0.00	0.00	0.61	0.07	0.72	0.72	0.72	0.72	0.00	0.00	0.00	0.00	0.00
F	0.08	0.08	0.00	0.00	0.00	0.06	0.04	0.01	0.08	0.05	0.06	0.00	0.00	0.00	0.00	0.00
	0.02	0.02	0.00	0.00	0.00	0.02	0.10	0.04	0.01	0.11	0.03	0.00	0.00	0.00	0.00	0.00
	0.02	0.02	0.00	0.00	0.00	0.02	0.01	0.04	0.08	0.01	0.10	0.00	0.00	0.00	0.00	0.00
	0.17	0.17	0.00	0.00	0.00	0.10	0.04	0.11	0.03	0.02	0.01	0.00	0.00	0.00	0.00	0.00
P	0.00	0.00	0.04	0.04	0.05	0.00	0.00	0.00	0.00	0.00	0.00	0.12	0.12	0.04	0.04	0.00
	0.00	0.00	0.43	0.23	0.42	0.00	0.00	0.00	0.00	0.00	0.00	0.06	0.06	0.16	0.16	0.00
	0.00	0.00	0.21	0.08	0.20	0.00	0.00	0.00	0.00	0.00	0.00	0.26	0.26	0.57	0.23	0.00
	0.00	0.00	0.08	0.40	0.09	0.00	0.00	0.00	0.00	0.00	0.00	0.56	0.56	0.23	0.57	0.00
D	0.09	0.09	0.00	0.00	0.00	0.00	0.00	0.00	0.00	0.00	0.00	0.00	0.00	0.00	0.00	1.00

Table 8-5 Its 89th power

	M			S			U			F			P			D
M ⎰	0.00	0.00	0.00	0.00	0.00	0.00	0.00	0.00	0.00	0.00	0.00	0.00	0.00	0.00	0.00	0.00
⎱	0.00	0.00	0.00	0.00	0.00	0.00	0.00	0.00	0.00	0.00	0.00	0.00	0.00	0.00	0.00	0.00
S ⎰	0.00	0.00	0.00	0.00	0.00	0.00	0.00	0.00	0.00	0.00	0.00	0.00	0.00	0.00	0.00	0.00
⎱	0.00	0.00	0.00	0.00	0.00	0.00	0.00	0.00	0.00	0.00	0.00	0.00	0.00	0.00	0.00	0.00
U ⎰	0.00	0.00	0.00	0.00	0.00	0.00	0.00	0.00	0.00	0.00	0.00	0.00	0.00	0.00	0.00	0.00
⎱	0.00	0.00	0.00	0.00	0.00	0.00	0.00	0.00	0.00	0.00	0.00	0.00	0.00	0.00	0.00	0.00
F ⎰	0.00	0.00	0.00	0.00	0.00	0.00	0.00	0.00	0.00	0.00	0.00	0.00	0.00	0.00	0.00	0.00
⎱	0.00	0.00	0.00	0.00	0.00	0.00	0.00	0.00	0.00	0.00	0.00	0.00	0.00	0.00	0.00	0.00
P ⎰	0.05	0.05	0.06	0.06	0.06	0.06	0.06	0.06	0.06	0.06	0.06	0.06	0.06	0.06	0.06	0.00
⎪	0.14	0.13	0.14	0.14	0.14	0.14	0.16	0.16	0.16	0.16	0.16	0.16	0.14	0.14	0.14	0.00
⎪	0.34	0.34	0.37	0.36	0.36	0.36	0.41	0.41	0.41	0.41	0.41	0.41	0.36	0.36	0.36	0.00
⎱	**0.43**	0.43	0.46	0.45	0.45	0.45	0.51	0.51	0.51	0.51	0.51	0.51	0.45	0.45	0.45	0.00
D	0.10	0.09	0.00	0.00	0.00	0.00	0.00	0.00	0.00	0.00	0.00	0.00	0.00	0.00	0.00	1.00

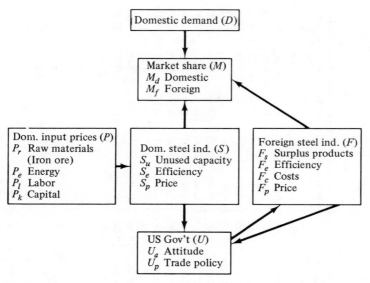

Figure 8-6

REMARK It may be helpful to conclude this Chapter by pointing out that dependence among the elements of a given component of a system may be computed as indicated in Chapter 5. The result is then weighted by the independence priorities computed in this chapter.

SCALING AND MULTICRITERIAN METHODS

9-1 INTRODUCTION

Our approach to prioritization and hierarchies has an interface with scaling methods, utility theory, and with multicriterion methods. Principal component analysis, logarithmic least squares, and the method of least squares are also discussed. Over several rewritings the chapter had to be shortened to nearly skeletal size. The reader should consult the references for additional readings.

9-2 SCALES AND MEASUREMENT

Fundamental measurement is the construction of scales by mapping an *empirical* relational system isomorphically into a *numerical* relational system. Derived measurement derives a new scale from other given scales. A good example of a derived scale is the scale for density derived from the fundamental scales for mass and volume.

A scale is perhaps best thought of in terms of the class of transformations of it which leave it invariant, i.e., which preserves the information it contains. Scales which are available, in increasing order of strength, are as follows.

(1) The *nominal scale*, unique up to any 1-1 transformation, which consists essentially of assigning labels to objects.
(2) The *ordinal scale* which gives the rank order of objects and is invariant under monotone increasing transformations.
(3) The *interval scale*, unique up to positive linear transformations of the form $y = ax+b$, $a > 0$.
(4) The *difference scale*, invariant under a transformation of the form $y = x+b$.
(5) The *ratio scale* (the scale used in setting priorities), invariant under positive linear transformations of the form $y = ax$, $a > 0$.

The essential difference between the ratio scale and the interval scale is that the former requires an origin as a point of reference, whereas the latter does not. The ratio scale originated historically in the measurement of frequencies in the calculation of probabilities.

Technically a scale is a triple consisting of a set S of elements, a binary operation "∘" on the elements and a transformation F of the elements to the real numbers. In our case S is a set of activities or objects $A_1, \ldots, A_n$. The binary operator "∘" is a binary or pairwise comparison of elements as to relative dominance with respect to a given property. For example, we write $A_i \circ A_j$ to indicate that A_i is compared with respect to A_j as to its relative dominance, e.g., with respect to weight if the A's are stones. To define the transformation F we translate the pairwise comparisons in the form of numerical values to represent pairwise comparisons and arrange them in a matrix A, then solve the eigenvalue problem to define the exact correspondence between activities and the real numbers. This entire process defines the transformation.

Why do we have a ratio scale when we use the AHP? We need to show that the pairwise comparisons defined by the binary operation map into the ratio scale of real numbers corresponding to the elements being compared. For example, if

$$A_1 \xrightarrow{F} w_1$$

$$A_2 \xrightarrow{F} w_2$$

$$A_1 \circ A_2 \xrightarrow{F} w_1/w_2$$

In general, to show what kind of scale one has is difficult when the transformation is complicated and involves physical operations such as the rise and fall of mercury with temperature change. For a problem using a physical system, the kind of scale one uses is established empirically. However, when we are dealing with an abstract system, we must have a theoretical method for establishing what kind of scale we have. Now we know that the solution of the principal eigenvalue problem for positive matrices is unique to within multiplication by a positive constant. Thus our transformation generates (or associates) a set of real numbers, $(aw_1, \ldots, aw_n)$, one for each activity $(A_1, \ldots, A_n)$ where a is an arbitrary positive number. This is precisely the definition of a ratio scale. We should note that this ratio scale derived from the judgment matrix is our estimate of an assumed underlying ratio scale that one would obtain, were one's matrix of judgments consistent.

The following are useful observations about ratio scales. We may add elements from the same ratio scale to obtain a third element which belongs to the same ratio scale. Thus if $y = ax$, $y' = ax'$ then $y + y' = a(x + x')$ and the multiplier is still a. However, neither the product nor the quotient of two such elements belong to the same ratio scale. Thus $yy' = a^2 xx'$ and $y/y' = x/x'$, neither of these two elements belongs to the ratio scale $y = ax$ since the multiplier $a \neq 1$ is absent from both.

It is useful to observe that the sum of two elements from two different ratio scales does not belong to a ratio scale. However, the product and quotient do, although it is not the same as either of the original ratio scales unless a or b are equal

to unity. To see this we write $y = ax$, $y = bx'$ yielding $y+y' = ax+bx'$ and $yy' = (ab)xx'$, $y/y' = (a/b)x/x'$. In conclusion when dealing with two different ratio scales and still desiring to attain meaningful ratio scale numbers, we must multiply or divide, but never add or subtract. This is why it is meaningless to add such quantities as time and distance, but we can make sense out of dividing length by time to get velocity.

Measurement theory is concerned with the few areas of representation theory, uniqueness theory, measurement procedures, and the analysis of error.

Representation theory involves the representation of the required relationships by a scale; uniqueness is concerned with acceptable homomorphisms which preserve relationships; measurement procedures deal with the construction of the homomorphisms, and the analysis of error is concerned with the ways in which error ran arise.

In his dissertation, Luis Vargas shows that the AHP is a method of measurement. First, he states a set of axioms which characterize the existence of a homomorphism between the set of alternatives and set of positive real numbers (representation theorem). Second, he shows that the homomorphism is unique up to a similarity transformation (uniqueness theorem), i.e., the set of admissible transformations of the homomorphism is the set of similarity transformations. Therefore, the triple consisting of the set of alternatives, the set of positive real numbers (or a non-denumerable subset) and the homomorphism is a ratio scale. However, this ratio scale is only a ratio scale in the narrow sense; i.e., the elements do not change under the transformation.

He also points out that hierarchical measurement involves fundamental and derived measurement, and that the final scale is a ratio scale unique up to the same similarity transformation as the second level of the hierarchy.

9-3 UTILITY THEORY

Utility theory is concerned with the representation of an individual's relative preferences among the elements of a set by using real numbers.

An ordinal utility function lists the rank order of the elements. Cardinal utility includes information on the strength of preferences. (There are also ordered metric ranking and multidimensional utility theory.)

How does one obtain comparisons of the utilities of decision alternatives when each utility must take into account the contributions of many relevant factors?

Additive utility theories offer one possible approach to this problem through the assumption that, roughly speaking, the utility of a whole equals the sum of utilities assigned to its parts.

A procedure developed by Keeney (1973) and applied to solve the problem of the Mexico City Airport is based essentially on the use of a multiattribute utility function.

It is desired to evaluate a set of alternatives in terms of their impacts on n attributes in order to choose the best alternative. The impacts are described by a vector of numbers $(x_1, \ldots, x_n)$. At the time the decisions must be made we cannot be sure what consequence will result. Thus a probability density function $p(x_1, \ldots, x_n)$ is given describing the likelihood of each consequence. Using this, a utility function

$$u(x_1, \ldots, x_n) \equiv u(x)$$

is "assessed". One can then calculate the expected utility of each alternative. The alternative with the greatest expected utility is selected.

Utility assessments, with more than two attributes simultaneously, are extremely difficult to do; hence, simplifying assumptions are made to derive a function f such that

$$u(x) = f[u_1(x_1), \ldots, u_n(x_n)]$$

where $u_i(x_i)$ is a utility function over the attribute.

9-4 BRIEF COMPARISON OF THE EIGENVALUE METHOD WITH OTHER METHODS OF RATIO SCALING

In his summary paper, Shepard (1972) indicates that research on dominance matrices and corresponding measurement has not been as extensive as those on the other three types: proximity, profile, and conjoint. We have been essentially interested in dominance matrices and their use in deriving ratio scales, and furthermore in the measurement of hierarchical impacts. Let us compare this method with work done by others. We hope that we may be forgiven if our comparison is not as complete as some may like to see. As it was, the core of the ideas was improvised and grew completely out of applications. Then it had to be integrated in the main stream of the literature.

Thurstone's model of comparative judgment demands pairwise comparison of the objects but only to the extent that one is more preferred to another. He recovers information on the stimuli by imposing assumptions of normality on the judgmental process. Under additional assumptions on the parameters; e.g., equal variances or zero covariances, he recovers various "metric" information on the stimuli.

If k judges compare n objects and if f_{ij} is the empirical frequency corresponding to the number of times object j is favored over object i by the judges, then p_{ij}, the proportion of times j is favored over i, is given by

$$p_{ij} = f_{ij}/k$$

Thurstone (1927) postulated that the distribution of all discriminal processes aroused by stimulus i is normal about the modal discriminal process (or mean). The mean discriminal process associated with stimulus i, $\bar{s}_i$, is called the scale value of the stimulus and the dispersion of the discriminal process is denoted by σ_i. Assuming normality, p_{ij} can be expressed as a standard normal deviate $z_{ij} = s_i - s_j$.

Thus $p_{ij} = 0.5$ when $z_{ij} = 0$ and this is the case when $\bar{s}_i = \bar{s}_j$. When $z_{ij} > 0$, j is assumed to have a higher modal discriminal process than i. We have

$$p_{ij} = \frac{1}{2} \int_{-\infty}^{z_{jj}} e^{-x^2/2} \, dx$$

The distribution of the differences $s_i - s_j$ is likewise normal with standard deviation

$$\sigma_{i-j} = (\sigma_i^2 + \sigma_j^2 - 2r_{ij}\sigma_i\sigma_j)^{1/2}$$

where r_{ij} is the correlation between s_i and s_j.

We have the law of comparative judgment.

$$s_j - s_i = z_{ij}\sigma_{i-j}$$

Each pair will have such an expansion. There are 6 such equations for 4 objects in 14 unknowns: 4 desired scale values, 4 standard deviations, and 6 intercorrelations. Only the z_{ij} are known. Thus it is not possible to obtain a unique solution to the system. As a first approximation one may assume all the standard deviations to be equal to σ^2 and then also all intercorrelations are equal to r. The result is

$$\bar{s}_i - \bar{s}_j = z_{ij}[2\sigma^2(1-r)]^{1/2}$$

The quantity in brackets is a constant and may serve as the common unit of the scale-separation of the various pairs of stimuli; it can be set equal to unity.

If we put

$$\bar{s} = \frac{1}{n} \sum_{i=1}^{n} \bar{s}_i, \qquad \bar{z}_j = \frac{1}{n} \sum_{i=1}^{n} z_{ij}$$

we can show, on putting $\bar{s}_1 = 0$, that

$$\bar{s}_j = \bar{s}_{j-1} + (\bar{z}_j - \bar{z}_{j-1})$$

A number of restrictions are associated with Thurstone's approach. For example, Guilford (1928) recommends limiting the range of probabilities.

Torgerson (1958) has systematized and extended Thurstone's method for scaling; in particular, concentrating on the case in which covariance terms are constant, correlation terms equal, and distributions homoscedastic.

Luce has proposed what Coombs (1964) calls the Bradley–Terry–Luce (BTL) model using the logistic curve which is a log transform of the probability distribution. Although this is different from assuming normality, in practice it is difficult to distinguish between the BTL model and the case in Thurstone's work where he assumes normal distributions and equal variances. The BTL model is more rigorously grounded in a theory of choice behavior. Coombs discusses the essential distinction between the two models.

We can contrast our assumptions with psychometric tradition. We do not begin with the supposition that ratio judgments are independent probabilistic processes. Instead, we investigate the consequences of changes in the judgments through perturbations on the entire set of judgments. This type of approach leads to the criterion of consistency. Thus, obtaining solutions in our method is not a statistical procedure.

Briefly, many psychometric methods perform aggregation of judgments in the course of solving for a scale. We assume that if there is aggregation of judgments, it occurs prior to the ratio estimate between two stimuli. Therefore, our solution procedure is not concerned with assumptions of distributions of judgments. However, if we want to compare any solution with the criterion of consistency, we appeal to statistical reasoning and perturbations over the entire matrix of judgments.

Our use of metric information in the matrix of subjects' judgments generates strong parallels with principal component analysis, except that the data give dominance rather than similarity or covariance information. See the end of this section for further discussion. In principal component analysis λ_{max} is emphasized, but one also solves for all the λ's. However, the results must be interpreted differently (see Hotelling, 1933).

In our analysis, the nature of the stimuli and the task presented to subjects are also similar to "psychophysical" scaling, as typified by Stevens and Galanter (1964) and recently used widely in many attempts to construct composite measures of political variables including "national power". Stevens' technique imposes consistency by asking the subjects to compare simultaneously each stimulus with all others, producing only one row of our matrix. This means the hypothesis of unidimensionality cannot be tested directly. If Stevens' method is used, one should take care that the judgments over stimuli are known to be consistent or nearly so. In addition, there is no way of relating one scale to another, as we do with the hierarchy.

Krantz (1972) has axiomatized alternative processes relating stimuli to judgments and derived existence theorems for ratio scales. Comparable axiomatization has not been extended to hierarchies of ratio scales.

Some have approached problems of scaling as if the cognitive space of stimuli were inherently multidimensional, but we choose instead to decompose this multidimensional structure hierarchically in order to establish a quantitative as well as qualitative relations among dimensions. The individual dimensions in multidimensional scaling solutions functionally resemble individual eigenvectors on any one level of our hierarchy.

The formal problem of constructing a scale as the normalized eigenvector w in the equation $Aw = \lambda w$, for λ a maximum, is similar to extracting the first principal component. When subjects are asked to fill the cells of only one row or one column and the other cells are computed from these (to insure "perfect consistency") the first eigenvalue, n, represents 100 percent of the variation in the matrix. If, however, "perfect consistency" applies to the data except that a normally distributed random component is added to each cell of the matrix, then one's theory of data would lead to principal factor analysis, and a "single-factor" solution would result. Thus, the imposition of perfect consistency by the experimenter produces an uninteresting result of exact scalability, which was assured by the experimental design of single-comparisons. In fact, one can see that if the subjects fill only one row or column of the matrix, and if the subjects' task is to generate ratios between pairs of stimuli, then the procedure is formally equivalent to having the subjects locate each stimulus along a continuum with a natural zero at one end: this is the "direct-intensity" technique of psychophysical scaling.

There is no simple relationship of the eigenvalue solution to least square solutions though there have been papers (for example, by Eckart and Young (1936), Keller (1962), and Johnson (1963) concerned with approximating a matrix of data by a matrix of lower rank, minimizing the sum of the square of the differences. In general, the two solutions are the same when we have consistency. A widely accepted criterion for comparison is not known. Thus, it is not clear which is superior. Iterating the eigenvalue procedure helps us approach consistency, which is our preferred criterion.

Tucker (1958) presents a method for the "determination of parameters of a functional relation by factor analysis". He states, however, that "the rotation of axes problem remains unsolved . . .," that is, the factor analysis determines the parameters only within a linear transformation. Cliff (1975), suggests methods for the determination of such transformations where a priori theoretical analysis or observable quantities provide a criterion toward which to rotate the arbitrary factor solution.

The hierarchical composition is an inductive generalization of the following idea. We are given weights of independent elements in one level. We generate a matrix of column eigenvectors of the elements in the level immediately below this level with respect to each element in this level. Then we use the vector of (weights of) elements in this level to weight the corresponding column eigenvectors. Multiplying the matrix of eigenvectors with the column vector of weights gives the composite vector of weights of the lower level elements.

Because the matrix of eigenvectors is not an orthogonal transformation, in general the result cannot be interpreted as a rotation. In fact, we are multiplying a vector in the unit n-simplex by a stochastic matrix. The result is another vector in the unit simplex. Algebraists have often pointed to a distinction between problems whose algebra has a structural geometric interpretation and those in which algebra serves as a convenient method for doing calculations. Statistical methods have a convenient geometric interpretation. Perturbation methods frequently may not.

In the works of Hammond and Summers (1965) concern is expressed regarding the performance of subjects in situations involving both linear and nonlinear relations among stimuli before concluding that the process of inductive inference is primarily linear. In our model subjects response to linear and nonlinear cues seems to be adequately captured by the pairwise scaling method described here, by using the hierarchical decomposition approach in order to aggregate elements which fall into comparability classes according to the possible range of the scale used for the comparison.

Note that our solution of the information integration problem discussed by Anderson (1974) is approached through an eigenvalue formulation which has a linear structure. However, the scale defined by the eigenvector itself is a highly nonlinear function of the data. The process by means of which the eigenvector is generated involves complex addition, multiplication, and averaging. To perceive this complexity one may examine the eigenvector as a limiting solution of the normalized row sums of powers of the matrix.

Anderson (1974) also makes a strong point that validation of a response scale ought to satisfy a criterion imposed by the algebraic judgment model. Such a criterion in our case turns out to be consistency.

Finally, it may be useful to mention briefly a graph-theoretic approach to consistency. A directed graph on n vertices which is complete (i.e., every pair of vertices is connected by a directed arc) is called a tournament. It can be used to represent dominance pairwise comparisons among n objects. Its cycles would then represent intransitivity. For example, every three vertices define a triangle, but not all triangles form 3-cycles. The number of cycles of given length is used to define an intransitivity index for that order, e.g., between triples or quadruples. Inconsistency is then defined (see Marshall (1971)) in terms of the ratio of the number of three, four, or more cycles in a given graph to the maximum number of cycles of that order. For 3-cycles the maximum number is $(n^3 - n)/24$ for n odd, and $(n^3 - 4n)/24$ for n even. For 4-cycles it is $(n^3 - n)(n - 3)/48$ for n odd, and $(n^3 - 4n)(n - 3)/48$ for n even. These results have not been generalized to k-cycles. However, the average number of k-cycles for a random orientation of the arcs of a complete graph is

$(k-1)! \binom{n}{k} \left(\frac{1}{2}\right)^k$. As yet we have found no relationship between this definition of

inconsistency and our eigenvalue-related definition. It is not likely that there will be. The above 3-cycle result is due to Kendall together with its statistical implications. It is nicely discussed in standard statistical references (see, for example, Moroney, 1968).

We referred above to principal component analysis. Let us consider this procedure very briefly.

Consider a random vector X with p components, zero mean vector and covariance matrix C. The distribution of X is unspecified. Let b be a p-component column vector with $b^T b = 1$.

Now $E(b^T X)^2 = E(b^T X X^T b) = b^T C b$; E denotes the expected value.

The normalized linear combinations $b^T X$ with maximum variance subject to $b^T b = 1$ is obtained from the Lagrangian function defined by

$$b^T C b - \lambda (b^T b - 1)$$

with λ as the Lagrange multiplier.

Equating the derivative with respect to b to zero gives

$$(C - \lambda I) b = 0$$

This has a nontrivial solution for λ an eigenvalue of C.

If we multiply on the left by b^T and use the constraint condition, we get $b^T C b = \lambda b^T b = \lambda$. This shows that λ is the variance of $b^T X$. Thus, for the maximum variance we should use $\lambda_{\max}$. If we normalize the corresponding solution b_1 by dividing by the sum of the squares of its coefficients, we have $b_1^T X$ as a normalized linear combination with maximum variance. One next makes a new normalized combination $b^T X$ with maximum variance of all linear combinations uncorrelated with $b_1^T X$, i.e., we want

$$0 = E(b^T X b_1^T X) = E(b^T X X^T b_1)$$
$$= b^T C b_1 \qquad = \lambda_{max} b^T b_1$$

But $C b_{max} = \lambda_{max} b_1$ and hence $b^T X$ is orthogonal to $b_{max}^T X$. Using $b^T b_1 = 0$ as a new constraint we form a new Lagrangian function

$$b^T C b = \alpha(b^T b - 1) - 2\beta(b^T c b_1)$$

with Lagrange multipliers α and β. Proceeding in this manner one can show that $\beta = 0$ and α is the second largest eigenvalue of C. (Note that since C is symmetric as a correlation matrix, all its eigenvalues are real.) We take the eigenvector corresponding to it and proceed as before, now imposing the condition that $b^T X$ has maximum variances of all normalized linear combinations uncorrelated with $b_1^T X$ and with $b_2^T X$ and so on.

When the eigenvectors are obtained in this fashion, the ratio of each eigenvalue to the total sum of the eigenvalues gives the percentage of the total variance reflected in its corresponding component. Thus as a first (and important practical) approximation, one concentrates on the principal component and looks for variations in conditions that lead to variations in the expression $b_1^T X$.

Pinski and Narin (1976) attempt to determine the influence of specific journals by examining the number of citations. They set up a citation matrix of the number of articles from each journal cited in every journal. The columns are then normalized to account for the different sizes of the journals. An eigenvalue procedure based on a general matrix they developed (that is not ratio scale oriented) is followed to calculate the influence weights.

9-5 PERTURBATION APPROACH: LOGARITHMIC LEAST SQUARES

Our problem in the inconsistent case may be stated as follows:
We wish to determine $w_1, \ldots, w_n$ such that

$$a_{ij} = f_{ij}(w_i, w_j; \alpha_i, \alpha_j; \ldots; \omega_i, \omega_j) = \frac{w_i}{w_j} \cdot g_{ij}(\cdot)$$

where we have with respect to the perturbation parameters

$$\lim g_{ij}(\cdot) = 1$$

Here the argument in $g_{ij}(\cdot)$ involves the same variables and parameters as in f_{ij}. Note, for example, that a multiplicative parameter should be allowed to tend to unity, an additive parameter to zero. In other words, if there is any hope of retrieving good estimates for w_i/w_j from a_{ij}, the perturbations must be small. Note, for example, that

$$a_{ij} = \frac{\alpha_i w_i + \omega_i}{\alpha_j w_j + \omega_j} = \frac{w_i}{w_j} \frac{\alpha_i}{\alpha_j} \frac{1 + \omega_i/\alpha_i w_i}{1 + \omega_j/\alpha_j w_j} \tag{9-1}$$

We may write (9-1) above in the form

$$a_{ij} \frac{w_j}{w_i} = g_{ij} \tag{9-2}$$

This basic underdetermined set of n^2 equations in the $n^2 + n$ w_i and g_{ij} requires n additional equations to be determinate. The choice of these relations seems open. However, it turns out that the n relations may be derived on the basis of the perturbation argument of the paradigm case given above. From that infinitesimal generation argument we require that the following set of relations should always hold:

$$\sum_{j=1}^{n} g_{ij} = \lambda_{\max} \qquad i = 1, \ldots, n$$

a set of conditions which depend on $A = (a_{ij})$.

Problem 1: Find w_i, $i = 1, \ldots, n$, which satisfy

$$\sum_{j=1}^{n} a_{ij} w_j = \lambda_{\max} w_i \qquad i = 1, \ldots, n \tag{9-3}$$

The set of conditions (9-2) and those of (9-3) have often been used as the necessary conditions which arise from the solution of an optimization problem. For example, (9-2) may be written as $\log a_{ij}(w_i/w_j) = \log g_{ij}$, and on squaring both sides and taking the sum over i and j the problem becomes one of minimizing error with respect to w_i, $i = 1, \ldots, n$. Problem 2 is to find w_i which minimize

$$\sum_{i,j=1}^{n} \left[\log a_{ij} - \log \frac{w_i}{w_j} \right]^2 = \sum_{i,j=1}^{n} (\log g_{ij})^2$$

This is the logarithmic least squares problem. However, this problem has precisely the same solution

$$w_i = \left[\sum_{j=1}^{n} a_{ij} \right]^{1/n} \left[\sum_{j=1}^{n} w_j \right]^{1/n} = \left[\sum_{j=1}^{n} a_{ij} \right]^{1/n} \qquad \text{if } a_{ji} = \frac{1}{a_{ij}}$$

obtained by taking products with respect to j on both sides of (9-2) and putting $\sum_{j=1}^{n} g_{ij} = 1$, a set of n conditions independent of $A = (a_{ij})$. This solution may be interpreted as one yielding the nearest consistent matrix to a given matrix in the sense of logarithmic least squares.

In statistics, principal component analysis uses the system (9-3) as the set of necessary conditions for the following kind of optimization problem. Minimize the quadratic form

$$f(w_1, \ldots, w_n) = \sum_{i,j=1}^{n} a_{ij} w_i^{-1} w_j, \; a_{ji} = a_{ij}$$

subject to

$$g(w_1, \ldots, w_n) = \sum_{i=1}^{n} w_i^2 = 1$$

The Lagrangian of this problem is

$$L(w_1, \ldots, w_n; \lambda) \equiv f - \lambda(g - 1)$$

The parameter λ appears in the problem as the Lagrangian multiplier (which is also a perturbation parameter for the optimization problem) rather than a direct parameter as in (9-3). In fact, one may construct a wide class of optimization problems which use either (9-2) or (9-3) as a set of necessary conditions.

It is useful to take the perturbation equations (9-2) and tabulate the assumptions made by different methods together with the corresponding solutions. We shall call the left eigenvector, which is the solution of the harmonic mean formulation, the antipriority vector. It provides a measure of how much an element is dominated by other elements in its level. The corresponding vector obtained by hierarchical composition measures the impact of the hierarchy on each element of a level. We have Table 9-1.

REMARK The logarithmic least squares solutions associated with the two matrices of the optics problem of Chap. 2 are $(0.61, 0.24, 0.10, 0.05)$ and $(0.61, 0.23, 0.10, 0.06)$.

Table 9-1 is self-explanatory as it relates the arithmetic, geometric, and harmonic means to our problem of scaling.

9-6 LEAST SQUARES FOR APPROXIMATING A MATRIX BY ANOTHER MATRIX OF LOWER RANK

The matrix $W = (w_i/w_j)$ of rank one is obtained by solving the eigenvalue problem. It is an approximation to $A = (a_{ij})$. We shall need the fact that any matrix may be approximated by another matrix of lower rank. This is done in the following fashion. First we note that

$$\text{Trace } (AA^T) = \sum_{i,j=1}^{n} a_{ij}^2$$

$$\text{Trace } (A - W)(A - W)^T = \sum_{i,j=1}^{n} \left[a_{ij} - \frac{w_i}{w_j} \right]^2$$

$$\text{Min trace } (A - W)(A - W)^T = \min \sum_{i=1}^{n} \alpha_i$$

where the α_i are the eigenvalues of $(A - W)(A - W)^T$.

Now, for any matrix X, XX^T is symmetric and all its eigenvalues are real. Also, X and X^T are positive. Thus XX^T is positive and has a unique real positive largest eigenvalue.

Table 9-1 Four perturbation methods with $a_{ij}\dfrac{w_j}{w_i} = g_{ij}$

	Consistent case assumptions	Problem	Solution	General case assumptions	Problem	Solution
Arithmetic mean	$g_{ij} = 1,\quad \sum_{j=1}^{n} g_{ij} = n$	$\sum_{j=1}^{n} a_{ij}\dfrac{w_j}{w_i} = n$, $i = 1,\ldots,n$; $Aw = nw$	$w_i = \dfrac{a_{ij}}{\sum_{i=1}^{n} a_{ij}}$;	$\sum_{i=1}^{n} w_i = 1,\quad \sum_{j=1}^{n} g_{ij} = \lambda_{\max}$, $j = 1,\ldots,n$	$\sum_{j=1}^{n} a_{ij}\dfrac{w_i}{w_j} = \lambda_{\max}$; $Aw = \lambda_{\max} w$	Normalized right eigenvector, and consistency index $\dfrac{\lambda_{\max} - n}{n-1}$
Row geometric mean	$g_{ij} = 1,\quad \prod_{j=1}^{n} g_{ij} = 1$	$\prod_{j=1}^{n} a_{ij}\dfrac{w_j}{w_i} = 1$, $i = 1,\ldots,n$	$w_i = (\pi a_{ij})^{1/n}$	$\prod_{j=1}^{n} g_{ij} = \mu$	$\prod_{j=1}^{n} a_{ij}\dfrac{w_i}{w_i} = \mu$ Conveniently replaced by log least squares criterion: $\min \sum_{i,j=1}^{n} \left[\log a_{ij} - \log \dfrac{w_i}{w_j}\right]^2 = \min \log^2 \mu$	Same as in consistent case; no measure of consistency
Harmonic mean	$g_{ij} = 1,\quad \sum \dfrac{1}{g_{ij}} = n$	$\sum_{i=1}^{n} \dfrac{1}{a_{ij} u_j/u_i} = n$; $uA = nu$	$u_i = \dfrac{\sum_{i=1}^{n} a_{ij}}{a_{ij}}$; (Reciprocal of first case above)	$\sum_{i=1}^{n} u_i = 1,\quad \sum_{j=1}^{n} \dfrac{1}{g_{ij}} = \lambda_{\max}$	$uA = \lambda_{\max} u$	Normalized left eigenvector, and consistency index $\dfrac{\lambda_{\max} - n}{n-1}$
Column geometric mean	Same for columns as for row geometric mean					

According to Johnson (1963)

$$AA^T \equiv P\Lambda P^{T'}$$
$$A^T A \equiv Q\Lambda Q^T$$

where Λ is a diagonal matrix whose entries are the eigenvalues of A in descending order of magnitude; the eigenvectors of AA^T are the corresponding columns of P and those of $A^T A$ are the corresponding rows of Q^T. As a final result we mention that the best least squares approximation of A by a matrix of rank r is given by

$$P_r \Lambda^{1/2} Q_r^T$$

where P_r and Q_r^T are the parts of P and Q^T associated with the first r columns of Λ.

Let $r = 1$, then P_1 is the eigenvector of AA^T associated with the maximum eigenvalue. Q_1 is the eigenvector of $A^T A$ associated with the maximum eigenvalue. If, as in the consistent case

$$Q_1 = \left[\frac{1}{p_{11}}, \frac{1}{p_{12}}, \ldots, \frac{1}{p_{1n}} \right]$$

where

$$P_1 = (p_{11}, p_{12}, \ldots, p_{1n})$$

then our consistent case solution is the best least square approximation. This need not be so in the inconsistent case.

Let us illustrate the best least square approximation idea on one of the optics example matrices A, by forming AA^T, $A^T A$ and obtaining their eigenvalues and eigenvectors. The eigenvalues, which are the same for both, are the diagonal elements of Λ in descending order of magnitude. The eigenvectors of AA^T are the corresponding columns of P and those of $A^T A$ the rows of Q^T.

We have

$$A = \begin{bmatrix} 1 & 4 & 6 & 7 \\ \frac{1}{4} & 1 & 3 & 4 \\ \frac{1}{6} & \frac{1}{3} & 1 & 2 \\ \frac{1}{7} & \frac{1}{4} & \frac{1}{2} & 1 \end{bmatrix}$$

$$\Lambda = \begin{bmatrix} 132.9000 & & & \\ & 1.4710 & & 0 \\ & & 0.1283 & \\ 0 & & & 0.0007 \end{bmatrix}$$

$$\Lambda^{1/2} = \begin{bmatrix} 11.528 & & & \\ & 1.213 & & 0 \\ & & 0.358 & \\ 0 & & & 0.027 \end{bmatrix}$$

$$P = \begin{bmatrix} 0.875 & -0.475 & 0.087 & -0.041 \\ 0.436 & 0.690 & -0.568 & 0.109 \\ 0.188 & 0.512 & 0.669 & 0.505 \\ 0.097 & 0.192 & 0.471 & 0.855 \end{bmatrix}$$

$$Q^T = \begin{bmatrix} 0.089 & 0.349 & 0.589 & 0.723 \\ 0.158 & 0.819 & 0.146 & -0.533 \\ -0.347 & -0.341 & 0.767 & -0.418 \\ 0.920 & -0.303 & 0.207 & -0.136 \end{bmatrix}$$

$$P\Lambda^{1/2}Q^T = \begin{bmatrix} 0.796 & 3.034 & 5.879 & 7.586 \\ 0.655 & 2.508 & 2.931 & 3.279 \\ 0.221 & 1.178 & 1.554 & 1.136 \\ 0.099 & 0.516 & 0.827 & 0.611 \end{bmatrix}$$

From the maximum eigenvalue approach we obtain a vector as an estimate of an underlying ratio scale. From the least squares approach we obtain a matrix $P_r\Lambda_r^{1/2}Q_r^T$ of lower rank (unit rank in our case) which is the best least squares fit to the given matrix of judgments. Naturally this matrix is a *better* fit than the matrix $W = (w_i/w_j)$ in the sense of least squares, i.e., if we define $F = A - P_r\Lambda_r^{1/2}Q_r^T$ and $G = A - W$ and take the sums of the squares of their entries, we can easily show that the first is equal to trace $(FF') = $ trace Λ_s where Λ_s is the diagonal matrix of eigenvalues not included in Λ_r (in our case Λ_r corresponds to the largest eigenvalue of A^TA and trace Λ_s is the sum of the remaining eigenvalues.) In fact we can show that trace$[(A - W)^T(A - W)] \geqslant$ trace(FF') as indeed it must. However, the problem is how to derive a scale vector from the least squares approximation matrix $P_r\Lambda_r^{1/2}Q_r^T$. If we arbitrarily assume that this matrix is nearly consistent, we may use any of its columns (normalized) as an approximation to the underlying scale. But now the problem is how good this vector is when compared with the maximum eigenvector. For our illustration, we used the root mean square deviation of each of these from the known underlying scales in problems where it was desired to make the comparison. As we show in the example below, the maximum eigenvector is clearly superior to the least squares vector (as we have interpreted it) as an approximation to reality.

If we form Λ_r by putting all diagonal elements but the first, which is the largest, equal to zero in Λ then we have

$$P_r\Lambda_r^{1/2}Q_r^T = \begin{bmatrix} 0.90 & 3.52 & 5.94 & 7.29 \\ 0.45 & 1.76 & 2.97 & 3.64 \\ 0.19 & 0.76 & 1.28 & 1.57 \\ 0.10 & 0.39 & 0.66 & 0.81 \end{bmatrix}$$

If we form $F_r = A - P_r\Lambda_r^{1/2}Q_r^T$ and take the sum of the squares of its elements, we obtain 1.6 which is precisely the trace of Λ_s, i.e., the sum of the remaining eigenvalues. If we assume that the above matrix is consistent, in order to derive a scale vector from it, we normalize its first column and obtain $s = (0.548, 0.274, 0.118, 0.061)$. It is interesting to note that all the other columns give the same result since the matrix has unit rank.

Although the vector is visibly not as good an approximation as the eigenvector we find that its mean square deviation from the actual vector $(0.61, 0.22, 0.11, 0.06)$ is $0.00\ 155$ as compared with $0.000\ 05$ for the maximum eigenvector $w = (0.62, 0.22, 0.10, 0.06)$ corresponding to $\lambda_{max} = 4.1$. This shows that the eigenvector solution for this example is superior to the least squares solution.

Let us now use the elements of w and of s, to form the matrices of ratios $W = (w_i/w_j)$ and $S = (s_i/s_j)$. We then compute $A - W$ and take the sum of the squares of its entries to obtain 13.42. Doing the same for $A - S$ we have 11.45, which is close to the first but somewhat better. This means that the least squares approximation is better if we wish to minimize the sum of the squares of the differences. Overall we conclude for this example, that since we are interested in the scale and not in the matrices of ratios, the eigenvector answer is better; this despite the fact that it does not satisfy the minimum squares criterion.

9-7 MULTICRITERION METHODS

A variety of methods are available for the analysis of multiple objective decisions. Some of them are structured to deal with predicting actions and choices in future decision situations. Others are structured to assist the decision maker with practical techniques which he can use to improve his decision making.

Weighting Methods

Srinivasan and Shocker (1973) review an earlier summary of methods of weight estimation given in Sluckin (1956) and in Blum and Naylor (1968). These methods are as follows:

(1) Weighting subcriteria on the basis of their predictability (using canonical correlation).
(2) Weighting subcriteria proportional to their average correlation with other subcriteria.
(3) Weighting subcriteria to maximize the difference in the composite's value between stimuli.
(4) Weighting subcriteria to maximize explained variance (using factor analysis).
(5) Weighting subcriteria proportional to their reliabilities.
(6) Equal weighting of subcriteria.
(7) Weighting subcriteria to equalize "effective weights" (i.e., proportion of composite's variance).
(8) Weighting on the basis of a dollar criterion.
(9) Weighting subcriteria using expert judgment.

(10) Weighting subcriteria by multiple regression on an intervally scaled global criterion.

They are examined or criticized using three basic criteria: relevance, multi-dimensionality, and measurability. Methods (1) through (7) lack relevance by either ignoring it by using an arbitrary statistical objective, or in an indirect and incomplete way by other subcriteria than the global criterion. Methods (5) through (9) involve biased estimation as one judges in terms of one subcriterion and then in terms of another independently, and hence the resulting multidimensional vector has bias between its components, sometimes double counting the importance of a subcriterion. Methods (8) through (10) suffer from a good way of producing measures that together make sense for weighting with respect to the global criterion. Examples of weighting methods are:

Outcomes versus objectives
Let us assume we have the outcomes $O_1, O_2, \ldots, O_m$. The procedure steps are as follows: (See Ackoff, et al., 1962, and Fishburn, 1972.)

(1) Rank the objectives in their order of value.
(2) Assign the value 1.00 to the first objective and assign values to the other objectives in a suitable form.

Objective	Value
O_1	$v_1 = 1$
O_2	v_2
$\vdots$	$\vdots$
O_m	v_m

(3) Compare the most important objective with the combination of all the others. In short, compare O_1 with $O_2 + \cdots + O_m$. If $1 \geqslant v_2 + \cdots + v_m$, then compare O_2 with $O_3 + \cdots + O_m$, if $v_2 \geqslant v_3 + \cdots + v_m$, then compare O_3 with $O_4 + \cdots + O_m$, and so on, until the comparison of O_{m-2} versus $O_{m-1} + O_m$ is completed.
(4) If $1 < v_2 + \cdots + v_m$, then compare O_1 with $O_2 + \cdots + O_{m-1}$. If $1 < v_2 + \cdots + v_{m-1}$ still holds, then compare O_1 with $O_2 + \cdots + O_{m-2}$, etc., until either O_1 is preferred to the rest, or until the comparison of O_1 versus $O_2 + O_3$ is completed, then proceed to step (3) again.
(5) Once the values, v_i, have been found, normalize them dividing by $\sum_i v_i$.

The assumptions underlying this procedure are as follows:

For each outcome we have associated a real nonnegative value.
If O_i is prefereed to O_j then $v_i > v_j$.
If O_i and O_j are equally preferred than $v_i = v_j$.
If the outcomes O_i and O_j have associated the values v_i and v_j, respectively, then the outcome $O_i + O_j$ has associated the value $v_i + v_j$. This assumption fails if O_i and O_j are mutually exclusive.

When a large number of outcomes is involved, this procedure is very laborious. In addition it does not produce unique scales and cannot cope with hierarchical type of problems. Klee (1971) has used a method of direct comparison of n objects. He first arranges the objects ordinally from most to least preferred. He compares the most preferred with the second most preferred, the second with the third and so on, each time assigning a numerical value to this ratio. When the process is completed, he assigns the number 1 to the least preferred or nth object and multiplies it by the ratio of the comparison of the $(n-1)$st to the nth to get the weight of the $(n-1)$st and so on, working backwards and obtaining a relative scale estimate for the n objects. There does not seem to be an intrinsic way of estimating consistency with this method.

Outcomes versus functions of objectives

Fishburn (1964, 1967) suggests an approach using additive utility theory through the assumption that the utility of the whole equals the sum of utilities assigned to its parts. Once all the objectives o_j's are properly identified and the measurable contributions are determined for each plan, the results can be put in the following matrix form.

Plan	Objectives					
	o_1	o_2	$\cdots$	o_j	$\cdots$	o_n
u_1	x_{11}	x_{12}	$\cdots$	x_{1j}	$\cdots$	x_{1n}
u_2	x_{21}	x_{22}	$\cdots$	x_{2j}	$\cdots$	x_{2n}
$\vdots$	$\vdots$	$\vdots$		$\vdots$		$\vdots$
u_i	x_{i1}	x_{i2}	$\cdots$	x_{ij}	$\cdots$	x_{in}
$\vdots$	$\vdots$	$\vdots$		$\vdots$		$\vdots$
u_m	x_{m1}	x_{m2}	$\cdots$	x_{mj}	$\cdots$	x_{mn}

For each plan u_i one assigns a vector $(x_{i1}, x_{i2}, \ldots x_{in})$ to the objectives. What is desired is to weight the plans in order to determine which one to use. From utility theory, an overall measure of the contribution of u_i (which we denote by $V(u_i)$) is obtained as a function of the n-dimensional vector $(x_{i1}, x_{i2}, \ldots x_{in})$, that is, $V(u_i) = V(x_{i1}, x_{i2}, \ldots, x_{in})$. Using the additivity assumption

$$V(u_i) = v_{i1} + v_{i2} + \cdots + v_{ij} + \cdots + v_{in}$$

the value of the objective for each plan is determined by the product of the relative importance of the objective $v(o_j)$ and the utility for the numerical measure x_{ij}, denoted by $v(x_{ij})$. In our notation

$$v_{ij} = v(o_j)v(x_{ij})$$

Estimating $v(x_{ij})$

As a first attempt to estimate $v(x_{ij})$ one may assume linear utility functions which are normalized so that they take on values between 0 and 1. For objectives whose measures are directly related to utility levels (e.g., contribution to national income), we may assume

$$v(x_{ij}) = \frac{x_{ij}}{\sum\limits_{i=1}^{m} x_{ij}}$$

and for those which are inversely related to utility levels (e.g., contribution to pollution)

$$v(x_{ij}) = \frac{1}{(n-1)} \sum\limits_{i=1}^{m} \frac{(1-x_{ij})}{\sum\limits_{i=1}^{m} x_{ij}}$$

Estimating $v(o_j)$

(1) Ranking methods The $v(o_j)$ are ranked from smallest to largest, such as $v(o_1)$, $v(o_2), \ldots, v(o_n)$, where the numbering of the objectives corresponds to the rank positions. Sometimes, a judge is asked to place a numerical value on each objective, indicating by 1 that which is most important, by 2 the next important, and so on. Other ordering methods exist which are variants of this method.

(2) Direct rating method The objectives may be presented next to a continuum or a finite number of discrete values marked off in units from 0 to 10. Then, for each $v(o_j)$, a judge is asked to mark on the continuum the importance of the given objective. The judge may be permitted to select points between integers, like 2.7, and may assign more than one objective on a scale position.

(3) Method of outcomes versus objectives (described above).

(4) Half-value sum Let us assume that $0 < v(o_1) < \cdots < v(o_n)$. The basic approach is to form half-value chains as follows. Begin with k near n and estimate a_j such that $v(o_j)+v(o_{j+2}) = v(o_k)$ and set $v(o_{j+1}) = (1/2)v(o_k)$. Repeat the process with $v(o_{j+1})$ replacing $v(o_k)$ and continue to get half-value chains as long as possible. A smooth curve tracing the different half-value chains may be used as an estimate of the desired utility function. For example, suppose thirty objectives have been ranked as follows $0 < v(o_1) < v(o_2) < \cdots < v(o_{30})$. Suppose $v(o_{22})+v(o_{24}) = v(o_{30})$, $v(o_{17})+v(o_{19}) = v(o_{23})$, $v(o_9)+v(o_{11}) = v(o_{18})$, $v(o_2)+v(o_4) = v(o_{10})$.

Using a half-value chain $[v(o_{30}), v(o_{23}), v(o_{18}), v(o_{10}), v(o_3)]$ and setting $v(o_3) = 1$, the estimated utility function may be represented graphically.

(5) Ordered metric methods Suppose $0 < v(o_1) < v(o_2) < \cdots < v(o_n)$, then the ordered metric ranking in the binary case is a ranking of the adjacent differences $v(o_1)-0$, $v(o_2)-v(o_1)$, $v(o_3)-v(o_2), \ldots, v(o_n)-v(o_{n-1})$.

In one instance, the $v(o_i)$ differences may be judged directly. In another instance, a comparison between $v(o_2)-v(o_1)$ and $v(o_4)-v(o_3)$, for example, may be made by comparing $v(o_1)+v(o_4)$ with $v(o_3)+v(o_2)$. When the same $v(o_i)$ is in both differences, such as a comparison of $v(o_3)-v(o_2)$ with $v(o_2)-v(o_1)$, then comparison is made directly.

(6) Indifference curve method In many problems it is desirable to determine the utility or worth function of an allocation of resources to various activities and to maximize it subject to constraints imposed by the quantities available, their price, and the amount of funds available. But it is usually difficult to find such a function, and instead *indifference curves* are determined for the activities in pairs bypassing the numerical approach. To find such a curve an individual is asked questions to determine tradeoff between the two attributes being compared. The indifference curve is where values of the two attributes have equal worth. Here one has two dimensional curves from which a reasonable multidimensional surface needs to be derived and the maximum found on that surface. An objection to the method is that quantitative information is lost.

Sequential Elimination Methods

Lexicographic order
The term "lexicographic" reflects the similarity between this method and the method by which words are ordered in a dictionary. The lexicographic approach requires that the attributes be ranked in terms of importance, and that the attribute values be placed on an ordinal scale. Once the most important attribute is selected, the alternative having the highest value for this attribute can be determined. If a single alternative emerges, this alternative is chosen, and the procedure stops. If there are several alternatives with the same highest value on the specified attribute, then the attribute ranked second in importance is compared across all these alternatives. The process continues in this way until a single alternative emerges, or until all attributes have been examined.

A weakness of lexicographic ordering is that an infinitesimal movement along one of the components does not outweigh large movements along others. A weaker criterion is: the *Principle of Pareto* optimality. One alternative is considered superior to another if it exceeds the latter in at least one dimension, and is no worse than the second in any other dimension. If an alternative satisfies this property with respect to all other alternatives, then it is said to be Pareto optimal.

Mathematical Programming Methods

Global objective function
The main problem here is to pool together multiple objectives to optimize the result subject to constraints in a linear programming framework. The idea is to take a convex combination of these objective functions with different parameters, and solve the resulting parametric programming problem. We obtain a finite family of solutions corresponding to a tesselation of parameter space into cells.

Judgment is used to select the solution that seems most appropriate.

Goals in the constraints; Goal programming

All global optima are, in a large context, local optima. We know that the solutions are optimal only in a restricted context. The optimal solution is not a strategy to be followed, but an additional information, to be evaluated in the context of the large system of which the problem was a component. Most of the time our objective is to maximize profit from all production. This gives the impression that we have only one objective—profit. But suppose we take a larger viewpoint. One which involves a number of separately identifiable goals, which cannot be easily combined into one function to be optimized. For example, we may wish to consider production levels for two different products that do the most for (a) net profit, (b) gross profit, and (c) cash position, subject to a set of restrictions on resources.

Clearly the solution which maximizes net profit is unlikely to be the same as that which maximizes the other two goals. To resolve the uncertainty of our larger purpose, we should re-determine whether maximization is our objective at all.

We do not really seek to maximize or minimize in making policy decisions, but rather we seek to "satisfy". Satisfying suggests setting goals and then seeking the particular allocation which offers the best promise of achieving those goals. This is the purpose of goal programming. Let us consider the following example

$$\text{Goal 1}: \quad 60x_1 + 50x_1 = 1{,}500 \text{ (net profit goal)}$$
$$\text{Goal 2}: \quad 2x_1 + 4x_2 \leqslant 80$$
$$\text{Goal 3}: \quad 3x_1 + 2x_2 \leqslant 60, \qquad x_1, x_2 \geqslant 0$$

x_1 and x_2 represent the number of units of products 1 and 2, respectively; 80 is the number of hours on machine A and 60 on machine B not to be exceeded. The three goals are not compatible. To solve the incompatibility problem, let us assign first priority to goal 1, second to goal 2, and third to goal 3. Let us attach the following strict meanings to the priority assignments:

Goal 1 should be satisfied as closely as possible, whatever the consequence in approximating goals 2 and 3.

Once goal 1 is achieved, goal 2 should be satisfied as closely as possible, so long as deference to goal 2 does not compromise goal 1.

Once goal 2 is achieved, goal 3 should be satisfied as closely as possible, so long as deference to goal 3 does not compromise goal 2.

So, the problem is planned as follows: minimize

$$P_1(d_1^- + d_1^+) + P_2 d_2^+ + P_3 d_3^+$$

subject to

$$60x_1 + 50x_2 + d_1^- - d_1^+ = 1{,}500$$
$$2x_1 + 4x_2 + d_2^- - d_2^+ = 80$$
$$3x_1 + 2x_2 + d_3^- - d_3^+ = 60$$

and to a nonnegativity condition on all variables. Here d_i^- and d_i^+ are shortage and surplus variables, respectively.

If P_1, P_2, and P_3 are regarded as coefficients of the variables we would be dealing with incommeasurables, since d_1^- and d_2^+ are measured in dollars, and the remaining variables are measured in machine hours. To resolve this difficulty, let us think of P_1, P_2, and P_3 as labels that specify the priority ordering of the goals to which they correspond, rather than as coefficients. Thus $P_1(d_1^- + d_1^+)$ means: First make $d_1^- + d_1^+$ as small as possible, subject only to the nonnegativity restriction on all variables. And $P_2 d_2^+$ means: make d_2^+ as small as possible without compromising achievement of the first goal, and so on to $P_3 d_3^+$.

One must consider the priorities P_1, P_2, and P_3 as being of such magnitude relative to each other, that P_1 is much larger than P_2 which in turn is much larger than P_3.

The connection between goal programming and hierarchies is through the concept of consistent scenarios in planning.

In a complex planning situation, the use of a hierarchical approach yields a composite scenario which suits all decision makers. However, this scenario must be realistic and compatible with all the dimensions of the problem. For example, realistic means that one cannot use more resources than one has. Compatible means that objectives must not conflict. If we define a scenario by a vector of state variables, X, and a set of decision variables, Y, then the scenario (X, Y) is consistent if $X = g(Y)$, where g is the model of the process functions of the system, i.e., of the physical flows in the system. The eigenvalue method and the principle of hierarchical composition may be used to construct a composite scenario whose state variables have the value R. If R cannot be obtained as a function of the decision variables, in the form $g(Y^*)$ where Y^* is a particular set of values for the problem, then R is not consistent and goal programming is used to revise the planning targets represented by R.

Specifically, assume that A is the matrix of technological coefficients of a given economy. Let X be the industrial outputs and Y be the final demands. It is known that $X = (I-A)^{-1} Y$. Suppose that the state variable X^* provide the level of consumption of a certain resource, the cost associated with its processing and also the emissions of pollutants in this processing. The total impact coefficients and the input-output model D represent the system process functions. We have $X^* = DX$, with $X = (I-A)^{-1} Y$. In order for the composite scenario values R to be consistent, we must have $X^* = R$.

If this is not true, the following optimization problem provides the framework to make R realistic and compatible:
Minimize

$$z = p_- d^- + p_+ d^+$$

subject to

$$BU + Id^+ + Id^- = R \qquad U \geqslant 0$$

where

$$B = \begin{bmatrix} (I-A) \\ D \end{bmatrix}$$

The solution U of this problem provides a consistent scenario suited to the specific real-life situation.

Local objectives: Interactive programming
The multiple criterion problem which we consider may be written as

$$\underset{x \in X}{\text{Max}} \ U\{f(x)\}$$

where f is an r-dimensional vector of real-valued functions, x is an n-dimensional vector of real-valued variables, X is the feasible region of R^n associated with x and U is the decision-maker's utility function defined on the range of f. One can assume that U is increasing in each f_i, and that X is convex and compact. U and each component of f are concave and continuously differentiable.

The decision-maker's marginal substitution rates among the criteria at a particular point may be used to estimate the direction of the gradient of his utility function at that point. This information may be used in the context of existing nonlinear mathematical programming algorithms to obtain an optimal solution to the problem.

Spatial Proximity Methods

Conjoint measurement
This is concerned with combining a set of independent variables in some functional form (generally a polynomial) to predict the values of a dependent variable. The coefficients or parameters of the function are usually estimated by regression techniques. There are several algorithms or approaches as to how to do this estimation by weighting the importance of the variables to the people involved (see Green and Wind, 1973). For various aspects of product/marketing decision applications see Wind (1979).

Multidimensional scaling
The fundamental objective of multidimensional scaling is to recover the underlying spatial structure of the perception process by a configuration in which each stimulus (alternative) is represented by a point in such a way that two stimuli that are subjectively viewed as being similar are closer together than those that are viewed as being less similar.

The process follows as below:

(1) A dissimilarity matrix is built, δ_{ij}; the main diagonal is composed of zeros, and the matrix is symmetric to the main diagonal.
(2) From the δ_{ij}-matrix it is possible to obtain a matrix of distances between stimuli, d_{ij}.
(3) Monotonicity is required

$$\delta_{i_1 j_1} < \delta_{i_2 j_2} \Rightarrow d_{i_1 j_1} < d_{i_2 j_2}$$

(4) One defines stress $S = \sqrt{S^*/T^*}$ where $S^* = \sum_{i<j} (d_{ij} - \hat{d}_{ij})^{(*)}$ and $T^* = \sum d_{ij}^e$.

---

* $\hat{d}_{ij}$ is the distances of the points which have been fitted from the initial configuration.

The problem is: minimize $\sqrt{S^*/T^*}$ over all the $\hat{d}_{ij}$ satisfying the hypothesis of monotonicity.

Green and Wind (1973) in their approach to marketing studies, examine five attributes of a project including name, price, package design, and whether or not it is guaranteed. In this specific problem, there are 108 combinations of these five attributes. Eighteen of these alternatives are chosen and ranked. The computer then searches for scale values for each attribute. Scale values are chosen such that when added together, the total utility of each combination corresponds to the ranks. No measure is given of how much better each alternative is.

Douglas Carroll (1977) designs an aid to planners in formulating strategies and forecasting outcomes for successful implementation of these strategies. He forms a matrix of cross impacts of conditional probabilities. He then calculates measures of dissimilarities of pairs of events by determining the Euclidean distance measure between the rows of the cross impact matrix (causes) and then determines the Euclidean distance between columns (effects).

Wigand and Barnett (1976) establish a dissimilarity (distance) matrix. The row and column headings are a set of concepts where each now defines a concept's relationship to all other concepts. The data are gathered by a series of direct paired comparisons and then treated as points in a spatial manifold (non-Euclidean N dimensional space). The location of these points is determined and then the squared distances between points minimized.

Tversky (1967) explores the mathematical structure of polynomial measurement theory (satisfied by a data structure if and only if it satisfies the irreflexivity axiom), and interrelates various measurement models within a unified conceptual framework leading to some mathematical problems whose solution is regarded as useful or illuminating. The theory has no simple empirically testable conditions. This approach allows for data analyzed by multidimensional scaling and by factorial methods. Performance (express order) between pairs is an ordering of distances between them which can be expressed as a polynomial function of the coordinates; the theory characterizes embedding this polynomial in a real n-space with fixed dimensionality.

Patrick Rivett (1977) has done work on "the selection of 'best' policies from a range of alternative possibilities where each policy is assessed in terms of its degrees of attainment of a set of objectives". The method proposed is based on multidimensional scaling techniques as further developed by Kendall for drawing maps based on fragmentary information.

An experimental test of the analytic hierarchy process was conducted by Schoemaker and Waid (1978) to compare it with the multiple regression approach (MR), the multi-attribute utility approach (MAU) of Keeney and Raiffa (1976), and simple direct assessment (DA). The above four methods differ in several ways: (1) they require different types of judgments, (2) they require different response modes (from ordinal to ratio), and finally, (3) each has domains of application to which the others make limited claims.

In the Schoemaker–Waid experiment, subjects were asked to evaluate hypothetical admission candidates, in pairwise comparisons, using four attributes only:

quantitative SAT, verbal SAT, high school cumulative average, and an index of extra-curricular activity. After these prior judgments subjects were asked for further judgments from which linear additive representations could be constructed on the basis of the above four methods. The experiment followed a with-in subject, factorial design. Thirty-three subjects were asked to make prior judgment among 20 pairs of alternatives, indicating direction as well as strength of preference within each pair. The linear additive models derived from AHP, MR, MAU, and DA produced 84 percent, 57 percent, 86 percent, and 84 percent correct predictions for these prior judgments, respectively. The Pearson product–moment correlations between the predicted and observed strengths of preference were 0.72, 0.19, 0.75, and 0.77, respectively.

These methods were compared only in a limited sense.

The authors examined only what each method had to offer with respect to additive, linear representations of multi-attribute preferences. The priorities of the attributes or criteria determined by the AHP were used as weights of a linear value function. This enabled the authors to compare them.

Although the methods are different, each has advantages over the others. The AHP need not assume consistency among preferences, while the construction of a utility function by the MAU approach requires a transitive preference relation. Also, there is a greater detail of information on pairwise comparisons in the AHP which uses a systems approach, and it is applicable in areas where non-measurable attributes exist.

The MAU possesses some advantages. It has a well-developed methodology for handling situations with risk and encompasses utility functions that are not linear (i.e., additive linear on each variable, multiplicative, and multilinear), Keeney and Raiffa (1976) discuss techniques to estimate the utility function. However, the process leads to the choice of one of a few established types of functions. The AHP generates functional values of a utility function rather than the function itself. For repetitious decision-making situations, having a utility function would be more advantageous. However, in practice, the utility function changes rapidly in time and hence has to be re-evaluated. Thus, the MAU does not do better operationally than the AHP. The former takes too much time and effort, and does not have the benefit as a group process that the AHP has been shown to have. The latter can perturb the judgments within the hierarchy to get a new set of priorities. With the AHP protocol, this represents less trouble than to construct the utility function for each period of time.

In relation to the MR method, one of the authors points out that "he would use the AHP rather than the MR method in any non-repetitive decision-making situation such as strategic planning or technology forecasting because these situations do not allow an easy derivation of measurable attributes. However, the AHP presents one operational problem, it takes time to get judgments in one session and must be spread out over a number of sessions. This inconvenience appears to be of no greater importance compared with the fact that the MAU provides utility functions, a process with which the people may not feel naturally comfortable. Their own preferences may later be inconsistent with the utility function.

9-8 OTHER COMPARISONS

Hirsch has conducted a thorough analysis of axiomatic methods used to study ranking, both ordinal and cardinal. By synthesizing the information contained in the axioms he was able to formulate a minimal set of axioms from which he derived a set of about forty analytical conditions for judging the goodness of multicriteria methods. Presumably, the more desirable conditions a method satisfies, the more preferred it should be.

Three main groups of multicriterion methods are defined in the following way. *Automatic methods* (A^+), in which the final ranking of the elements is obtained from the initial data, general assumptions, and conditions, and a specified algorithm based on an additional set of axioms. There is no interaction with the decision-maker nor feedback process. *Semi-automatic methods* $(A^=)$, in which the decision-maker can make choices only at specified stages of the method, and according to certain rules. There exists specification of feedback processes which brings flexibility and adaptivity to the real situation. *Non-automatic methods* (A^-), in which the decision-maker can make decisions at any moment, and changes in the axioms and assumptions are permitted.

To compare and evaluate multicriterion methods, he defines their major structural characteristics. Each characteristic is to be defined on a characteristic scale, so that any multicriterion method is identified by the set of its characteristic levels measured on each characteristic scale. First of all, he defines measurement scales which are: cardinal absolute, cardinal ratio, cardinal interval, ordered metric, ordinal, and nominal. Over these measurement scales he defines the characteristic scales which are five; namely, I-characteristic scale, O-characteristic scale, G-characteristic scale, D-characteristic scale, and W-characteristic scale. The I-characteristic scale shows the degree of specificity required in the measurement scales for the several criteria (degree of cardinality). The O-characteristic scale indicates the quality of the ranking obtained. The W-characteristic scale gives some information about the relative importance of the criteria. The measures of the relative importance of the criteria are unidimensional indicators. They might be ordinal or cardinal. However, the ordinal measures of relative importance are not sufficient because they cannot be used to get a global ranking. Thus, he develops two more different scales based on interscale distance comparisons. They are the G and D characteristic scales. Based on these scales, he defines some objective measures of performance of multicriterion methods: the rational conditions.

Among the methods he studied are: goal programming, multiple linear objectives, and several others of recent vintage. He considered the "preanalytical" conditions of: neutrality/independence, ordinality, stability, responsiveness, pareto optimality, degree of structure, anonymity, and homogeneity.

The eigenvalue method does not require strict independence, ordinality, anonymity, or homogeneity. However, it has stability, responsiveness, pareto optimality, and certain structural properties. It also has a normalized scale. As yet Hirsch's approach does not enable one to say how much better one method is than another and in what value system.

REMARK   Although we have not made a serious attempt to axiomatize our approach which admits intransitivity, we give a short sketch of ideas which need to be considered in attempting such axiomatization. Ordinarily axioms are used to give non-constructive existence types of proofs for utility functions. We have used existing mathematical theory to do the same. However, we have made certain assumptions in this process. Examples are as follows.

(1) A system can be decomposed into comparability classes (the components) in the framework of a directed network.
(2) Elements in each component may be compared with respect to some or all the elements in an adjacent component (the initial vertex of an arc).
(3) Comparisons can be made in terms of an absolute numerical scale to form ratios.
(4) The pairwise comparisons utilize reciprocal matrices (optional).
(5) Intransitivity is allowed and its effect on the consistency of the outcome measured.
(6) The priority or composite index of dominance of an element is derived through a composition or weighting principle.
(7) Any element which appears in the hierarchy is considered relevant, although its priority may be low. It does not make sense to speak of 'irrelevant alternatives' introduced into the hierarchy to test for independence from them.

MATRICES AND EIGENVALUES

INTRODUCTION

In this Appendix we give a brief introduction to the algebra of matrices and eigenvalue problems.

MATRICES AND LINEAR SYSTEMS OF EQUATIONS

A matrix is a rectangular array of mn numbers arranged in m rows and n columns. The number, element, or entry of the matrix A in the ith row and jth column is denoted by a_{ij}. Thus, we have for the m by n matrix A

$$A = \begin{bmatrix} a_{11} & a_{12} & \cdots & a_{1n} \\ a_{21} & a_{22} & \cdots & a_{2n} \\ \vdots & & & \vdots \\ a_{m1} & a_{m2} & \cdots & a_{mn} \end{bmatrix}$$

Generally, we denote the matrix A by (a_{ij}) and specify the number of its rows and columns. The subscripts i and j refer to the row and column, respectively, in which the entry is located. A is said to be a square matrix of order n if $m = n$.

The rows and columns of A are called vectors. The matrix A may consist of a single row vector or a single column vector. In that case, a single subscript on its entries suffices. For example, $A \equiv (a_1, \ldots, a_n)$ is a row vector. The diagonal elements of a square matrix A of order n are $a_{ii}, i = 1, \ldots, n$. A *diagonal* matrix A has the property that $a_{ij} = 0$, for all i and j with $i \neq j$. Some of the diagonal elements are nonzero. If also all $a_{ii} = 0$ for all i, A is called the *zero* or *null* matrix and is denoted by bold face zero or by bold face capital O. The unit or *identity* matrix I is a diagonal matrix with $a_{ii} = 1$ for all i. A *triangular* matrix A is a square matrix with $a_{ij} = 0$ for $i > j$ or $a_{ij} = 0$ for $i < j$. The *transpose* of $A = (a_{ij})$ denoted by $A^T = (a_{ji})$ is defined by replacing the element in the i, j position of A by the element in the j, i position; that is, we interchange the rows and columns of A by rotation around the main diagonal to obtain A^T. Since two matrices are equal if their corresponding elements are equal, we can define a *symmetric* matrix by $A = A^T$; that is, $a_{ij} = a_{ji}$. We define a *skew symmetric* matrix by $A = -A^T$; that is, $a_{ij} = -a_{ji}$ with $a_{ii} = 0$; *Hermitian* by $a_{ji} = \bar{a}_{ij}$ ($\bar{a}_{ij}$ is the complex conjugate of a_{ij}). We also define a *reciprocal* matrix by $a_{ji} = 1/a_{ij}$ with $a_{ii} = 1$. $A = (a_{ij})$ is said to be positive if $a_{ij} > 0$ for all i and j and nonnegative if $a_{ij} \geqslant 0$. We also have $A \geqslant B$ if $a_{ij} \geqslant b_{ij}$ for all i and j.

There are rules by which matrices A and B can be added, subtracted, multiplied, and "divided". These operations constitute an algebra of matrices, somewhat similar to the algebra of ordinary numbers, but care must be taken as all the rules that work with ordinary numbers do not work with matrices, which have a more general algebra. Indeed, a matrix of order one by one is a single number, called a scalar, and all laws which apply to matrices in general must also apply to this special kind of matrix and, hence, to ordinary numbers.

Historically, matrices arose as a shorthand method of listing coefficients of a system of equations. A general set of m equations in n unknowns is given by

$$a_{11}x_1 + a_{12}x_2 + \cdots + a_{1n}x_n = y_1$$
$$a_{21}x_1 + a_{22}x_2 + \cdots + a_{2n}x_n = y_2$$
$$\vdots \qquad\qquad\qquad \vdots \qquad\quad \vdots$$
$$a_{m1}x_1 + a_{m2}x_2 + \cdots + a_{mn}x_n = y_m$$

It simplifies the writing of such a system if the coefficients, the array (a_{ij}), are separated from the variables, the x_j. Then the x_i, which are repeated in each row, need be written only once, thus

$$\begin{bmatrix} a_{11} & a_{12} & \cdots & a_{1n} \\ a_{21} & a_{22} & \cdots & a_{2n} \\ \vdots & & & \\ a_{m1} & a_{m2} & \cdots & a_{mn} \end{bmatrix} \begin{bmatrix} x_1 \\ x_2 \\ \vdots \\ x_n \end{bmatrix} = \begin{bmatrix} y_1 \\ y_2 \\ \vdots \\ y_m \end{bmatrix}$$

If we write the x_j as a column then the rule to reassemble the original system is: with every a_{ij} associate the corresponding x_j, i.e., a_{32} and x_2 yield $a_{32}x_2$. That is, as you move across the rows of coefficients, move *down* the column of x's for the proper association. This simple operation is the basis for the general matrix multiplication rule.

We may refer to $x_1, x_2, \ldots, x_n$ as the vector x and $y_1, y_2, \ldots, y_m$ as the vector y. Notice that in general the number of elements in x is not the same as that in y. The product of an m by n matrix and a p by q matrix is only possible when $p = n$ and results in a matrix of size m by q. Thus, if $q = 1$, that is, the second matrix is a vector, the product is also a vector. To prevent confusion, keep in mind that subscripted letters refer to elements of matrices or vectors and unsubscripted letters refer to a whole matrix or vector.

The origins of matrix addition and multiplication may be related to operations on systems of equations.

Consider again a system of equations

$$y_1 = a_{11}x_1 + a_{12}x_2$$
$$y_2 = a_{21}x_1 + a_{22}x_2$$

and suppose we have a second system of equations

$$z_1 = b_{11}x_1 + b_{12}x_2$$
$$z_2 = b_{21}x_1 + b_{22}x_2$$

If we wish to combine these two systems, since the x's are what the two systems have in common, we would add the first equation of the first set to the first equation of the second set, grouping corresponding terms and go to the second equations doing the same, and so on.

$$y_1 + z_1 = (a_{11} + b_{11})x_1 + (a_{12} + b_{12})x_2$$
$$y_2 + z_2 = (a_{21} + b_{21})x_1 + (a_{22} + b_{22})x_2$$

This gives the same result as working with the matrices of coefficients using matrix addition. Suppose A is the matrix of coefficients of the first set and B is the matrix of coefficients of the second set. Then to add in the way described above, A and B must be of the same order. Their sum will also have this order. The rule is $A + B = (a_{ij}) + (b_{ij}) = (a_{ij} + b_{ij})$; corresponding elements in the matrices are added.
We have

$$\begin{bmatrix} a_{11} & a_{12} & a_{13} \\ a_{21} & a_{22} & a_{23} \end{bmatrix} + \begin{bmatrix} b_{11} & b_{12} & b_{13} \\ b_{21} & b_{22} & b_{23} \end{bmatrix} = \begin{bmatrix} a_{11}+b_{11} & a_{12}+b_{12} & a_{13}+b_{13} \\ a_{21}+b_{21} & a_{22}+b_{22} & a_{23}+b_{23} \end{bmatrix}$$

More concretely

$$\begin{bmatrix} 1 & -2 & 3 \\ 0 & 2 & -4 \end{bmatrix} + \begin{bmatrix} 0 & 3 & -3 \\ 0 & 2 & -8 \end{bmatrix} = \begin{bmatrix} 1+0 & -2+3 & 3+(-3) \\ 0+0 & 2+2 & -4+(-8) \end{bmatrix} = \begin{bmatrix} 1 & 1 & 0 \\ 0 & 4 & -12 \end{bmatrix}$$

The rule of addition may be extended to any number of matrices of the same order: $A + B + \cdots + Z = (a_{ij} + b_{ij} + \cdots + z_{ij})$.

The additive inverse of a matrix $A = (a_{ij})$ is the matrix $-A = (-a_{ij})$ such that $A + (-A) = 0$.

We have with respect to addition both associativity

$$(A+B)+C = A+(B+C)$$

and commutativity

$$A+B = B+A$$

Suppose we wish to multiply the equations by some constant (or scalar) α (another trick we used to use in elementary algebra when trying to solve systems of equations) as follows

$$\alpha y_1 = \alpha a_{11}x_1 + \alpha a_{12}x_2 + \cdots + \alpha a_{1n}x_n$$
$$\alpha y_2 = \alpha a_{21}x_1 + \alpha a_{22}x_2 + \cdots + \alpha a_{2n}x_n$$

$$\cdot \quad \cdot \quad \cdot \quad \cdot \quad \cdot \quad \cdot \quad \cdot \quad \cdot \quad \cdot$$

$$\alpha y_n = \alpha a_{n1}x_1 + \alpha a_{n2}x_2 + \cdots + \alpha a_{nn}x_n$$

then
$$\alpha A = \alpha(a_{ij}) = (\alpha a_{ij})$$

or, the rule is: to multiply a matrix A by a scalar α, multiply every element in A by α.

For example
$$-3\begin{bmatrix} -2 & 0 & 4 \\ 3 & 6 & 1/2 \end{bmatrix} = \begin{bmatrix} 6 & 0 & -12 \\ -9 & -18 & -3/2 \end{bmatrix}$$

Scalar multiplication and addition may now be combined in a rule for the linear combination of matrices

$$\alpha A + \beta B + \cdots + kZ = (\alpha a_{ij} + \beta b_{ij} + \cdots + kz_{ij})$$

where $\alpha, \beta, \ldots, k$ are scalars.

Consider the following set of equations expressing $y_j, j = 1, 2, 3$ in terms of x_i, $i = 1, 2, 3, 4$.

$$y_1 = 2x_1 + 4x_2 - x_3 + x_4$$
$$y_2 = x_1 - 3x_2 + 2x_3 - 2x_4$$
$$y_3 = 2x_2 + x_3 - x_4$$

Then also consider a second set of equations expressing $z_k, k = 1, 2$ in terms of y_j.

$$z_1 = 3y_1 + y_2 + 2y_3$$
$$z_2 = y_1 - y_2 + 5y_3$$

We want to express z_k in terms of $x_i, i = 1, 2, 3, 4$. We do this by substituting for $y_j, j = 1, 2, 3$ from the first system into the second. We have $z_k, k = 1, 2$, in terms of $x_i, i = 1, \ldots, 4$

$$z_1 = 3(2x_1 + 4x_2 - x_3 + x_4) + (x_1 - 3x_2 + 2x_3 - 2x_4) + 2(2x_2 + x_3 - x_4)$$
$$= (3 \times 2 + 1 \times 1 + 2 \times 0)x_1 + [3 \times 4 + 1 \times (-3) + 2 \times 2]x_2 +$$
$$[3 \times (-1) + 1 \times 2 + 2 \times 1]x_3 + [3 \times 1 + 1 \times (-2) + 2 \times (-1)]x_4$$
$$= 7x_1 + 13x_2 + x_3 - x_4$$

Thus, the coefficient of x_1 is obtained by taking sums of products. The products are those of the coefficients of y_1, y_2, and y_3, respectively in the expression for z_1, each multiplied by the corresponding coefficient of x_1 from the three equations for y_1, y_2, and y_3, and then taking the sum. Similarly for the coefficients of x_2 and x_3. For z_2 we have $z_2 = x_1 + 17x_2 + 2x_3 - 2x_4$. All this can be accomplished by multiplying the matrix of coefficients of the first system by those of the second.

Thus we write for these matrices

$$\begin{array}{c} \\ z_1 \\ z_2 \end{array} \overset{\begin{array}{ccc} y_1 & y_2 & y_3 \end{array}}{\begin{bmatrix} 3 & 1 & 2 \\ 1 & -1 & 5 \end{bmatrix}} \overset{\begin{array}{cccc} x_1 & x_2 & x_3 & x_4 \end{array}}{\begin{bmatrix} 2 & 4 & -1 & 1 \\ 1 & -3 & 2 & -2 \\ 0 & 2 & 1 & -1 \end{bmatrix}} = \overset{\begin{array}{cccc} x_1 & x_2 & x_3 & x_4 \end{array}}{\begin{bmatrix} 7 & 13 & 1 & -1 \\ 1 & 17 & 2 & -2 \end{bmatrix}}$$

z_k in terms y_j in terms of x_i z_k in terms of x_i
of y_j

The multiplication is carried out to obtain the coefficients in brackets associated with x_1, x_2, x_3, and x_4 for z_1. Thus, the entry in the 1, 1 position in the matrix on the right is obtained by multiplying the elements in the first row of the matrix on the left by the corresponding elements in the first column and adding, that is

$$3 \times 2 + 1 \times 1 + 2 \times 0 = 7$$

The entry 2 in the 2, 3 position is obtained by multiplying the second row of the first matrix on the left by the third column of the second matrix on the left. We have

$$1 \times -1 + -1 \times 2 + 5 \times 1 = 2$$

In general then, if we multiply matrices $A = (a_{ij})$, $B = (b_{ij})$ to obtain $C = (c_{ij})$, that is, $AB = C$ we have for the entry in the i, j position of C

$$c_{ij} = \sum_{k=1}^{n} a_{ik}b_{kj}$$

Taking the ith row of A with the jth column of B, multiplying coefficients in corresponding positions as indicated by the index k and then adding. It is clear that multiplication is meaningful only when A is an m by n matrix and B is an n by q matrix.

Suppose A and B are as shown below, then C is as indicated on the right.

$$\begin{bmatrix} a_{11} & a_{12} & a_{13} \\ a_{21} & a_{22} & a_{23} \end{bmatrix} \begin{bmatrix} b_{11} & b_{12} \\ b_{21} & b_{22} \\ b_{31} & b_{32} \end{bmatrix} = \begin{bmatrix} c_{11} & c_{12} \\ c_{21} & c_{22} \end{bmatrix}$$

where

$$c_{11} = a_{11}b_{11} + a_{12}b_{21} + a_{13}b_{31}$$
$$c_{12} = a_{11}b_{12} + a_{12}b_{22} + a_{13}b_{32}$$
$$c_{21} = a_{21}b_{11} + a_{22}b_{21} + a_{23}b_{31}$$
$$c_{22} = a_{21}b_{12} + a_{22}b_{22} + a_{23}b_{32}$$

Products of matrices satisfy:

(1) The associative law $C(BA) = (CB)A$.
(2) The distributive law with respect to addition

$$C(A + B) = CA + CB, \qquad (C + B)A = CA + BA$$

(3) Associativity with respect to product by a number: $(kA)(k'B) = kk'AB$. Thus if k and k' are equal to 1 or -1, we have $(-A)B = A(-B) = -AB$, $(-A)(-B) = AB$.

In general, the product of matrices is noncommutative. For example, if

$$A = \begin{bmatrix} 2 & 2 & 0 \\ -3 & 4 & 7 \end{bmatrix} \qquad B = \begin{bmatrix} 1 & 4 \\ -1 & -4 \\ 1 & 4 \end{bmatrix}$$

$$AB = 0 \qquad \text{but } BA = \begin{bmatrix} -10 & 18 & 28 \\ 10 & -18 & -28 \\ -10 & 18 & 28 \end{bmatrix}$$

which also shows that $AB = 0$ with $A \neq 0$, $B \neq 0$. Also from $AB = AC$ we have $A(B - C) = 0$ but we cannot conclude that either $A = 0$ or $B = C$ as we have just seen.

However, sums of matrices satisfy all the properties of sums of numbers. For example $A + B = A + C$ implies $B = C$.

Multiplying any matrix by a scalar matrix (a diagonal matrix with the same constant for all the diagonal elements) is the same as multiplying it by a constant. Thus, for example

$$\begin{bmatrix} k & 0 \\ 0 & k \end{bmatrix} \begin{bmatrix} a & b & c \\ a_1 & b_1 & c_1 \end{bmatrix} = \begin{bmatrix} ka & kb & kc \\ ka_1 & kb_1 & kc_1 \end{bmatrix}$$

Note that $AI = IA = A$. The inverse of A, if there is one, is a matrix A^{-1} such that $AA^{-1} = I$. We have $(AB)^{-1} = B^{-1}A^{-1}$ and $(AB)^T = B^T A^T$. Two matrices A and B are called orthogonal if $AB = 0$. The matrices AA^T and $A^T A$ are symmetric.

REMARK In the matrix product $AB = C$, we note that c_{ij} is formed by using the ith row vector of A and the jth column vector of B. In general, we have for the multiplication of two vectors $v = (v_1, \ldots, v_n)$ and $w = (w_1, \ldots, w_n)$, called their *scalar* or *dot* product and denoted by $(v, w) = v_1 w_1 + v_2 w_2 + \cdots + v_n w_n$, obtained by multiplying corresponding components and adding. The length of a vector $v = (v_1, \ldots, v_n)$ is denoted by $|v|$ and is defined as $|v| = (v_1^2 + \cdots + v_n^2)^{1/2}$ which is euclidean length. Now we know from analytic geometry that the angle θ between any two lines whose directional numbers are $(v_1, \ldots, v_n)$ and $(w_1, \ldots, w_n)$ satisfies the relation $\cos \theta = (v_1 w_1 + \cdots + v_n w_n)/|v| \, |w|$. Thus $(v, w) = |v| \, |w| \cos \theta$. Note that the two vectors $(1, 3, 2)$ and $(4, 0, -2)$ are orthogonal.

We can associate with a matrix A of order n a number called its determinant and denote it by $|A|$ or by $\det(A)$. It is defined as the algebraic sum of all possible products of n of the entries in each of which there is precisely one element from each row and each column of A. Now we can arrange the elements in each term in the order of the successive columns of A. We would have n choices for the element taken from the first column, then $n - 1$ choices for the element taken from the second column...two choices for the element taken from the next to last column and the element of the last column is therefore determined. This gives $N = n(n-1) \ldots 2$ choices. (The product of the first n positive integers is called n factorial and represented by $n!$.) With each choice corresponds a different term. Thus, the determinant of order n has $n!$ terms.

In the algebraic sum, each term is preceded by a plus or a minus sign according to the following rule. We arrange the elements of each term in the order of the columns and note the sequence of indices of corresponding rows. This sequence may be constructed by interchanging pairs of elements in the sequence of natural numbers $1, 2, \ldots, n$. If the number of interchanges is even (odd), the sign of the term would be positive (negative). Thus, the sign is simply $(-1)^s$ where s is the number of interchanges. For example, the term $a_{21}a_{32}a_{13}$ in the determinant of a 3 by 3 matrix A, gives rise to the sequence of row indices 2, 3, 1. To put it in the form 1, 2, 3, we need two interchanges: (1) interchanging 1 and 2 and then interchanging 2 and 3. The two interchanges lead to a positive sign for the term. The term $a_{11}a_{32}a_{23}$ with row indices 1, 3, 2 needs one interchange of the elements 3 and 2 to put it in the form 1, 2, 3. Thus, the term receives a negative sign. Using this definition, it is easy to see that the determinant of the matrix

$$
\begin{vmatrix}
2 & 1 & 4 \\
3 & 0 & -5 \\
1 & -1 & -1
\end{vmatrix} = (2)(0)(-1)+(1)(-5)(1)+
$$

$$
(4)(3)(-1)-(4)(0)(1)-(1)(3)(-1)-(2)(-5)(-1) = -24
$$

Among the many known properties of determinants are $|AB| = |A|\,|B|$; if a row or column is multiplied by α the determinant of A is multiplied by α; however, $|\alpha A| = \alpha^n |A|$, $|A| = |A^T|$; interchanging a row with the corresponding column leaves $|A|$ unchanged; an interchange of two rows or two columns in A changes the sign of $|A|$; $|A|$ is zero if two columns or two rows of A are the same or one is a constant multiple of the other; if a column of A, e.g., the first, has the form $a_{11}+b_{11}, a_{21}+b_{21}, \ldots, a_{n1}+b_{n1}$, then $|A|$ is the sum of two determinants; the first has $a_{11}, a_{21}, \ldots, a_{n1}$ as its first column and the second has $b_{11}, b_{21}, \ldots, b_{n1}$ as its first column, all other columns remaining as in A. It follows that a determinant is unchanged if we add to any column a constant multiple of another column; if A is triangular $|A| = a_{11}a_{22}, \ldots, a_{nn}$.

The *rank* of a matrix A is the order of the largest square array (submatrix) whose determinant is not equal to zero. A square matrix is *nonsingular* if its rank is equal to its order, i.e., $|A| \neq 0$. If $|A| = 0$, A is said to be *singular*. For example, a matrix in which every row is a constant multiple of one row is not only singular but has unit rank.

A systematic way for developing (expanding) a determinant is as follows: The minor D_{ij} of the element a_{ij} is the determinant of the matrix obtained by striking out the ith row and jth column. The cofactor A_{ij} of a_{ij} is $(-1)^{i+j}D_{ij}$.

We have for the expansion of det (A) with respect to the ith row:

$$
|A| = a_{i1}A_{i1} + \cdots + a_{in}A_{in} \qquad i = 1, \ldots, n
$$

Similarly for expansion with respect to a column.

The adjoint of A denoted by adj (A) is the matrix whose i, jth element is A_{ji}. From the above equation we see that $A \cdot \mathrm{adj}\,(A) = |A| \cdot I$. It follows that A is invertible (i.e., has an inverse) if and only if $|A| \neq 0$ (i.e., A is nonsingular), and that $A^{-1} = \mathrm{adj}\,(A)/|A|$ in this case.

Consider the linear system of equations

$$\sum_{j=1}^{n} a_{ij}x_j = b_i \qquad i = 1, \ldots, n$$

In matrix notation this system may be written as

$$Ax = b$$

where A is the matrix of coefficients.

$$A = \begin{bmatrix} a_{11} & a_{12} & \cdots & a_{1n} \\ a_{21} & a_{22} & \cdots & a_{2n} \\ \vdots & & & \vdots \\ a_{n1} & a_{n2} & \cdots & a_{nn} \end{bmatrix}$$

and x and b are the column vectors

$$x = \begin{bmatrix} x_1 \\ x_2 \\ \vdots \\ x_n \end{bmatrix} \qquad b = \begin{bmatrix} b_1 \\ b_2 \\ \vdots \\ b_n \end{bmatrix}$$

When $b \neq 0$, i.e., some of the b_i are nonzero, the system is called a *nonhomogeneous* system; otherwise, it is called *homogeneous*.

If A is nonsingular, it has an inverse A^{-1} and we can uniquely solve the nonhomogeneous system by writing $x = A^{-1}b$. Cramer's rule provides a convenient way for solving a nonhomogeneous system and is equivalent to the above but involves the use of determinants rather than matrix inversion. The ith component x_i of the vector x is a fraction whose numerator is the determinant of the matrix obtained from A by replacing the ith column of A by the column vector b and whose denominator is the determinant of A. Note that for the solution of a homogeneous system, the numerator of x_i is always equal to zero and, hence, unless A is singular so that its determinant vanishes, there is no solution other than the trivial one $x = (0, 0, \ldots, 0)$. If $|A|$ is also zero, we need a convenient way to obtain a nonzero solution since Cramer's rule leads to an indeterminant expression (zero over zero) for the x_i. There are various ways for obtaining the solution in this case. The best known are elimination methods which solve for an unknown in one equation and substitute its value in the others. If there are more variables than equations, then the surplus or independent variables are assigned arbitrary values to be used to determine the remaining (dependent) variables.

We may adopt the convention that all vectors should be thought of as column vectors and use the transpose to indicate the corresponding row vectors. But we occasionally use a symbol without a transpose superscript when there is no chance for confusion.

A set of vectors $v_1, \ldots, v_n$ are said to be *linearly independent* if for all numbers $a_1, a_2, \ldots, a_n$ the equation

$$a_1v_1 + a_2v_2 + \cdots + a_nv_n = 0$$

(where the right-hand side is the zero vector of n components) implies that $a_1 = a_2 = \cdots = a_n = 0$.

Thus none of the vectors can be obtained by multiplying others by a constant and adding. Otherwise, they are said to be *linearly dependent*, i.e., the above relation holds with not all a_i, $i = 1, \ldots, n$, equal to zero.

A *linear combination* of vectors $v_1, v_2, \ldots, v_n$ is a sum of the form $\sum\limits_{i=1}^{n} a_i v_i$ where a_i are arbitrary numbers. A linear combination is called a *convex combination* of $v_i, i = 1, \ldots, n$ if $a_i \geqslant 0$, and $\sum\limits_{i=1}^{n} a_i = 1$.

A set of vectors $v_1, v_2, \ldots, v_n$ is said to form a *basis* for the space of vectors of n components (n-vectors) if

(1) they are linearly independent;
(2) every vector is a linear combination of them (which is the same as saying that they span the space).

In the space of n-vectors, a basis must consist of n vectors. In particular, the set of vectors $v_i, i = 1, \ldots, n$ whose n entries are zero except for the ith entry, which is equal to unity, form a basis for the space of n-vectors.

Note for example that $v_1 = (1, 0, 0)$, $v_2 = (0, 1, 0)$, and $v_3 = (0, 0, 1)$ are linearly independent since

$$a_1 v_1 + a_2 v_2 + a_3 v_3 = (a_1, 0, 0) + (0, a_2, 0) + (0, 0, a_3)$$
$$= (a_1, a_2, a_3)$$

In order for this vector to be the zero vector $(0, 0, 0)$, we must have $a_1 = 0$, $a_2 = 0$, $a_3 = 0$. The vectors $v_1 = (1, 0)$, $v_2 = (0, 1)$, $v_3 = (1, 1)$ are linearly dependent since the requirement that

$$a_1 v_1 + a_2 v_2 + a_3 v_3 = (a_1 + a_3, a_2 + a_3) \text{ be } (0, 0)$$

gives $a_1 + a_3 = 0$, $a_2 + a_3 = 0$ which are satisfied by $a_1 = -a_3$, $a_2 = -a_1$, which need not be all zero. To find the coefficients in $v = a_1 v_1 + \cdots + a_n v_n$ we must solve a system of linear equations. For example, $(2, 3) = a_1(1, 7) + a_2(4, 2)$ leads to the two equations $2 = a_1 + 4a_2$ and $3 = 7a_1 + 2a_2$.

The set of all vectors that are convex combinations of n linearly independent vectors (unit vectors) is called an n-simplex (the unit n-simplex).

Since the rows and columns of a matrix are vectors, it turns out that the rank of a matrix is the maximum number of linearly independent rows which it has. This is the same as the maximum number of linearly independent columns. In a matrix of rank one, every row (or column) vector is a constant multiple of a single row (or column).

Two vectors v_1 and v_2 (like two matrices) are orthogonal if $v_1 v_2 = 0$ where v_1 is written as a row vector and v_2 is a column vector. There is a standard procedure for transforming a set of n linearly independent vectors to a set of vectors that are orthogonal in pairs. If the original set forms a basis, so will the new set and it is called an orthogonal basis.

CHARACTERISTIC EQUATION: EIGENVALUES AND EIGENVECTORS

A proper vector (characteristic vector or eigenvector) of A is a non-null vector w such that $Aw = \lambda w$ or $(1/\lambda)A$ transforms w to w, i.e., leaves w fixed. The values of λ corresponding to such a w are called the proper values (characteristic values or eigenvalues) of A. Thus, w would be a proper vector or eigenvector if it is a non-trivial (i.e., nonzero) solution of $(A - \lambda I)w = 0$ for some number λ. The components of w constitute a set of solutions of a homogeneous linear system with matrix $A - \lambda I$. Such a system, in fact, has the trivial solution $w_1 = \cdots = w_n = 0$ where $w = (w_1, \ldots, w_n)$. But in order that there be a nontrivial solution, the matrix $A - \lambda I$ must be singular, i.e., its determinant $|A - \lambda I|$ should be zero. This determinant is an nth degree polynomial in λ. It has the form $\lambda^n - a_1 \lambda^{n-1} + \cdots + (-1)^n \det(A)$ and is called the characteristic polynomial of A. The condition that the determinant should equal zero leads to an nth degree equation called the characteristic equation of A which, by the Hamilton and Cayley theorem is identically zero if λ is replaced by A, thus yielding a matrix equation. The roots λ_i $i = 1, \ldots, n$, of the characteristic equation $|A - \lambda I| = 0$ are the desired eigenvalues. The fundamental theorem of algebra assures the existence of n roots for a polynomial equation of degree n. The eigenvectors are obtained by solving the corresponding systems of equations, $Av_i = \lambda_i v_i$. Care must be exercised in getting all the eigenvectors when there are multiple roots.

Note that

$$a_1 = \sum_{i=1}^{n} a_{ii} \equiv \text{trace } (A)$$

and that the roots of the characteristic equation as roots of an nth degree equation satisfy

$$\sum_{i=1}^{n} \lambda_i = a_1 = \text{trace } (A)$$

and

$$\prod_{i=1}^{n} \lambda_i = |A|$$

We can see this by expanding the factorization $(\lambda - \lambda_1)(\lambda - \lambda_2) \ldots (\lambda - \lambda_n)$ of the characteristic polynomial. We note that the characteristic equation may have multiple roots and, hence, the total number of distinct roots may be less than n. Obviously, a multiple root λ_i of multiplicity k would appear in the factorization in the form $(\lambda - \lambda_i)^k$. For a simple root $k = 1$.

From $Aw = \lambda w$ and $A\lambda = \lambda A$ since λ is a constant, we have $A^2 w = A(Aw) = A(\lambda w) = Aw = \lambda(\lambda w) = \lambda^2 w$. Thus, λ^2 is an eigenvalue of A^2 and similarly λ^k is an eigenvalue of A^k. Thus, trace $A^k = \lambda_1^k + \cdots + \lambda_n^k$.

Example Consider the matrix

$$A = \begin{bmatrix} 1 & 2 \\ 3 & 4 \end{bmatrix}, \quad I = \begin{bmatrix} 1 & 0 \\ 0 & 1 \end{bmatrix}, \quad \lambda I = \begin{bmatrix} \lambda & 0 \\ 0 & \lambda \end{bmatrix}$$

$$(A - \lambda I) = \begin{bmatrix} 1 - \lambda & 2 \\ 3 & 4 - \lambda \end{bmatrix}$$

$$|A - \lambda I| = (1 - \lambda)(4 - \lambda) - 6 = \lambda^2 - 5\lambda - 2 = 0$$

Since the characteristic equation is a quadratic we solve it by using the well-known quadratic formula for the roots of such an equation. We have for the eigenvalues

$$\lambda_1 = \frac{5 + \sqrt{33}}{2}$$

$$\lambda_2 = \frac{5 - \sqrt{33}}{2}$$

and to obtain the eigenvector corresponding to λ_1, we write $Aw = \lambda_1 w$, that is

$$\begin{bmatrix} 1 & 2 \\ 3 & 4 \end{bmatrix} \begin{bmatrix} w_1 \\ w_2 \end{bmatrix} = \lambda_1 \begin{bmatrix} w_1 \\ w_2 \end{bmatrix}$$

or

$$w_1 + 2w_2 = \lambda_1 w_1$$

that is

$$w_1 = -\frac{2}{1 - \lambda_1} w_2$$

$$3w_1 + 4w_2 = \lambda_1 w_2$$

Since the matrix $A - \lambda_1 I$ is singular there is dependence between its rows and hence the second equation yields no new information. Thus the eigenvector w is obtained by assigning an arbitrary value to w_2 and calculating w_1 from the above relation. We assign w_2 the value 1. We then have

$$w = \left[\frac{2}{\lambda_1 - 1}, 1 \right]$$

We can normalize w by making its coefficients sum to unity. We do this by dividing each coefficient by the sum $w_1 + w_2$ which is $(\lambda_1 + 1)/(\lambda_1 - 1)$. The resulting normalized vector is

$$\left[\frac{2}{\lambda_1 + 1}, \frac{\lambda_1 - 1}{\lambda_1 + 1} \right]$$

Since multiplying by a constant does not affect the solution of $Aw = \lambda w$, we shall think of the eigenvectors w to be always given in normalized form. We may similarly obtain the eigenvector corresponding to λ_2. The eigenvalues as the roots of any polynomial equation are obtained by standard numerical methods of which there are several. There are nowadays canned computer programs for getting these roots. When the equation is the characteristic equation of a matrix, there are computer programs which, knowing the matrix, also find the eigenvectors.

The eigenvalues of a matrix, as roots of its characteristic equation, may be complex numbers and, hence, would occur in pairs as complex conjugates. Recall that a complex number is of the form $a + ib$ where $i = \sqrt{-1}$ and a and b are real. The modulus of such a number is denoted by $|a + ib|$ and is equal to $(a^2 + b^2)^{\frac{1}{2}}$. If the matrix has real entries and is symmetric, all its eigenvalues are real. The eigenvectors corresponding to different eigenvalues are orthogonal. The same property also applies to a Hermitian matrix. A and A^T have the same eigenvalues but generally not the same eigenvectors.

The following theorem (see Franklin, 1968) may be adapted to

$$a_{ij} = \frac{w_i}{w_j} \varepsilon_{ij}$$

by using a continuous transformation such as a logarithmic function. It asserts that the eigenvalues of a matrix depend continuously on its coefficients (the same as proving that the roots of a polynomial depend continuously on its coefficients).

Theorem If an arbitrary matrix $A = (a_{ij})$ has the eigenvalues $\lambda_1, \lambda_2, \ldots, \lambda_s$ where the multiplicity of λ_j is m_j with $\sum_{j=1}^{s} m_j = n$, then given $\varepsilon > 0$ sufficiently small, there is a $\delta = \delta(\varepsilon) > 0$ such that if $|a_{ij} + \varepsilon_{ij} - a_{ij}| = |\varepsilon_{ij}| \leq \delta$ for $i, j = 1, \ldots, n$, the matrix $B = (a_{ij} + \varepsilon_{ij})$ has exactly m_j eigenvalues in the circle $|\mu - \lambda_j| < \varepsilon$ for each $j = 1, \ldots, s$ where $\mu_1, \ldots, \mu_n$ are the eigenvalues of B.

PROOF Define $f(\mu, B) = \det(\mu I - B)$.

Let $\varepsilon_0 = 1/2 \min |\lambda_i - \lambda_j|$ $1 \leq i < j \leq s$ and let $\varepsilon < \varepsilon_0$. The circles $C_j: |\mu - \lambda_j| = \varepsilon, j = 1, \ldots, s$ are disjoint. Let $r_j = \min |f(\mu, A)|$ for μ on C_j. Note that $\min |f(\mu, A)|$ is defined because f is a continuous function of μ. Also $r_j > 0$ since the roots of $f(\mu, A) = 0$ are the centers of the circles.

The determinant $f(\mu, B)$ is a continuous function of the $1 + n^2$ variables and $a_{ij} + \varepsilon_{ij} i, j = 1, \ldots, n$ and hence for some $\delta > 0, f(\mu, B) \neq 0$ for μ on any $C_j, j = 1, \ldots, s$ if $|\varepsilon_{ij}| \leq \delta, i, j = 1, \ldots, n$. From the theory of functions of a complex variable, the number m_j of roots μ of $f(\mu, B) = 0$ which lie inside C_j is given by

$$n_j(B) = \frac{1}{2\pi i} \int_{c_j} \frac{f'(\mu, B)}{f(\mu, B)} d\mu, \qquad j = 1, \ldots, s$$

which since $f(\mu, B) \neq 0$ is a continuous function of the $1 + n^2$ variables in $|\mu - \lambda_j| = \varepsilon, |\varepsilon_{ij}| \leq \delta, i, j = 1, \ldots, n$. In particular it is a continuous function of $a_{ij} + \varepsilon_{ij}$ with $|\varepsilon_{ij}| \leq \delta$.

Now for $B = A$ we have by assumption $n_j(A) = m_j, j = 1, \ldots, S$. Since the integral is continuous it cannot jump from $n_j(A)$ to $n_j(B)$ and the two must be equal and have the common value m_j, $j = 1, \ldots, s$ for all B with $|a_{ij} + \varepsilon_{ij} - a_{ij}| \leqslant \delta$ $(i, j = 1, \ldots, n)$.

There are various ways of estimating $\lambda_{\max}$ and here is a well-known one.

$$\lambda_{\max} = \lim_{k \to \infty} (\text{trace } A^{2k})^{1/2k}$$

For example, we find for a 3×3 reciprocal matrix the following

$$\text{trace } A^4 = 3 \left[19 + \frac{4a_{12}a_{23}}{a_{13}} + \frac{4a_{13}}{a_{12}a_{23}} \right]$$

Similar calculation for a 4×4 reciprocal matrix yields

$$\text{trace } A^4 = 4 \left[34 + \frac{4a_{12}a_{23}}{a_{13}} + \frac{4a_{13}}{a_{12}a_{23}} + \frac{4a_{12}a_{24}}{a_{14}} \right.$$

$$+ \frac{4a_{14}}{a_{12}a_{24}} + \frac{4a_{13}a_{34}}{a_{14}} + \frac{4a_{14}}{a_{13}a_{34}} + \frac{a_{12}a_{24}}{a_{13}a_{34}}$$

$$+ \frac{a_{13}a_{34}}{a_{12}a_{24}} + \frac{a_{13}a_{24}}{a_{14}a_{23}} + \frac{a_{14}a_{23}}{a_{13}a_{24}} + \frac{a_{12}a_{23}a_{34}}{a_{14}}$$

$$\left. + \frac{a_{14}}{a_{12}a_{23}a_{34}} \right]$$

Note that terms tend to compensate since a coefficient which is in the numerator of one term also appears in the denominator of the next one. Thus an increase in this coefficient increases one term and decreases the other. Generally this is not true for a non-reciprocal matrix.

One often encounters functions of a matrix A such as powers and exponentials. Meaning has been given to such functions. We have the following theorem in this field due to Sylvester (see Frazer, Duncan, and Collar, 1955).

$$f(A) = \sum_{i=1}^{k} \sum_{m=0}^{m_i - 1} \frac{(A - \lambda_i I)^m}{m!} f^{(m)}(\lambda_i) Z(\lambda_i)$$

Here k is the number of distinct characteristic values of the matrix A, m_i is the multiplicity of the ith root λ_i, $f^{(m)}(\lambda_i)$ is the mth-order formal derivative of f evaluated at λ_i, and the $Z(\lambda_i)$ are complete orthogonal idempotent matrices of the matrix A; that is, they have the properties

$$\sum_{i=1}^{k} Z(\lambda_i) = I; \qquad Z(\lambda_i)Z(\lambda_j) = 0, \qquad i \neq j; \qquad Z^2(\lambda_i) = Z(\lambda_i)$$

where I and 0 are the identity and null matrices, respectively.

When the characteristic values are all distinct, one has, for an nth-order matrix A (Hildebrand, 1952)

$$f(A) = \sum_{i=1}^{n} f(\lambda_i) Z(\lambda_i)$$

where

$$Z(\lambda_i) = \frac{\prod_{j \neq i} (\lambda_j I - A)}{\prod_{j \neq i} (\lambda_i - \lambda_j)}$$

To illustrate how these are obtained when f is a polynomial in A, note from the nth-degree polynomial $|\lambda I - A| = 0$ that A^n can be expressed in terms of lower powers of A and hence that f can always be reduced to a polynomial of degree not exceeding $n-1$. If we write

$$f(A) = \sum_{i=1}^{n} \alpha_i \prod_{\substack{j=1 \\ j \neq i}}^{n} (A - \lambda_j I)$$

and multiply on the right successively by v_i, $i = 1, \ldots, n$ the characteristic vector of λ_i and use the fact that $Av_i = \lambda_i v_i$, and hence that $f(A)v_i = f(\lambda_i)v_i$, we have

$$\alpha_i = \frac{f(\lambda_i)}{\prod_{j \neq i} (\lambda_i - \lambda_j)}$$

which gives the desired result.

If $f(A) = e^{At}$ and the characteristic values of A are distinct, we have the spectral resolution of $f(A)$ given by

$$e^{At} = \sum_{i=1}^{n} e^{\lambda_i t} Z(\lambda_i)$$

The case of multiple characteristic roots is derived from the confluent form of Sylvester's theorem. If we write, for brevity

$$f(A) = \sum_{i=1}^{k} T(\lambda_i)$$

where k is the number of distinct roots, then

$$T(\lambda_i) = f(\lambda_i) Z_{m_i - 1}(\lambda_i) + f'(\lambda_i) Z_{m_i - 2} + \frac{f''(\lambda_i)}{2!} Z_{m_i - 3}(\lambda_i) + \cdots$$

Here m_i refers to the multiplicity of the root λ_i, and

$$Z_{m_i}(\lambda_i) = \frac{1}{m_i!} \frac{d^{m_i}}{d\lambda^{m_i}} \frac{F(\lambda)}{\Delta_{m_i}(\lambda)} \bigg|_{\lambda = \lambda_i}$$

where

$$F^{(m)}(\lambda_i) = m!(-1)^{n-m-1} (\lambda_i I - A)^{m_i - m - 1} \prod_{j \neq i} (\lambda_j I - A)$$

gives the mth-order derivative of F, and

$$\Delta_{m_i}(\lambda) = \prod_{j \neq i} (\lambda - \lambda_j)$$

Note, for example, that

$$Z_1(\lambda) = \frac{d}{d\lambda} \frac{F(\lambda)}{\Delta(\lambda)} = \frac{\Delta(\lambda)F'(\lambda) - F(\lambda)\Delta'(\lambda)}{[\Delta(\lambda)]^2}$$

Consider the system

$$\dot{x} = x+y \qquad \dot{y} = x-y$$

or simply

$$\dot{X} = AX; \qquad X = \begin{bmatrix} x \\ y \end{bmatrix}, \qquad A = \begin{bmatrix} 1 & 1 \\ 1 & -1 \end{bmatrix}$$

Using Sylvester's formula with $\lambda_1 = \sqrt{2}$, $\lambda_2 = -\sqrt{2}$ we have

$$e^{At} = \frac{e^{\lambda_1 t}}{\lambda_1 - \lambda_2} (A - \lambda_2 I) + \frac{e^{\lambda_2 t}}{\lambda_2 - \lambda_1} (A - \lambda_1 I)$$

and use it to obtain the solution of the system. Similarly we can show that if

$$B = \begin{bmatrix} 2 & 1 \\ 1 & 2 \end{bmatrix}$$

then

$$B^{100} = \begin{bmatrix} \dfrac{3^{100}+1}{2} & \dfrac{3^{100}-1}{2} \\[2ex] \dfrac{3^{100}-1}{2} & \dfrac{3^{100}+1}{2} \end{bmatrix}$$

SOME CONCEPTS FROM GRAPH THEORY

DEFINITIONS

A graph is a set of points V called *vertices* or *nodes* and a set of simple curves E called *edges* with a rule (of incidence) which associates each edge with vertices which are called its end points. The vertices are said to be incident with the edge. An *open* edge is incident with precisely two distinct vertices. A *closed* edge (called a loop) is incident with precisely one vertex and hence its end points coincide. No edges have points in common other than vertices.

In Fig. A-1, v_1 and v_2 are examples of vertices; e_1 is a loop whose end point is v_5; e_2 is an open edge whose end points are v_2 and v_3.

Two edges with a common vertex or two vertices that are the end points of an edge are said to be *adjacent*. A vertex is *isolated* if it is not incident with any edge. We denote a graph by $G = (V, E)$.

A *subgraph* of a graph G is a subset V_1 of the set of vertices V and a subset E_1 of the set of edges E with the same incidence between vertices and edges as in G.

A graph is called *simple* if it has neither loops nor parallel edges, i.e., multiple edges between pairs of vertices. Most of the time we shall be concerned with simple graphs, but since we have allowed for loops and parallel edges in our definition of graphs we will usually make it clear when we are considering nonsimple graphs.

With each edge, one may associate a direction or orientation indicated by an arrow. The resulting graph is then called a *directed graph* and its edges are called arcs. (See Fig. A-2.) A directed graph is denoted by $D = (V, A)$.

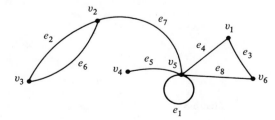

Figure A-1

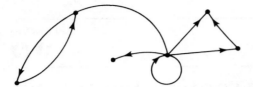

Figure A-2

The number of edges incident with a vertex $v \in V$ is called the degree of the vertex and is denoted by $d(v)$. We denote by $d^-(v)$ the number of arcs directed toward v, and by $d^+(v)$ the number of arcs directed away from v. A loop incident with a vertex is counted twice in determining the degree. For an isolated vertex we have $d(v) = 0$.

For a graph $G = (V, E)$ we denote the number of vertices and the number of edges by $|V|$ and $|E|$, respectively, and $|V|$ is called the order of the graph. The graph in Fig. A-3 has $|V| = 7$ and $|E| = 10$. A graph is called finite if both $|V|$ and $|E|$ are finite, and infinite if either is infinite. We shall be concerned exclusively with finite graphs. In the graph of Fig. A-3, the degree of v_1 is 5; v_7 is isolated.

It is easy to show that in every graph the number of vertices of odd degree is even. To see this note that $\sum_{v \in V} d(v) = 2|E|$ since each edge is counted twice. If we denote by V_o and V_e the sets of vertices having odd and even degrees, respectively, then we obtain the result by observing that $\sum_{v \in V_e} d(v) + \sum_{v \in V_o} d(v) = \sum_{v \in V} d(v) = 2|E|$ and hence $\sum_{v \in V_e} d(v)$ is an even number. This can only be if the sum has an even number of terms.

A sequence of n edges $e_1, \ldots, e_n$ in a graph G is called a *walk* or *edge progression* if there exists an appropriate sequence of $n+1$ (not necessarily distinct) vertices $v_0, v_1, \ldots, v_n$ such that e_i is incident with (v_{i-1} and v_i), $i = 1, \ldots, n$. The walk is *closed* if $v_0 = v_n$ and *open* otherwise. If $e_i \neq e_j$ for all i and j, $i \neq j$, the walk is called a *tour* or a *chain*. A closed chain is called a *circuit*. If all the vertices are distinct, a walk is called a *simple chain* while, if $v_0 = v_n$ and all other vertices are distinct, we have a *simple* circuit provided that $n \geqslant 3$. An example of a simple chain is given by the edge sequence $\{e_3, e_4, e_7, e_2\} \equiv \{(v_6, v_1), (v_1, v_5), (v_5, v_2), (v_2, v_3)\}$ in Fig. A-1. Here we have replaced each edge in the sequence by the pair of vertices that are its

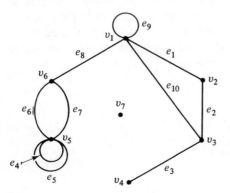

Figure A-3

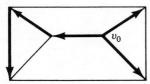

Figure A-4

end points as they succeed each other in the walk v_6, v_1, v_5, v_2, v_3. Similar definitions may be given for directed graphs giving attention to the direction on each arc. There we speak of *arc progressions, paths* and *cycles*, and *simple paths* and *simple cycles*.

A graph is said to be *connected* (strongly connected) in the undirected (directed) sense if there is a simple chain (path) between any pair of vertices. A graph of $n+1$ vertices is *n-tuply connected* if the removal of $n-1$ or less vertices does not disconnect it. Two chains are said to be disjoint if they have no vertices in common, except perhaps for their end points.

A component C of a graph G is a connected subgraph which is maximal (i.e., every vertex that is adjacent to a vertex in C is also in C and all edges of G incident with vertices in C are also in C).

A *subtree* is a connected subgraph which has no circuits. A *spanning tree* is a (maximal) subtree which contains all the vertices of the graph. An edge of the graph that is not in the tree is called a *chord*. An edge of the graph that is in the tree is known as a *branch*. When a chord is added to a spanning tree, the result is a circuit called a *fundamental circuit*. Figure A-4 shows a spanning tree for a directed graph. The tree is *rooted* at v_0, from which all paths that are in the tree begin.

A special type of circuit in a graph, important for practical applications, is named after the famous Irish mathematician William Rowan Hamilton (1805–65). We call a circuit which passes through every vertex of the graph once and only once a *Hamiltonian circuit*. By contrast, the name of the Swiss mathematician Leonard Euler (1707–83) is associated with an *Eulerian graph* in which the edges form a chain with each edge of the graph included in the chain once and only once. The chain may be open or it may form a circuit.

Two graphs $G = (V, E)$ and $G' = (V', E')$ are *isomorphic* to each other if there exists a 1 to 1 correspondence between V and V' and between E and E' which preserves incidences. For instance, the two graphs shown in Fig. A-5 are isomorphic.

A simple graph $G = (V, E)$ having $|V| = n$ and such that every pair of vertices is joined by an edge is called a *complete graph on n vertices*. It is easily verified that a complete graph has $n(n-1)/2$ edges. Since any two complete graphs having the

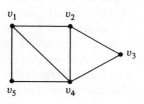

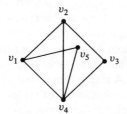

Figure A-5

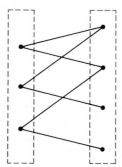

Figure A-6

same number of vertices are isomorphic we speak of the complete graph on n vertices.

A graph is called *bipartite* if its vertices can be partitioned into two disjoint sets such that the only edges in the graph are those which connect vertices from one set to those in the other. (See Fig. A-6.)

Discussion

An important elementary concept associated with a graph G on n vertices is that of connectedness. Intrinsically, much of algorithmic graph theory is concerned with connectivity, its redundance and even absence in the graph.

A graph is not connected (or disconnected) when the set of vertices V can be separated into two sets V_1 and V_2 with no edge joining a vertex in V_1 to a vertex in V_2, otherwise it is said to be connected. Although two vertices may not be directly connected by an edge, it may be possible to reach one of them from the other by a simple chain. If there is such a chain connecting every pair of vertices, then the graph is said to be connected. Sometimes people prefer to use the first definition, but more frequently the equivalent second definition is used. In fact, the second definition is much richer as it opens up the entire area of problems of *reachability* or *traceability* of a graph or of subgraphs of that graph. For example, we can begin to ask for more. Can we start at a vertex and travel or trace the edges of the graph sequentially without repetition? Can we do so and still terminate at the starting vertex? Can we, by starting at a vertex, trace a simple chain through all the vertices with or without returning to our initial vertex? Can we do so if we considered only subgraphs of $n-1$ vertices?

Another type of question is concerned with how much connectivity there is in a graph. There are two ways to look at this type of question: (1) through the edges of the graph; and (2) through its vertices. A graph may be disconnected by the removal of several edges taken together. A minimum collection of such edges is known as a *cut set* and the smallest number of edges in a cut set is called the *degree of connectivity* of the graph. A tree is connected of degree one. Clearly a tree is the weakest type of connected graph. On the other hand, in a circuit, the removal of an edge leaves a connected graph (in fact a tree) behind.

In terms of edge connectivity, how much connectivity there is in a graph may be measured by the minimum number of chains connecting any pair of vertices or by the existence of simple circuits of different sizes. Chains and circuits on the one hand and cut sets on the other are two complementary ways of studying connectedness and the lack of it. Even questions of *planarity* (embedding the graph in the plane without intersections of edges at points that are not vertices), and *nonplanarity* of graphs are related to connectivity. By reducing the number of edges of a nonplanar graph, it can be made planar.

There are also two ways to look at how vertices disconnect a graph. The first is associated with the concept of the *degree* of a vertex. For example, if in a tree we have a vertex of degree two and we remove it together with its incident edges, the remaining graph is disconnected. On the other hand, if the graph is a simple circuit and hence every vertex has degree two, the removal of a vertex does not disconnect the graph. It seems reasonable that the higher the degrees of the vertices, the stronger the connectivity should be. But this type of statement is too general and needs to be made specific in the context of a particular problem.

A vertex of a graph is called a *point of articulation* or *cut-vertex* if its removal disconnects or separates the graph. The *multiplicity* of a cut-vertex is the number of components which result from its deletion. There may be more than one vertex which is a point of articulation. For example, in Fig. A-1, v_2 and v_5 are points of articulation. However, v_6 is not. The collection of articulation points forms a set of articulation vertices which, in the context of communication networks, may be regarded as the vulnerability set of the graph. Of course, a graph may have no point of articulation (such a graph is said to be nonseparable) but the removal of k vertices together disconnects it. Such a set is known as *articulation set of order k*.

A graph is k-connected, $0 \leqslant k < n$ if the removal of $k-1$ vertices or less does not disconnect it. Any pair of vertices of such a graph can be connected by k disjoint chains (no two of which have vertices in common). A graph which has no articulation set of order k is called *k-irreducible*. Otherwise, it is known as *k-reducible*.

So far we have been speaking of a general undirected graph. Connectivity questions are somewhat more complicated if a direction is assigned to the edges of the graph. Here a graph may be connected in the undirected sense, yet be only *weakly connected* in the directed sense. Thus, there may be a path from one vertex to another, but not conversely; i.e., it is not strongly connected. It is clear that cycles play an important role in strongly connected graphs.

REFERENCES AND BIBLIOGRAPHY

Ackoff, R. L., S. K. Gupta and J. S. Minas: "Scientific Method," Wiley, 1962.

Alexander, Joyce, and T. L. Saaty: The Forward and Backward Processes of Conflict Analysis, *Behavioral Science*, vol. 22, pp. 87–98, March 1977.

—— and ——: Stability Analysis of the Forward–Backward Process, *Behavioral Science*, vol. 22, pp. 375–382, November 1977.

Anderson, N. H.: Information Integration Theory: A Brief Survey, in D. H. Krantz, R. C. Atkinson, R. D. Luce, and P. Suppes (Eds.) *Contemporary Developments in Mathematical Psychology*, vol. II, Freeman, San Francisco, 1974.

Arrow, Kenneth J.: "Social Choice and Individual Values," Yale University Press, New Haven and London, p. 28, 1970.

Ball, W. W. Rouse: "Mathematical Recreations and Essays," MacMillan, New York, 1947.

Batschelet, E.: "Mathematics for Life Scientists," Springer-Verlag, New York, 1973.

Bauer, Louis, H. B. Keller, and E. L. Reiss: Multiple Eigenvalues Lead to Secondary Bifurcation, *Siam Rev.*, vol. 17, no. 1, January 1975.

Baumol, W.: "Business Behavior, Value and Growth," MacMillan, New York, 1959.

Bell, R. and R. Wagner: "Political Power," Free Press, New York, 1969.

Bellman, R. E. and L. A. Zadeh: Decision-Making in a Fuzzy Environment," *Management Sci.*, vol. 17, 1970.

Berge, C.: "Theory of Graphs and Its Applications," Wiley, New York, 1962.

Blum, M. L. and Naylor, J. C.: "Industrial Psychology—Its Theoretical and Social Foundations," Harper and Row, New York, 1968.

Bogart, Kenneth P.: Preference Structures I: Distances between Transitive Preference Relations, *J. Math. Sociology*, vol. 3, pp. 49–67, 1973.

——: Preference Structures II: Distances between Transitive Preference Relations, (publication status unknown).

Bouteloup, Jacques: "*L'Algebre Lineaire*," Presses Universitaires de France, Paris, 1967.

——: "Calcul Matriciel Elementaire," Presses Universitaires de France, Paris, 1972.

Bronson, Gordon: The Hierarchical Organization of the Central Nervous System, in "International Politics and Foreign Policy: A Reader in Research and Theory," Rev. edn, James A. Rosenau (Ed.), Free Press, New York, 1969.

Buck, R. C. and D. L. Hull: The Logical Structure of the Linnaean Hierarchy, *Systematic Zoology*, vol. 15, pp. 97–111, 1966.

Carroll, J. Douglas: "Impact Scaling: Theory, Mathematical Model, and Estimation Procedures," Bell Laboratories, Murray Hill, New Jersey, 1977.

Chipman, J.: The Foundations of Utility, *Econometrica*, vol. 28, no. 2, 1960.

Churchman, C. West and Philburn Ratoosh (Eds.): "Measurement—Definitions and Theories," Wiley, New York, 1959.

—— and H. B. Eisenberg: Deliberation and Judgment, Chapter 3, in M. W. Shelley II and G. L. Bryan (Eds.), "Human Judgments and Optimality," Wiley, New York, 1969.

Cliff, N.: Complete Orders from Incomplete Data: Interactive Ordering and Tailored Testing, *Psychological Bull.*, vol. 82, no. 2, pp. 289–302, 1975.

Cogan, E. J., J. G. Kemeny, R. Z. Norman, J. L. Snell, and G. L. Thompson: "Modern Mathematical Methods and Models," vol. II, Committee on the Undergraduate Program, Mathematical Association of America, 1959.

Coombs, Clyde H.: "A Theory of Data," Wiley, New York, 1964.

David, H. A.: "The Method of Paired Comparisons," Griffin, London, 1969.

Dobson, Ricardo, T. F. Golob, and R. L. Gustafson: Multidimensional Scaling of Consumer Preferences for a Public Transportation System: An Application of Two Approaches, *Socio-Economic Planning Science*, vol. 8, pp. 23–36, 1974.

Dulmage, A. L. and N. S. Mendelsohn: Graphs and Matrices, "Graph Theory and Theoretical Physics," Frank Harary (Ed.), Academic, pp. 167–227, New York, 1967.

Dyer, J. S.: An Empirical Investigation of a Man–Machine Interactive Approach to the Solution of the Multiple Criteria Problem, in "Multiple Criteria Decision Making," Cochrane, James L., and Milan Zeleny, University of South Carolina Press, Columbia, S.C., 1973.

Eckart, Carl and Gale Young: The Approximation of One Matrix by Another of Lower Rank, *Psychometrika*, vol. 1, no. 3, pp. 211–217, September 1936.

Eckenrode, R. T.: Weighting Multiple Criteria, *Management Sci.*, vol. 12, no. 3, pp. 180–192, November 1965.

Eisler, Hannes: The Connection Between Magnitude and Discrimination Scales and Direct and Indirect Scaling Methods, *Psychometrika*, vol. 30, no. 3, pp. 271–289, September 1965.

Emshoff, J. R. and T. L. Saaty: Prioritized Hierarchies as a Vehicle for Long Range Planning, May 1978 (to appear)

Encarnation, J.: A Note on Lexicographical Preferences, *Econometrica*, vol. 32, no. 1–2, 1964.

Farquhar, Peter H.: A Survey of Multiattribute Utility Theory and Applications, *Studies in the Management Sciences*, vol. 6, North-Holland Publishing, Amsterdam, pp. 59–89, 1977.

Fechner, G.: "Elements of Psychophysics," vol. 2, translated by Helmut E. Adler, Holt, Rinehart, and Winston, New York, 1966.

Feller, W.: "An Introduction to Probability Theory and Its Applications," Wiley, New York, 1950.

Feraro, T.: "Introduction to Mathematical Sociology," Wiley, 1973.

Fishburn, P. C.: "Decision and Value Theory," Wiley, New York, 1964.

———: Independence in Utility Theory with Whole Product Set, *Operations Research*, vol. 13, pp. 28–45, 1965.

———: Additive Utilities with Incomplete Product Set: Applications to Priorities and Assignments, *Operations Research*, 1967a.

———: Methods of Estimating Additive Utilities, *Management Sci.*, vol. 13, no. 7, pp. 435–453, 1967b.

———: Arrow's Impossibility Theorem: Concise Proof and Infinite Voters, *J. Econ. Theory*, vol. 2, pp. 103–106, 1970.

———: "Utility Theory for Decision Making," Wiley, New York, 1972.

———: "Lexicographic Orders, Utilities and Decision Rules: A Survey," July 1974.

Fitz, Raymond and Joanne Troha: "Interpretive Structural Modeling and Urban Planning," University of Dayton, 1977.

Franklin, Joel N.: "Matrix Theory," Prentice-Hall, Englewood Cliffs, N.J., 1968.

Frazer, R. A., W. J. Duncan, and A. R. Collar: "Elementary Matrices and some Applications to Dynamics and Differential Equations," Cambridge University Press, 1955.

Frobenius, G.: Uber Matrizen aus nicht negativen Elementen, *Sitzber. Akad. Wiss. Berlin, Phys. Math. Kl.*, pp. 456–477, 1912.

Gal, T. and J. Nedoma: Multiparametric Linear Programming, *Management Sci.*, vol. 18, no. 7, 1972.

Gale, David: "The Theory of Linear Economic Models," McGraw-Hill, New York, 1960.

Gantmacher, F. R.: "Applications of the Theory of Matrices," Interscience, New York, 1960.

Gardner, Martin: The hierarchy of Infinites and the Problems it Spawns, *Scientific American*, vol. 214, pp. 112–118, March 1966.

Geoffrion, A. M., J. S. Dyer, and A. Feinberg: An Interactive Approach for Multicriterion Optimization with an Application to the Operation of an Academic Department, *Management Sci.*, vol. 19, no. 4, 1972.

Gillett, J. R.: The Football League Eigenvector, *Eureka*, October 1970.

Green, P. and F. Carmone, "Multidimensional Scaling and Related Techniques in Marketing Analysis," Allyn and Bacon, Boston, 1970.

———— and Yoram Wind: "Multiattribute Decision in Marketing," Dryden, Hinsdale, Ill., 1973.

Guilford, J. P.: The Method of Paired Comparisons as a Psychometric Method, *Psychological Rev.*, vol. 35, pp. 494–506, 1928.

Guttman, Louis: The Principal Components of Scalable Attitudes, in "Mathematical Thinking in the Social Sciences," Paul F. Lazarsfeld (Ed.), pp. 216–257, Russell and Russell, New York, 1969.

Hammond, K. R. and D. A. Summers: Cognitive Dependence on Linear and Nonlinear Cues, *Psychological Rev.*, vol. 72, no. 3, pp. 215–224, 1965.

Harris, E. E.: Wholeness and Hierarchy, Chapter 7 in *Foundations of Metaphysics in Science*, Humanities Press, New York, 1965.

Herbst, Ph. G.: "Alternatives to Hierarchies," H. E. Stenfert Kroese b.v., Leiden, Netherlands, 1976.

Hildebrand, F. B.: "Methods of Applied Mathematics," Prentice-Hall, Englewood Cliffs, N. J., 1952.

Hill, J. Douglas and John N. Warfield: Unified Program Planning, *IEEE Transactions on Systems, Man, and Cybernetics*, vol. SMC-2, no. 5, pp. 610–621, November 1972.

Hirsch, G.: Logical Foundation, Analysis and Development of Multicriterion Methods, Ph.D. Thesis, Operations Research, University of Pennsylvania, 1976.

Hotelling, H.: Analysis of a Complex of Statistical Variables into Principal Components, *J. Ed. Psychology*, vol. 24, pp. 417–441, 498–520, 1933.

Huber, George P.: Multi-Attribute Utility Models: A Review of Field and Field-Like Studies, *Management Sci.*, vol. 20, no. 10, June 1974.

Intriligator, Michael D.: A Probabilistic Model of Social Choice, *Rev. of Economic Studies*, vol. XL, pp. 553–560, October 1973.

Isaacson, Dean L. and Richard W. Madsen: "Markov Chains, Theory and Applications," a volume in the Series in Probability and Mathematical Statistics: Probability and Mathematical Section, Wiley, New York, 1976.

Johnson, Charles R., Theodore Wang, and William Beine: A Note on Right-Left Asymmetry in an Eigenvector Ranking Scheme, *J. Math. Psychology*, January 1979.

Johnson, Richard M.: "On a Theorem Stated by Eckart and Young," *Psychometrika*, vol. 28, no. 3, pp. 259–263, September 1963.

Johnson, Stephen C.: Hierarchical Clustering Schemes, *Psychometrika*, vol. 32, pp. 241–254, September 1967.

Julien, Pierre-Andre, P. Lamonde, and D. Latouche: "La Methode Des Scenarios," University of Quebec and Ministère D'Etat Sciences et Technologie, Quebec, Canada, 1974.

Kahneman, Daniel and Amos Tversky: Subjective Probability: A Judgment of Representativeness, *Cognitive Psychology*, vol. 3, pp. 430–454, 1972.

———— and ————: Prospect Theory: An Analysis of Decision Under Risk, *Econometrica*, in publication.

Keeney, Ralph L.: Decision Analysis with Multiple Objectives: The Mexico City Airport, *Bell J. Econ. Management Sci.*, Spring 1973.

———— and Craig W. Kirkwood: Group Decision Making Using Cardinal Social Welfare Functions, *Management Sci.*, vol. 22, no. 4, December 1975.

———— and H. Raiffa: "Decisions with Multiple Objectives: Preference and Value Tradeoffs," Wiley, New York, 1976.

Keller, J. B.: Miscellanea, Factorization of Matrices by Least-Squares, *Biometrika*, vol. 49, pp. 1–2, 1962.

Kemeny, John G. and J. Laurie Snell: "Mathematical Models in the Social Sciences," Blaisdell, New York, 1962.

Klee, A. J.: The Role of Decision Models in the Evaluation of Competing Environmental Health Alternatives, *Management Sci.*, vol. 18, no. 2, 53–67, October, 1971.

Knorr, K.: *Power and Wealth*, Basic Books, New York, 1973.

Koestler, Arthur and J. R. Smythies (Eds.): "Beyond Reductionism: New Perspectives in the Life of the Sciences," MacMillan, London, 1970.

Krantz, David H., R. Duncan Luce, Patrick Suppes, and Amos Tversky, "Foundations of Measurement," vol. 1, Academic, New York, 1971.

——: A Theory of Magnitude Estimation and Cross-Modality Matching, *J. Math. Psychology*, vol. 9, no. 2, pp. 168–199, May 1972.

——: Fundamental Measurement of Force and Newton's First and Second Laws of Motion, *Philos. Sci.*, vol. 40, no. 4, pp. 481–495, December 1973.

Kruskal, J. B.: Multidimensional Scaling by Optimizing Goodness of Fit to a Nonmetric Hypothesis, *Psychometrika*, vol. 29, no. 1, 1964.

——: Nonmetric Multidimensional Scaling: A Numerical Method, *Psychometrika*, vol. 29, no. 2, 1964.

——: "How to Use MDSCAL, a Multidimensional Scaling Program," The Bell Telephone Lab., Inc., Murray Hill, N.J., 1967.

Kunreuther, H. and Paul Slovic: Economics, Psychology, and Protective Behavior, *Amer. Econ. Rev.*, vol. 68, November 1978.

Lindgren, B. W.: *Elements of Decision Theory*, Macmillan, New York, 1971.

Linstone, H. A. and Murray Turoff, "The Delphi Method: Techniques," Addison-Wesley, Reading, Ma., 1975.

Lootsma, F. A.: "Saaty's Priority Theory and the Nomination of a Senior Professor in Operations Research," University of Technology, Delft, Holland, 1978.

Luce, R. D. and P. Suppes: Preference, Utility and Subjective Probability, in *Handbook of Mathematical Psychology*, vol. III, 1964.

MacCrimmon, K. R.: An Overview of Multiple Objective Decision Making, in "Multiple Criteria Decision Making," Cochrane, James L., and Milan Zeleny (Eds.), University of South Carolina Press, Columbia S.C., 1973.

Malone, David W.: An Introduction to the Application of Interpretive Structural Modeling, *Proc. IEEE*, vol. 63, no. 3, pp. 397–404, 1975.

Manheim, Marvin L.: *Hierarchical Structure: A Model of Planning and Design Processes*, The M.I.T., Cambridge, Mass., p. 222, 1966.

Marcus, Marvin and Henryk Minc: "A Survey of Matrix Theory and Matrix Inequalities," Allyn and Bacon, Boston, 1964.

Marshall, C. W.: *Applied Graph Theory*, Wiley-Interscience, New York, 1971.

May, Kenneth O.: Intransitivity, Utility, and the Aggregation of Preference Patterns, *Econometrica*, vol. 22, no. 1, January 1954.

McCracken, R. F.: "Multidimensional Scaling and the Measurement of Consumer Perception," University of Pennsylvania (Thesis) 1967.

McNeil, D. R. and J. W. Tukey: Higher-Order Diagnosis of Two-Way Tables, Illustrated on Two Sets of Demographic Empirical Distributions, *Biometrics*, vol. 31, no. 2, June 1975.

Mesarovic, M. D. and D. Macko: Scientific Theory of Hierarchical Systems, in "Hierarchical Structures," L. L. White, A. G. Wilson, and D. Wilson (Eds.), American Elsevier, New York, 1969.

——, ——, and Y. Takahara: "Theory of Hierarchical Multilevel Systems," Academic, New York, 1970.

Miller, G. A.: The Magical Number Seven Plus or Minus Two: Some Limits on our Capacity for Processing Information, *Psychological Rev.*, vol. 63, pp. 81–97, March 1956.

Moreno, J. L.: "Fondements de la Sociometrie," translated by Lesage-Maucorps, Presses Universitaires de France, Paris, 1954.

Moreney, M. J.: "Facts from Figures," Penguin, Baltimore, 1968.

Morris, Peter C.: Weighting Inconsistent Judgments, *Pi Mu Epsilon J.*, 1979.

Nikaido, H.: "Introduction to Sets and Mappings in Modern Economics," North-Holland, Amsterdam/American Elsevier, New York, 1970.

Patee, H. H.: The Problem of Biological Hierarchy, in *Towards a Theoretical Biology*, vol. III, C. H. Waddington (Ed.), Edinburgh University Press, 1969.

——— (Ed.): "Hierarchy Theory, the Challenge of Complex Systems," George Braziller, New York, 1973.

Perlis, Sam: "Theory of Matrices," Addison-Wesley, Reading, Ma., 1952.

Perron, O.: Zur Theorie der Matrices, *Math. Ann.*, vol. 64, pp. 248–263, 1907.

Pinski, Gabriel and Francis Narin: Citation Influence for Journal Aggregates of Scientific Publications: Theory, with Application to the Literature of Physics, *Information Processing and Management*, vol. 12, Pergamon, Oxford, pp. 297–312, 1976.

Proceedings of the IEEE, Special Issue on Social Systems Engineering, Chapter 2, "Binary Matrices in System Modeling," March 1975.

Rabinovitch, I.: "The Dimension Theory of Semiorders and Interval Orders," Ph.D. Thesis, Dartmouth College, June 1973.

Rivett, Patrick: Policy Selection by Structural Mapping, *Proc. R. Soc. Lond.*, vol. 354, pp. 407–423, 1977.

Rosen, Robert: Hierarchical Organization in Automata Theoretic Models of Biological Systems, in *Hierarchy Theory: the Challenge of Complex Systems*, Howard H. Pattee (Ed.), Braziller, New York, 1973.

Rosenblatt, M.: "Random Processes," Oxford University Press, New York, 1962.

Russell, Bertrand: A History of Western Philosophy, Simon & Schuster, New York, 1945.

Saaty, Thomas L.: "An Eigenvalue Allocation Model for Prioritization and Planning," Energy Management and Policy Center, University of Pennsylvania, 1972.

———: "Measuring the Fuzziness of Sets," *J. Cybernetics*, vol. 4, no. 4, pp. 53–61, 1974.

———: "Hierarchies and Priorities—Eigenvalue Analysis." University of Pennsylvania, 1975.

———: Hierarchies, Reciprocal Matrices, and Ratio Scales, *Modules in Applied Mathematics*, Cornell University, The Mathematical Association of America, 1976a.

———: Interaction and Impacts in Hierarchical Systems, *Proceedings of the Workshop on Decision Information for Tactical Command and Control*, Robert M. Thrall and Associates, Rice University, Houston, pp. 54–102, 1976b.

———: Theory of Measurement of Impacts and Interactions in Systems, *Proceedings of the International Conference on Applied General Systems Research: Recent Developments and Trends*, Binghamton, New York, 1977a.

———: A Scaling Method for Priorities in Hierarchical Structures, *J. Math. Psychology*, vol. 15, no. 3, pp. 234–281, June 1977b.

———: Scenarios and Priorities in Transport Planning: Application to the Sudan, *Transportation Research*, vol. 11, no. 5, October 1977c.

———: The Sudan Transport Study, *Interfaces*, vol. 8, no. 1, pp. 37–57, 1977d.

———: "The Faculty Tenure Problem—Determination of Requirements," in publication, with Anand Desai, 1977e.

———: "A New Paradigm for Queueing and Its Application," in publication, with J. J. Dougherty III, 1977f.

———: Exploring the Interface Between Hierarchies, Multiple Objectives and Fuzzy Sets, *Fuzzy Sets and Systems*, January 1978.

———: Modeling Unstructured Decision Problems: Theory of Analytical Hierarchies, *Mathematics and Computers in Simulation*, vol. 20, no. 3, pp. 147–157, September 1978. Also appeared in *Proceedings of the First International Conference on Mathematical Modeling*, University of Missouri-Rolla, vol. 1, pp. 59–77, 1977g.

——— and J. P. Bennett: A Theory of Analytical Hierarchies Applied to Political Candidacy, *Behavioral Science*, vol. 22, pp. 237–245, July 1977a.

——— and ———: "Terrorism: Patterns for Negotiations; Three Case Studies Through Hierarchies and Holarchies," Study for the Arms Control and Disarmament Agency, 208 pp.,

1977b. See also "Facing Tomorrow's Terrorist Incident Today," U.S. Department of Justice, LEAA, Wash. D.C. 20531, 28–31, 1977.

—— and M. W. Khouja: A Measure of World Influence, *J. of Peace Sci.*, Spring 1976.

—— and Reynaldo S. Mariano: Rationing Energy to Industries; Priorities and Input-Output Dependence, *Energy Systems and Policy*, January, 1979.

—— and Paul C. Rogers: Higher Education in the United States (1985–2000): Scenario Construction Using a Hierarchical Framework with Eigenvector Weighting, *Socio-Econ. Plan. Sci.*, vol. 10, pp. 251–263, 1976.

—— and Luis Vargas: "A Note on Estimating Technological Coefficients by Hierarchical Measurement," *Socio-Econ. Plan. Sci.*, vol. 13, no. 6, 333–336, 1979.

Sankaranarayanan, A.: "On a Group Theoretical Connection Among the Physical Hierarchies," Research Communication No. 96, Douglas Advanced Research Laboratories, Huntingdon Beach, California, 1978.

Savage, C. Wade: Introspectionist and Behaviorist Interpretations, of Ratio Scales of Perceptual Magnitudes, *Psychological Monographs: General and Applied*, vol. 80, no. 19, whole no. 627, 1966.

Schoemaker, P. J. H. and C. C. Waid: "A Comparison of Several Methods for Constructing Additive Representations of Multi-Attribute Preferences," Wharton Applied Research Center, University of Philadelphia, August 1978.

Scott, Dana: Measurement Structures and Linear Inequalities, *J. Math. Psychology*, vol. 1, pp. 233–247, 1964.

Shepard, R. N.: The Analysis of Proximities: Multidimensional Scaling with an Unknown Distance Function, *Psychometrika*, vol. 27, 1962.

——: Analysis of Proximities as a Technique for the Study of Information Processing in Man, *Human Factors*, no. 5, 1963.

——: A Taxonomy of Some Principal Types of Data and of Multidimensional Methods for their Analysis, *Multidimensional Scaling : Theory and Applications in the Behavioral Sciences*, vol. 1, R. N. Shephard (Ed.), Seminar Press, New York, 1972.

——, A. Kimball Romney, and Sara Beth Nerlove (Eds.): "Multidimensional Scaling, Theory and Applications in the Behavioral Sciences," Vol. 1, Seminar Press, New York, 1972.

Shinn, A.: An Application of Psychophysical Scaling to the Measurement of National Power, *J. Politics*, vol. 31, pp. 132–951, 1969.

Simon, H. A.: The Architecture of Complexity, *Proc. Amer. Philosophical Soc.*, vol. 106, pp. 467–482, December 1962.

—— and A. Ando: Aggregation of Variables in Dynamic Systems, *Econometrica*, vol. 29, no. 2, pp. 111–138, April 1961.

Sluckin, W.: Combining Criteria of Occupational Success, *Occupational Psychology*, Part I, vol. 30, pp. 20–26, 1956, and Part II, vol. 30, pp. 57–67, 1956.

Srinivasan, V. and A. D. Shocker: Linear Programming Techniques for Multidimensional Analysis of Preferences, *Psychometrika*, vol. 38, pp. 337–369, 1973.

Stevens, S. S.: On the Psychophysical Law, *Psychological Reviews*, vol. 64, pp. 153–181, 1957.

——: Measurement, Psychophysics, and Utility, in "Measurement, Definitions and Theories," C. W. Churchman and P. Ratoosh (Eds.), Wiley, New York, 1959.

——: To Honor Fechner and Repeal His Law, *Science*, vol. 13, 13 January 1961.

—— and E. Galanter: Ratio Scales and Category Scales for a Dozen Perceptual Continua, *J. Experimental Psychology*, vol. 54, pp. 377–411, 1964.

Stewart, G. W.: Error and Perturbation Bounds for Subspaces Associated with Certain Eigenvalue Problems, *SIAM Review*, vol. 15, no. 4, pp. 727–764, October 1973.

——: Gershgorin Theory for the Generalized Eigenvalue Problem $Ax = \lambda B_x$, *Mathematics of Computation*, vol. 29, no. 130, pp. 600–606, April 1975.

Stoessinger, J. G. "The Might of Nations," Random House, New York, 1965.

Suppes, P. and J. L. Zinnes: "Basic Measurement Theory," *Handbook of Mathematical Psychology*, vol. 1, 1963.

Sutherland, John W.: "Systems: Analysis, Administration, and Architecture," Van Nostrand Reinhold, New York, 1975.

Thurstone, L. L.: A Law of Comparative Judgment, *Psychological Review*, vol. 34, pp. 273–286, 1927.

Torgerson, Warren S.: *Theory and Methods of Scaling*, New York, 1958.

Tucker, Ledyard R.: Determination of Parameters of a Functional Relation by Factor Analysis, *Psychometrika*, vol. 23, no. 1, pp. 19–23, March 1958.

Tversky, Amos: A General Theory of Polynomial Conjoint Measurement, *J. Math. Psychology*, vol. 4, pp. 1–20, 1967.

——— and D. Kahneman: Judgment under Uncertainty: Heuristics and Biases, *Science*, vol. 185, pp. 1124–1131, 27 September 1974.

Van der Waerden, B. L.: Hamilton's Discovery of Quaternions, *Mathematics Magazine*, vol. 48, no. 5, pp. 227–234, November 1976.

Vargas, L.: Note on the Eigenvalue Consistency Index, 1978.

———: "Sensitivity Analysis of Reciprocal Matrices," Chapter 3 in Ph.D. dissertation, The Wharton School, University of Pennsylvania, 1979.

Waid, Carter: "On the Spectral Radius of Non-negative Matrices," (to appear).

Waller, Robert J.: The Synthesis of Hierarchical Structures: Technique and Applications, *Decision Sciences*, vol. 7, no. 4, pp. 659–674, October 1976.

Warfield, John N.: On Arranging Elements of a Hierarchy in Graphic Form, *IEEE Transactions on Systems, Man, and Cybernetics*, vol. SMC-3, no. 2, pp. 121–140, March 1973.

———: Developing Subsystem Matrices in Structural Modeling, *IEEE Transactions on Systems, Man, and Cybernetics*, vol. SMC 4, no. 1, pp. 74–80, January 1974a.

———: Developing Interconnection Matrices in Structural Modeling, *IEEE Transactions on Systems, Man, and Cybernetics*, vol. SMC-4, no. 1, pp. 81–87, January 1974b.

———: "Societal Systems: Planning, Policy and Complexity," Wiley, New York, 1976.

Wei, T. H.: "The Algebraic Foundations of Ranking Theory," Thesis, Cambridge, Mass., 1952.

Weiss, Paul A.: "Hierarchically Organized Systems in Theory and Practice," Hafner, New York, 1971.

Weyl, H.: Chemical Valence and the Hierarchy of Structures, Appendix D in "Philosophy of Mathematics and Natural Science," Princeton University Press, N.J., 1949.

Whyte, L. L.: Organic Structural Hierarchies, in "Unity and Diversity in Systems," Essays in honor of L. von Bertalanffy, R. G. Jones and G. Brandl (Eds.), Braziller, New York, 1969.

———: The Structural Hierarchy in Organisms, "Unity and Diversity in Systems," Essays in honor of L. von Bertalanffy, R. G. Jones and G. Brandl (Eds.), Braziller, New York, (in press).

———, A. G. Wilson, and D. Wilson (Eds.): "Hierarchical Structures," American Elsevier, New York, 1969.

Wielandt, H.: Unzerlegbare, nicht negative matrizen, *Mathematische Zeitschrift*, vol. 52, pp. 642–648, 1950.

Wigand, Rolf T. and George A. Barnett: Multidimensional Scaling of Cultural Processes: The Case of Mexico, South Africa and the United States, *International and Intercultural Communication Annual*, vol. III, pp. 140–172, 1976.

Wilf, Herbert S.: "Mathematics for the Physical Sciences," Wiley, New York, London, 1962.

Wilkinson, J. H.: "The Algebraic Eigenvalue Problem," Clarendon Press, Oxford, 1965.

Williamson, R. E. and H. F. Trotter: "Multivariable Mathematics," Prentice-Hall, Englewood Cliffs, N.J., 1974.

Wilson, A. G.: Hierarchical Structure in the Cosmos, in *Hierarchical Structures, Proc.*, American Elsevier, New York, 1969.

Woodall, D. R.: A Criticism of the Football League Eigenvector, *Eureka*, October 1971.

Yu, P. L.: "A Class of Solutions for Group Decision Problems," Center for System Science, University of Rochester, New York, 1972a.

———: "Cone Convexity, Cone Extreme Points and Nondominated Solutions in Decision Problems with Multiobjectives," University of Rochester, New York, 1972b.

────── and M. Zeleny: "The Set of all Nondominated Solutions in the Linear Case and a Multi-criteria Simplex Method," University of Rochester, New York, 1973.

Zeleny, M.: Linear Multiobjective Programming, Ph.D. thesis, University of Rochester, New York, 1972.

──────: On the Inadequacy of the Regression Paradigm Used in the Study of Human Judgment, *Theory and Decision*, vol. 7 pp. 57–65, 1976.

AUTHOR INDEX

SUBJECT INDEX